Dark Religion

Fundamentalism from The Perspective of Jungian Psychology

by

Vladislav Šolc & George J. Didier

PUBLISHED BY CHIRON PUBLICATIONS

www.ChironPublications.com

Interior and cover design by Danijela Mijailovic
Printed primarily in the United States of America.

ISBN 978-1-63051-398-6 paperback
ISBN 978-1-63051-399-3 hardcover
ISBN 978-1-63051-400-6 electronic
ISBN 978-1-63051-673-4 limited edition paperback

Library of Congress Cataloging-in-Publication Data Pending

To my beloved children Immanuel and Veronika (Vladislav Šolc)

To my two wonderful sons Michael and Brian
(George J. Didier)

Foreword

These are the times that try men's souls.
(Thomas Paine, December 1776)

We live in an era of extremism in political discourse, religious life, the news cycle, and our personal lives. For centuries under the banner of God, human societies amassed countless rounds of ethnic cleansing, deaths, and untold human suffering. We are left wondering how it is that the religious impulse, in which deep calls to deep, is so frequently perverted into a war cry that justifies murder, torture, rape, and other atrocities. Furthermore, despite breathtaking scientific advances in the past few centuries, we have more reason than ever to be concerned that our destructive capacity might cause the extinction of our species and multitudes of other species.

Vladislav Šolc and George Didier have entered this morass of unfathomable horrors and possibilities, to bring insightful, psychologically well-informed explorations to the field of religion and religious extremism. They remind us that the religious impulse inheres to the psyche and that this mysterious encounter with the numinous while transcending cultures, epochs, and historical figures becomes embodied in everyday life for weal or woe. They explore the roots of this impulse from a depth psychological perspective that is heavily informed by the writings of Carl Gustav Jung, the founder of Analytical Psychology.

Dark Religion is a double *entendre.* Not only are the shaping forces of our religious experience rooted in the dark, but when we remain *in the dark* about the roots of our religiosity there is enormous potentiality for misunderstanding, perversion, manipulation, and exploitation of our hunger for the transcendent. The religious impulse—in its essence an encounter with the *holy (and wholly) other*—can overtake a person and provoke intense projections onto the *other.* How are any of us supposed to distinguish healthy passionate belief from passionate belief that goes awry and becomes destructive?

Dark Religion From the Perspective of Jungian Psychology is a thoughtful, penetrating examination of humankind's encounter with the universal, transcendent mystery that is most commonly spoken of as God. It stands on its merits as a scholarly investigation of religion, and it is especially timely given the extremism that continues to flare up around the world.

The authors propose that psychology, especially depth psychology, offers a remedy for the affliction of dark religion. Serious seekers must bring light to bear upon the dark recesses of our experience of the numinosum. For Jungians, this means illuminating the individual recesses including the collective ones as well.

A genuine encounter with the numinous can be so powerful that it overtakes a person. It is the *wholly other* quality of such moments that imparts a *holy* dimension. But the psyche naturally divides experiences into polarities and if one consciously over identifies with one aspect of the polarity, the other is not abolished, it is simply driven into the unconscious.

We puzzle over moments of sudden, brutal violent eruptions like the Rwandan genocide of Tutsis by Hutus. We ask ourselves how people, who peacefully coexisted, as neighbors and friends, could unleash such destruction. The answer can be found in this book. Split off parts of our psyche's encounter with the numinous can become like dry kindling ready to be ignited by a well-timed spark.

Time and again we have seen such moments consume countless human beings in the pyre. The fact that a website exists that compiles the death tolls for man-made *multicides* www.necrometrics.com attests to our urgent need to hear what Didier and Šolc have to say about dark religion.

There is good news for the reader who takes to heart this book's underlying message. *Dark Religion* lays bare the underlying causes of religious extremism and fanaticism. It reminds the reader that each one of us is called to the mysterious task of shedding light, consciousness, upon our own encounter with the numinous.

Each of us faces a challenge to illuminate the unconscious domains of our psychological and religious life and then recover what we have projected onto others. With proper care, the original spark from the numinous encounter can flower as compassionate, soul-building action in the world. Those who recover their projections are less likely to cast their burdens on the *other* and less likely to perpetrate violence. The Sermon on the Mount captures this sentiment nicely, "Blessed are the peacemakers for they shall be called children of God."

Dr. Leonard Cruz, Asheville, N.C.

Acknowledgments

I am very grateful to George J. Didier who wrote and edited this book with me. I am thankful for his knowledge, enthusiasm and personal openness with which he approached this project. I would also like to thank Arlo Compaan and Fred Gustafson for their ideas and input when I was working on my Diploma thesis that preceded this book. I would also like to thank my wife Rebecca, Greg Baima and Amy Smart-Dumouchel for their editing and grammar recommendations. I am thankful to Andrea Scheans for her comments on the manuscript of the book *In the name of God* that was published in Czech Republic. Finally, George and I would like to thank Robert Mikulak for his editing and especially Leonard Cruz for providing his expertise and essential feedback.

-Vlado Šolc

I would like to express my sincere appreciation and depth of gratitude to Vlado Šolc for inviting me to make this creative journey with him. We traveled together through many winding paths, detours and wide-open highways that brought this book into being. Vlado had written many of his seminal ideas and insights into extreme religion when he invited me into the creative process of expanding on his work and sharing my own insights and reflections on the religious function of the psyche and the deleterious effects of extreme religion. I would also like to thank Nadine for reading, editing and commenting on the developing manuscript as it took shape and Suzi Naiburg for her brief but essential insights and reflections into creative writing and editing early on in our process. As always, at the end of a long odyssey, I am most grateful to my family, Nadine, Michael and Brian. Thanks for your patience as I spent weekends and evenings reading, writing and editing.

-George J. Didier

Introduction

There has never been a greater urgency than there is now to understand fanatical religion and religious fundamentalism. The phenomenon of extreme religion not only threatens the body politic, international relations, but our very existence. What turns religion into such a destructive force that it produces extreme conflict and division leading to cultural clashes, religious wars, and international terrorism? We have termed this phenomenon: Dark Religion. Almost everyone in one-way or another is affected by this development in our world: from the consulting room, to our families, our churches, our mosques and our temples, not to mention our public arenas and political platforms.

In Dark Religion, we explore the dynamics and causes of extreme religion, fundamentalism and fanaticism. Dark Religion, we discovered, is radically *uprooted* from spirituality. The striving for connection to the Transpersonal, which Jung saw as instinctive, becomes perverted. In short, dark religion hinders a healthy religious approach to the symbolic and thus inhibits one's on-going connection to the Self. In its stead one finds a static belief system derived from literalist and concretistic thinking.

This approach obscures the true nature of spirituality and eclipses one's symbolic relationship to numinous experiences. As a result, fundamentalists believe they have established a literal one-to-one correspondence of identity with God and thus confuse their own will and actions with the will and actions of God; they believe they speak directly for God (vox Dei est scriptor). Hence, the most violent acts of aggression are committed "in the name of God." In this religious endeavor, the "I" (ego) of the fundamentalist hides behind the image of God while assuming God's authority as one's own. Religious extremists, as we will show, identify with their literalized image of God, substituting an awe of the mystery of things for an absolute certainty of knowing the will of God.

Our argument is that religion is not only a connection to the numinosum as a source of life and renewal, but also a source of extreme power that can lead to radically perverted states of mind and creeds that kill the soul's relationship to the transpersonal. The so-called radicalized religions masquerade as if they are enlightening and religious however, they are flawed at the core and, in the end, are the opposite of religion. This book offers an in-depth-psychological analysis of what happens when a person becomes possessed by the energies of the Self that are not made conscious. We coin the term "dark religion" to describe all forms of fanatical, radical and unhealthy religion.

Analytical psychology is particularly well suited for analyzing this phenomenon due to its unique resources Jungians have gathered over decades while studying the dynamics and religious functions of the psych. *Dark Religion* offers new insights and a fresh perspective on how religion is used in the mind of the individual to hide behind their image of God. In *Dark Religion*, we explore and explicate these dynamics of religion, whether embodied by the radical extremist or by the fundamentalist next door, by submitting them to a critical analysis using the tools and knowledge of depth psychology. Supported by numerous examples in the world today and in our own clinical practices, our study reveals how dark religion leads to profound conflicts on both the personal, interpersonal and cultural levels

In an attempt to understand the excessive proliferation of radical creed and fundamentalism in our culture today, *Dark Religion* surveys the contemporary religious and spiritual land-scape all the while discovering the emergent forms of spiritual praxis in light of postmodernism and the rise of fundamentalism. Our study reveals that spirituality, besides being an inherent dimension of human nature; is one of our most essential needs. Religion only becomes "dark," we argue, when we ignore, deny or separate it from its own living roots in the unconscious.

How does one recognize dark religion? What are its psychological and religious signs? Who are most vulnerable to its seduction and alluring energy? What can one do about it? It is as close as your local church or synagogue or mosque. This book begins to answer these and other compelling questions on the nature of dark religion.

Vlado Šolc and George J. Didier, October 10, 2017, Whitefish Bay, WI and Rockford, IL.

Table of Contents

I.
RELIGION: A DEPTH PSYCHOLOGY PERSPECTIVE

Indeed, man is completely modern only when he has come to the very edge of the world, leaving behind him all that has been discarded and outgrown, and acknowledging that he stands before the Nothing out of which All may grow (Jung, 1931, [CW 10, para. 151]).

Religion is one of the most significant determinants of human actions. Religious practices, such as the ritualized burial of the dead, creation of sacred places, and the fashioning of symbolic artifacts can be traced back more than 100,000 years.[1] Early humans were mostly driven by instinct; in all likelihood, their religion reflected this developmental need. Religion and religious practices can be seen as an evolutionary and creative force, without which man would have remained a *non-symbolic* animal and might never have evolved to the current cognitive and cultural levels of development.[2] Religion is a faculty that forms culture and the mind. The appearance of religion coincides with the mind's ability to relate to a transcendent aspect of being that exists beyond immediate, palpable sense reality. Religion depends upon the imaginative and symbol-forming ability of the human psyche.

---

[1] D. Bruce Dickson, *The Dawn of Belief: Religion in the Upper Paleolithic of Southwestern Europe* (1990)

[2] When we use the term "man" we use it in the sense Jung and others used, i.e., human being. (For example: *Man and His Symbols*)

Aristotle (as cited in Field, 1931/1932) states, "the soul never thinks without an image" (p. 46). Thus, we might also say that the soul never thinks without religion. According to, Jung, religion "is incontestably one of the earliest and most universal expressions of the human mind ..." (Jung, 1940 [CW 11, para. 1]). During Jung's descent into the underworld, he discovered that: "The wealth of the soul exists in images" (Jung, 2009, 232). Such premises apply to the varieties of religious experience. Islamic scholar Henry Corbin[3] asserts that the imaginal world (*mundus imaginalis*) is an order of reality all its own. This order of reality is an intermediary world of image having an ontological foundation that accords with the sensate world and the world of thought and intellect. We believe that human beings are naturally religious; we are *homo religiosus*, a term used by Hegel, James, Otto, Eliade, Tillich and others.

A fundamental question presents itself immediately. Is religion a function of our relationship to something transcendent or is it simply a psychological aspect of being without reference to anything beyond the psyche? The varieties of questions pertaining to what is religion and what are religious experiences are shaped by how those questions are answered.

We intend to adopt a fairly narrow set of parameters pertaining to the fundamental operational definition of religion. The psyche is incapable of suspending its own subjectivity: when the psyche considers itself, it is simultaneously being experienced and is the subject of experience. The phenomena of religion, like the phenomena of mind, can become the object of scientific exploration. As theologian John Hick (1990) pointed out, religion can be viewed as an attempt to represent and comprehend the emergence of various phenomena that are responses to the experience of the God—the *experience* of God is available for study, but never God himself. Any attempt to study God, or the numinosum (a quality associated with archetypes that inspires fear, mystery, and awe), directly falls squarely in the domain of

[3] Henry Corbin, (1972) "*Mundus Imaginalis: or The Imaginary and the Imaginal*", Spring.

metaphysics. It is important to stress that this book is not a theological inquiry, and the study of metaphysics or theology is not its purpose. Furthermore, this book does not provide an exhaustive answer to the question "what is religion?" Rather, it explores various possibilities of how this question may be answered while ultimately hoping to advance the conversation.

Jungian psychology's unique, in-depth perspective has far-reaching implications for the study and practice of religion. Jung's approach to religion was empirical and phenomenological, though he did not avoid occasional philosophical cogitations or metaphysical speculation. Again and again, he claimed that all the conclusions he arrived at were based on careful observation and documentation of his lived experience, including the observations of the contents produced by the conscious and unconscious mind. He believed any observer could repeat those observations "all the time and everywhere" (Mathison, 2001). He pointed out that the language of the psyche is universal, because the "organs" of the psyche are common to all humanity (Jung, 1990).[4]

Functions of Religion

This book explores the *function* of religion from various angles and explores how the *religious function of the psyche* manifests itself to use Corbett's (1996) language. It is an investigation from a Jungian perspective on the nature of various psychological phenomena and the dynamics underlying the extreme religious creeds (i.e., fundamentalism) that make their appearance in radical religions. It is also an exploration of how archetypes influence the way a person uses religion (e.g., clinging, defensive, etc.), its creeds and what constitutes radical, excessive, or unhealthy adherence to a system of belief. An even broader, underlying goal of this book is to shed light on the possible causes

[4] Jung, C.G. (1990). *The archetypes of the collective unconscious*. Hull, R. F. C. (Trans.). *Bollingen Series XX. The Collected Works of C.G. Jung, 9* i. Princeton, NJ: Princeton University Press. First published in 1959.

and phenomenology of strong, radical, and fanatical religious persuasions. To a great extent, we hope to show how archetypes influence action and cognition not only in religious behavior but in ways that might not necessarily be religious.

Religious Extremism is Potentially Dangerous

During the twentieth century the three Abrahamic religions experienced a surge of fundamentalism. The rise of Christian fundamentalism can be traced to the publication of The *Fundamentals: A Testimony To The Truth*, a set of 90 essays published from 1910 to 1915 by the Bible Institute of Los Angeles. This was followed by the rise of the Christian evangelical right in the United States from 1940 through the 1970s. In the later part of the twentieth century, figures like Jerry Falwell and Pat Robertson galvanized a renewed vigor to the Christian fundamentalist movement in America. The rise of Islamic fundamentalism corresponds roughly with the Iranian Revolution (1979).[5] The substantial financial support provided by Saudi Arabia to madrasa's teaching a fundamentalist doctrine of Islam known as Wahhabism is thought to have played a critical role in the worldwide spread of Islamic fundamentalism. Modern Jewish fundamentalism began to claim attention with the beginning of the State of Israel, and gained momentum as ultra-orthodox groups increasingly gained power in the Israeli parliament.

Recently, religious fundamentalism sought to combine political and religious goals. The implications of such a conflation of goals provoked concerns in Europe and the Unites States. The past thirty years witnessed the rise of Christian fundamentalism in America under various monikers like Religious Right, the Moral Majority, and the Tea Party movement as well as the rise of many religiously-inspired jihadist movements across Europe

[5] "Indeed the Islamic revolution in Iran was perhaps the most important factor in the rise of contemporary Islamic fundamentalism." (Martin E. Marty, R. Scott Appleby, *Religion, ethnicity, and self-identity: nations in turmoil*; University Press of New England, 1997, p. 40).

and the Middle East. History teaches that when politics and extreme religion combine a potential for mass hysteria comes into play. What drives such movements can be understood as archetypal energy, also known as numinous energy. These forces can heal or harm; they can create or destroy. The archetypal undercurrents that propel fundamentalist movements may become tools for coming to terms with the most important human questions of meaning and value. At the same time they may also become tools for self-deception, providing the necessary substrata for mass manipulation. It depends on how wisely the archetypal energy is managed and used.

The fact that extreme religious fervor fuels so many of the current political and social developments makes the question of religions' role in this phenomenon a pressing question. Above C.G. Jung's door of his home in Küsnacht is an inscription that states *VOCATUS ATQUE NON VOCATUS DEUS ADERIT*, "Called or not called God is present." We are all called to make a deeply responsible and conscious decision regarding how we use religion to inform us and serve as our guide.

The Numinosum and the Development of Religion

Jung discovered that the archetypal dimension of the psyche and the powerful numinous affects it produces, is the source of religious experience. Certain aspects of an archetype are religious, and conversely, certain aspects of the religious experience are archetypal. Religion comes about when there is an attempt to come to terms with a primary archetypal experience. That is not to say that encounters with archetypes always produce faith or belief in a supernatural reality or in God, however God may be conceived. What does commonly occur from archetypal experience is a *change* of consciousness, which may or may not result in a theistic or atheistic stance.

Symbolic and Mythopoetic

The symbolic and mythopoetic dimensions of the psyche provide a structure-forming fabric for development. Psyche comes alive through this symbol-creating function. We benefit from this symbol-making function only to the extent that we become willing to consciously recognize symbols and myth. Failure to acknowledge the symbol-creating function of the unconscious does not depotentiate it; the function remains operative. In fact, the symbol-creating function intensifies the more it is overlooked. This may lead to the development of symptoms that are symbolic of unresolved and conflicted intrapsychic forces. To a great extent, one's level of conscious awareness and experience of the symbol-making function, determines the way one's religiosity manifests.

The Jungian Approach Is About Seeking, Not About Certitude

Can we view Jungian theory as a form of natural religion?[6] Yes and no! Jung himself remained mostly agnostic in his professional writings.[7] He left his followers unsure about the

---

[6] Natural religion is naturally and universally human; it can be defended and identified through the use of reason as opposed to revelation; it is not in conflict with natural laws. Its object is a part of nature, not "above" it. Natural religion does not exclude a "Supreme Being" that commands and inspires humans towards piety and good conduct (Tyler, 2009, p. 97).

[7] ". . . The idea of God is an absolutely necessary psychological function of an irrational nature, which has nothing whatever to do with the question of God's existence. The human intellect can never answer this question, still less give any proof of God. Moreover such proof is superfluous, for the idea of an all-powerful divine Being is present everywhere, unconsciously if not consciously, because it is an archetype. There is in the psyche some superior power, and if it is not consciously a god, it is the "belly" at least, in St. Paul's words. I therefore consider it wiser to acknowledge the idea of God consciously; for, if we do not, something else is made God, usually something quite inappropriate and stupid such as only an "enlightened" intellect could hatch forth. Our intellect has long known that we can form no proper idea of God, much less picture to ourselves in what manner he

specifics of his private faith even though he spoke occasionally about his personal relationship to God. For example, he wrote in 1952:

> "I find that all my thoughts circle around God like the planets around the sun, and are as irresistibly attracted by Him. I would feel it to be the grossest sin if I were to oppose any resistance to this force" Jung, MDR, 1963, p. 42).

The conclusions reached in this book do not require faith in any specific doctrine or dogma. Instead, they are intended to be operationalized psychological principles. The validity of our conclusions rests on empirical evidence. The difference between science and theology mirrors the difference between phenomenon and noumenon, i.e., between the perceived world of our senses and the world beyond the senses. Gravity is real despite the physicists' inability to confirm the existence of the graviton; likewise, the representations and effects of the Self are real despite its "immaterial" nature. Because the Self belongs to the noumenon, we can speculate about its nature and like Jung, confirm our impressions empirically.

Jungian psychology is foremost a method or tool for approaching the numinosum in such a way that it provides a fuller, deeper, and healthier response to life—it is also a teaching that promotes spiritual growth. Reading between the lines of Jung's work reveals a sense of mystery pointing to a higher level of being. As Jung (1940, [CW 11 para. 2]) stated: "...it does not conflict with the principles of scientific empiricism if one occasionally makes certain reflections which go beyond mere accumulation and classification of experience." Jung was a Kantian at heart; he believed that any conceivable transcendental object has to remain a *Ding an sich* (German: unknowable as thing-in-itself)—this is true of archetypes, gods, or God. For Jung, the archetypes were real and they were congruent with the Platonic forms (see also *Platonic Jung, Chiron 2017*). Arche-

really exists, if at all. The existence of God is once and for all an unanswerable question." Carl Jung, CW 7, par.110

types possess emergent properties similar to those that appear in nonlinear, dynamical systems described by Complexity Theory.[8,9] Jung never attempted to prove or postulate any ethical, transcendent *being* of a monotheistic or a dualistic nature; instead he spoke about the effect of various forces operating upon the human psyche. In Jung's psychology, ethics emerges as a result of the *relationships* between the subjective and objective realms of the psyche, or more specifically between the ego and the Self. We will follow Jung's example and refrain from postulating metaphysical, eschatological, or eternal purposes to the experience of religion.

Psyche Is Real

Most Jungian scholars and psychoanalysts do not consider the unconscious to simply be a derivative of consciousness; they understand it to be ontologically real and *a priori*—existing before consciousness. This is Jung's axiomatic foundation, his *sine qua non* for psychic life. The unconscious is vastly more than the residue of psychic life that is barred from conscious awareness; it is like a deep, life-sustaining aquifer. This distinguishes Jung from many other psychologists. Religion is more than a psychological phenomenon. Jung recognizes the autonomous and transcendent nature of archetypes, but assigns to human beings moral responsibility for how they to respond to the archetype. Jung's spirituality returns the gods to the psyche. He says:

But since the development of consciousness requires the withdrawal of all projections we can lay our hands on, it is not possible to maintain any nonpsychological doctrine about the

---

[8] See: Cambray, J., Carter, L., *Analytical Psychology, Contemporary Perspectives in Jungian Analysis, Chap. Archetypes: Emergence and psyche's Deep Structure*, Hogenson, G., p. 32-82, Routledge, London and NY, 2004.

[9] See Cruz, Leonard. "Fellowship of the Word: On Complexes, Chaos, and Attractors." *The Unconscious Roots of Creativity*, Chiron Publications, 2016.

gods. If the historical process of world despiritualization continues as hitherto, then everything of a divine or daemonic character outside us must return to the psyche, to the inside of the unknown man, whence it apparently originated (Jung, 1940, [CW 11, para. 141]).

Jung never tried to prove nor disprove the existence of God. Making the psyche the object of reflection and examination does not go against religion. After all, as Jung wrote to Pastor Damour (1941), "God has never spoken to man except in and through the psyche." If believers and researchers confine themselves to observable psychological processes, no leap of faith is necessary.

Jung recognized that archetypes have the ability to influence and change things within a person and this can produce change in the material world. This is one source of evidence that archetypes are real: *Wirklichkeit ist, was wirkt.* [10] Thus, for Jung, the real is anything that has an ability to cause an effect on something else. Therefore, archetypes must be real. In addressing the issue between metaphysics and religious psychology, Jung (1931, [CW 13, para. 73]) writes: "To understand metaphysically is impossible; it can only be done psychologically. I therefore strip things of their metaphysical wrappings in order to make them objects of psychology." (Jung, Wilhelm, 1970, *The Secret of the Golden Flower.*)

Individuation is both a psychological and a religious process. The *"organic unity"* of psychological and religious experiences, described by Dourly (1984), elevates everyday existence in ways that makes the flesh holy and brings the divine close to the human. Nonetheless, Jung recognized the risk and dangers of unconscious material possessing an individual (1940, [CW 11, para. 141]), "Wherever [the] unconscious reigns, there is bondage and possession." It is imperative that a reciprocal, mutual relationship and dialogue exist between the conscious and unconscious realms. It is a delicate and fragile balance

[10] German: The real is what works.

between the conscious and unconscious that protects us from fanatic entrapment on one hand and a feeling of spiritual desertion on the other.

What Constitutes Unhealthy

This book should not be viewed as an attempt to pathologize religion. Pathology produces suffering (*pathos*) and sometimes, in excess. Of course, religion can fall prey to pathological influences. When certain forces are not sufficiently contained by religion, the mind can become sick, but religion does not necessarily cause sickness in the mind. Radical religions and creeds are the expressions of inadequate, non-credible, or poorly contained numinous archetypal energy by the ego. This does not say anything about the nature of the energies themselves, which are ineffable. The Jungian perspective does not pathologize or moralize archetypal processes, nor does it reduce them to anything fully knowable. It does provide a means for recognizing that seemingly evil phenomena also possess elements of opposites that are good and unhealthy psychological elements.

Questions

A host of questions emerge from the inquiry into the archetypal level of religion. Can archetypal experiences be considered religious? Are all "isms" with religious overtones rooted in archetypal possession? Is the psyche *essentially* religious, and if it is, can we assume a degree of religiosity is present anytime we deal with the psycho-symbolic process? If not, what specific features distinguish something as religious? Are archetypal influences always at play when dealing with human passions? And finally, what distinguishes religious fanaticism from other forms of fanaticism? According to Jung, (Jung, 1954d, [CW 9i, para. 129]):

> The archetype behind a religious idea has, like every instinctive force, its specific energy, which it does not

> lose even if the conscious mind ignores it. Just as it can be assumed with the greatest probability that every man possesses all the average human functions and qualities, so we may expect the presence of normal religious factors, the archetypes, and this expectation does not prove fallacious.

In this sense, we don't really have an option to be religious or irreligious. For all we know, the earliest humans may have lived in a state of ever-present anxiety about retributive justice from the gods.

It is evident that nobody can afford to ignore archetypal energies without expecting consequences. Here we are not talking about the belief in God, but about the conscious awareness of the reach of archetypal power. Either there is a conscious effort to integrate archetypal energies, or the archetypes take the lead, and our possession by the archetypal forces becomes our fate. Jung stressed over and over that the greatest danger to humanity are humans themselves.

Reality

In his *Four Quartets*, T.S. Eliot (1916) speaks of human nature as that which "cannot bear much reality" (CPP. 172). Religion provides a tool for "framing" reality. It is a force that can hold the world together; without religion the world may appear chaotic, meaningless, and unintelligible.

Religion, like fire, is a good servant, but a bad master. Without any religion a person may become lost, but with too much religion a person may become trapped. As Stein (1985) reiterates, regarding spiritual endeavors, humans have to hold the imaginary rod neither too tight nor too loose. Our clinical experience suggests that people holding strong religious convictions are often prone to magical thinking, selective morality, and denial—none of which are useful in solving the great problems facing humankind.

Deed

Religious conviction by itself does not make us good, though good deeds do make a difference. The *Bible* says: "Beware of false prophets, who come to you in sheep's clothing, but inwardly they are ravenous wolves. You will know them by their fruits" (Matt 7:15-17, *English Standard Version*). The task of individuation rests in part on the ability to resist the destructive lure of archetypal forces that can foster depravity and instead, use these energies to discover mundane affairs as sacramental. In this respect individuation is more than an exercise in human development it is a moral quest. Too often archetypal energies are viewed as *goals* and not the *means* for fostering spirituality. Such an approach permits the same influences that are capable of freeing a person to also entrap them.

Paradox Is a Constituent of Reality

Jung's approach does not ask for faith. It opens a way of living in the world that embraces paradox instead of opposing it. The path of individuation is a life lived in the midst of doubt and moral conflict. There may be paths with more certainty but in the end they may be more painful. Jung pointed out (Jung, CW 13, 1967, p. 265X) "Until you make the unconscious conscious, it will direct your life and you will call it fate." His was not a nihilistic, resigned message; what shines through this observation is a genuine gnosis. Jungian psychology recognizes that phenomena present themselves to the psyche as polarities existing in a dynamic tension. Jung (1951e) believed that when the individual remains unconscious about his or her inner tensions, one aspect of the polarity will inevitably be acted out in the form of fate. We termed this specific fate (i.e., consequence of unconsciousness) *theonemesis*, a topic we explore at the end of this book.

Theodicy

We come to the problem of evil. Theodicy is defined as the vindication of divine goodness and omnipotence in light of the existence of evil. This theological conundrum penetrates one's daily life for those aspiring to live morally.[11] Whether or not God, the transcendent reality, is supremely good, *Summum Bonum,* and therefore worthy to be worshiped, may not serve well as a moral imperative for those committed to right action and right being-in-the-world. Philosophical concepts like the Trinity, Sunyata, Brahman, Absolute Spirit, Divine Will, or Omega Point remain rational abstractions unless they have a meaningful connection to action. Jung's work offers a framework for understanding the connection between spirit and matter and good and evil. The path of individuation involves a sincere and open relationship to symbols radiating out of the Self and fosters a progressive, constructive morality anchored in conscious deeds. The opposite of this process is a regressive movement leading to detachment and the disintegration of wholeness. A

---

[11] We are using here the term "morality" in accordance with teaching of Immanuel Kant as used in the theory of C. G. Jung. The term morality is used here not as moral conventions, but as a conscious decision to act responsibly with respect to knowledge and conscience. Kant says: "An action from duty has its moral worth not in the aim that is supposed to be attained by it, but rather in the maxim in accordance with which it is resolved upon; thus that worth depends not on the actuality of the object of the action, but merely on the principle of the volition, in accordance with which the action is done, without regard to any object of the faculty of desire. It is clear from the preceding that the aims we may have in actions, and their effects, as ends and incentives of the will, can impart to the actions no unconditioned and moral worth. In what, then, can this worth lie, if it is not supposed to exist in the will, in the relation of the actions to the effect hoped for? It can lie nowhere else than in the principle of the will, without regard to the ends that can be effected through such action; for the will is at a crossroads, as it were, between its principle *a priori*, which is formal, and its incentive *a posteriori*, which is material, and since it must somehow be determined by something, it must be determined through the formal principle in general of the volition if it does an action from duty, since every material principle has been withdrawn from it." Immanuel Kant, *Groundwork for the Metaphysics of Morals*, Edited by Allen W. Wood, Yale University Press, p.15.

central tenet of Jungian psychology proposes that whatever is split off and disconnected from the original unity appears in the form of re-enactment and compulsion that will confront us again and again no matter how big our pitchfork is.[12] Jung stated that compulsion is one of the great mysteries of life. (1955, par. 151) The compulsive urge to seek (desire) is ingrained in living organisms. Whether this involves a plant seeking the sun (heliotropic) or a creature seeking to procreate, seeking is a basic principle of evolution. For human beings seeking can become *locked* in its attachment to one specific object or thought structure. Excessive attachment is likely to drive other, incompatible elements into the unconscious. The ego that becomes disconnected from the original unity is apt to become more vigorous in its compulsions and attachments. We are called to respond to Socrates' proclamation that the unexamined life is not worth living. (Plato, *Apology*, 38A)

Jung's thought was anchored in Platonic forms and ideology. It reflected Enlightenment ideals, and sought to combine Romantic discourse with medieval philosophy and mystical teaching. Though theists and atheists criticized Jung, they both found refuge in the wisdom and the theory he offered.

The main goals of this book are to determine what constitutes a religion from a depth psychological perspective and what can be learned from a depth psychological examination about the domain of radical, excessive, maladaptive, or extreme forms of religious worship and belief. We begin with a brief outline of the development of religion over the last several centuries with a special emphasis on major features leading to our present crisis. This outline includes a survey of Jung's prophetic vision (1934) and the foreshadowing of a new dispensation. In this review we will survey the contemporary religious and spiritual landscape, the new emergent forms of spiritual praxis in light of modernism, and the rise of fundamentalism in the new millennium.

---

[12] Horace said: "*Naturam expellas furca, tamen usque recurret.*" You can drive nature out with a pitchfork, but she always comes back. (About 20 B.C.)

II.
THE EMERGENT DISPENSATION AND THIRD MILLENNIUM SPIRITUALITY

"No matter what the world thinks about religious experience, the one who has it possesses a great treasure, a thing that has become for him a source of life, meaning, and beauty, and that has given a new splendor to the world and to mankind."

C.G. Jung, *Psychology and Religion,*
(1940, [CW 11, par. 167])

"Divinity is an Underground river that no one can stop and no one can dam up."

(Meister Eckhart[13])

We are witnessing a radical change in religious life and culture throughout the modern and post-modern world, particularly among the three monotheistic Abrahamic religions: Christianity, Islam, and Judaism. Various figures have approached these changes differently. Goethe dramatized it, Nietzsche distilled its essence with Zarathustra's utterance, "God is dead," while Freud characterized religion as an illusion. The God Image of earlier dispensations—most particularly the narration of the divine as existing *out there,* distant, external to human beings, one-sidedly patriarchal, and mediated through traditional religious hierarchy is changing as Western religious conscious-

[13] Quoted from *One River, Many Wells*, Fox, p. 5, (2000).

ness evolves. As mainline traditional Christianity loses its foothold in the world, depth psychology[14] has been extending its influence in the realm of religion and soul.

Religion plays a vital and indispensable role in our personal lives, in our communities, and in the larger political world we inhabit. We are witnessing the reengagement of the U.S. military in Syria and Iraq as it attempts to counter the extreme fundamentalist group ISIS. Uncontained and unrecognized religious impulses are undergoing major transformations that defy neat categorizations. Contrary to what several modern and postmodern scholars predicted regarding religion's demise (e.g., Nietzsche, Freud, Weber, Durkheim, Dawkins, Karl Marx, etc.), religion, is not in danger of extinction.

THE TASK OF THE POSTMODERN WORLD

Since the 18th century, science has challenged religion and claimed a pre-eminent position as arbiter of truth. This movement has wielded tremendous influence over religious beliefs regarding what is real and credible. As a response, the evolutionary movement of the religious impulse is being challenged and transformed into new spiritual forms. As these challenges to conventional religion become known as movements of the evolving spirit, we may, hopefully, anticipate a reduction in reckless and violent acting-out. This may be an answer to the fundamentalist's response to a modernity that has lost touch with the sacred. The task, in the postmodern world, is to find a path between the Scylla of withdrawing projections (returning the gods to their source) and the Charybdis of overwhelming numinous energy (Nietzsche's Ubermenschen) that the ego needs

[14] The term, depth psychology, from the German *Tiefenpsychologie,* was first coined by psychiatrist Eugen Bleuler and later used by Freud (1914) to refer to the practice and research of the science of the unconscious, both psychoanalysis and analytical psychology. This approach to consciousness recognizes that the psyche is a complex process involving levels that are partly conscious, partly unconscious, and still other parts that remain completely unconscious.

to contain. The challenge involves the inherent need to critical examine and then retrieve one's projections (gods, demons, etc.) restoring them to their source in the inner recesses of one's own psyche.

As people lose their *raison d'etre* through a loss of faith in traditional religion, they often transfer (unconsciously) these needs to culturally relevant phenomena and objects like material success, status symbols, and other achievements for self-identity and meaning. However, these cultural objects have a short shelf life; once satisfying they easily, in time, lose their appeal, they no longer provide meaning nor meet the individual's deeper longing for identity and fulfillment.. Restless ensues. Fundamentalists are often sharply aware of this distressing development and hence are more determined to cleave to the past. Jung, among other scholars, like Derrida and Foucault, recognized that we are living in a period that has lost its way, its orienting myth.

There is a deep unrest and thirst for experiences of the sacred that institutional and traditional religions no longer mediate. Witness the exodus from mainline Protestant denominations and the increasing numbers of Catholics who are becoming more indifferent to the notion that Catholicism is the only path to salvation.[15] Meanwhile, those who claim no particular faith identity are increasing at such an alarming pace that worldwide "unbelief" now represents the "world's third largest religion."[16] Collective religious symbols and forms like cathedrals, spires, churches, rituals, liturgies, and sacraments no longer serve the religious function of the psyche (soul) for many people today. These religious images and forms of spirituality no longer lead one to, or remind one of the living spirit.

Ironically, while institutional religion appears to be losing its influence in American culture[17] *spirituality* is on the ascendancy. Spirituality has become highly marketable as attested to by publishers, bookstores, public speakers, and celebrities. It has

---

[15] See: *National Catholic Reporter* 36, October, 1999, pp.11-20.
[16] See: *Belief without Borders*, Mercadante, L. 2014.
[17] Mercadante, L. *Belief without Borders*, 2014.

even gained credibility as an independent research discipline in academia.[18] These broad cultural shifts and movements, from institutional membership to individual seekers and from believers to spiritual nonbelievers, are indicative of the changing landscape of our religious imagination. It reflects the loss of meaning in our traditional institutional religions and the heralding of new spiritual forms and practices. Indeed, the Western world is undergoing an evolutionary mythic transition to a new dispensation—a time of uncertainty, liminality, and anxiety.

SPIRITUAL BUT NOT RELIGIOUS

In the West we are witnessing different responses to this situation. There is a simultaneous rise of fundamentalism on one hand and a rise of what researchers have termed the "spiritual but not religious" on the other (SBNRs; Bender, 2010; Mercadante, 2014; Heelas and Woodhead, 2005).[19] According to the most recent Pew Research Center's Forum on Religion and Public Life survey, (PEW, 2014) there appears to be a dramatic rise of those claiming to be "spiritual" but "not religious." The "spiritual but not religious" (S.B.N.R.s) comprise a unique population that seek spiritual alternatives by looking to develop their own spirituality apart from traditional religious structures and institutions.[20] This term is relatively new but is popular in the United States, where one study reports that as many as 33% of people identify as spiritual but not religious.[21] According to Robert Wuthnow, we have become a nation of "seekers" of the esoteric rather than "dwellers" in traditional religious structures.[22]

---

[18] See: *APA Handbook of Psychology, Religion, and Spirituality.*

[19] See: *The New Metaphysicals: Spirituality and the American Religious Imagination*, Bender, 2010; Mercadante, *Belief without Borders*, 2014.

[20] See Mercadante, L. *Belief without Borders*, Oxford University Press, 2014. (pp. 50-67)

[21] See *"American Spiritual Searches Turn Inward,"* Gallup.com Retrieved 2014-10-10

[22] Robert Wuthnow, *After Heaven: Spirituality in America since 1950s*

SPIRITUALITY AND ITS COMMERCIALIZATION

When inquiring into a patient's religious affiliations, in the consulting room, the response is often, "I'm spiritual but not religious." At that moment, one is likely to hear that traditional religion is viewed as authoritarian and limiting, while spirituality is viewed as personal and liberating. Is this response simply an expression of the patient's deep interest in all things spiritual or does it reflect the patient's alienation from traditional institutional religion? Is it a justification? Is it a narcissistic preoccupation? Is there such a thing as a generic, commoditized spirituality: McSpirituality? To be spiritual but not religious may be symptomatic of what is happening in our culturally shared religious life.

Critics have denounced the commercialization and marketing of spirituality. For example, the shadow side of one of the most popular and newest psycho-religious movements, "The McMindfulness Craze,"[23] has been heavily criticized for its image and commercialized packaging. Mindfulness is presented as a panacea with almost miraculous efficacy. From changing one's brain to alleviating all stress to promising enlightenment, advocates of mindfulness have promised quick cures. Though mindfulness and meditation can have tremendous transformative effects, their limitations are often overlooked. Most particularly, as we have noted in our clinical practices and documented by authors Rubin, Kornfield, and Brown, are the ongoing developmental issues that depth psychology addresses that are entirely left untouched by meditation (e.g., early childhood wounds, unconscious conflicts and fears, difficulties with intimacy and what is most important to our present work is the fact that "meditation neglects meaning." One might ask: Did Osama Bin Laden meditate?

(Berkeley and Los Angeles: University of California Press, 1998).

[23] For example see Jeffrey Rubin's article, 2015,*The McMindfulness Craze: The Shadow Side of the Mindfulness Revolution*, http://www.truthout.org.

Nonetheless, researchers are also clarifying some of the misconceptions of this burgeoning (S.B.N.R.) phenomenon. For example, Courtney Bender, a professor of religion at Columbia, went into the streets of Cambridge, Massachusetts, where she studied the S.B.N.R. folks in their own environment and discovered that they were not solitary seekers at all, but involved in an assortment of diverse groups.[24] This fact alone conflicts with the stereotype of S.B.N.R.s as anti-institutional loners. The S.B.N.R. phenomena and its many "forms of spirituality" appear to be, from a Jungian perspective, a movement toward direct and immediate experiences with the energies of the unconscious that are not mediated through institutional religion or its priests. For it is precisely this energetic (spiritual) dimension that traditional institutional churches *and* fundamentalism have inadvertently lost touch with — the source of numinous life sustaining and renewing energy.

The nature of this shift is complex and it is directly related to the fact that traditional religious symbols have lost their capacity to contain and mediate access to the numinous unconscious. Jungian theory and scholarship can make a major contribution in understanding and responding to these newly emerging religious phenomena, such as the S.B.N.R.s.

The best-selling author and former Catholic Monk Thomas Moore offers guidance for developing a "custom spirituality" or "a religion of one's own" in his book, A *Religion of One's Own.*[25] He writes:

"Every day I add another piece to the religion that is my own. It's built on years of meditation, chanting, theological study and the practice of therapy – to me a sacred activity."[26]

Fundamentalism, we believe, is one maladaptive and aberrant response to these cultural changes. It is a transitional phenomenon, which attempts to keep alive the spirit of the

---

[24] Bender, C. *The New Metaphysicals: Spirituality and the American Religious Imagination*, Chicago, 2010.

[25] More, 2014 *A Religion of One's Own*. New York: Gotham Books.

[26] Ibid., p. 26

previous dispensation by returning to a literal rendition of institutional faith. While fundamentalism clings to a literal interpretation to avoid the anxiety of change and the unknown, the S.B.N.R.s tend toward the other extreme by avoiding any trappings of traditional institutional religions in order to assert the greatest personal freedom in determining their spirituality. The S.B.N.R.s also tend to easily cross over and freely borrow fascinating (numinous) religious practices or objects that resonate with their own personal spiritual sensibilities.

FUNDAMENTALISM ACROSS ALL DISCIPLINES

Fundamentalism of all kinds, (religious, political, cultural, etc.) poses one of the most dangerous threats to our contemporary world. Significantly, today we are hearing from many different schools of thought about the dangers of fundamentalism. When asked what he believed to be the greatest menace and threat to individual liberty and freedom, Anthony Gibbons, director of the London School of Economics, stated:

Contrary to the received wisdom of the moment, I believe we should oppose all forms of moral absolutism. The simplest way to define fundamentalism is as a refusal of dialogue—the assertion that only one way of life is authentic or valid. Dialogue is the very condition of a successful pluralistic order.[27]

William Lafleur, professor of religion, reiterates this idea.

Much of what we recognize as "fundamentalism" in any religious tradition is, at least in its hermeneutic posture, a wholesale rejection of all modern critical approaches and a professed return to a given scripture as authoritative in this sense. It tries to be premodern.[28] (Lafleur, 1998 pp. 75-89).

Understanding this dichotomous religious development worldwide provides a clue as to what is happening in our world today. Religious experience is being dichotomized throughout

[27] Giddens, 1997 p. 82.

[28] Lafleur, 1998 pp. 75-89.

the world such that a tension arises between fundamentalism and personally meaningful spiritual paths. In *After God,* Mark Taylor, a contemporary philosopher, states "You cannot understand the world today if you do not understand religion. Never before has religion been so powerful and so dangerous" (Taylor, 2007, p. XIII). Taylor attempts to redefine religion through a theology of culture; his work resonates with Jungian psychology's understanding of the dynamics of the (religious) psyche.

Despite widespread rejection of religion we are left asking, "What makes religion so powerful and dangerous today?"

Beginning with the age of the Enlightenment and continuing through the age of Modernism, many scholars have characterized religion as a product of infantile projections, superstition, and archaic beliefs. The slogan has been "God is dead!" However, even Nietzsche's madman in *The Gay Science* foresees a dialectical *coincidentia oppositorum* when he first declares that he seeks God only to later pronounce God is dead. Nietzsche's, *Übermensch,* became a sort of archetype that calls to both the fundamentalist and the S.B.N.R. types. In the breakdown of traditional religious structures and beliefs—in its liminal transformative realm—the religious impulse becomes either creative and/or dangerous. To paraphrase the American humorist Mark Twain, The news of God's death has been greatly exaggerated. In many quarters of the world religion flourishes and it still exerts deep and profound effect on our culture. Taylor points out that scholars' undue focus on the microanalysis of religion overlooked the foundational questions like "What religion is?" therefore missing religion's ubiquitous nature and its pervasive cultural influence.[29] For example, Taylor (2007, p.1) cites the 1966 Easter cover story of Time magazine, asking the question: "Is God Dead?"—citing philosophers, theologians and historians.

> For many, that time has arrived, nearly one of every two men on earth lives in thralldom to a brand of

[29] Taylor, *After God*, 2007. p. 11 Chicago: University of Chicago Press).

> totalitarianism that condemns religion as the opiate of the masses – which has stirred some to heroic defense of their faith but has also driven millions from any sense of God's existence. Millions more, in Africa, Asia, and South America, seem destined to be born without any expectation of being summoned to the knowledge of the one God.

Ironically, not more than a decade later, Taylor cites Newsweek's article, again, however now declaring "'the most significant – and overlooked – religious phenomenon of the '70s was 'the emergence of evangelical Christianity into a position of respect and power.' Today evangelicalism is alive and well in this country, and Pentecostal Protestantism is the fastest-growing religion in Africa, Asia, and South America."[30] Hence, Taylor asks the poignant question, "Why did this apparent reversal occur in such a short span of time?" The 1960s heralded the death of God, but it eventually gave birth to the Moral Majority and New Religious Right. Both academics and non-academics suffer from a very narrow, limited perception and understanding of the influence and workings of religion and culture. At the same time as the number of individuals who identify with the decline of religion increases, a space is left into which fundamentalism enters and thrives. We concur with Taylor's analysis.

RELIGION AS THE FABRIC OF HUMAN LIFE

Similar to Jung, Taylor sees religion as being innate to human life. Without understanding the nature, origin, and ground of religion, both lay and scholarly religious writers can easily become preoccupied with their own idiosyncratic ideas, whether consciously or unconsciously. These idiosyncrasies may emphasize myriad aspects of religion such as: inerrancy of scriptures, doctrine, belief, dogma, etc., thereby failing to

[30] Taylor, *After God,* p. 1. 2007

recognize the universality of religion (the larger picture) and its pervasive presence in culture. Because it is so easy to lose sight of the forces that create and shape the contemporary religious, Taylor offers the following *foundational definition of religion*:

> Religion is an *emergent*, complex, adaptive network of myths, symbols, rituals and concepts that simultaneously figure patterns of feeling, thinking, and acting and *disrupt stable structures of meaning and purpose.* When understood in that way, religion not only involves ideas and practices that are manifestly religious but also include a broad range of *cultural phenomenon not ordinarily associated with religion.*[31]

Taylor devotes himself to establishing religion as native to human life; that is, the divine is the "groundless ground" of *both* religion *and* culture. In a similar manner, Jung discovered the native religious function of the psyche and began to conceptualize how that dynamic is played out, not only in history, but also in the lives of individuals and culture. For Taylor, the "Groundless ground" allows one to view the inherent dialectical relationship in religion as both a *stabilizing and destabilizing* force in culture and in one's personal life. Taylor arrives at this position by understanding religion as uniting the opposites of transcendence and immanence; thus religion is a dialectical relationship of "immanent transcendence."[32] The immanent nature of religion provides a stabilizing force by furnishing a sacred ground for human existence. Religious expression rests on immanent concretization that transcends its immediate incarnation. It is this very interplay of religion's immanent nature that leads to transcendence that makes immediate, concrete manifestations. Therefore, religion stabilizes when it gives the numinous concrete form and destabilizes by providing the means to transcend that form. The present concrete form that the sacred takes on will also prove to be destabilizing since it ultimately cannot fully satisfy the religious

---

[31] Taylor, *After God,* 2007

[32] Ibid., 41.

impulse which leads to transcendence. In its dialectical nature and tension, even the present concretizations of the sacred (e.g., sacramental and iconoclastic) are also the destabilizing forces. This is similar to Jung's view of the evolution of archetypal consciousness, both personal and collective. As Jung writes, unconscious fantasy is a cauldron: "Formation, transformation, Eternal Mind's eternal recreation..."[33] Jung's archetypal unconscious forever transcends its incarnations, thus denying any historical and particular incarnation's ultimate supremacy.

Taylor's definition and appreciation of religion as an emergent, creative, relational, and encompassing force allows him to appreciate the deconstructive chaotic aspects of religion. This permits him to enter fully into the postmodern conversation. Unlike fundamentalists who are afraid and anxious of the implications of postmodernism, Taylor's embrace of the dialectical nature of religion proves to be well suited to contemporary society. In fact, the destabilizing nature of contemporary religion brings about a new stabilizing incarnation. The traditional structures and forms of religion deteriorate when the renewing energies of the religious imagination are being extinguished by oppressive attitudes toward the unconscious. For both Taylor and Jung, this provides an opportunity for religious and cultural transformation. We are on the cusp of an epochal change, what Jungian scholar Edward Edinger has termed a "new dispensation."[34]

[33] Jung, CW 5, par. 400.

[34] See Edinger, 1981

III.
ARCHETYPAL PROCESSES AND PHENOMENA OF RELIGION IN JUNGIAN THEORY

1. RELIGIO

> Numinous experience arises from an autonomous level of the psyche that is either the source of, or the medium for, the transmission of religious experience; empirically, we cannot say which. We cannot know whether religious experience arises 'beyond' the psyche, or from within it. But having such an experience immediately implies the presence of the psyche, without which there would be no experience, or no experiencer (Corbett, 1996).

Wach (1951/1958), defines religion as follows: "A system of thought, feeling, and action that is shared by a group and that gives the members an object of devotion"; "a code of behavior by which individuals may judge the personal and social consequences of their actions"; and

> (...) a frame of reference by which individuals may relate to their group and their universe. Usually, religion concerns itself with that which transcends the known, the natural, or the expected; it is an acknowledgment of the extraordinary, the mysterious, and the supernatural. The religious consciousness generally recognizes a transcendent, sacred order and elaborates a technique

to deal with the inexplicable or unpredictable elements of human experience in the world or beyond it (p. 28).

Religion may be used to refer to a faith, or a religious belief, or to an organized religion. A faith or religious credence is a strong belief in a supernatural power or powers that act beyond or outside of the natural laws that control human destiny. An organized religion is an institution that proscribes certain conduct and espouses certain beliefs in a divine power. This describes what is meant when one says "He was raised in the Protestant religion." Here is Webster's Universal Encyclopedic Dictionary (2010) etymology and definition of the word religion: Middle English *religioun,* from Anglo-French *religiun,* Latin *religion-, religio,* supernatural constraint, sanction, religious practice, perhaps from *religare* to restrain, tie back: *relien* to rally, from Anglo-French *relier* to retie, gather, rally, from Latin *religare* "to tie out of the way", from *re-* + *ligare* to tie. (p.1)

1: a) the state of a religious;
   b) 1: the service and worship of God or the supernatural,
   b) 2: commitment or devotion to religious faith or observance.
2: a personal set or institutionalized system of religious attitudes, beliefs, and practices.
3: *archaic*: scrupulous conformity: *conscientiousness* (governed by or conforming to the dictates of conscience: Latin *conscientia,* from *conscient-, consciens,* present participle of *conscire* to be conscious (be conscious of guilt), from *com-* + *scire* to know).
4: a cause, principle, or system of beliefs held to with ardor and faith.

According to Cicero (n.s.), religion is derived from Latin relegare "go through again, read again," from re- "again" + legere "read" (p.1). However, popular etymology among the later ancients and modern writers connects it with religare "to bind fast," via notion of "place an obligation on," or "bond between humans and gods" (Douglas & Harper, 2010). *Re-ligare* can also mean "to bind back" or to "re-connect" (with something lost, disconnected) (Nydahl, Ako Sa Veci Maju, & Kagju, 2007, p. 16).

Connection, in the religious sense, does not mean simple perception or experience; it means conscious observation with respect to the meaning of that experience. Jung (1940) builds upon the etymological idea of connection and *re-connection* with the gods, and from an analytical perspective, he understood the word *religio* in the following way:

Careful consideration and observation of certain dynamic factors that are conceived as "powers": spirits, daemons, gods, laws, ideas, ideals, or whatever name man has given to such factors in his world as he has found powerful, dangerous, or helpful enough to be taken into careful consideration, or grand, beautiful, and meaningful enough to be devoutly worshipped and loved (p.8).

Religion As Connection

The antonym of the Latin *religens* is *negligens.* What this implies is that religion involves some sort of special, conscious connection to the divine, as compared with a negligent, vague, or unconscious connection to it (Jung, 1946).[35] Jung (1946 [CW 16, par. 395]) writes: "...Equilibrium does in fact exist between the psychic ego and non-ego, and that equilibrium is a *religio"* (p. 196). From a Jungian perspective, there is an archetypal *energy* behind the *powers* (i.e., spirits, daemons, gods, laws, ideas, and ideals) that is the source of the intensity or temper of religious devotion. Anytime ego-consciousness recognizes this relationship between the human and the supernatural, and responds with this *peculiar attitude*, it can be spoken of as a *religious connection.* Whenever the ego pays careful and responsible attention to the emerging content of the unconscious (i.e., images, symbols, feelings, intuitions, and

[35] Negligens - Lat. *negligentia*, from *neglegere*, to neglect, literally "not to pick up something"; disambiguation.

synchronistic events) we are talking about a spiritual or religious attitude of the ego.

This generates a number of questions. Does the specific nature of the relationship between ego and the unconscious deserve to be called religious? Can we say that any relationship between ego and archetypal experience is basically religious? What distinguishes devotion as religious and are these distinctions valid? For example, a scientist possessed by the object of her exploration, a politician consumed by his ideas, or a person in love may think and act toward the object of their devotion as if it were sacred; though they would be unlikely to label such devotion religious. The zeal and passion of a strident atheist would reject the label of religious despite his or her devotional and unwavering belief that there is no God. It appears that Jung's definition of religion is basically interchangeable with the definition of spirituality.

Image-Representation of Deity

How do we distinguish between *sacred* and *profane* experiences, between ordinary experience and experience of the numinous? If a person displays a subjective attitude and frame of reference toward something that they believe deserves to be worshipped then we should refer to those experiences as religious. Although this is a subjective and an individual matter, it always refers to the *Imago Dei*, the God Image, a fantasy-image of the "higher power." That is, anything involving a thought or fantasy structure that makes reference to a god, a deity, or some objective referent that includes a transcendent, numinous dimension can be thought of as religion. This holds true even when a person is possessed by an archetypal energy and formulates an accompanying ideological structure. For example, if a fanatic member of the Khmer Rouge acts under the powerful belief in a *perfect social order,* but does not associate this with a conscious idea of a deity or a higher, transcendent power, we would not classify this form of possession as religious. We will speak of religion where a God

Image—*Imago Dei*—is present as a frame of reference. In addition, *spiritual* objects or rituals that people develop that involve a higher, transcendent power should be considered religious even when they are not tethered to a commonly recognized, collective form of doctrine or dogma. Led by instinct, or unconscious motivation, such actions and attitudes may share quite a bit with the religious experience. Even a psychotic individual who may worship and prostrate himself before a tree that he believes to be sacred can be likened to a devout follower of any of the Abrahamic traditions that prostrate themselves before God. One's personal faith is not only derived from archetypal influences; a person's inner temperament and memory makes a personal faith possible. For the ego, the common elements of religious experience are archetypal influences of the Self and the presence of the *Imago Dei* that provides a symbolic basis for incarnating and *containing* the experience of the numinous.

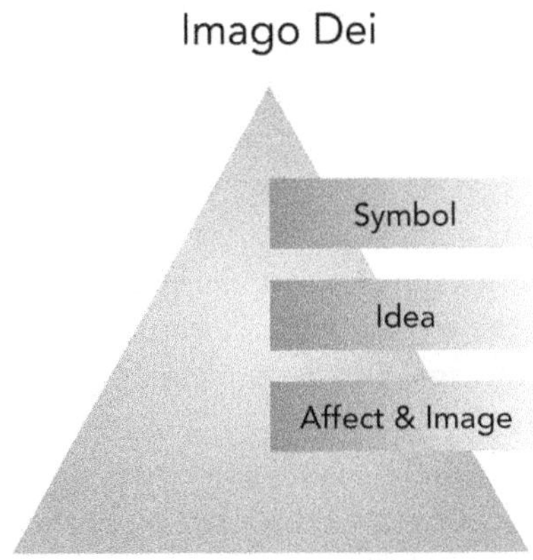

Rational and Non-Rational Aspect of Religion

Religious experiences consist of *rational* and *non-rational* components and contain an intellectual and an emotional component (Stein, 2006). The rational aspects are grounded in ideas, whereas the non-rational aspects are grounded in feelings and affects. When God's presence is experienced through intense feelings it is not difficult to have faith, states, Fox (2000). Contrast this with religious experience residing in a rational frame that is sustained by means that are only secondary to the immediate experience. What constellates around one's *Imago Dei* is an elaborate system of individual references to anything based on archetypal knowledge, memory, and prior experiences or a combination of these is still to be considered religious. We consider religious experience as an active conscious connection with the archetypal energies, i.e., the Self. This connection can be direct or indirect. Without the conscious recognition of an experience as religious it remains just an experience. Psychoanalysis can be very helpful in fostering a deeper understanding that transforms experiences from the profane to the sacred.

Archetypes Are The Sources of Psychic Energy

Is the presence of the archetype necessary to meet the criteria for an experience to be called religious? Jung (1919, [CW 8, para. 270]), in his essay on *Instinct and the Unconscious*, spoke of archetypes as "necessary *a priori* determinants of *all* psychic processes" (emphasis authors'). He went on to say that, "Just as his instincts compel man to a specifically human mode of existence, so the archetypes force his ways of perception and apprehension into specifically human patterns" (Jung, 1948a, [CW 8, para. 270]).

When speaking about anything *endowed* by spiritual energy we are referring to archetypes and their energies projected onto external objects. Therefore, we are speaking about *inner* energy-dominants and patterns whose primary source is the psyche and not the objective world.[36] Jung (1935, [CW 11, para. 857]) wrote,

[36] Psyche is "in" the world the same way the world is "in" the psyche. The objective and the subjective are only auxiliary terms while dealing with the object-subject continuum. We cannot know how this "objective" world would look like without the "subject." Would there be a sound from a

"The world of gods and spirits is truly 'nothing but' the collective unconscious inside me." If projected outside their *source* (psyche), they are perceived as objective and external. Palpable objects of external reality play an important and indispensable role when experiencing and apperceiving the unconscious. Religion is considered to be a way of responding to unconscious energies that influence the experiencing ego. Unconscious energy that significantly touches the ego (in positive or negative ways) is considered archetypal. This specific aspect of the unconscious, with its effect on ego-consciousness, has been traditionally referred to as divine or daemonic. In Jungian literature this influence is referred to as *numinous*; hence numinosum.

2. THE NUMINOSUM

We might say . . . that the term "religion" designates the attitude peculiar to a consciousness which has been changed by experience of the numinosum (Jung, 1938, [CW 11, para. 857]).

---

branch falling from the tree if there was nobody in the forest? What (and how) we are able to touch, see and hear is determined by the innate faculties of our senses. For example, humans cannot see electromagnetic wavelength outside of the spectrum of 390 - 700 nm. We cannot detect vibrations in our ears which are lower than 20 Hz and greater than 20 KHz and the like. We know they "exist" because of technological devices that extend our senses. The same is true about a priori categories of pure reason determining *how* we are able to think and *what* we are able to think. Categories of feeling and imagination (archetypes) allow us to experience the world in a very determined way as to what we can feel and know about the "objective" world; therefore, one cannot go beyond the frame of those inner structures. Another phenomenon complicating our experience of the world is projection, or unconscious attribution of unconscious states to the object. According to the theory of Lévy-Bruhl later adapted by Jung, ancient humans, or children, naturally live in the state of *participation mystique*, or unconscious unity. In that state object and subject overlap and are experienced as one. Hence magical thinking or belief that external beings are directly responsible for one's mental states. According to Jung, realization of unconscious contents, i.e., withdrawal of projections and transforming unconscious content to conscious content creates a more accurate (real) picture of the world. He termed this individuation (See for example: Jung, CW 6, par. 781).

Jung was a product of the Enlightenment, but he was also a child of Romanticism. Philosophers like Goethe, Herder, Nietzsche, Schelling, Schopenhauer, Feuerbach, Schiller and especially Schleiermacher influenced Jung more than is generally recognized. Jung's idea of religion rests upon an *experience* of archetypal energy and that is one of the major reasons he emphasized its emotional aspect. The nature of such an experience was thoroughly explored by the German theologian Rudolf Otto (1869-1937).

Otto and numinosum

In *Das Heilige,* written in 1917, he introduced the term *numinosum*. Otto wrote: "... I adopt a word coined from the Latin *numen*.[37] Omen has given us *'ominous,'* and there is no reason why from *numen* we should not similarly form a word *'numinous.'*" For Otto, human encounters with "the Holy" (through religious experience, imagery, ritual, prayer, etc.) are experienced as "unworldly" feelings of dependence, awe and fear at the same time. He coined the phrase *mysterium tremendum et fascinans* (awful and fascinating mystery). A religious experience, thus, consists of three components: mystery, fear (dread) and fascination (attraction). Otto stressed the inherent ambiguity of a numinous experience. It is tremendous, absolutely overpowering, but seducing and captivating at the same time. It is a mixture of positive attraction, mystical absorption and fear all at once. Hence, there is a certain complexity and peculiar bipolarity of this mystery. It is wholly paradoxical. Jung recognized the identity of the experience of the archetypal and the *wholly other* described by Otto and came to the conclusion that archetypes, when activated, always produce numinous affect. Otto, in his work *Das Heilige*, was actually describing what Jung called archetypal encounters. Otto says:

[37] *Numen* - hint, or sign (authors)

> . . . The feeling of it may at times come sweeping like a gentle tide pervading the mind with a tranquil mood of deepest worship. It may pass over into a more set and lasting attitude of the soul, continuing, as it were, thrillingly vibrant and resonant, until at last it dies away and the soul resumes its 'profane,' non-religious mood of everyday experience. It may burst in sudden eruption from the depths of the soul with spasms and convulsions, or lead to the strangest excitements, to intoxicated frenzy, to transport, and to ecstasy... It may become the hushed, trembling, and speechless humility of the creature in the presence of – whom or what? In the presence of that which is a *mystery* inexpressible above all creatures. (Rudolf Otto and John W. Harvey, *The Idea of the Holy*, 2004, p. 12).

Mystery

Mystery denotes enigma, inexplicability, inexpressibility and incomprehensibility, which are "above all creatures." Otto says (1923): "Conceptually mysterium denotes merely that which is hidden and esoteric, that which is beyond conception or understanding, extraordinary and unfamiliar."

> (...) It implies the first application of a category of valuation which has no place in the everyday natural world of ordinary experience, and is only possible to a being in whom has been awakened a mental disposition, unique in kind and different in a definite way from any 'natural' faculty. (p. 13)

Mysterium is the "wholly Other", that still possess an element of intelligibility, meaning that it involves a meaningful directive to the perceiving ego. It feels, as Grof described it, as a "more real reality" (Grof, 1984)[38] imposing its effect on the ego.

---

[38] *Stanislav Grof interviews* Dr. Albert Hofmann, Esalen Institute, Big Sur, California, 1984, p1.

James and Mystical Experiences

William James (1842-1910), who studied the phenomenology of religious experience, also influenced Jung's thoughts about encounters with archetypal energy. In his initial voyage to the United States to deliver lectures at Clark University with Freud, Jung was very impressed with William James. He states: "I spent two delightful evenings with James alone and I was tremendously impressed by the clearness of his mind and the complete absence of intellectual prejudices" (Jung, 1949, Letters). James' (1902) *Varieties of Religious Experience* expounds on the phenomena of religious experience. James adopts a natural theology wherein religious experience is normalized and rendered simply as human experience.[39]

James explained the following characteristics of mystical experience:

1) Ineffability: A state that defies expression. This quality "must be directly experienced; it cannot be imparted or transferred to others. In this peculiarity mystical states are more like states of feeling than like states of intellect," says James.

2) Noetic quality: "They are states of insight into depths of truth unplumbed by the discursive intellect," describes James.

3) Transiency: About this aspect of mystical experience James says: "Mystical states cannot be sustained for long. (...). Often, when faded, their quality can but imperfectly be reproduced in memory; but when they recur it is recognized; and from one recurrence to another it is susceptible of continuous development in what is felt as inner richness and importance."

[39] "Natural theology is a program of inquiry into the existence and attributes of God without referring or appealing to any divine revelation. In natural theology, one asks what the word "God" means, whether and how names can be applied to God, whether God exists, whether God knows the future free choices of creatures, and so forth. The aim is to answer those questions without using any claims drawn from any sacred texts or divine revelation, even though one may hold such claims." (Internet Encyclopedia of Philosophy, n.d., p.1)

Prolonged states of mystical experience may produce destabilizing effects on the ego that can be observed with psychotics.

4) Passivity: "The mystic feels as if his own will were in abeyance, and indeed sometimes as if he were grasped and held by a superior power." This characteristic describes the subordinate position of the ego toward the archetypal energy. (pp. XVII-XVIII)

Abraham Maslow

Jung, James, Otto, Eliade and others were pioneering explorers of the psychological states of humans from our earliest beginnings. Their discoveries led to increased interest in those states in the field of psychology. The introduction of Eastern philosophies to the West, together with the introduction of psychedelic drugs, gave rise to experimental studies led by people like Grof, Leary, Brentano, Rogers and others. Another important contribution to the understanding of religious (i.e., numinous) experiences came from Abraham Maslow's: *Religions, Values and Peak-Experiences.* In this work Maslow popularized the term "peak-experience," using the term to describe an encounter with numinosum. He (1976) says:

> The very beginning, the intrinsic core, the essence, the universal nucleus of every known high religion (unless Confucianism is also called a religion) has been the private, lonely, personal illumination, revelation, or ecstasy of some acutely sensitive prophet or seer. The high religions call themselves revealed religions and each of them tends to rest its validity, its function, and its right to exist on the codification and the communication of this original mystic experience or revelation from the lonely prophet to the mass of human beings in general. But it has recently begun to appear that these "revelations" or mystical illuminations can be subsumed under the head of the "peak-experiences" or "ecstasies" or "transcendent" experiences which are now being eagerly investigated by many psychologists. (p. 30)

As noted, Rudolf Otto also highlighted the awful, tremendous nature of the encounter with numinosum. The Bible also makes frequent mention of God who is to be feared and obeyed. For example:

"O LORD, God of vengeance,
O God of vengeance, shine forth!"
(Psalm 94; *The Bible*, English Standard Version)

> (...) Therefore, my beloved, as you have always obeyed, so now, not only as in my presence but much more in my absence, work out your own salvation with *fear* and *trembling*, for it is God who works in you, both to will and to work for his good pleasure, (Phil 2:1; emphasis ours).

Tremendum, according to Otto, implies a feeling of fear or religious *awe* (Ger. *des Schauervollen*), *majesty (Ger. des Übermächtigen*). It is an overpowering and unapproachable quality of the numinosum that is absolutely prodigious and vital (Ger. *das Energischen*). Otto writes that the tremendum evokes a sense of dependence and induces submission. According to Otto the *mysterium tremendum* is "wholly Other," coming from a completely strange God (Ger. *Das Ganz Andere*). It is unlike anything that consciousness encounters in ordinary states. It typically arouses in one a state of stupor, a "blank wonder, an astonishment that strikes us dumb, amazement absolute" (p. 26). In this state, "the soul is held speechless, trembles inwardly to the farthest fiber of its being (...) it implies that the mysterious is beginning to loom before the mind, to touch the feelings," (p. 17).

In mythology, we find numerous examples of encounters with the tremendum. Tremendum is variously represented as Chaos, a destructive dragon or monster, the underworld, extreme weather conditions, destructive fire, or stormy seas. Ancient Greeks projected the experience of tremendum onto the god of the sea, Poseidon. The *Orphic Hymn to Poseidon* begs him not to show his frenzied power to the sailors:

> Hear, Poseidon, ruler of the sea profound, whose liquid grasp begirds the solid ground; who, at the bottom of the stormy main, dark and deep-bosomed holdest thy watery reign. Thy awful hand the brazen trident bears, and sea's utmost bound thy will reveres. Thee I invoke, whose steeds the foam divide, from whose dark locks the briny waters glide; shoe voice, loud sounding through the roaring deep, drives all its billows in a raging heap; when fiercely riding through the boiling sea, thy hoarse command the trembling waves obey. Earth-shaking, dark-haired God, the liquid plains, the third division, fate to thee ordains. 'Tis thine, cerulean daimon, to survey, well-pleased, the monsters of the ocean play. (*Orphic Hymn 17 to Poseidon*; trans. Taylor. Greek hymns C3rd B.C. to 2nd A.D., p.1)

Fascinans

Fascinans consist of elements of awfulness and wonderfulness. This element of numinosum produces overflowing affection (Ger. das Überschwengliche). "And here too the unique nature of the experience of bliss is immediately noticeable," states Otto. This bliss is also *ganz andere*-beyond ordinary experience. He refers to fascinans as something awesome and delightful. In mythology this experience is symbolized by an encounter with the Other and falling in love with profound beauty, *femme fatale*, finding lost paradise, drinking aeternal water (*aqua permanens*), and discovering the alchemical stone of wisdom, *lapis philosophorum,* receiving divine deliverance and the like. This *fascination* and *attraction* is often constellated by the opposite sex, traditionally, and then projected by men onto women and women onto men. We read in *Songs of Songs* (*Holman Christian Standard Bible* 4:1-7) about the perfect beauty of the bride:

> How beautiful you are, my darling. How very beautiful! Behind your veil, your eyes are doves. Your hair is like a flock of goats streaming down Mount Gilead. Your teeth are like a flock of newly shorn [sheep] coming up from

> washing, each one having a twin, and not one missing. Your lips are like a scarlet cord, and your mouth is lovely. Behind your veil, your brow is like a slice of pomegranate. Your neck is like the tower of David, constructed in layers. A thousand bucklers are hung on it- all of them shield of warriors. Your breasts are like two fawns, twins of a gazelle, which feeds among the lilies. Before the day breaks and the shadows flee, I will make my way to the mountain of myrrh and the hill of frankincense. You are absolutely beautiful, my darling, with no imperfection in you.

In the *Odyssey* (800 B.C.), Odysseus falls in love with a nymph named Calypso, who, besides other qualities, represented feelings of excitement, attraction and infatuation. Fascinans is sometimes described as a sublime, perfect world or the state of being in paradise.

In *Revelation* (*Bible New International Version*, 22:1-5) we find following passage describing an image of eternal bliss capturing the emotional state and feelings of *fascinans*:

> Then the angel showed me the river of the water of life, as clear as crystal, flowing from the throne of God and of the Lamb down the middle of the great street of the city. On each side of the river stood the tree of life, bearing twelve crops of fruit, yielding its fruit every month. And the leaves of the tree are for the healing of the nations. No longer will there be any curse. The throne of God and of the Lamb will be in the city, and his servants will serve him. They will see his face, and his name will be on their foreheads. There will be no more night. They will not need the light of a lamp or the light of the sun, for the Lord God will give them light. And they will reign forever and ever.

Jung and Otto

The ego's encounter with the archetypal numinosum, like its encounter with the Holy, always humbles and changes the ego. Jung understood religion to be the attitude evoked in the mind after it has been affected by an encounter with the numinous, (Jung 1940, [CW 11, par. 9]). Jung's definition of religion then, is basically synonymous with what we understand spirituality to be.[40] Encounters with the numinosum may be ushered in by any number of human experiences: the death of a loved one, or the birth of a new life. Or, for someone like a scientist, it may arrive upon recognizing the profound mysteries and awe involved in studying the natural world. Immanuel Kant believed that there were two things that filled his mind with ever new and increasing admiration and awe: "The starry sky above me and the moral law within me." (*Idea for a Universal History from a Cosmopolitan Point of View*; 1784, p. 22). In the face of infinite incomprehensibility the intellect is humbled by the numinosum. Within the Christian tradition the ego seized by the Holy may experience its own sinfulness and undergo a moral catharsis. When the ego withstands and relates to the encounter with the Holy, without splitting it off, human beings relate more deeply with love and compassion to one another and the world. But if the overwhelmed ego responds with rigid defenses, the result can be selfishness, aggression, and hatred.

Jung adopted Otto's affective and phenomenological inquiry into the numinosum and applied it to his archetypal theory. According to Jung, the numinosum is a dynamic agency or affect not produced by an arbitrary act of will. The experience seizes and possesses the human subject. The numinosum is central to understanding religious experiences and encounters with the Self. Jung states:

> A great many ritualistic performances are carried out for the sole purpose of producing at will the effect of the *numinosum* by means of certain devices of a magical nature, such as invocation, incantation, sacrifice, meditation and other yoga practices, self-inflicted tortures of various descriptions, and so forth. But a

[40] For what is often referred to as religion, i.e., the organized set of beliefs and practices; Jung used the term creed as we will see later on.

> religious belief in an external and objective divine cause is always prior to any such performance (Jung 1969, [CW 11, para. 7]).

Religion: An Experience and An Idea

As we have stated, activation of the unconscious always produces, a certain degree of numinous experience. The ego may secondarily decide whether or not to assign a religious value to a numinous experience. Nonetheless, an experience ought to be considered *numinous* when it can be described as an apperception of unconscious content and energy of a greater intensity than is typical for everyday life. It produces an experience that feels "wholly Other." The experience becomes *religious* when an element of meaningful consideration, idea or an image, i.e. *Imago Dei*, is attached to it. So, we see that religion arises from a living experience of the numinosum as Jung (1957, [CW 10, para. 521]) explains:

> People call faith the true religious experience, but they do not stop to consider that actually it is a *secondary* phenomenon arising from the fact that something happened to us in the first place which instilled Πίστις (pistis) into us—that is, trust and loyalty (emphasis ours)

Thus, numinous experience is not necessarily to be understood as a religious experience unless it is connected to a spiritual frame involving the idea of god/God. Thus, both, a palpable *experience* of archetypal energy and a peculiar attitude of the mind are needed to form the whole gestalt of what we call religion.

Clinical Aspects of Interaction With the Numinosum

The numinosum always arises from the interaction between the ego and the "wholly Other," the Self. As Lionel Corbett (1996) points out, "...Numinous experience is always felt like a personal revelation; importantly, its significance may be accepted or rejected to [a] varying degree" (p. 14).

Whether the numinous experience will have a transformative effect or produce a dissociative influence depends on the strength of the ego and on the degree to which the ego manages to establish a personal relationship to the numinosum. We can say that the ego requires a certain degree of resistance and resilience to withstand the wholesale experience of unconscious forces; however, it also needs a degree of flexibility and openness to be changed by these experiences. Flexibility can be conceived of as the "right" degree of responsiveness to the influence of numinosum. The *tremendum* aspect of archetypal experience has a "crushing" influence on the ego, while *fascinans* has an integrative effect upon the ego—both are needed. Corbett stressed the importance of a balanced relation to numinosum as one of the key aspects of transformation in clinical practice. He (1996) states:

By 'religious' I refer to Jung's understanding of the activity of *religio* as the careful observation, and attempted integration, of important intrapsychic (soul-derived) images, including those considered pathological. We observe, we intuit, we feel, we reason, but above all we experience a kind of radiance and power from these experiences, a form of discovery which takes us beyond simple cognitive and affective categories into true gnosis, or experiential knowledge of the divine. Depending on the individual's temperament, and whether one wants to relate to the Self or realize one's identity with it, we believe that to pay attention to the personal experiences of the numinosum is either a form of prayer, or path to enlightenment, or both (p. 221).

Corbett stresses "Numinous experiences often occur during times of great personal turmoil." (Corbett, 2011, p. 55).

Andrew's Conversion

One of my (G.J.D.) patients, a 16-year-old male, presented with severe anxiety, racing thoughts, crying spells and different voices telling him how "bad and evil" he was. One voice suggested he kill himself and then he will be with the Lord. He attempted mightily to suppress these feelings and voices.

Several weeks prior to this symptomatic outbreak, this young adolescent, who comes from a divorced family with his mother subsequently having numerous abusive boyfriends, had a "religious experience (conversion) and was baptized in the Holy Spirit." He stated that he had "found religion" and felt that he was getting his life together. In the following weeks he experienced tremendous excitement, joy and laughter ("I've got that joy, joy, joy, down in my heart," he would sing). This fulfilled a deep longing for feeling loved and good in light of his experience of parental neglect. However, these religious experiences also opened him to his unconscious repressed memories of parental neglect, abuse and personal failings—what he termed sin. These memories and images came back with a vengeance and a numinous darkness in the image of the evil one, Satan. This is the counterbalancing force of the dark tremendum. This young man's weak ego and a fragile self-structure opened him to energies that he was not prepared to deal with. He did not have the ego resiliency to resist, withstand and work through these energies and instead felt overpowered by intrusive, abusive and racing thoughts, feelings and voices. His overwhelming anxiety led him to conclude he was "losing it." In this young man's struggle, we see evidence of the delicate balance that must be struck between remaining open to numinous experiences and the tendency for such experiences to overwhelm and flood the psyche. He oscillated between a desire for complete surrender to the *fascinans* in the form of the Lord who would unite him with the Holy and the counter-vailing forces of the *tremendum* that tormented him with the idea of his utter unworthiness.

3. CREED

A creed coincides with the established church, or at any rate, forms a public institution whose members include not only true believers but vast numbers of people who can only be described as 'indifferent' in matters of religion and who belong to it simply by force of habit (Jung 1957, [CW 10, para. 508]).

Creeds are another expression of the human relationship to the divine. This relationship represents a collective, structured and institutionalized form of relationship to the numinosum and its representations. Creeds are "*codified and dogmatized forms of original religious experiences,*" says Jung (1940, [CW 11, para. 10; emphasis added). Creed and religion need to be distinguished based on codes of subjective and objective components constituting the frame of reference explaining and preserving religious experience.

Creed rests upon at least four pillars:

1) the *experience* of the numinosum (Holy, God);
2) *stories* and *ideas* that provide the frame for one's beliefs (theology and mythology);
3) *conduct*: set of religious practices, customs and rituals; and
4) *faith*, that is acceptance of certain claims which cannot be explained and justified by rational analysis (reason) alone.

A creed rests mainly on its theological foundation and codified conduct, while religion, i.e., spirituality is rooted primarily in experience. Religion is more theologically flexible than creed. Creed prescribes and proscribes what is to be believed and what is to be rejected based on a frame provided by those in authority. Religion and spirituality are not bound by an established creed and thus are more likely to change frames based on lived experience. In the case of creed, the task of passing on knowledge of the numinosum is carried out by an implied or explicit authority. The danger is, knowledge of the numinosum is often articulated and passed on without any numinous experiences or what we might call a living relationship to the numinosum. In creedal communities numinous experiences are often implied but are not necessary and are often relegated to a secondary or tertiary position. The ideological framework of a creed is firmly anchored and established, it is not something that is in the process of formation. Although the ideas involved in a creed may have originally emerged from experience, subsequent followers do not partake in this original memory. Adherents to a creed typically accept ideas by means of unconscious participation. Jung:

> It is true that every creed is originally based on the one hand upon the experience of the numinosum and on the other hand upon Πίστις, that is to say, trust or loyalty, faith and confidence in a certain experience of a numinous nature and in the change of consciousness that ensues (Jung 1958, [CW 11, para. 9]).

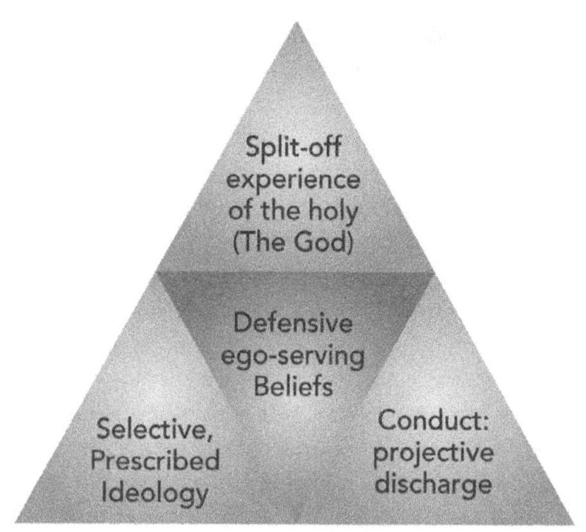

Creed, a Prescribed Religion

Creed As Trust

For Jung, the term "religion" designates the attitude peculiar to a consciousness that has been changed by the experience of the numinosum; whereas the term creed refers to the attitude of mind that accepts certain religious ideas as truths and perpetuates them by institutionalized means. Etymologically, the Middle English word *crede* comes from Old English *crēda*, which has its root in Latin *credo* (first word of the Apostles' and Nicene Creeds – "I believe…"). Latin credo is from *credere*, which means to believe, trust, or entrust. *Webster's Dictionary* (2011) defines the word as: 1) a brief authoritative formula of religious belief; and 2) a set of fundamental beliefs; also as 3) a guiding principle (p.1). *The Free Dictionary* defines creed as a "religious doctrine": "The written body of teachings of a religious group that are generally accepted by that group" (p.1). Creeds are *by definition* established, elaborate, structures of ideas; they can be written or unwritten and can create an established body of knowledge for a group. Creed can be religious only to the extent that it allows for individual experiences of the numinosum. Too often this is not the case. A creed can represent one's formalized relationship to God and the numinosum, but it may also become a powerful tool of indoctrination intended to control, deny, constrain, or dictate to others the nature of their relationship to the numinosum. In this respect, the creed is *antithetical* to religion.

> The disadvantage of a creed as a public institution is that it serves two masters: on the one hand, it derives its existence from the relationship of man to God, and on the other hand, it owes a duty to the State, i.e., to the world, in which connection it can appeal to the saying 'Render unto Caesar…' and various other admonitions in the New Testament (Jung 1957, [CW 10, para. 520]).

Creed can be understood as a statement of the collective, it is a common consensus of the group's view of religious ideas and experiences. Taken together, individual experiences are collectivized over time and in the course of this transition subjective experience is often lost or diminished. Creeds can disfigure an individual religious experience. Conversely, when an individual allows a unique religious experience to be subsumed under a codified creed important emotional elements and archetypal properties may be excluded. Such exclusion does not lead to the extermination of those elements; it merely splits them off psychologically, a process that increases the pressure to relegate these energies to the shadow where they may manifest as compulsiveness, group identification, one-sidedness, projection, and the like.

Borrowed Religiosity

Individuals who are too eager or in desperate need to join a religious group, often sacrifice or disown their personal God-image in favor of the collective God image. This psychological maneuver of denying or merging God images, results in the formation of a religious persona that fits the group's expectations. Such a persona lacks a living connection to the Self though the persona serves well enough for playing the role of an adherent. The religious persona tends to be a false and distorted image of the source of religious experience, the numinosum. In such situations, the objects of religious worship cannot be experienced in a true symbolic manner.

Enactment of Numinous Energy

The movement that proceeds from personal experience of the Holy to a formal religious creed often results in the ego excluding its own unique and personal experience of the numinosum. In the same way that we have come to understand from physics, that energy can neither be created nor destroyed, the exclusion of archetypal energies from conscious awareness does not abrogate these energies – they simply work unconsciously. However, what emerges instead are shadowy psychological features that possess an inexorable urge toward "enacting" unconscious and undifferentiated aspects of the numinosum. In psychoanalysis, the term enacting refers to those occasions when an analysand and analyst first act out their unconscious dynamics and conflicts instead of bringing that material consciously into the consulting room for examination.[41] We use the term enactment here rather broadly, as a manifestation of unconscious material without accompanying reflection. When we speak of enactment in the context of the numinosum being excluded from conscious awareness, one sees actions arising from unconscious energies that have not been adequately and critically reflected on—leading to a type of archetypal possession resulting in a distortion of reality (enactments, conspiracies, idealization and the like). A split-off or unrecognized pole of one's numinous experience does not disappear simply because it remains unrecognized. This missing "piece" of the Self will often make its presence known through fate. There is a tendency for religious phenomena to become dichotomized such that indirect encounters (sacred stories, traditions, etc.) with the numinosum that are filtered through creeds may evoke destructive, unconscious renderings of the God image while direct experiences tend to evoke more integrating, benevolent perspectives.

In the Old Testament, Yahweh often appears vengeful, punitive, and cruel, qualities that resemble how gods are sometimes rendered in mythology. The New Testament image of God emphasizes qualities that are gentle, loving, and inviting. The Old and New Testament offer very different frames of reference through which the numinosum may be assimilated and these different frames can evince different creeds. We could speculate that the evolution of the image of God from the Old to the New Testament parallels an evolution of consciousness in which the Self became more fully integrated. As Erich Neumann observed, "The first half of life is largely taken up with adapting to the powers of the outside world and their suprapersonal demands. (...) The unconscious activity of the self dominates the whole of life, but it is only in the second half that this activity becomes conscious. (Neumann, E., *The Origins and History of Consciousness*, 1962, p. 409)

---

[41] "Enactment is (...) defined as a pattern of nonverbal interactional behavior between the two parties in a therapeutic situation, with unconscious meaning for both. It involves mutual projective identification between therapist and patient." (Plakun EM, Erik H. Erikson Institute for Education and Research, 1998, p.1)

The difference between the Old and New Testament's images of God informs us of two distinctly different ways that the ego deals with archetypal energies. These have enormous psychological implications and potential. The ego can develop "filters" that effectively make it impenetrable to archetypal energies as Compaan (2010) notes:

> [Archetypal] energies might be so disliked or shamed by the ego that they have no opportunity to emerge into the material world. The ego remains unconscious about these archetypal energies. It may be that the archetypal energy still gets expressed but the ego thinks that it is not happening (p.16).

Later, we explore how such psychological maneuvers are reflected in the notion of karma in both the Hindu and Buddhist traditions.

Analysis Serves The Realizations of Different Aspects of The Self

Analytical psychotherapy serves the highest function when it is able to bring split-off energies into conscious awareness that can lead to their realization, meaning, emotional experience, and thus greater degrees of volitional relationship. Failing to accomplish the integration of split-off energies fosters the *projection* of these forces that coalesce as the shadow.[42] Wallin (2007) explains it this way:

---

[42] Jung defines the shadow succinctly as "the thing a person has no wish to be", (CW 16, para. 470). The shadow is one's negative side of their personality; the hidden, inferior and unpleasant aspects of oneself that one wishes to hide. The shadow manifests in one's attitudes, behavior and emotions. Furthermore, Jung states: "The shadow personifies everything that the subject refuses to acknowledge about himself (...) and a tight passage, a narrow door, whose painful constriction no one is spared who goes down to the deep well. (...) and when an individual makes an attempt to see his shadow, he becomes aware of (and often ashamed of) those qualities and impulses he denies in himself but can plainly see in others—such things as egotism, mental laziness, and sloppiness; unreal fantasies, schemes, and plots; carelessness and cowardice; inordinate love of money and possessions...[a] painful and lengthy work of self-education." (M-L von Franz, "The Process of Individuation" in C. G. Jung, *Man and his Symbols* (London, 1978, p.174)

> Experiences, memories, representations, and feelings that are unintegrated and denied seem, figuratively speaking, to seek a home. If they can't be psychologically accommodated within the [patient], they must be relocated in the other (p. 249).

Projective Identification

The process of projective identification can intensify the grip that one person's unconscious exerts on another person's unconscious. Projective identification can produce what Jung (1954b, [CW 8, para. 61]) refers to as "breaking the pair of opposites." To clarify, projection occurs when an element of the unconscious is projected onto another person and then perceived as if it originated in the other person. Projective identification occurs when the recipient of someone's projection identifies with what is being projected on them and acts accordingly. In both, social processes and therapy, conscious *mentalization* is needed to avoid raw reactivity that is typical for any gradated conflict, (Zosky, 2003).[43] Analysis strives for the patient to own his or her own unconsciously born responses, and that only happens through the analyst's ability to do the same.

---

[43] "Mentalization is a term used by both developmental psychologists and psychoanalysts to refer to a core process of human social functioning and self-regulation, involved in the establishment of robust links between personally meaningful early experiences and their representation. More elaborate mentalization, sometimes called 'reflectiveness,' is linked with attachment, insofar as a caregiver's mindfulness about a child's mental states appears as a key mediator of the transmission of attachment. (...) Fonagy and Target (1997, 2002) *Understand mentalizing as resulting from the development of representations of psychological states in the mind of the human infant.* (Koren-Karie, Oppenheim, Dolev, Sher, & Etzion-Carasso, 2002; Meins, Fernyhough, Wainwright, Clark-Carter, Das Gupta, Fradley, & Tuckey, 2003)." In *Mentalization in adult attachment narratives: Reflective functioning, mental states, and affect elaboration compared*; 2008, Peter Fonagy, PhD et al.

Redefining Creed

Typically, a person adheres to a certain creed only after an experience in which archetypal energies break through. Under such circumstances the ego can no longer hold sway against the breakthrough of archetypal messages. The conversion of Saul of Tarsus on the road to Damascus may be one such example of the archetypal energies breaking through. If a creed is established too firmly the ego is prevented from integrating new experiences and insights—even powerful emotional experiences. One of the functions of a creed is to serve as a safe container of archetypal affect; however it also serves as a protection against the awful and disintegrating aspects of the numinosum. The proper balance of these opposing forces helps maintain consensual reality and preserves the moral compass of the collective. If the protective function dominates over the containing function, creed becomes subservient to a religious persona, instead of serving the Self.

Even those who strictly follow an organized set of religious rules develop their own positions that may at times contradict the established teachings. A person may assume views that depart from a creed in ways that may be deemed liberal, personal, or contradictory. For example, some areas of potential departure from creeds in contemporary Christianity include: abortion, whether or not homosexuality constitutes a sin, the second coming, and whether or not God ordains men to have authority over women within the family.

One of my patient's daughter, who is lesbian, states that she believes and accepts everything that her church teaches, except "they still have not caught up with contemporary medical findings." (V.Š.)[44] As the ego develops, an individual's frames evolve in ways that contain the numinosum, accommodates and assimilates it, and integrates it into a personal worldview. In the religious zeitgeist today, people are beginning to create "a

---

[44] V.Š. Identifies Vladislav Šolc, G.J.D. identifies George J. Didier as authors of corresponding text.

religion of one's own" outside the confines of their traditional creed. We speak about spirituality when a person discovers greater freedom from the binding dogmas of a prescribed philosophy and simultaneously differentiates one's identity from social structures of that philosophy or religion. It does not mean that church or ritual will necessarily be abandoned; it means that their functions become more consciously accepted. Spirituality represents an individual consciousness coming to terms with, and understanding, the common playing field of our archetypal heritage; whereas, creed represents the collective archetypal understanding on the platform of unconscious identification. Jung says:

> (...) in Christianity, Christ is an exemplar who dwells in every Christian as his integral personality. But historical trends led to the imitatio Christi, whereby the individual does not pursue his own destined road to wholeness, but attempts to *imitate* the way taken by Christ. Similarly in the East, historical trends led to a devout imitation of the Buddha. That Buddha should have become a model to be imitated was in itself a weakening of his idea, just as the imitatio Christi was a forerunner of the fateful stasis in the evolution of the Christian idea. (MDR, 1963, p. 337; emphasis author's)

Healthy Fruits of Creed

Healthy religion takes both, creed and personal spirituality into account. It is important to state again that creed yields negative fruits only when it emerges from the shadow where it may manifest as authoritarian, exclusivist, xenophobic, and mind-closing, etc. For many people organized religion, along with creeds, provide healthy opportunities for spiritual experiences and connection in loving and meaningful ways. Barack Obama said (*National Prayer Breakfast*, Feb. 6, 2009):

I didn't become a Christian until many years later, when I moved to the South Side of Chicago after college. It happened not because of indoctrination or a sudden revelation, but because I spent month after month working with church folks who simply wanted to help neighbors who were down on their luck no matter what they looked like, or where they came from, or who they prayed to. (p.1)

Creed can be viewed as unhealthy when the frame it provides is too narrow and tight or is simply unmalleable. Likewise, individual spirituality untethered to collective norms can be as misguided as uncritical adherence to a creed without any involvement of individual spirituality.

Creed (identification)	Spirituality (individuation)

Creed versus Spirituality

4. RELATIONSHIP BETWEEN CREED AND RITUAL

The very essence of myth is that haunting awareness of transcendental forces peering through the cracks of the visible universe (Wheelwright, 1968, p. 32)

Unconscious energy is an ever-present force that influences development of consciousness. That is true from an ontogenetic and phylogenetic perspective. The ego development, understood as coinciding with the development of consciousness, is based on a dialectical relationship between conscious and unconscious. Consciousness of archetypal patterns and forces gives the ego a unique advantage; awareness fosters differentiation from the inner other. Ego needs fluidity to navigate archetypal energy, but it also needs material to build upon. If there's a lack of differentiation between conscious and unconscious, the ego becomes a mere passenger rather than a driver. Fluidity, therefore, can foster a meaningful and dialectical relation between ego and the Self.

Symbolic Process

This meaning-creation is fostered by a symbolic process of ritual that has been studied by scholars like Turner (*The Ritual Process: Structure and Anti-Structure*; 1969), and van Gennep (*The Rites of Passage*; 1960). From an anthropological perspective, the use of symbols during a ritual (symbolic) process enables the "dissolution" of the previous order and the creation of malleable situations that establish new world views, positions, institutions, and customs. Because ego draws meaning from the external structure and inner patterns, both are crucial to the process of adaptation. Analytical psychology understands symbolic process as a function in which symbols are utilized to produce a change of consciousness (individuation). Ritual *objectifies* symbols in a more or less concrete way and involves them in playing when the ego is receptive to what they represent. We can say that ritual is a tool for holding and containing numinous energies while working toward their integration into consciousness. When functioning normally the ego serves as a filter that lets through only so much unconscious archetypal energy. The amount of archetypal energy that gets through is proportional to the ego's disposition: strength and level of development. Inflation, possession, disintegration, and other similar phenomena are symptoms of impaired ego function, and thus symptoms of the dominion of the Self. The loss of one's ego is equivalent to a state of complete unconsciousness, possibly a return to the primordial state. Ritual creates access to and a protective barrier against a return to an overwhelming primordial state of unity. At the same time rituals are building blocks the ego utilizes to make meaning. Jung spoke on being immersed in the unconscious:

> The unconscious no sooner touches us than we *are* it—we become unconscious of ourselves. That is the age-old danger, instinctively known and feared by primitive man (...) [primitives] are afraid of uncontrolled emotions, because consciousness breaks down under them and gives way to possession. All man's strivings

> have therefore been directed towards the consolidation of consciousness. This was the purpose of rite and dogma; they were dams and walls to keep back the dangers of the unconscious, the 'perils of the soul.' Primitive rites consist accordingly in the exorcising of spirits, the lifting of spells, the averting of the evil omen, propitiation, purification, and the production by sympathetic magic of helpful occurrences. It is these barriers, erected in primitive times, that later became the foundations of the Church. It is also these barriers that collapse when the symbols become weak with age. Then the waters rise and boundless catastrophes break over mankind (Jung, 1951a, [CW 9i, para. 47]).

Thus the function of ritual is not only to protect the ego from the numinosum, but also to create psychological conditions under which the ego can allow the numinosum to enter and eventually integrate the experiences of the Self. Probing the ego and employing its "elasticity" beyond its everyday limits ensures approximation to one's inner world and the Self.

Ritual Is Relation To The Sacred That Changes Personality

Ritual conducted "between the profane and the sacred," to use Eliade's terminology, was practiced for the purpose of the development of personality. This happened when the sacred was manifested and found its meaningful place in the mind of the one who practiced it. The development of personality happens as a development of new realizations, of acceptance of one's position in life, tribe and family; or the letting-go of feelings of remorse, sadness due to the death of a close person, transition in hierarchy, and the like.

Myth and Ritual Are Intertwined Aspects of The Religious Conduct

Myth (image)	Ritual (behavior)

"Ritual is simply myth enacted; by participating in a rite, you are participating directly in the myth."
Joseph Campbell, Pathways to Bliss, 2008, Introduction, xvii

Myth also serves as a *container* of the archetypal energy passing through the fortifications of the ego (Corbett, 1996). Mythology and its enactment in ritual can be viewed as an attempt to define or consciously structure otherwise unstructured archetypal energies. Ritual bridges the animal and human components of the psyche by establishing cosmogonic or mythical doctrines in the minds of participants. Ritual provides the form for the unconscious content. One realizes and accepts his or her place in the universe on the platform of collective norms. The saying, "It has always been done that way, so it makes sense to continue," is in accordance with established meaning. A parent must release their child to marry and cleave to another person; the suffering of loss is accepted because it represents a sacrifice to a higher order. Ritual helps the individual become a bearer of archetypal knowledge, of principles that transcend their individual existence. Indeed, the very essential utility of the human mind is the creation of meaning. Mind's nature is such that it does not accept chaos and ambivalence; therefore, it consistently seeks to create comprehensible structures of meaning. Mind could not do that without the feeling-forms, namely the archetypes, assisting in the creation of meaning. Religion has to do with the process of utilizing the ability of mind creating meaning. Ritual can be viewed as container, catalyst, and preserver of archetypal knowledge.

Through the power of ritual process, archetypal energies and knowledge of the collective unconscious take on human form. Ego evolved out of the complex web of social and symbolic relations that were captured in outward expressions as sounds, images, and acts. Those are still needed as they provide a very specific frame of incarnating unconscious material. Ritual, mythology, and theology are parts of such a frame.

Defense Against Numinous Affect

Mythology appears to have a dual, paradoxical function. It can reconcile a human's need for constant connection with the numinosum (sacred energy) and the need to differentiate by creating unique, individual structures needed to function in the everyday life.

Sacred (collective; participation mystique)	Profane (individual; unique)

Myth Bridges Universal and Daily

When ritual and mythology begins to wane in providing transcendent (archetypal) communication between the two worlds creed can be used as a *defensive* tool.

That is why Jung (In Neumann, 1970) cautioned:

> Only when we have recognized how the personal develops out of the transpersonal, detaches itself from it but, despite the crucial role of ego consciousness, always remains rooted in it, can we restore to the transpersonal factors their original weight and meaning, lacking which a healthy collective and individual life is impossible (p. xxiii)

Ritual consolidates and protects against the numinosum and permits us to utilize the numinous energy constructively. These functions are complementary. Just like cell membranes cannot fulfill the function of exchange of information and energy if its permeability is too low; so the ego cannot form its relationship to numinosum if its defenses are too rigid. The reverse is also true. If a cell becomes too permeable it may rupture; so the ego, if it becomes too permeable, being overwhelmed by the numinosum, may rupture and thus the alchemical vessel of the psyche may split or fracture. Ritual process can foster the ego's permeability to the numinosum, all depending on which perspective we are viewing the process. The ego instinctively defends against disintegration and loss of connection with the body, while the unconscious at the same time wants to be transformed into consciousness by becoming part of the ego-structure, inhabiting the ego, so to speak. Defenses strengthened with development of culture where instinctive demands ran contrary to culture. Taboos, accommodating instinctive and numinous energies, arose as split-off areas and could exist in parallel with societal boundaries, religions among them. This duality that developed within human nature promoted a continuous battle of opposites that would be impossible without mutual relationship. Alchemists were aware of this cyclic interdependence of nature and used their knowledge in seeking a *lapis*, a stone of salvation. Pseudo Demokritos said: "Nature rejoices in Nature, Nature subdues Nature, and Nature rules over the Nature." (In Jung 1977a, [CW 84, para. 86)

Containing Numinosum

Neumann uses term the *creative unconscious* as the force energizing every process of ego development. Encounters with the numinosum and consequent transformations are desirable aspects of religious practices. Ritual and its meaning-structure provide a container protecting the ego from being swallowed up by the numinosum. The controlled enlargement of consciousness during ritual is religious in its function, because the participant can experience profound insight into reality and the original wisdom of the psychic cosmos. Jung (1950) gave an example of this change in an initiation ritual:

> The initiate may either be a mere witness of the divine drama or take part in it or be moved by it, or he may see himself identified through the ritual action with the god (...). This participation in the ritual event gives rise, among other effects, to that hope of immortality which is characteristic of the Eleusinian mysteries. A living example of the mystery drama representing the permanence as well as the transformation of life is the Mass (...) The mass is an extramundane and extra-temporal act in which Christ is sacrificed and then resurrected in the transformed substances; (...) The experience of the Mass is therefore a participation in the transcendence of life, which overcomes all bounds of space and time. It is a moment of eternity in time (pp. 117-118).

In the above example, Jung writes from his own personal experience of initiation. During the years of his "creative illness" (1913 to 1930), Jung underwent a ritualistic confrontation with his personal unconscious and the collective unconscious that led to his transformation. He states:

> The years when I was pursuing my inner images were the most important in my life — in them everything essential was decided. It all began then; the later details are only supplements and clarifications of the material that burst forth from the unconscious, and at first swamped me. It was the prima materia for a lifetime's work (MDR, 1961, p. 199).

He captured his experience in word and image in his now-famous *Liber Novus, (The Red Book).* Jung's own experience of initiation was an encounter with the numinous, a "confrontation with the unconscious," an experience of fear and awe in the face of a tremendum most difficult to define or understand. In this ritual process of self-guided active imagination, Jung was initiated into the deeper mysteries of the creative unconscious and granted grace on the mere ground of his presence and active participation. In this initiation, Jung experienced himself as both participant and witness through imaginal ritual action with numerous collective figures. It was in this personal experience that he discovered the creative source of all mythology, religions and spirituality.

Ritual helps to maintain the precious balance between the conscious and unconscious worlds. There are numerous indications that this was done in indigenous societies in a purely instinctive way. The process of ritual carried by humans was already widespread in the late mid-Paleolithic times (at least about 90,000-70,000 years ago; Cochran, Harpending, 2010, p. 31)[45]. Religious practices have been performed not only by primitive societies, but by modern man as well, to fulfill the same function.

Creative Unconscious

With the protection against unmitigated archetypal power afforded by ritual, the unconscious comes to build new structures from this raw material. For Erich Neumann, it was the process of creation "from within and from outside" or the reproduction of the natural process. Neumann (1970) asked why mankind "reproduces the natural process in his cults and rituals, so indefatigably" ...and answered it: "...by means of analogous set of symbols, he [human] produces in his own soul the same creative process which he finds outside himself in nature" (p. 211). According to Neumann, each culture finds through ritual the synthesis between consciousness and the creative unconscious. Over hundreds of thousands of years, the creative evolution of consciousness—via mythology and ritual—has been integrating unconscious contents that have led to its progressive extension of its frontiers. The creative process of ritual has served humans' spiritual needs since its beginnings.

---

[45] However, there is evidence of proto-human made first ritualistic artifacts much earlier, dating 430,000 and 540,000 years ago (*Nature*, DOI: 10.1038/nature, 13962).

We would like to pose some questions that have naturally emerged: How does the continuation of this process look today? Has modern man encountered something totally new, something that hinders the creative process? How has development of the scientific attitude complicated the experience and use of rituals?

Loss of Symbol

The emergence of religion during the era that Jaspers (1953) called the Axial Age launched the rapid evolution of consciousness accompanied by a slow but steady withdrawal of projections from the objective world. This caused the natural and instinctive relationship to archetypal reality to change its form. Archetypal forces became objectified. Science and religion, on the playing field of the Middle Eastern and Mediterranean regions, emerged practically simultaneously with the nascent ability of humans to inquire about the phenomena of their own existence. This process continued through the Hellenistic era, when gods began to be recognized more clearly as projections and through the establishment of one God (monotheism). It proceeded via the medieval struggle between expanding scientific thinking and religious adherence to traditional explanations of the world. Following this, consciousness took another form in nihilistic philosophy and the Age of Enlightenment that created, for many, an apotheosis of reason and resulted in the denial and repression of the unconscious elements of reality. A dichotomy arose in which the numinosum became split into either a natural force that can be fully explained by reason or a supernatural entity that can be only related to via faith. As a result of this "horizontal split" religious scriptures during 17th- and 18th-century Europe began to be approached with more literal understanding than ever before.

Expanded literacy of the wider population brought about the fear that reason would lead to the dissolution of God. The process culminated in a modern and postmodern era of psychological imbalances and relativization of moral values. This relativization produced two extreme perspectives: one consisting of the uncritical adherence to anything perceived as traditional and, the other depended on an overvaluation of reason in ways that sacrificed the vitality of the instinctive life. So, two million years of man's evolution of consciousness was tossed aside, thereby throwing out the baby with the bathwater. The last 500 years in particular (beginning roughly with the Protestant Reformation) have been marked by an increased polarization between the ability of human consciousness to look at the world from a distance (science) and adherence to traditionally established worldviews (religion). Both of these approaches are legitimate attempts to grasp the nature of the world, but the extreme polarization weakened and devalued both approaches. While science attempts to explain how the universe works, religion strives, and sometimes claims, to know the purpose behind the workings of the universe. To synthesize and transcend this split appears to be the challenge of the modern age.

Religion and sience both strive for understanding of reality

The rise of reason allowed the numinosum to be parsed into comprehensible shapes and portions that are more easily contained and integrated into an emerging frame in which God is no longer needed. The energy of the numinosum became split-off as if it had a life of its own. Modern man suddenly stood alone. Under the influence of reason and rationality, projections onto numinosum were withdrawn without an accompanying embrace of the numinous world within. This puts enormous pressure on modern man's conscious capacity to withstand the painful split of opposites. Sooner or later such splits demand to be reconciled or transcended. Failing to do so can lead to various maladaptive positions. One of the primary maladies arising from this split between reason and numinosum is the loss of connection to the symbol. A leap of faith into an unknown realm is required in order to connect the symbols that lie hidden in the labyrinth of psyche waiting to be discovered through devoted conscious work.

Sapientia

Modern man's impoverished symbolic skills led to increased rigidity when dealing with the realities of archetypal energies. Under such circumstances, a person is more inclined to identify with the numinosum instead of developing a conscious relationship with it. This accounts for the relatively recent rise of fundamentalism, a movement of strong adherence to the teaching of religious *fundamentals*. The rapid expansion of formal scientific knowledge and quantitative data occurs at the expense of deeper knowledge, what might be called wisdom, *sapientia.* Wisdom provides a spiritual frame of understanding that is necessary for creating a meaningful relationship to the numinosum.

Fundamentalism Is The Revolt Against The New

Karen Armstrong (2005) defined fundamentalism as a revolt against modern secular society, as a tendency to withdraw from mainstream society to create enclaves of "pure faith." Fundamentalists, according to her,

> ...build a counter-culture, in conscious defiance of the Godless world that surrounds them, and from these communities some undertake a counter-offensive designed to drag God or religion from the sidelines to which they have been relegated in modern secular culture, and bring them back to center stage (p.5).

Her sociological and historical interpretations are very important for understanding the psychological processes when it comes to marginalizing and relegating modernity and the accompanying *new worldviews* to the sidelines. Becoming modern entails being exposed to an overwhelming ambiguity arising from the multicultural aspects of the modern world, science and philosophy with its contradictions and spirituality with its indispensable impression on individual choice. Fundamentalists choose to avoid this individuating struggle and escape to images that pretend to offer a solution to suffering, but at its core it is just an unrealistic fantasy of paradise on earth. Graeme Wood (2015) in his article *What ISIS Really Wants?* explains the motivation of the fanatical Islamic movement that rapidly spread its influence in just a few months.

> In fact, much of what the group does looks nonsensical except in light of a sincere, carefully considered commitment to returning civilization to a seventh-century legal environment, and ultimately to bringing about the apocalypse. (...) They refer derisively to "moderns." In conversation, they insist that they will not—cannot—waver from governing precepts that were embedded in Islam by the Prophet Muhammad and his earliest followers. They often speak in codes and allusions that sound odd or old-fashioned to non-Muslims, but refer to specific traditions and texts of early Islam. (p. 1)

Any creedal container eventually begins to weaken naturally, so it is understandable that the containers will need to be strengthened. But as Jesus cautioned, "no one pours new wine into old wineskins" (Mark 4:22). Similarly, new insights and understandings about the numinosum, when poured into old, outmoded vessels are likely to produce stale, bitter results. One cost of retrenching into old beliefs—to fundamentalism—is self-deception as one adheres more strictly to traditional dogma. This is truly paradise lost. Unfortunately, the psyche does not simply forgive such a betrayal; it tends to punish us with the very things we tried to avoid. Jungian psychology long recognized the need for continual Περιπέτεια (Greek: change) ways of approaching the questions of religiosity and offered the concept of depth spirituality, which did not require uncritical clinging to the past. It also did not recommend forgetting the past, but fostered the acceptance of the *present* by giving it a new focus: awareness of the numinous unconscious. The future can restore paradise only when the past and present are connected in a new way.

5. SPIRITUALITY

The return of the Gods to their psychic origins would have great societal and personal value. On the social level it would mean that each community bonded by a totally transcendent divinity would have to come to realize that its allegedly unique and exclusive divinity was a valued variant of the family of monotheistic Gods created by the psyche as humanity now moves through and hopefully beyond its once much needed monotheistic moment. Such a realization would produce a moderating and humanizing relativity in the claims for universal and exhaustive religious validity made by each of the contending one and only Gods and free their constituencies from the need to convert or kill each other (Dourley, 2006, pp.)

A knowledge of the existence of something we cannot penetrate, of the manifestations of the profoundest reason and the most radiant beauty—it is this knowledge and this emotion that constitute the truly religious attitude; in this sense, and in this alone, I am a deeply religious man (Einstein, 1956 in Tippet, 2010, p. 78)

In this section, we will 1) briefly review the origins and evolution of the term spirituality up to and including contemporary culture; 2) outline pressing issues and concerns facing the 21st century; 3) in light of our present cultural and religious zeitgeist offer a Jungian spiritual perspective.

In our contemporary culture there is an extraordinarily broad movement of interest in and hunger for spirituality and spiritual experiences. The topic of spirituality is not only being addressed by contemporary pop culture, but it has become the focus of study for various disciplines and professions that include psychology, integrative medicine, social sciences, business, and management, the military, and the world of entertainment and professional sports.[46] In the field of psychology alone, the American Psychological Association (APA) published the *APA Handbook of Psychology, Religion and Spirituality;*[47] a 2-volume set (Vol. 1: *Context, Theory and Research;* and Vol. 2: *An Applied Psychology of Religion and Spirituality*) with over 75 chapters covering almost every topic of interest in psychology, religion and spirituality today.

In addition, the APA recently inaugurated and published a quarterly journal titled *Psychology of Religion and Spirituality,* designed to study and explore the contributions of spiritual and religious constructs in psychology and related fields. In the field of applied psychology, the APA has launched a new quarterly journal titled *Spirituality in Clinical Practice*. The focus of this journal is to inform practitioners by publishing clinical research and guidelines on spiritually oriented interventions: meditation, prayer, forgiveness, mindfulness, etc.

This field of study has now achieved mainstream scientific status. In addition, a further development has been the movement from research to practice, thus the field of *applied psychology of religion and spirituality*. A timely and simple example:

> During a recent psychotherapy seminar at Columbia University, psychologist Lisa Miller, Ph.D., watched an Orthodox Jewish student listen to a Baptist neuro-scientist explain how prayer increases focus and decreases stress. The student had an "aha" moment, saying the research helped explain why she felt less

---

[46] NBA Coach Phil Jackson's, *Sacred Hoops: Spiritual Lessons of a Hardwood Warrior,* 1995.

[47] *APA Handbook of Psychology, Religion and Spirituality*, (2013) American Psychological Association, Kenneth Pargament, Editor-in-Chief, Washington, D.C.

clearheaded in the United States than in Israel, where prayer was a bigger part of her life.[48]

In this simple vignette, we see the interdisciplinary relation among a psychologist, a neuroscientist, and a student. Further, we witness the teaching by a Baptist neuroscientist explaining the benefits of prayer (spirituality) to an Orthodox Jewish student who has a spiritual "aha" moment about a present life situation. What we are discovering today and finding most convincing is the approach that regards spirituality as an autonomous discipline that can function in partnership and in mutuality with not only theology, but with a host of disciplines. This evolution begins to liberate spirituality from its relatively oppressive and domineering relationship to dogma. As we will see, the term spirituality has evolved and developed over the centuries.

Defining Spirituality

The term spirituality, like the term religion, is unavoidably ambiguous and multifaceted; there is any number of definitions, all depending on one's individual and cultural experience and religious perspective. In contemporary pop culture, the term spirituality has become the newest buzzword denoting anything from personal connection with the sacred, to ecology and Gai spirituality, to new age physics, crystals, and numerous forms of meditation. It is also being used by all manner of religions and even nonreligious movements such as feminism and Marxism. Meanwhile, the term religion has been denigrated by association to the malevolence often displayed by institutional religion.

Neither religion nor spirituality is superior to the other. Because there is no single, agreed-upon definition, we choose to define spirituality as broadly as possible without becoming too vague by including anything that anyone believes—a usage that would render the term meaningless.

[48] APA Monitor, Vol. 44, No. 9, p. 73

Let us explore the origins of the term spirituality and its development from its origins as a Pauline term. This will help us understand the roots of the historical split between spirit and matter and, the attending deleterious effects upon people's spiritual life and practices that developed over the ensuing centuries. It is our contention that Jung—doctor of the soul—sought to address and heal the wound evinced by this split.[49] The following is a brief summary highlighting the essential evolution of the term "spirituality" up to the 20th century.

The History

The term spirituality[50] has its origins in St. Paul's creation of the term spiritual (*pneumatikos*), which was developed from the Greek word for the Spirit of God, (*pneuma*).[51] Originally, the adjective spiritual was composed by St. Paul to refer to any person who was influenced by the Spirit of God (1 Corinthians 2:12, 15) and the gifts of the Spirit of God (Romans 15:27; charisms, speaking in tongues, blessings, etc.). He also differentiated between the Spirit of God and the spirit of man. More importantly, St. Paul used the term to differentiate the spiritual person (Greek: *pneumatikos*) from the natural person (Greek: *psychikos anthropos*). It is questionable whether St. Paul intentionally meant to contrast spiritual with material (nature) or simply intended to differentiate the natural human being from the person under the influence of the Spirit of God.[52] Either way, this distinction continued to influence the development of the theological terms spirit, its adjectival form "spiritual," and its substantive "spirituality."

---

[49] See Stein, M. (1986). *Jung's Treatment of Christianity: The psychotherapy of a Religious Tradition*

[50] For a fuller discussion see: *World Spirituality: An Encyclopedic History of the Religious Quest,* New York: Crossroad, 1985.

[51] See Principe, Walter, (1983). *Toward defining spirituality*, Studies in Religion/Sciences, 12, 127-41.

[52] Schneiders, Sandra (1989). *Spirituality in the Academy*, Theological Studies, 50

In the 12th century a further philosophical definition of spirituality developed that placed spirituality in opposition to materiality or corporeality. This philosophical perspective became firmly established and accepted as the standard. Further splitting and bifurcation between the world of spirit and the world of materiality continued in the centuries that followed. The term spirituality emerged during the 13th century and reflected the contrast between the jurisdiction and property of the religious and secular powers. It was also during this century that the splitting of theology from its "spiritual matrix was sown" as philosophy began to compete and finally superseded scripture in supplying the categories for dogmatic and systematic theology.[53] Hence, it is important to note that spirituality lost its influence and rightful place in the midst of theology, it was relegated to a lesser and subsidiary branch of theology. With developments in the 17th and 18th centuries, the supposedly "golden age of spirituality," the term came to represent the "interior life of the Christian," the search for "the life of perfection" as opposed to one's ordinary life of faith, with a concomitant elitist emphasis on a direct search for the divine.[54] Late medieval spirituality was characterized by an intense search for the direct experience of God, whether through the private, interior ecstasy of mystical illumination, or through the personal scrutiny of God's word in the Bible. Mystical experience was potentially available to everyone, lay or cleric, man or woman, learned or illiterate. Conceived of as a personal gift of God, it stood sharply removed from social rank or cultural attainment. It was unworldly, irrational, private and authoritative. Devotional reading of the Bible, in its turn, brought an awareness of a church strikingly different from the all-encompassing, worldly medieval institution.[55]

Because of its major focus on the *affective aspect* of the interior life, spirituality was depreciated and viewed pejoratively

[53] Ibid. p. 681
[54] Ibid. p. 683
[55] University of California-Santa Barbara's website (n.d., p.1).

by theologians and church authorities. Consequently, spirituality carried a rather dubious reputation and was associated with heretical views and forms of spiritual praxis. Spirituality became an isolated subdivision, to a particular branch of theology thereby losing its ability to influence and inform theology in general. This resulted in a bifurcation between theology and its spiritual matrix, and thus a split between Christian thought and Christian living. This gave rise to institutional religion without a lived spirituality. These institutional religions can easily regress to become an *ideology* (creed) that is primarily a system of collective beliefs with which one identifies.

In the 18th and 19th centuries, spirituality became associated with the life of perfection that took on an aura of elitism, for the cleric and religious, in contrast to the ordinary life of the faithful. When the professional religious class lays claim to the layperson's spirituality the role of the spiritual director tended to emphasize articles of faith and doctrine and relied on theological expertise. Spirituality became dominated and unduly influenced by creed, dogma, and the assertion of inerrancy. What was accepted as the actual movement of the spirit (personal experience) was subjected to scrutiny in accord with theological traditions. For most of the 20th century, spirituality was viewed as the lived practice of the interior life by those pursuing personal growth and perfection.

These developments have resulted in two basic schools of thought defining spirituality: one with a dogmatic emphasis relying on a "definition from above" and the other a more anthropological view offering a "definition from below."[56] Traditional spirituality is found primarily among conservative religionists and fundamentalists. Fundamentalists are often most comfortable with a spirituality defined from above, where one's approach to the sacred is contained, outlined, and formulated by someone vested with authority (e.g., biblically based theologies, hierarchical institutions, or formal religious

[56] Sandra Schneiders, (1989). *Spirituality in the Academy, Theological Studies, 50*

societies). This spirituality is often determined by one's affiliation to a particular religious tradition, typically deriving from one's family of origin.

The spiritual developments of the last two millennia have resulted in what Bechtle[57] has termed a "dissociation of sensibility" and what Lovelace[58] has called a "spirituality gap" in the evangelical Christian experience. These rationalistic developments leave little room for one's personal embodied journey of spiritual growth. Bechtle believes that this has led to a "post-Enlightenment lobotomizing of Western culture": the divorce of thought from feeling and mind from heart, which is reflected in the historical split between theology and spirituality. [59] We are in full agreement with Bechtle's insights and would tend to phrase it as a mind/soul - body/affect split. As a result, two traditionally different (dichotomous) paths to the divine developed. One was the way of knowledge and theory (mind), and the other was the path and journey of the heart, consisting of prayer, devotion, and action.

Spirituality from the Middle Ages up to the 20th century was heavily theoretical, otherworldly, elitist, ahistorical, relying too exclusively on thought and doctrine while concentrating on the interior life of perfection. In contrast, today's focus on spirituality is described by Heagle as: "The emerging spirituality of our age is intensely personal without being private. It is visionary without becoming theoretical...it is incarnational without becoming worldly."[60] It emphasizes personal response and interior commitment but it radically changes the context within which this response takes place.

---

[57] Bechtle, (1985). *Convergence in Theology and Spirituality,* in *The Way,* 305

[58] Lovelace, Richard, (1973). *The Sanctification Gap*, in *Theology Today* 29, 365-366

[59] Bechtle, in "Convergence," 305

[60] Heagle, John (1985). *"A New Public Piety: Reflections on Spirituality,* Church I, 7

Though the term spirituality originated from the Christian experience and lexicon,[61] its anthropological definition, as "defined from below," has undergone an exponential period of evolution in the last two decades. It has been transformed into a generic term (i.e., spirituality that has no brand name such as Benedictine spirituality or Buddhist spirituality, or Wicca spirituality, etc.) descriptive of the human capability for self-transcendence irrespective of whether that experience is formally religious or not. In essence, spirituality has been liberated from its subjugation to religious doctrine and dogma to encompass the whole person; it has become a search for transcendent integration and wholeness. The spirit was recognized as the spiritual core, the deepest center of a person. It is here that the person is open to the transcendent dimension; it is here that the person experiences ultimate reality."[62]

With these most recent developments, the term "spirituality" lost its sole referencing to the influence of the "Spirit of God" and instead came to refer to the action of the "human spirit." Peter Van Ness, assistant professor of philosophy of religion at Union Theological Seminary who specializes in nonreligious or secular spirituality, describes spirituality as "the quest for attaining an optimal relationship between what one truly is and everything that is," whether or not that experience is religious or secular.[63] In essence, Van Ness is saying that spirituality is the ability to relate to a universal, cosmic reality in a healthy and positive way, as an emerging whole individual. This is an extremely broad definition that encompasses both religious and secular spiritualties. This development has permitted spirituality to become independent of creed:

---

[61] See Principe, H. Walter, (1983). *Toward defining spirituality*, Studies in Religion/Sciences, p. 12, pp. 127-41

[62] *World Spirituality: An Encyclopedic History of the Religious Quest.* (1996). The Crossroad Publishing Company: New York.

[63] van Ness, Peter (1996). *Introduction: Spirituality and the Secular Quest*, in *Spirituality and the Secular Quest,* Crossroads: New York.

[Spirituality]... has come to describe a religious consciousness and discipline entirely free of a relation to any religious institution (Wulff, 1998, pp. 5).

The meaning of spirituality has shifted from the spiritual practice of a given tradition to a wider universal meaning involving either one's relationship to all reality including the transpersonal or a transcendent being. Thus, spirituality itself is regarded as an autonomous discipline, of the human spirit, which can function in mutual partnership with many other fields of interest and disciplines. The spirit, in this new dispensation, is now being accessed through one's individual relationship with the unconscious through the use of symbols, images, via meditation, dreams, active imagination, autonomic writing, etc.

The factors responsible for this exponential development of spirituality are complex. In today's postmodern world, for example, with its rejection of master narratives, its anti-foundationalism, and thoroughgoing relativism, makes it difficult for the traditional structures of religion to flourish, let alone survive. It is exactly in this cultural context that spirituality as *lived experience* can flourish and consequently has become inordinately popular. This is also the essence of Jung's insight and insistence on the importance of one's personal experience in regard to religion and one's spirituality.

As Schneider[64] exhorts, Christians have to recognize the present developments in spirituality and the linguistic fact that neither Christianity in particular nor religion in general have dominion over the meaning and use of the terms spiritual or spirituality as it once had. This is a fortuitous development since it brings about the necessary means to liberate spirituality from its traditional confinement and, from its oppression by rigid dogmatism and creed. The evolutionary widening of the term "Spirit of God" to signify and denote the realm of the "human spirit" has ramifications that reverberate across all religious

---

[64] Schneider, Sandra *Religion and Spirituality: Strangers, Rivals, or Partners?* Public Lecture Santa Clara Lecture, Santa Clara University, Feb. 6, 2000. Vol. 6, No. 2

boundaries; and is one example of the historical process of restoring the gods to their rightful place. Ideally these movements are a catalyst and call for the inter-dialogue and mutual respect for all religions. The esteemed theologian Karl Rahner, S. J., architect of *Vatican II*, makes such a point in emphasizing the necessity for the interdisciplinary study of religious phenomena, similar to James and Jung, as constitutive elements of human experience, particularly mysticism. He states:

When and to whatever extent such experiences (mystical phenomenon of a psychological kind such as altered states of consciousness, paranormal experiences, etc.) occur (to the point of enjoying "essential" differences of a psychological kind), it is the mystic and the experimental psychologist within whose competence an investigation of these phenomenon falls, not that of the dogmatic theologian.

Rahner appears to suggest that psychology, not theology, ought to be the arbiter if religious (mystical) experience is a constituent factor in human development and individuation. Both Jung and Rahner tap deeply into the German mystical tradition.

As many theologians (Rahner, K., Tillich, Teilhard de Chardin, etc.), psychologists (Jung, Maslow, Sutich, Grof etc.), cultural anthropologists (Becker, etc.), and psychoanalytic authors (Bion, Hillman, Moore, Eigen, Milner) have reflected, human beings can be described as spirit in the world. The process of spirituality is an effort to understand and actualize the inherent potential of this sublime and vast paradoxical condition. After years of studying the human condition, Pulitzer Prize-winning author Ernest Becker writes in *Denial of Death*[65]: "The distinctive human problem from time immemorial has been the need to spiritualize human life..." C.G. Jung spent his life vocation wrestling with that need and, with his voluminous work, he offers one of the more cogent responses for the 21st century.

---

[65] Becker, Ernest, *The Denial of Death,* 1973.

An Alchemist's Laboratory, Public domain.

Four Essential and Constituent Aspects of Spirituality

Most definitions of spirituality have four essential components in common:

1) *Individual experience of the numinosum*. The emphasis here is on experience and the numinosum, terms that are difficult to define. Nonetheless, this definition highlights the fact that spirituality is not a theory, or belief, or an abstract idea, or an ideology. It is a phenomenological reality that every human being has the inherent potential to experience. This experience is self-explanatory, and even though it is highly subjective, it is the source of transcendence, enlargement of one's personality, meaning, conversion, and the source of faith and relatedness to the *cosmic Whole*. Jung says:

> I thank God every day that I have been permitted to experience the reality of the [Image] of God in me. (...) Thanks to this act of grace, my life has meaning and my inner eye was opened to the beauty and grandeur of dogma. No matter what the world thinks of religious experience, the one who has it possesses a great

> treasure, a thing that has become for him a source of life, meaning, and beauty, and that has given a new splendor to the world and to mankind. (...) Is there, as a matter of fact, any better truth about the ultimate things than one that helps you to live? (Jung, [CW 11, par. 167, *Word and Image*]).

2) *Spirituality involves a conscious involvement in the individuation project*. That is, it is an evolving and cohering process and approach to life consciously engaged as an ongoing endeavor. To this end, one's spirituality is relatively independent from any institutionalized body of knowledge (i.e., a prescribed theology or tradition; e.g., Celtic spirituality, feminist spirituality, Jesuit spirituality, etc.).

3) *Spirituality is a process and endeavor involving differentiation and life-integration.* Hence it is holistic and encompasses body, mind, heart, soul, feelings, thoughts, intuitions, and social and cultural dimensions of life. This process of differentiation includes one's relationship to established religions (as defined above) in terms of religious practices, conduct, customs (ritual), and faith. Spirituality is distinct in its requisite of individual experience of the numinosum as a necessary condition for moral volition. Religion in this sense is a personal relation to archetypal forces and the morality that follows as an imperative of one's conscience. Creed, on the other hand, often understands morality simply as a code of prescribed, collective ethics. While spirituality puts emphasis on the creative dialogue between the ego and the Self, creed relies on traditionally approved or tested methods such as certain types of prayers and exercises: fasting, pilgrimages, the rosary, novenas, petitions, confession, etc. The art of spirituality, in Jungian terms, delineates individual maxims of conduct, which thus yields to a morality based on the continuous, responsible, and individual assessment of reality. Such communication requires sustained work; only then can the rich fruits of this encounter be harvested. It is also understood here that one's spirituality can be deceiving or hypocritical in the same way that "creed" can be.

4) *Individuation moves toward transcendence.* Individuation is pursued and empowered by one's experience of ultimate value in one's psychic economy—that which moves one toward egoic-transcendence. The focus of egoic-transcendence is on what one regards as ultimate in relation to oneself and in some sense what one views as *objective.* For example, one could experience and perceive love, money, sexuality, social justice, ecology, or individual union with God (*unio mystica*) as ultimate values.

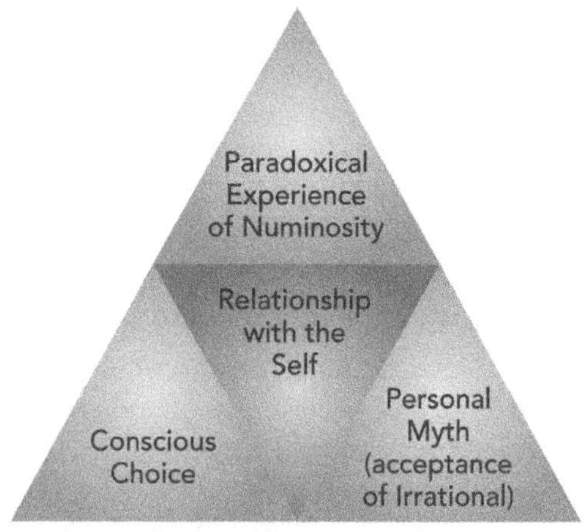

Spirituality, an Individual Religon

Spirituality and The New

Because spirituality originates in one's personal encounter with the numinosum, it is more receptive to anything new, including cross-religious[66] and philosophical ideas, dreams, altered states of consciousness, and as well as scientific insights.

---

[66] The religious and spiritual journey of Bede Griffiths is an excellent contemporary example; his journey from Protestantism to Catholicism (Benedictine/Camaldolese) to his conversion to Hinduism. See Shirley du Boulay in an excellent work title, *Beyond the Darkness: A Biography of Bede Griffiths* (New York: Continuum, 1998)

It is an attempt to redefine or rediscover a place for the numinosum and the Image of God amid various influences and pressures of modernity, at the same time retaining sovereign primacy of an individual's mandate in seeking happiness.

Jung's work gave considerable attention to this aspect of the human attempt to continually rediscover the depths of the divine (i.e. the Self) within human experience and culture, all the while outlining theoretical and specific practical guidelines and advice for such a process.

Herewith, we would like to introduce a depth-analytical perspective of spirituality as presented in Jung's work and expanded by neo-Jungians like Dourley (2006), Stein (1996, 2005, 2014), Corbett (1996, 2002, 2005, 2007), Edinger, (1986), and others. Stein and Corbett (2005) in their paper *Contemporary Jungian Approaches to Spiritually Oriented Psychotherapy* stated:

Jungian psychology makes the radical claim that psychotherapy is an intrinsically spiritual discipline. The rationale for this idea is that the psyche does not consist only of personal material; rather, human consciousness is seamlessly connected to a larger, transpersonal field of Consciousness, referred to as the objective psyche. ...For the spiritually oriented psychotherapist, the archetypes are not only important in the spiritual traditions; they act as deep structures (processes) in the psyche that govern the organization of experience and the development of personality and psychopathology. ...The Jungian approach does *not* try to *codify* the experience and apply it to everyone. We do not try to write a universally applicable sacred text based on any particular experience (such as the handing down of the law on Mt. Sinai), because every person experiences the numinosum in his or her own way. ...This type of experience led Edinger (1984) to suggest that we are entering a new phase of religious consciousness, a new way of understanding our experience of the sacred. Instead of divine grace being mediated by law, by faith, or by the intervention of a savior, the psychological dispensation stresses our relationship—indeed our dialogue—with transpersonal levels of Consciousness. (Stein & Corbett, 2005, pp. 1-29; authors' emphasis)

The God Image

According to the abovementioned authors, spirituality can gain a new meaning when viewed through the prism of Jungian thought, in particular the theory of the unconscious. It can satisfy those who follow institutionalized religion and creeds, while being willing to interpret dogmas symbolically. It can also satisfy those seekers of transcendence who accept little from the prisms of organized religion, but are open to looking within. As John Dourley pointed out, Jung traced the origins of both institutional religion and the now-emerging spirituality of the individual seeker to their common originator, the archetypal unconscious, i.e., the Self. Jungian psychology has not presented us with new gods but has brought to our attention the reality of the collective unconscious. Jung's genius discovered that it is impossible to seek the living God if the unconscious is bypassed. Otto, (1919), Corbin (1972), Corbett (1996), and others, point out that God is manifested *through* the numinous experience of the collective unconscious. As a modern perspective, Dourley, said:

> From this point of common agreement only two options about God's existence remain open. Either the unconscious creates the spirits and Gods as projections of its major psychic energies, or God creates the unconscious as the medium through which God makes itself known to humanity (p. 3).

Dourley continues by stating:

> When Jung's total work is weighed and considered, the first of Corbett's options prevails. The unconscious creates the Gods and spirits wholly out of its own archetypal resources and the evolution of human religious consciousness, and its attendant spirituality is presently coming to realize this fact (p. 4).

Spirituality As Consciousness

The Jungian view of spirituality rests upon the claim that archetypes of the collective unconscious are the par excellence sources of information about the world. Archetypes are the "building blocks" of reality. While Freud thought of the ego as a rather interiorized objective world, the Jungian idea of archetypes suggests that the objective world is an exteriorization of the unconscious, or in other words, psyche and matter are essentially opposites sides of same coin. Jung (1953) writes in a letter to Wolfgang Pauli:

> Psyche and matter, as a "matrix," are both an X - i.e., a transcendental unknown quantity and thus indistinguishable in conceptual terms, which makes them *virtually identical*; only on a secondary level are they different, as different aspects of Being. (In Meier, Atom and Archetype, 64 J, p. 126)[67]

Jung's view on spirituality is partly Platonic, for it entails discovering profound meaning and an intelligence or creative force that is *a priori.*[68] In this sense, the scientific approach can be an asset to spirituality and not its adversary. While religion endows life with meaning in the sense of a feeling value, science can help understand it in terms of rational and structural values. Religion points to life's purpose while science points to the means of existence. We essentially believe that there is no either-or argument for science versus religion. We advocate for a *complementary* view that produces a reality that is holistic.

---

[67] The psychoid archetype, where "psychic" and "material" are no longer viable as attributes or where the category of opposites becomes obsolete and every occurrence can only be asymmetrical; the reason for this is that an occurrence can only be the one or the other when it proceeds from an indistinguishable One. (Jung, In Meier, *Atom and Archetype*, 76 P, p. 169)

[68] There has been ongoing discussion among Jungians and neo-Jungians if the archetypes and the collective unconscious have an *a priori* nature (substantial quality) or emerged (emergent theory) as a result of interaction with environment. (See: "*Analytical Psychology: Contemporary Perspectives in Jungian Analysis*, Edited by Joseph Cambray and Linda Carter, Hove, UK: Brunner-Routledge, 2004.

This spirituality unites religion and science in recognizing the validity of both as sources of knowledge. Jung taught that archetypes *"know"* something about the world in the sense that they are "of" the world and contain partial information that participates in the greater gestalt that is formed in consciousness. A psychization, or integration of unconscious into consciousness, allows for the enlargement of meaning. We can find parallels in the marvelous and complex cooperation that takes place in ant colonies. The individual ant has no idea about the holistic aspect of the system but instinctively participates in it. Similarly, with the human brain, the combination of over 80 billion neurons operates individually, but together they form more complex operations. Consciousness is the representation of such coordination and complexity. Consciousness does not happen in each neuron proportionally but *emerges* as a whole, and there it can apprehend the object (whatever it is) in its holistic (and definite) form. Archetypes appear to be both *containers* and *mediators* of consciousness. Their nature allows human consciousness to make meaning out of experience and may allow for experiencing reality not in the relative sense, but in the universal sense where world is experienced as it is.. Archetypes can be viewed as the "letters," while consciousness is the "reader" of the letters. Without the ability of abstracting meaning, the reader would only see the succession of the signs. Archetypes appear to provide the energy that is needed for the transformation: creation of conscious meaning.

The knowledge of the archetype can be decoded via analysis of the symbol, as previously latent meaning is revealed. When irrational forces are experienced and reflected upon, a new, rational meaning arises. The result is personal. Spirituality *is* the means of elevating each individual human above the autonomy of his or her instinctive dispositions and giving him or her a perspective needed to make a good enough choice. The process of spirituality allows one to view the greater picture—like an ant that is suddenly able to comprehend its place in the entire ecology. Spirituality is a process of *transformation* from unconsciousness to consciousness.

Spirituality As Redemption

Another implication of the spirituality that Dourley saw in Jung's work was that the human and the divine are in a *mutual* relationship—in a state of *redemption* together. With the gradual arrival of self-knowledge projections are withdrawn. One discovers that archetypes work from the objective world leading to the realization of archetypes as factors that work nowhere else but *in* human life and no other way than through human life. Every human understanding sheds a bit of light on the darkness of the unconscious. God, if understood as unconscious intelligence, gets to know himself in time and space. Conscious free will depends upon consciousness interacting with the Self so that a union between conscious and unconscious is created. Likewise, one may propose that God would be incomplete without the interaction of human beings.[69] This interaction permits us to form a union with the numinosum and in turn, it permits God to fully experience finality, transience, mortality, and the conflicts that emerge from these human experiences. To that purpose, says Jung, God *created* a human and *became* a human. Jung's *Answer to Job* (1952a, [CW 11, par. 631]) is a deep exploration of this idea:

> One should make clear to oneself what it means when God becomes man. It means nothing less than a world-shaking transformation of God. It means more or less what Creation meant in the beginning, namely an objectivation of God. At the time of the Creation, he revealed himself in nature; now he wants to be more *specific* and become man (emphasis ours).

Jung's idea of individuation no longer involves a perfect and detached God who supervises man's futile and sinful attempt to become good. Individuation proposes an involved and evolving God whose consciousness is interdependent upon human consciousness. We might say that human being's self-

[69] See also: Peter B. Todd, *The Integration of God: Integrating Science and Religion (Chiron, 2012)*

knowledge depends on the ability to know God, and conversely God's self-knowledge depends on God's capability to participate in human experience. In the continuing process of individuation, both God and human have been redeeming each other. Thus, the individuation of mankind is the individuation of (its) God.

Consciousness for man, therefore, equals consciousness for God. Conversely, Jung's findings reveal that the state of being unconscious inevitably leads to the manifestation of evil in the world. What follows from this is that to rid the world of evil requires that man undertake the task of bringing the unconscious to light—evil is not to be found outside of man. This brings the reality closer to human reach. Jung (1952, [CW 11, para. 631) put it this way:

"It was only quite late that we realized (or rather, are beginning to realize) that God is Reality itself and therefore—last but not least—man. This realization is a millennial process."

Spirituality Has No Artificial Limits of Discovery

Spirituality in the Jungian paradigm is a continuing process of becoming, *creatio continua*. Cultivating self-knowledge and self-love every day is an inexhaustible goal, Dourley (2006) stated:

In thus revisioning the process of incarnation as wholly within the psyche, it is important to note that the fecundity of the archetypal will always outstrip its incarnations in consciousness. There will always be more to become incarnate. This understanding of incarnation denies to any religion or archetypal equivalent the status of unqualified ultimacy or finality (p. 6).

Organic Unity of The Divine and The Human

According to Jung, religious and psychological experiences are *de facto* "organically one." One can only experience the numinosum through the psyche. Thus, the psyche has a natural affinity to the unconscious and is the most natural container of the divine unconscious. Jung stated:

What one could almost call a systematic blindness is simply the effect of the prejudice that God is *outside* man (Jung 1940, [CW 11, para. 100]).

Orthodox theologies created a split between humankind and God with all of the attending consequences. Jung's (1913) study of Eckhart brought about a painstaking insight in light of his own encounter with the unconscious, the concept of God denoted a relative and not an absolute relation to man. Jung noted that God is not "wholly cut off from man" and does not exist beyond the human conditions but is

> in a certain sense dependent on him; which implies a reciprocal and essential relation between man and God, whereby man can be understood as a *function* of God, and God as a psychological function of man (Jung 1921a, [CW 6, para 412]).

Jung (1940) viewed the birthing of the Self, or the birth of the divine Son, within the individual as a spiritual process of utmost importance. Reductive approaches to psychoanalysis do not view this process of gradual integration of the unconscious as spiritual at all. A reductive approach would see the birth of the Self primarily as an adaptation to external reality. Jung went much deeper. Archetypes of the collective unconscious are not *a posteriori* formed structures but emergent phenomena and creative forms of wisdom and intelligence par excellence. It is through the archetypes of the collective unconscious that God and the Universe emanated. The unconscious does not derive from human consciousness but is an autonomous, living, intelligent, and creative power—the deepest well of wisdom. It is a bottomless abyss, a mystery and before the unconscious one experiences awe and humility. The unconscious (Self) serves as a guide that can nurture a conscientious way of living. Edinger spoke about the spiritual process of the ego-Self axis as a creation of consciousness, which establishes a conscious connection to the Self. Jung claimed repeatedly that the mystery of the living well of life is already present in humans. A severed connection with the numinous, a lost connection with the symbol, an overly defensive ego-position, and an inability to engage the archetypal world can bring about a neurosis and a "loss of the soul." The subjects of this work: intellectual entrapment, one-sided rationality and concretism, fanatical adherence to dogma, religious absolutism, and irrational persuasions of a destructive nature are all potential results of the loss of soul. The absence of a conscious relation to archetypal realities can lead to an unmitigated possession and a painful life lived under the veil of illusion.

A New Myth

Quite frequently, Jung spoke about the spiritual crisis of contemporary times and proposed the creation, or rather, the evolution of a new myth—a myth which would reconnect our psyche with its deeper roots. Such a myth would offer a wider spiritual consciousness than what was previously known. The new myth would not be a doctrine of the collective, but an ever-changing created image that is recreated over and over by each individual person. Dourley (2006) wrote:

> In this sense the individual's surfacing of one's individual myth from the power that gives birth to them all is the greatest contribution the individual can make to a now emerging religious sensibility of wider universal sympathy and inclusion (p. 16).

Let us recall that spirituality is an expression of the individual's religious experiences of the numinosum, whereas creed too easily becomes an impersonal expression of religion that does not offer a living organic connection to the Self. The new myth proposed by Jung strives for the unity of opposites, the *complexio oppositorum*. This comprises the whole of the numinosum and is a vehicle for returning religious experience to its original natural function.

IV.
THE EMERGING PSYCHOLOGICAL DISPENSATION

"The new psychological dispensation finds man's relation to God in the individual's relation to the unconscious" (Edinger, 1984).

"As Jung rightly foresaw, our age is an age in quest of its soul. The anxiety, the despair, the suffering, and the dis-orientation of the inner life have deeply scarred the twentieth century" (Christou, 1976).

Jung had foreseen a new development in the evolution of religion, in particular, Christianity. As early as 1934, Jung asserts, "we stand on the threshold of a new spiritual epoch; and that from the depths of man's own psychic life new spiritual forms will be born."[70] The new spiritual epoch is nothing less than a revolutionary new worldview, a new myth, in essence a new dynamic dispensation that fosters a personal connection to the transpersonal psyche (the Self). The Christian mythos for Jung forms part of the foundational (archetypal) bedrock of our Western culture and cannot simply be jettisoned or arbitrarily replaced without violence to our personal and collective psyche. Jung is not seeking the demise of Christianity but simply to "dream the myth onward" (Jung 1959 [CW 9i]). He seeks to move Christianity beyond its own literalism, its dogmatic thinking and its clericalism. We might say that Jung is announcing the

[70] McGuire and Hill, 1977, p. 6.

end of an epoch or stage of Christian faith. This period was invested in the external authority of the scriptures, of tradition, the magisterium and the historical Christ. Jung wishes to shift the focus from the external Christ to the inner Christ, as the archetype of the Self. As Jung asserts, it is from the "depths of man's own psychic life" that "new spiritual forms will be born." The word depth is a metaphor for the unconscious—the new *terra incognita* (Latin: unknown land). The exploration of the unconscious opens up new territory, a new frontier, and a new sphere that now can be freely and creatively explored and worked with, though not without its danger. Why we might ask? Well, first, as noted above, organized religion had a "religious formula for everything psychic" (Jung 1934/54 [CW 11]) hence there was no need to look within and discover one's own psychic unconscious and spiritual life. This indeed is a tragic reality that the public forms of religious traditions are often helpless in providing the assistance we need with our psychospiritual development and individuation. As we have outgrown old traditional forms we will need to embrace a new dispensation standing in openness and vulnerability. One of the cornerstones of the new dispensation will be the recovery of individual spiritual experiences of the transpersonal (God within) to foster growth and individuation.

> In a recent interview, the Dalai Lama stated:
> I believe deeply that we must find, all of us together, a new spirituality. [Interviewer: Which wouldn't be 'religious'?] Certainly Not. This new concept ought to be elaborated alongside the religions, in such a way that all people of good will could adhere to it. [Interviewer: Even if they have no religion, or are against religion?] Absolutely. We need a new concept, a lay spirituality. We ought to promote this concept with the help of scientists.[71]

---

[71] Fox, 2000, p. 3.

Various scholars including Edinger, (1981, 1984), Moore (1990, 2002, 2003), Corbett, (1981, 2007, 2011), Dourley (1984; 1990; 2014) and other scholars like, Maslow and Sutich (1971), Grof (1994), Smith (1958; 1976), have continued researching and developing the idea that activation of one's interiority, creates new forms of spirituality. Though this new dispensation is built upon the three Abrahamic religions, the primary focus of this exploration will be on the Jewish and Christian. We hold that these new forms in which the sacred will be explored and experienced are fundamental to the individuation process. The previous religious dispensations can be reinterpreted in light of *analytical* psychology and the discovery of the psyche. We are in the midst of a major transitional period moving from the old dispensations of traditional Christianity (i.e., hierarchical institutions, sacerdotal clergy, fossilized dogma, etc.) and all that has been denied and corrupted in institutional religion.

For Jung, modernity (and postmodernity) is nothing short of a 'rite of passage' into new and deeper experiences with the 'Holy' and the sacred. It is the opposite of fundamentalism, understood as a premature closing of all religious dialogic enterprises and inquiries, particularly with one's interior life. This is the essence of Jung's psychology of religion, its dialogic approach with one's interiority. However this dialogic approach to one's interior life is far more complex than one typically imagines, inordinately so, if one starts out without any preparation. For example, let's look at the basic reality of the living psyche.

THE REALITY OF THE PSYCHE

"What most people overlook, or seem unable to understand, is the fact that I regard the psyche as real.[72]

"The psyche is not inside man; it is we who are inside the psyche."[73]

---

[72] CW 11, par. 751

[73] Christou, *1976; p. 6*

Jung's genius was his uncanny and powerfully sensitive perceptual abilities into the interior *depths* of the human soul. His personal predilection and capacity for containing and working with interior states of consciousness is evident in his early childhood experiences and dreams (Jung, 1961, MDR pp. 6-83). His highly sensorial and creative genius led him to explore and map his own personal unconscious. This eventually led to one of the greatest discoveries of the 20th century: the reality of the psyche and the collective unconscious.[74] Jung has been heralded as an "epochal man; the first to experience and articulate fully a new mode of existence."[75] Jung discovered that the psyche is as objective and real as the material world. It is the counterpart to the physical material world. The reality of the psyche is the foundation and keystone of what Jung envisioned as a new myth for the modern world.[76] However, the psyche is a very elusive reality that is difficult to recognize and identify; as Jung states: *it is we who are inside the psyche*. One's dreams and inner work during analysis makes it clear to the analysand that he or she possesses a psyche and that identity is contained within it. Jungian scholar and analyst Marie-Louise von Franz recounts her first encounter with Jung in discussing the idea of the objective reality of the psyche:

> I met Jung when I was eighteen, and at that time he told me about a vision that one of his patients had had of being on the moon, and then the man on the moon grabbed her with his black wings and didn't let her go. She was possessed by this black figure, you see. And Jung talked as if this weren't just a vision but actually as if she really *had* been on the moon. So, having a rational nature, I got irritated and said, "But she wasn't on the real moon. That was just a vision." And Jung looked at me seriously and replied, "She *was* on the moon." And I said, "Wait a minute. It can't be. She wasn't up there."

---

[74] Edinger, 1972; Jaffe, 1999, p. 27

[75] Edinger, 1984; Jung, *Letters* II, p. 139.

[76] CW 10, par. 148

> I pointed to the sky, and he just looked at me again, penetratingly, and repeated, "She was on the moon." Then I got angry and thought, "Either this man's crazy or I'm stupid." And then I slowly began to realize that Jung meant that what happens psychologically is the real reality — I started to comprehend his concept of the reality of the psyche. And that was a big revelation.[77]

Jung's exceptional gift of navigating and mapping the inner world is evident in "Confrontation with the Unconscious" (*MDR*, 1989), and in *The Red Book* (aka: *Liber Novus*). *Liber Novus*, as Shamdasani points out, clearly differentiates Jung from Freud and all other early psychoanalytic theorists.[78] It was in his dialogues with Philemon, the Wise Old Man, recorded in *The Red Book*, that Jung discovered the reality of the objective psyche.

Philemon ... It was he who taught me psychic objectivity, the reality of the psyche. Through the conversations with Philemon, the distinction was clarified between myself and the object of my thought ... psychologically; Philemon represented superior insight.[79]

SPIRIT OF THE DEPTHS

In Jung's early *Red Book* encounters (*Liber Primus),* he contrasts the "spirit of the times" with the "spirit of the depths". This opposition is fundamental to Jung's query concerning the possibility of another source of knowledge than the zeitgeist of the scientific age.[80] In this new approach, knowledge is conveyed not through the conventional signs, concepts, or ideas but through the symbol. Jung's definition of symbol in *The Red Book* (2009) conveys the path to this new knowledge.

---

[77] "Forever Jung," pp. 83-84. Rolling Stone Magazine, Nov. 21, 1985.
[78] *The Red Book, (Liber Novus)* 2009, 245; fn 163, 246.
[79] *MDR*, pp. 207-9
[80] Jung, (2009). *The Red Book,* p. 264

> The symbol is the word that goes out of the mouth, that one does not simply speak, but that rises out of the depths of the self as a word of power and great need and places itself unexpectedly on the tongue. It is an astonishing and perhaps seemingly irrational word, but one recognizes it as a symbol since it is alien to the conscious mind. If one accepts the symbol, it is as if a door opens leading into a new room whose existence one previously did not know (p. 311).

Symbols, Jung maintained, originated from the unconscious and "the creation of symbols was the most important function of the unconscious" (Jung 2009, 210). The symbol combines products of consciousness (sense and reason) and the unconscious (non-sense, knowledge that initial does not make sense; depth) bringing them into a new relation that creates something original and innovative. Throughout *The Red Book,* the symbol offers a third way of knowing between believing and scientific knowledge. Philemon, the archetype of the Wise Old Man, is the principal teacher of this new symbolic form of knowledge, which makes the unconscious a source of spiritual knowledge. Essentially, the symbol is an image pointing to the unknown or unknowable (the mysterious) and thus the golden gateway to the greatest unknown, the unconscious. The symbolic nature of *The Red Book* suggests that a new vision and a new religious idea are emerging, and thus new forms of spirituality are evolving. This new knowledge is not conveyed through concepts or thought but through symbols. As *The Red Book* categorically distinguishes Jung from Freud, so Jung's insights concerning new forms of spirituality differentiate him from Freud, who considered religion obsolete. Jung's critique of the religion of his day and the crisis of Christianity was the fact that by cutting off and thus denying the psyche's unconscious side, religion had lost its connection to the unconscious, thereby depotentiating the fullness of the symbol; becoming 'mono-tono-theistic.'

Throughout his continual liminal encounters documented in *The Red Book* (1913-28), Jung is confronted and wrestles with the notion that a new God Image is being conceived. In his confrontations with Salome and Elijah, Jung learns that his soul is heralding this new God Image and its mysteries (*"Oikonomia tou mysterious*:" Greek: the dispensation of the mystery).[81] This descent and journey (i.e., Nekuia) initiated Jung into the deeper mysteries of the human soul and determined his future work. As he writes,

> The years when I was pursuing my inner images were the most important in my life – in them everything essential was decided. It all began then; the latter details are only supplements and clarifications of the material that burst forth from the unconscious and at first swamped me. It was the prima material for a lifetime's work.[82]

Whereas Nietzche's Zarathustra proclaimed the death of God, *Liber Novus* proclaims "the rebirth of God in the soul."[83]

In his psychological research and personal Nekuia (i.e., night sea journey), Jung was to discover that the psyche naturally produces imagery and symbols that are numinous. That is, the natural language of the psyche is images and symbols. One hears echoes of St. Augustine's *"Anima autem est naturaliter religiosum*," (Latin, The soul is naturally religious.).

These initiatory experiences had deep and formative influences on shaping Jung's vision of the unconscious. These experiences of the numinous images of the psyche moved him to understand and interpret the unconscious as fundamentally a religious phenomenon par excellence.

Essentially, in this regard, Jung's interest was in developing a psychology of the religious-making process. Henceforth, Jung's rudimentary viewpoint that the experience of the unconscious is, at heart, a religious phenomenon. Hereafter, Jung found

[81] Edinger, (1984).

[82] MDR, p. 199.

[83] Shamdasani, *The Red Book, A Reader's Edition*. p. 31. 2009

himself dealing with the inherent dilemma of how to work and write scientifically about the soul's religious imagery and its transpersonal nature. Thus the task before him was the interpretation and illustration of numinous experiences into symbols and then studying the psychological function of such symbols (Jung 2009, p. 212). In the analytical case of a priest, named Joseph, (below) we will see how this process might unfold and what it might look like.

SOUL: THE SACRED SPACE SHARED BETWEEN RELIGION AND DEPTH PSYCHOLOGY

"The real reunion of religion and psychology is neither in dogma nor in ecumenical councils nor in action; it is taking place within the soul of the individual..." (Hillman, 1984).

"The soul is a mystery indeed, but this mystery is, on the one hand, the mystery of nature, which it is possible to explore scientifically, and, on the other hand, it is a mystery, which has been the object of religion to experience qualitatively and to cultivate (cultus)" (Christou, 1976, p. 53).

In recent years, particularly with the focus on spiritual seeking versus institutional dwelling, it has become popular and quite fashionable to speak of "soul" in both contemporary spiritual movements (S.B.N.R., yoga, mindfulness, energy medicine, etc.) and in the world of psychology and psychotherapy. Nonetheless, in the midst of all these different fields of study there is no ultimate homogeneity or uniformity of meaning. Thus, we will briefly explore the notion, the history and the experience of soul from several different perspectives.

First, we will review different facets of the traditional Christian understanding of soul and how it shares some similarities and many differences with depth psychology and Jung's experience and understanding of soul. Jung's is a psychology of the soul as opposed to an ego psychology, clinical psychology or cognitive-behavioral psychology. While these latter psychologies tend to focus exclusively on the mental constructs of consciousness and the everyday anxiety of the ego, in depth psychology, soul naturally implies accessing deeper (unconscious) and broader levels of the human psyche. For example, in cognitive-behavioral psychology, the belief is that if one can change one's cognitions (e.g., cognitive distortions, faulty thinking, etc.) one's life will be transformed. In working solely with strengthening the ego's adaptation, this approach can be efficacious. However, one's deeper emotional life (unconscious dynamics, conflicts, deficits, motivation, etc.) and relationship to the transpersonal, is simply nonexistent or ignored, or simply treated as not the domain of healing.

In sharp contrast, depth psychology attempts to embrace the full complexities of human experience, both conscious and unconscious, and in particular one's wounded and suffering soul, through dreams, conflicts, symptoms, reveries, active imagination, transference and countertransference, etc. In this approach, archetypal patterns for healing (e.g., archetype of the wounded healer) are intentionally activated and used within the deeper structures of the field between therapist and patient.

In traditional Christianity, the cure of the soul, *cura animarum*, (Note: feminine genitive plural of anima) referred to the formal office of the priest as mediator, confessor, and healer of broken hearts and wounded souls. In essence, the image of priest, as healer, was viewed as Doctor of Souls. Today this vocation and sacred art has been expanded on and developed in the art of depth psychotherapy.[84]

Similar to the word spirituality, the idea and concept of soul cannot be adequately defined nor concretized. It is a living symbol that cannot be tethered and made profane. Thus, as a symbol, it is not completely within our grasp or control; that is, one cannot use the word in an unambiguous way. Like all "ultimate symbols, which provide the root metaphors for the systems of human thought," it cannot be reified.[85] As we noted

[84] See Szasz, T.1974; Stein, 1985; 2014; Corbett, L.1996, 2011.

[85] Hillman, J. *Suicide and the Soul,* p. 44 (1964).

earlier, in today's world, it is very tempting to commercialize spirituality; it is lucrative to write or speak of the soul. It behooves one to be aware of the shadow side to our contemporary spiritual craze and bricolage.[86] One cannot study the soul using the rational inductive scientific method: The soul needs its own phenomenological and methodological approach. Transpersonal and spiritual experiences often have no rational understanding or explanation; thus, they lead one into the depths to create something original and unexpected that cannot simply be reproduced. As the late author on soul, Christou, states:

The soul remains the great unknowable. ... We know that the soul is an everyday experience, yet we have no language to talk of it which is not vitiated by abuses of the language of reason or sense perception (Christou 1971, p. 25).

RELATIONSHIP TO SOUL

Growing up in the Catholic faith (G.J.D.) during the '60s and 70's, emphasis was placed on the mysterious and elusive supernatural nature of soul. I was fascinated by the image and idea of soul. The popular Baltimore Catechism, the church's essential teaching guideline, taught that man is a creature composed of body and soul, made in the image and likeness of God, and the essential likeness to God was the eternal soul and its free will. It also taught that everyone had an "eternal soul" from birth and that it was more important to save one's soul from hell than one's body. The church taught, quite fearfully, that one's soul could easily become stained due to sin. Mortal sin meant that one would never see God and would be condemned to hell. In the Catholic mythos, it was considered essential to keep one's soul free from sin in order to obtain eternal life. Hence, relationship to one's soul was inherently conflictual. On one hand, we were created in the image and

[86] Jeffrey B. Rubin "The McMindfulness Craze: The Shadow Side of the Mindfulness Revolution.

likeness of God, but on the other hand, we were fearful and preoccupied with following and obeying the commandments, the church's laws and rules, and ultimately: fear of hell. Jung writes that Western religion 'speaks of an immortal soul but has very few kind words to say for the human psyche as such' (CW 11, 28). How true, this latter aspect is the source of much scrupulosity, suffering and religious psychopathology

This traditional understanding of soul refers to a supernatural reality, an ontological principle, a divine spark within the human person: "the originative seat of reason and will in the human person. Created by God, it is regarded as a spiritual reality that survives physical death."[87] There is no systematic development of soul in either the Old Testament or the New Testament. It wasn't until well into the middle ages (NB: second dispensation) and the emergence of Christianity into the Greco-Roman world with the introduction of Greek philosophy and Platonism that Christianity developed a systematic doctrine of the soul. For the Christian, the soul is the divine basis and home in which God and self meet. This is the secret dwelling place where God and self take up residence; the inner sanctuary where creativity comes to life and the sacred is encountered. This is the world between worlds in which one retreats to find respite and comfort.

GOD AND SOUL

Jung often uses the words "soul" and "psyche" (Greek: *psykhe*) interchangeably. Though it appears that when he wanted to write about the scientific understanding of this experience in contemporary thought, he would use the more biological, modern and feminine term "psyche." Psyche, to the modern reader, is less ambiguous and more acceptable. When he wanted to write or speak from a deeply personal, religious, or romantic place he preferred the term "soul." In using soul and

[87] *A Handbook of Theological Terms*, Harvey, V. 1964. p. 226.

psyche interchangeably, Jung is referencing that both concepts may speak to the same reality but emphasize different perspectives. Furthermore, Jung believed that both concepts spoke to the whole person and hence prevented the tendency to bifurcate the human being into two divisions one spiritual and one psychological. For Jung, the psyche and the reality of the soul are primary principles, that is, they are foundational propositions that cannot be deduced or reduced from any other proposition in their own right and thus are addressed as such. Jung posited that the reality of the soul (psyche) was a principle *sui generis,* in its own right. In this view, the psyche is a primary datum and creates the reality which one inhabits. That is, the way one experiences the world is an amalgam of the objective world and the world perceived by the psyche or soul through images and fantasies. Perhaps this is among the reasons that Jung wrote in *The Red Book*:

> If a man possessed his desire, and his desire did not possess him, he would lay a hand on his soul, since his *desire is the image and expression of his soul* ... if we possess the image of a thing, we possess half the thing. The image of the world is half the world. He who possesses the world but not its image possesses only half the world, since his soul is poor and has nothing. The wealth of the soul exists in images.[88]

This is Jung's grounding ontological position, a third position between *esse in intellectu* (the abstract introverted standpoint: reality of mental processes) and *esse in re,* (the objects of sense, extroverted standpoint: material reality) what he refers to as *"esse in anima"* ("being in psyche/soul": is a psychological fact),[89] in contrast to the reigning ontology of his day, *"esse in re"* (being in matter). In his depth psychological approach, Jung insisted that the recovery of the soul was a vital task for "modern man;" thus Jung's religious concern. He writes:

[88] The Red Book, A Reader's Edition, pp.127-28
[89] Collected Works 6. par. 77.

> *Esse in intellectu* lacks tangible reality, *esse in re* lacks mind. Idea and thing come together, however, in the human psyche, which holds the balance between them. What would the idea amount to if the psyche did not provide its living value? What would the thing be worth if the psyche withheld from it the determining form of the sense-impression? *What indeed is reality if it is not a reality in ourselves, an esse in anima?* [Writer's italics] Living reality is the product neither of the actual, objective behavior of things nor of the formulated idea exclusively, but rather of the combination of both in the living psychological process, through esse in anima.[90]

Jung uses a hands-on approach that is up-close, personal, engaging and deep. The soul for Jung is a living reality in the here and now that essentially involves a dynamic relationship to one's unconscious; one we can immediately experience and relate to. Soul for Jung, then, is not some elusive, ethereal, and otherworldly idea that evokes fear of damnation, "black marks on the soul," and hell. In fact, we might say Jung liberated the religious function of the soul from the extreme limitations of intellectual abstraction, ahistoricism, and otherworldly preoccupation. Jung's reflections and writings on soul are enlivening, practical, and engaging. In the broad swath of his voluminous work, Jung uses the word "soul" in a number of different ways. We will review several for our work.

JUNG'S EXPERIENCE OF SOUL

In his youth and early adult years, Jung had a naturally close affinity with his inner life[91] (i.e., soul) and her manifestations. However, some years later, as a young psychiatrist, Jung confesses that he had lost his soul during a period of his life in which he was focused entirely on his scientific work as a research psychologist. In this process, he attempted to objectify

[90] Jung, CW 6, Psychological Types, par. 66.

[91] See *Memories, Dreams and Reflections,* pp. 6-113.

his soul and thought that he could explain and control her; certain fields of psychology still believe this today: psychology without psyche! It was during this period that he won international acclaim for his research and work in discovering "complexes" all the while collaborating intimately with Freud. Following this research and his subsequent break with Freud, Jung had to rediscover his lost connection to his own inner depths. Tellingly, Jung had stopped writing in his journals (Black Books) from 1900-12 while he was immersed in his scientific psychological research. In 1912, he recommenced his writing in his famous *Black Book* (a "book of my most difficult experiment") recording his fantasies and confrontation with the unconscious. He writes in *The Red Book*:[92]

> My soul, where are you? Do you hear me? I speak, I call you-are you there? I have returned, I am here again. I have shaken the dust of all the lands from my feet, and I have come to you, I am with you. After years of long wandering, I have to come to you again.
>
> There is no other way, all other ways are false paths. I found the right way, it led me to you, to my soul. I return, tempered and purified. Do you still know me? How long the separation lasted! Everything has become so different. And how did I find you? How strange my journey was! What words should I use to tell you on what twisted paths a good star has guided me to you? Give me your hand, my almost forgotten soul. How warm the joy at seeing you again, you long disavowed soul. Life has led me back to you. (...) My soul, my journey should continue with you. I will wander with you and ascend to my solitude.

The general leitmotif of *The Red Book* is how Jung struggled to re-engage his soul and heal the modern predicament of spiritual alienation. This was accomplished through participating in the rebirth of a new God Image in the depths of his soul while

---

[92] Shamdasani, *The Red Book: A Reader's Edition,* W.W. Norton & Company, LTD. 2009. p. 127

simultaneously creating a new dispensation, in the form of a psychological and theological cosmology. Jung's new worldview offered a foundational orientation and framework of ideas, including a psychology, philosophy, and beliefs forming a comprehensive description through which he interpreted the world.

Jung's night sea journey was an engagement with the depths of his own soul and, through her, "the spirit of the deep," the collective unconscious.

> I have learned that in addition to the spirit of this time there is still another spirit at work, namely that which rules the depths of everything contemporary. (...)The spirit of the depths forced me to say this and at the same time to undergo it against myself since I had not expected it then. I still labored misguidedly under the spirit of this time, and thought differently about the human soul. I thought and spoke much of the soul. I knew I had learned many words for her, I had judged her and turned her into a scientific object. I did not consider that my soul cannot be the object of my judgment and knowledge. (...) Therefore the spirit of the depths forced me to speak (to my soul, to call upon her as a living and self-existing being. I had to become aware that I had lost my soul. From this we learn how the spirit of the depths considers the soul: he sees her as a living and self-existing being, and with this he contradicts the spirit of this time for whom the soul is a thing dependent on man, which lets herself be judged and arranged, and whose circumference we can grasp. I had to accept that what I had previously called my soul was not at all my soul, but a dead system. Hence I had to speak (to my soul as to something far off and unknown, which did not exist through me, but through whom I existed."

Jung had to realize that he lost his relationship to soul and now had to call upon her as a living and self-existing being. His soul, once rediscovered, became his intermediary and guide. His soul asks him, "Will you accept what I bring?" Operationally defined, Jung came to understand the soul as a personification that represented the connection between the personal and the archetypal (spiritual/ transpersonal). Here, Jung's use of soul refers to the deepest subjectivity of an individual, a dimension in one that leads to a deep sense of purpose, interiority, and meaning.[93] In this process, Jung referred to soul as "the function of relationship to the unconscious," the living connective tissue that leads to the deeper interior life and the transpersonal Self. Hence, the soul may be imagined as a bridge or gateway to the deeper collective unconscious. Jung writes:

> "We define the soul on the one hand as the relation to the unconscious, and on the other as a personification of unconscious contents" (Jung 1976, [CW 6, par. 420]).

SOUL AND SEXUALITY: THE GATEWAY TO THE SELF

Jung also envisioned the soul as the anima/animus, that is, an archetypal image of the eternal feminine in a man's unconscious or the eternal masculine in a woman's unconscious that provides a gateway or path between ego-consciousness and the collective unconscious. For example, Jung often refers to the possibility of dream figures of the *opposite* sex as "soul figures." In theory, he considered a male figure in a female's dream or a female figure in a man's dream as personifying parts of the psyche that are unconscious to the dreamer. Jung considered the male/female dyad as one of nature's most powerful opposites. Contrasexual figures in a dream serve as a symbolic bridge or psychopomp (guide) to deeper levels of one's psyche more than same-sex figures simply because opposite-sex figures are more unknown and thus symbolize the opposite.

---

[93] For further reflections see Corbett, L. 1996, pp. 114-126.

The soul, as anima/animus, is defined in terms of interiority, image, introversion, and inwardness. As a relation to the unconscious, the soul, or anima/animus, is not the experience of one's ego personality; it is the experience or encounter of something radically different and separate, the not-me. [That's why in dreams the psyche often uses one's contrasexual images to address or speak to one's opposite.] As the relation to the unconscious, anima/animus consciousness does not seek to explicate or make plain and simple. Its function is to point toward the unknown, the mysterious, and give an image to it. Thus, the soul does not seek control or manipulation or clear critical thinking, but the furthering and deepening of one's imagination. Clarity is not one of its hallmarks. Anima/animus reflection is quintessentially the mode of imagination. In this view, the anima (soul) becomes the psychopomp, the guide to the underworld and the collective unconscious.

The work of the late E. Christou[94] is by far one of the most thorough and penetrating works on the contemporary issue of "soul." Christou writes:

> The difference between a thinking automat or a photographic plate and a human being remains that indefinable something we call soul; this would mean that a human being is able to *experience* what he thinks or feels, where the concept "experience" means more than just perceive or think the content in question (Christou, *The Logos of the Soul* p. 23).

When one speaks of soul, as in an old soul, a troubled soul, a lost soul, an innocent soul, a moved soul, a poor soul, one is poetically expressing and reflecting on the state of the soul by the soul itself—what we might term soulful experience. These are descriptions of the soul in the language of thought and thus reflect the state of the soul of the one describing the experience. Thus the soul must be understood in the context of its experience. It is a form of experience.

[94] Christou, E. *The Logos of the Soul*. Zurich: Spring 1976

Christou insists that the *"soul has a logic of its own"* and an experience of its own not to be seized by languages appropriate to physical phenomenon on the one hand, and to mental processes on the other." Hence, Christou highlights that the soul is the experiencing subject and not the mind or body or behavior that is experienced. There is a categorical difference between mind and soul; soul is of a different order and "has its own developmental processes leading to psychic maturity." For example, talking about my feelings, fantasies, and thoughts is not the same as experiencing my feelings, fantasies, and thoughts. The order of soul is the path to meaning that is discovered and/or created as we explore, name, and reflect on our experience. One may be inspired or profoundly moved by an experience, whether it is of nature, art, ritual, music, joy, love, or grief. Soul-making is being in the experience, not simply noticing or observing it. This subtle shift in understanding and emphasis is essential to grasp the subtle and elusive nature of soul. The realm of the body, emotions, thoughts, and sensations comprises all the *sources* of our psychological experiences, not the experiences themselves. The soul is essentially about experience and what we do with our experience, our moods, our fantasies, and our mental and physical states.[95] Besides simply being an intellectual or aesthetic understanding of what we experience, soul is our visceral relationship to the experience. Thus, soul is the symbol and name we give to our ability to transform ideas and feelings in our imagination and experience them. In this process we use our imagination to incubate, gestate, and transform our bodily states, sensations, and emotions into an experience—of soul.

Jung also conceived of the soul as the originator of images and symbols in our dreams, visions, fantasies, and active imagination. The unconscious (the Self) cannot manifest or become conscious without some sort of connection or bridge and translator. One's individual relationship to *soul* provides the bridge or connection to the spirit and the larger psyche, the transpersonal Self.

---

[95] See Christou, E., 1976, pp .57-82.

Gustav Klimt, Public domain, via Wikimedia Commons.

Thus, as another function of soul in Jung's psychology, (2009) the soul acts as the recipient and transmitter for archetypes. That is, the soul is the organ that metabolizes and transforms the archetypes into human images, symbols, and emotions, and incarnates them in the body and psyche. By creating and working with imagery and concomitantly emotions, one's soul can respond to the spirit of the deep.

> ... how the spirit of the depths considers the soul: he sees her as a living and self-existing being, and with this he contradicts the spirit of the time for whom the soul is thing dependent on man. (...) If he possessed his desire, and his desire did not possess him he would lay a hand on his soul, since his desire is the image and expression of his soul. (p. 232)

When we have numinous experiences or dreams, it is the soul, which connects us to transpersonal levels of spirit; that is, the soul translates and embodies the experience of spirit into sensations, affects, and images into personal consciousness. Hence, what we experience and discover about the spirit is mediated through the soul. The soul expresses one's deepest desires and thus coagulates those desires in the body-mind-psyche. Archetypal images reflect the symbolic connections between the personal and the universal mediated by channels that transcend our present comprehension. For example, whether it's in one's religious ecstasy (e.g., Bernini's St. Theresa in ecstasy) or lovers making love (Munch's "The Kiss") or the visions of the visionary (shamanistic channeling). The operative factor here is the idea that each person has the opportunity to have a growing personal relationship with his or her own soul. Following the soul's yearnings and desires leads people to their own *Imago Dei*, (their psychic God Image). However, traditional religious institutions often fail to be aware of this living psycho-spiritual experience and thus subjugate and bind the soul to *outer authority*; the idealized Other (e.g., hierarchical institutions, leaders, etc.). Seductive and authoritarian institutional religions, particularly fundamentalist, may capture one's soul by "hijacking it" and enslaving it to the collective.

Jung's lifelong work became defined as he attempted to walk between the world of science and the world of psycho-spiritual experiences. He furthered this by translating and writing objectively as a scientist what he experienced in his inner life, wrote about in his journals, and practiced as doctor of the soul. The study of religious phenomena was one of the central and critical issues that played a major role in shaping Jung's concept of psychology and the interpretation of unconscious phenomenon.[96] Hillman, widely known as one of the most innovative and insightful writers on archetypal

---

[96] See Shamdasani, S. *The Red Book: A Reader's Edition*; 2009

psychology and soul, exemplifies Jung's notion that there will be "new forms of spirituality" in his own archetypal psychology. He defines soul as "That unknown human factor which makes meaning possible, which turns events into experiences, which is communicated in love and which has a religious concern."[97]

THE LANGUAGE OF THE SOUL

In working with his patients, as doctor of the soul, Jung clearly preferred the natural language of the psyche, its naturally religious imagery and symbols, which more aptly describe the natural psychic processes. However, he found that in using traditional religious imagery in his clinical work (e.g., interpreting dream images), he needed to reinterpret them from a depth psychological perspective, and once he did, soul became a living relational reality once again for his patient. That is, for many people today, the traditional religious language has lost its power to evoke, reveal and relate to the mystery and depth of one's soul. The traditional religious language for the modern person is unintelligible; it is no longer effective in communicating the transpersonal. That is, for many today, religious language no longer serves as a portal to the soul, nature, or the world-soul. This is particularly true for the youth and young adults who have the left the Church. Often in the consulting room, one hears from middle-aged parents lamenting the loss of the Church for their children. They wonder why.

Jung's overall approach to psychology, and in particular therapy, became focused on understanding and re-interpreting traditional images and symbols of one's soul from the perspective of depth psychology;[98] the new (third) dispensation. In this approach, Jung articulates in a new way images of the soul that speak to his patients and brings together, in potential harmony and balance (conscious and unconscious) one's relationship to the

[97] Hillman, 1972, p. 23
[98] Jung, *Letters, II,* p. 525

sacred. Jung was attempting to build a bridge (i.e., transcendent function) between consciousness and the unconscious.

> In all too many cases the old language [of traditional religion] is no longer understood, or is understood in the wrong way. If I have to make the meaning of the Christian message intelligible to a patient, I must translate it with a commentary. In fact this is one practical aim of my psychology, or, rather psychotherapy.[99]

One of Jung's fundamental movements was to hear religious language as discourse about the living soul and one's relation to her. He moves the language of religious discourse and experience away from rigidly defined, religiously bound terms and belief systems to the immediate presence of the living psyche. He states,

> In describing the living processes of the psyche, I deliberately and consciously give preference to a *dramatic, mythological* way of thinking and speaking because this is not only more expressive but also more exact than an abstract scientific terminology" (Jung 1959, [CW 9ii, para. 25]). Whether working in the consulting room with this patients or writing about the "living processes of the psyche" (i.e., imaginal work, dreams, visions, etc.), Jung preferred to use mythological language and images for the simple reason that this language captured the reality of psyche and was "experience-near."

A PSYCHOSPIRITUAL DISPENSATION

In my (G.J.D.) former ministry as a priest, one of my functions was to reflect on and interpret the traditional sacred scriptures for the community (i.e., the first two dispensations: Old Testament and New Testament). In my work as analyst, there is a very similar function, as I collaborate with another

[99] *Jung, Letters, II,* p. 22

(patient) in paying attention to and working with and embodying images and symbols in one's dreams, (sacred scriptures from the Self), and fantasies; though this time from the perspective of the third (psychological) dispensation. In this endeavor, we are using the religious and symbolic imagery of the psyche—not only from the Old or New Testament, but also from different religions of the world. Ironically, I am reminded of a remark by Lacan stated in a similar context: "The strength of the churches resides in the *language* they have been able to maintain" (Ecrits, p. 72).[100] Lacan is highlighting a basic principle about language that is not only relative to "the churches" but also to the language of Jungian psychology. Thus, we might ask what sort of *language* does the *ecclesia* of Jungian psychology use that is similar to "the churches"? With the discovery of the reality of the psyche, Jung's language is clearly one of deep interiority focusing on one's inner (soulful) experiences. This was also true with the traditional language of "the churches" in their use of metaphor and symbol in teaching, preaching, and proselytizing. "The churches" and Jungian psychology share the language of soul.

Jung develops a new hermeneutic in which he understands and reinterprets the religious impulse and its imagery and symbols. With the hermeneutical tools of depth psychology, religious and literary scriptures can now be understood as the phenomenology of the objective psyche (collective unconscious).

Living Reality

Who among traditional church attendees are not tired of the same old homilies interpreting the same old stories that happened eons ago, in the same old way. This is truly indicative of the interpreters' loss of connection to the ongoing revelation and immediacy of the numinosum for the individual and the world today. With Jung's discoveries and new perspective,

[100] Lacan, *Ecrits*, p. 72

traditional scriptures are no longer interpreted as something that happened once and for all, eons ago. They become a living reality that speaks to the soul with potential for transformation and incarnation. Religious and spiritual realities (experienced through the psyche) are ongoing psychospiritual dynamics in *everyone's psyche* (i.e., the new dispensation).

Jung believed that a deep spiritual life was everyone's birthright; it only had to be discovered in the depths of one's soul. Thus, religious experience is not simply the privilege of mystics and saints; it is privileged to every human being. What this means is that the Self is continually attempting to incarnate facets of it-Self in one's personal experience: individuation. When one begins to view personal experience in light of unconscious surprises and the unexpected, as revelatory, (new dispensation) spirituality becomes a living dynamic that he or she is now deeply involved with. As Jung once stated, the face you turn toward the unconscious will turn back toward you. One's spirituality is no longer limited to mediation through the historically limited and narrower channels of one's tradition or prescribed religious faith; but now through the collective unconscious, one has unlimited access to humankind's transpersonal treasure house of images and symbols. As Jung writes: "The unconscious mind of man sees correctly even when conscious reason is blind and impotent" (Jung 1952a, [CW 11, par. 608]).

This perspective heralds the new *psychological* dispensation: discovering and working with the sacred from one's inner life.

Dream of Buddha

A Christian analysand of mine (G.J.D.) dreamt of a simple image of the Buddha meditating, bringing equanimity to his troubled soul. He was puzzled as to why he did not have a dream of Christ or one of the Christian mystics meditating. Prior to his analysis he would have minimized or even ignored or suppressed this image because it did not fit his belief system. Hence, he would have lost this compensating image and sacred message that his personal predicament and personality (structure) needed. After this dream, he began to receive his dreams more seriously (affirming his inner life/soul) and enrolled in a meditation course. He works radically differently now with his own soul; she is no longer limited to his conscious belief system.

This new hermeneutic has the potential to renew and revitalize traditional religious imagery by understanding it in light of the reality of the psyche and the transpersonal. It opens one to the development of one's own living connection to the soul. It acts like a bridge for the myriad ways that the Self may manifest in one's personal psyche. This perspective also offers the possibility of bringing about a re-enchantment of one's world and a return of the feeling of soul to one's modern rationalistic and scientific vision of the world.[101]

PSYCHE AND RELIGION

With the discovery of the reality of the psyche, (i.e., re-discovery of experiential soul), Jung asserts that all experience, including the experience of the divine (spirit), is mediated through the psyche. Jung does not doubt the reality of spirit, he is simply stating that the experience of soul and spirit though real, is mediated through the human psyche and thus more accessible than most people realize. This approach is quite similar to the phenomenological approach used by William James.

The experience of spirit is an irreducible psychic fact. The source of the religious imagination, for Jung, is the psyche and the collective unconscious. It is Jung's insight that the religious impulse, its images, symbols, and language, is inherently the expression of the mythopoeic level of the human psyche (i.e., soul). This discovery and movement has profound significance for an understanding of the contemporary religious landscape and its evolution within the individual and the collective.

---

[101] See Hillman, Re-Visioning Psychology, 1975

Jung's critics, however, claim that he is reducing the divine to nothing but psychological phenomenon, similar to Freud. They claim (Fromm, 1950; Buber, 1952; Noll, 1997) that he is guilty of psychologism, a reductionist move that reduces a transpsychic reality (God) to something only psychological; thus, equating spirit and psyche. Again, Jung responds that the psyche is real, and to say that something is psychological is to insist that it is real. The experience of the divine, the numinosum, manifests itself psychologically—how else would it be experienced? Jung emphasizes the immanent and radical presence of the divine (similar to Eckhart and Taylor[102]) as opposed to more transcendent, otherworldly descriptions of the divine that has been characteristic of traditional Christianity. For Jung, "The Kingdom of God is within you."[103] Our knowledge of the divine, though, is limited to what the psyche allows us to know about the divine.[104] It is this extraordinary vision and depth of the human psyche that analytical psychology offers religion. This vision has the potential to bring about a healing alliance between science and religion, Eros and Logos, head and heart. Jung writes:

The unconscious is the only available source of religious experience. This is certainly not to say that what we call the unconscious is identical with God or is set up in his place. It is simply the medium from which religious experience seems to flow. As to what the further cause of such experience might be, the answer to this lies beyond the range of human knowledge (Jung 1957, [CW 10, par. 565]).

THE EVOLUTION OF RELIGION AND THE PSYCHOLOGICAL DISPENSATION

As we have noted, Jung had foreseen major epochal developments in the evolution of religion in the contemporary

---

[102] Taylor, *After God*, 2007

[103] Luke, 17:21.

[104] See p. 70 above

Western world. These religious developments were due, partially, to the failure of the Church and her traditional religious structures to contain, mediate and transform unconscious archetypal energies. Hence, these uncontained energies can become strongly activated within the individual. Previously, these contents were held dormant within the collective body by the hierarchical organization of the Church—until the dawn of the Enlightenment. With the gradual deterioration of the Church's symbolic life to mediate one's numinous experiences of the sacred, the Church lost its capacity to contain religious (numinous) energy and the individual's archetypal content. This has led to the activation of different levels of the personal, cultural, and collective levels of the unconscious. Presently, some individuals who remain in the church and those who pursue paths outside the Church (e.g. S.B.N.R.s) are forced to contain and transform the energies that have been activated. Failing to do so, individuals may become the victim of these forces that foster regressive tendencies in response to change. This can give rise to fundamentalism and other "isms" that can manifest as phenomena like ISIS.

Edinger states, "The new psychological dispensation finds man's relation to God in the individual's relation to the unconscious" (Edinger, 1984 p. 90). The first dispensation was the Judaic dispensation based on the Law; the People of God found their relationship to the sacred through the Law and the Ten Commandments. The second was the Christian dispensation, which was based on faith, in the God-man. The new (third) dispensation[105] is based on one's experiential relationship to one's own interiority, the unconscious, the Self. In this new dispensation, the official Church is no longer the sole retainer of the "franchise of revelation."

In Jung's assertion of a "new spiritual epoch,"[106] he believed that the first two dispensations were losing their vitality and energy and thus their ability to psychologically contain

[105] See Edinger, 1984.

[106] McGuire and Hill, 1977, p. 68

numinous energy and transform Western consciousness. In response to the masses leaving the churches, he stated: "Life has gone out of the churches and it will never go back. The gods will not reinvest dwellings once they have left."[107] In the new psychological dispensation, the individual must look within, discover the inner spark of divinity and become a conscious carrier of the divine. Thus, the innermost soul of the individual becomes the container, the Cathedral (i.e. tabernacle) for the divine. In working with these sacred energies and their embodiment in images and symbols, Jung writes in *The Red Book*:

> I should advise you to put it all down as beautifully as you can - in some beautifully bound book. It will seem as if you were making the visions banal - but then you need to do that -then you are freed from the power of them. If you do that with these eyes for instance they will cease to draw you. You should never try to make the visions come again. Think of it in your imagination and try to paint it. Then when these things are in some precious book you can go to the book & turn over the pages & for you it will be your church-your *cathedral*-the silent places of your spirit where you will find renewal. If anyone tells you that it is morbid or neurotic and you listen to them - then you will lose your soul - for in that Book is your soul.[108]

Transitioning Between Dispensations: Deacon James

James, an analysand (G.J.D.) and older Deacon in a large Catholic parish was struggling with his own internal religious authority and the Institutional authority of the Church. His experience is offered as an example and illustration of a minister feeling the tension between the traditional Christian dispensation and the new third (depth-psychological) dispensation.

---

[107] William McGuire and R.F.C. Hull, *C. G. Jung Speaking*, p. 97.
[108] Jung, *The Red Book*, p. 216

The deacon was often challenging his Pastor over certain religious practices that he felt were either oppressive or no longer relevant to the people of the parish.

In one case he was ministering to a dying parishioner who had been attending Sunday Eucharist for years without receiving Holy Communion because he had been divorced and had not received an annulment. As the deacon came to know and experience this dying man's deep faith, his devotion and continued religious practice through the years, he wrestled with the church's teaching forbidding divorcees from receiving Holy Communion. As the deacon struggled, he approached another priest (hierarchical authority) in the parish to gain his advice and possible permission for the parishioner to receive Holy Communion. The deacon did not trust his own religious authority. The priest upheld the Church's formal prohibition. The deacon was in anguish for weeks over this decision and felt that it was punitive but could not bring himself to offer communion to the parishioner.

A few weeks later, the parishioner died. After his death, the deacon became indignant with himself and the formal position of the Church hierarchy. He had an overwhelming regret that he did not engage his own religious authority and bring Holy Communion to the dying parishioner. Thereafter, the deacon had a compensatory dream in which he was encouraged to develop his own religious authority and return the hierarchical authoritative projection to his own soul.

THE RELIGIOUS DISPENSATION

What exactly does dispensation mean? Edinger makes reference to Ephesians 3:8-9, noting that the word dispensation was translated from the Greek, *"Oikonomia tou mysterious"* which was interpreted as dispensation of the mystery. Thus, in this view, "man's relation to the hidden mystery of God must be dispensed or administered ... as the "administration of a household" (1972, p. 18).

The Latin origin of the word dispensation is the verb *dispensare*, to manage, distribute, allot, arrange, dispense. There are two definitions in particular, which we need to understand in reference to our work. First, defined in psychic terms, dispensation refers to "the specific arrangement or system by which our perception of the world is ordered,"[109] the lens through which we view the world. Religions, by nature, order our world (mythically) by providing us with a perspective, a lens through which we view creation, discover meaning, and find purpose. Religion orients us to answering the most basic and fundamental questions of our lives.

Secondly, dispensation also refers to the disbursement or the act of dispensing numinous energy relating to the deity, one's *Imago Dei*. Hence, we might say, religion is the experience of the mystery of receiving the deity's grace and relationship.

In the first dispensation, one's world was ordered and arranged by the collective as the Chosen People of Israel and the Law. In the second Dispensation, one's world was ordered and arranged by one's relationship to the Church (the Bible, sacraments, Magisterium, etc.) and faith in the God-man. In the new Dispensation—one's world is ordered and arranged in accordance with one's experientially and reciprocal relationship to the personal and collective unconscious: one's worldview is a co-created process between consciousness and one's personal relationship to the unconscious.

In naming this present religious development the "new psychological dispensation,"[110] Edinger stresses the new vision and process through which one's world is ordered and how numinous energy (grace) is dispensed and received in daily life. This is an emergent phenomenon arising from the unconscious through dreams, visions, synchronicities, different ritual processes, intuition, altered states of consciousness, active imagination, Holotropic Breathwork, etc.

---

[109] Jaffe (1999), p. 18. (*Celebrating Soul*)

[110] William McGuire and R.F.C. Hull, *C. G. Jung Speaking*, p. 97.

Through discovering and working with one's psyche, one can submit to and develop a new relation (dispensation) to the hidden mystery of the divine. In this new dispensation, one encounters the divine through one's own relation to his or her psyche (soul); the psyche is sacramental, by nature.

In the first dispensation, God's favor was on those who kept the Law; while in the second dispensation, grace was dispensed through the Church, through faith and imitation of the God-man: De Imitatione Christi. In the new depth psychological dispensation, one's relation to the hidden mystery of the divine is now dispensed and received through one's experience and relationship to the psyche.

First Dispensation: Abraham's Call to Monotheism

As the ancient Hebrews distinguished between gods and the one God, Moses called the people into a covenant, which eventually developed into a monotheistic religion. Differentiation, as Jung writes, "is the essence, the *sine qua non* of consciousness,"[111] for once a psychic object is known, it *typically* does not carry archetypal projections. Thus one's *Imago Dei*, necessarily undergoes renewal and ongoing revelation. However, fundamentalists fail to differentiate between God qua God and the psychic experience of God (Imago Dei). The fundamentalists, who claim to know the God they worship, interpret this in literal and concrete ways; hence, their anxiety and strong reaction over changes in the deity's imago. As consciousness grows, differentiation increases, and projections become more defined and specific. Projections, particularly projections of archetypal material, still abound but they become more localized and specific. The Ancient Hebrews knew a deity by the name YHWH.

[111] CW 7, par. 339.

The First Dispensation, James Tissot, Public domain, via Wikimedia Commons.

In this first dispensation, numinous energy was projected onto the Law. The Law gave form, shape and order to the consciousness of the Chosen People. With this new development, their perception of the world became structured around their collective identity as the Israelites bound by the Law as conveyed by the Ten Commandments and the Torah. In this dispensation, personal experiences and opinions play an insignificant role. The collective law is dominant, and personal views and opinions are replaced with collective beliefs and values. After the Christian revelation, the first dispensation came to be known as the Jewish Dispensation. Obedience to the Law was the supreme value. Note the Pharisees condemning Jesus, who healed on the Sabbath! At this stage of development, there is no room for individual differentiation. Religious fundamentalists often take up residence in this formal stage of development.

The Second Dispensation: Christianity

With the emergence of the Christian faith, the projected psychic content of the *Imago Dei*, is now located, literally *and* symbolically, in the God-man (i.e. "Son of man," Anthropos). Grace and salvation are no longer mediated through the Law but now achieved through faith in the God-man, Jesus of Nazareth. Faith in the God-man supplants the Law. This is the heralding of the new religious evolution into the Christian dispensation. In this second dispensation, ultimate values and ideologies like faith, love, and hope assume the numinous power attributed to previously idealized objects like the Law and the Torah. The projections of unconscious material onto the God-man, Christ, are still viewed in both a literal and concrete way:[112] God is alive and exist in Heaven.

With the evolution and birth of the Christian faith, the Jewish Law was reinterpreted. The unconscious archetypal God (image) moves closer to humanity by taking on human form and becoming a part of the human family, however, in this version, God in Christ, is still distant and radically idealized as the *only* Son of God. This second dispensation is centered on faith and belief through projecting one's own inner Imago Dei onto the Christ figure. Jesus becomes Christ, the archetypal figure who receives the collective projections of savior. This religious movement, built upon the Jewish dispensation, is now called the "Christian dispensation,"[113]which became focused, organized and unified around the apocryphal life of Christ. Thus, we can speak of an Old Testament (Jewish Dispensation) and now a second, New Testament (Christian Dispensation), which announces the continuing evolution of God and humankind.

The Law was the first dispensation, faith in the Christ figure the second dispensation, and one's personal relation to their unconscious is the New Dispensation. If *psyche* is the source of religious experience the new dispensation is deeply psychological. This New (Psychological) Dispensation extends the first (Law) and second dispensations (Faith). In this psychological dispensation, the individual becomes the "sole carrier of life" (Jung 1977, [CW 16, par. 224]). Because the churches no longer contain the numinous energy emanating from the individual, this energy may flow over and potentially flood the individual. The individual may then become Self-aware and potentially burdened by the numinous transpersonal

[112] Jung, 1978, (CW 9ii, par. 68-126)
[113] Edinger, 1986; Jaffe, 1990

psyche. Where a minister once carried the weight of dispensing the numinous, in the new psychological dispensation this weighty responsibility falls to the individual. Jung continues the idea of the incarnation of the divine, but now through every human being mediated by the psyche.

The Form of Dispensation

A further meaning of dispensation refers to the "form" in which a thing is dispensed or distributed. So, we might ask, in the religious realm what is dispensed or distributed? For just as water or wine can be dispensed by means of a bottle or tap, so the spirit can be dispensed by means of images, symbols, sacraments, rituals, religious artifacts (e.g., the cross, Menorah, rosary, the circle, icons, Kittel, benedictions, etc.). In traditional Roman Catholic theology, grace was thought of as being dispensed through the sacraments. Ordained priests, who act in *Persona Christi*, were officially authorized to preside over the sacraments and were considered dispensers of sacramental grace (*Ex opere operato*[114]: regardless of the state of the priest—sacraments dispense God's grace). In the practice of the Church, Catholics were obligated to attend Mass weekly under the threat of mortal sin, and go to confession at least once a year to receive God's forgiveness and grace that came through the sacraments. This form of dispensation comes only from the sacerdotal priesthood. In this tradition, one's relationship to the divine (Numinous unconscious) is mediated through the dispensation of grace through the priesthood and sacraments: *Ecclesiae sacramentis*. A product of this theology is that the locus of God's grace is outside the individual, is hierarchical and mediated through a cleric, and is dependent on an Institution. Oddly enough, these realities can become an impediment or impingement to one's personal relationship to spirit.

---

[114] *Ex opere operato* is a Latin phrase meaning "from the work worked" referring to the efficacy of the Sacraments deriving from the action of the Sacrament as opposed to the merits or holiness of the priest or participant.

There is a powerfully strong shadow element to the church's traditional religious and hierarchical system. In the Christian dispensation, too much psychic reality had been denied including the reality of the body, sexuality, evil and a person's connections to the earth. Thus, the old forms of dispensing of soul and spirit are no longer as enlivening or viable as sources of life and spirit. As the Church's symbols and authority lose their vitality, where could an individual turn to experience the transpersonal?

The Third Dispensation: What Is Dispensed in The New Dispensation?

> *We don't know...how much of God...has been transformed...It can be expected that we are going to contact spheres of a yet transformed God when our consciousness begins to extend into the sphere of the unconscious.*[115]

In relating to the depths of one's psyche, one inherently connects to those religious stirrings of the numinosum. This in turn offers a transformation of consciousness by which our perception of the world is ordered. In the new (psychological) dispensation, one's perception of the world is ordered by one's view of their personal experience of the transpersonal, in particular their *Imago Dei*.

The new dispensation does not necessarily negate the prior dispensations; it builds on their historical and archetypal images and symbols. In addition, the new dispensation need not negate one's relationship to another religious body or institution. Ideally, for those to whom traditional religion continues to mediate the sacred, the new psychological dispensation can foster a greater balance between inner and outer, deepen one's

[115] Jung, *Letters*, II, p. 314.

awareness of the unconscious life of the soul, and enrich one's personal spirituality.[116]

FEAR OF ONE'S SELF

This movement toward a new dispensation has its own attending anxieties and fears as old structures and symbols give way to the "not-yet" known future or the "not-yet" known God. This state of being "in-between" threatens many, most particularly, the fundamentalists who cleave to their old creeds and beliefs. Creating even greater uncertainly and anxiety is the fact that among other things, the new dispensation is not mediated through the Church, its priests or ministers. One's soul and religious grounding has been emancipated, no longer tethered to traditional doctrines and beliefs, and is now more readily able to enter into the deeper waters of the unconscious. Hence the fruit of each individual's work and relationship to his or her soul will be the building blocks of the future God-Image and Church. One's religious work, then, is rooted in personal experience and the ongoing dialogue between the conscious and unconscious. Whereas the traditional teachings of the Church address the ego and its need for conversion, sin, guilt, confession, etc. The new dispensation acknowledges something deeper within one's personal unconscious and works with all of one's affective experience without proscribing what is acceptable and what is not acceptable. One's personal experience will be the key to listening to how the Self through one's complexes may incardinate.

Fr. Joseph (A Case Study)

An analysand of mine (G.J.D.) who was a young Catholic priest was in the throes of a personal and religious crisis while struggling with his vows, the Institutional Church and his

[116] Schneider, 2000, p. 12.

evolving spirituality. After several years of analysis he had the following dream:

> I am on a religious pilgrimage of some sort, walking on a dusty road in what appeared to be an ancient city. I notice off to my far right there are numerous steeples with crosses, cupolas, and religious domes filling the early evening skyline. There is lightning off in the distance. As I make my way along the road, there are fellow travelers making their way along the path. As I continue my journey, I pass a woman who appeared in need; she was off to the side. I stopped and assisted her briefly and then continued on the journey. In the next image, I am high up in the mountains inside a cave-like structure that opens out to a vast view of other mountains. I am sitting at an old table with a large book in front of me. Behind me to my right is Carl Jung, and behind me on my left is Christ. Jung says to me: "Open the book and study the Anthropos." Then the dream ended.

Fr. Joseph had learned to value his inner work and in particular his dreams, during his years in analysis using them for spiritual discernment. This was an extraordinarily numinous dream that had a profound effect on him; he was dumbfounded and amazed by it, particularly in that it addressed him so personally. Where did this dream come from, he would ask? The numinous affect, the images, the symbolism and his interpretation challenged his traditional religious beliefs (second Dispensation) and nudged him along his path of individuation. After this dream he began realizing how his own inner God-Image was changing. He immediately began studying the 5,000-year old history of the Anthropos and its relation to the Christ figure. Note that Anthropos is a Greek name that is commonly translated as human being, first man, the great man and "Son of Man" in the New Testament. The dream-addressed issues concerning his own religious life, his wounded narcissism, and his relationship to the feminine and critically raised the question: who was Christ? The dream liberated him to ask and address the deeper questions that he wanted to ask all along–

but anxious to inquire. He interpreted the dream as calling him to the task of making conscious the chthonic spirit in human nature; an aspect that he viewed as missing in the Christ figure. He also interpreted the dream as informing him that the Christ figure was a contemporary symbol of the ancient mythology of the Anthropos and thus preceded the Christian myth. Furthermore, he experienced the images of Christ and the Anthropos as living symbols—for him—of what Jung refers to as the Self; one's *Imago Dei*. This young man reexamined the role of the archetype of Christ and the priesthood for himself and his ministry. The dream inaugurated a great quest, an odyssey of the spirit, for this young cleric. He slowly developed a radically different relationship to the Christ figure and the authority of the Church. The dream may also be seen as announcing the end of one dispensation and the heralding of a new dispensation.

The experience of the sacred is not something experienced only in prayer or in church. In the new dispensation one's daily life and experience is the conduit for discovering and fostering a relationship to the divine. One must pay attention to what crosses one's path. Jung has many different views of the divine; in one such view he states:

> God is ...an apt name given to all overpowering emotions in my psychic system, subduing my conscious will, and usurping control over myself. This is the name by which I designate all things which cross my willful path violently and recklessly, all things which upset my subjective views, plans and intentions and change the course of my life for better for worse.[117]

There is no one-size-fits-all McSpirituality in the new dispensation. One's experience of the numinous is always relevant to one's personal psychology and psychopathology which directly addresses what one needs for healing and wholeness. Hence, personal experience of the transpersonal psyche is the new evolving form of one's spiritual life and practice. When one learns how to pay attention to the manifestations and

[117] Jung *Letters, II* p. 525.

revelations of the unconscious (Self) one can begin to respond personally to the divine. One discerns how the numinosum personally addresses them. Jung states:

> You are quite right, the main interest of my work is not concerned with the treatment of neuroses but rather with the approach to the numinous. But the fact is that the approach to the numinous is the real therapy and inasmuch as you attain to the numinous experiences you are released from the curse of pathology. Even the very disease takes on a numinous character.[118]

Note it is not *numinous de jour*, but an experience of the numinous that is tailored to each individual's psychological/ spiritual work that leads to liberation "from the curse of pathology." Numinous experiences of adversity, surprise, and distress can beckon us to transformation. This is how the divine becomes incarnate and participates in our lives.

This new dispensation offers a form of religious expression in which experience supersedes belief in creedal religion. One of the reasons for this is simply the fact that the sacred or the holy manifests directly through the unconscious. That is, one is often surprised by a religious experience, which indicates that the experience emerged from the unconscious. In this process, one has direct contact with it and does not need to rely on belief or be dependent on the intercession or mediation of a sacerdotal priesthood. In an interview for the BBC, John Freeman asked Jung if he believed in God[119] and Jung replied "...I know. I don't need to believe, I know."[120]

---

[118] Jung *Letters, I* p. 377.

[119] Jung clarified: "Mind you, I didn't say 'there is a God.' I said: 'I don't need to believe in God, I know.' Which does not mean: I do know a certain God (Zeus, Yahweh, Allah, the Trinitarian God, etc.) but rather: I do know that I am obviously confronted with a factor unknown in itself, which I call 'God' in consensu omnium (quod semper, quod ubique, quod ab omnibus creditur). Vincentian Canon: "What has been believed everywhere, always, and by all is the catholic Faith of Christianity"; authors), Jung, *Letters Vol. II*, Page 525.

[120] Jung, *Letters, II*, p. 271.

This was not the first time Jung spoke on "knowing" the divine. In an earlier interview Jung said, "I only believe in what I know. And that eliminates believing. Therefore, I do not take his existence on belief – I know that he exists."[121] Traditional religions assume that if you believe, you are initiated and you will have the experience (of God). Jung turns this upside down: "If you have the experience of God or the Self, you will believe, or more precisely you will know."

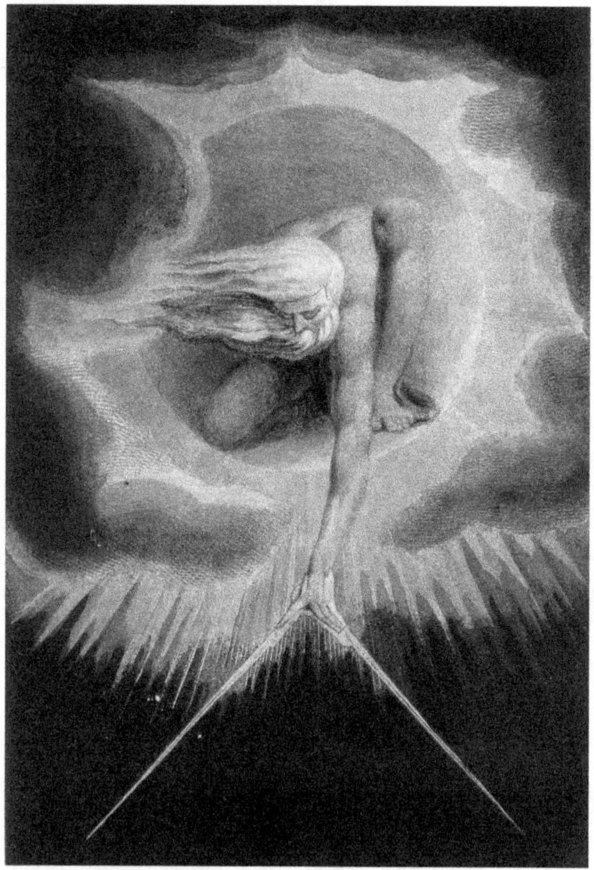

William Blake, Public domain, via Wikimedia Commons.

[121] Ibid.

In the new psychological dispensation, as Edinger notes, it is precisely in becoming "aware of the transpersonal center of the psyche, the Self," and by living "...out of that awareness, [one] can be said to be the incarnation of the (new) God Image."[122]

Nonetheless, Jung was adamant in his scientific research and work that he never wanted his psychology to become an official religion that would be codified with creeds and beliefs. He considered himself a consummate scientific psychologist who studied a process empirically and named it whilst refraining from becoming identified with the process under study. He did not set out to establish a body of beliefs. Yet, he asserted, in 1942, that analysis or psychotherapy might be considered a "religion *in statu nascendi*, in a state of being born."[123] How can these differing views be reconciled?

Jungian analysis and psychotherapy can be understood as providing a ritual vessel that cultivates a type of initiation process that fosters transformation. This analytic vessel provides the opportunity for a person to develop a relationship with his or her own deeper religious sensibilities and impulses; it is a means by which a connection to soul occurs. The religious flavor of Jung's psychology of the unconscious is one of many developing forms and practices emerging from earlier traditions that may lead to a new, postmodern, post-tradition, Christian religion. Analysis and psychotherapy provide a container in which the analyst or therapist functions like a midwife who aids in the birth of one's own *Imago-Dei*, one's *religion in statu nascendi.* This is the heart and soul of the new psychological dispensation. The call is to look within the depths of one's own soul and not outside. The new psychological dispensation discourages the idealizing of religious authorities that leads the follower to abdicate spiritual authority and autonomy to another.

---

[122] Edinger, 1984, p. 84

[123] CW 16, para. 181.

In the new dispensation, a person strives to find the value of his or her inner path by cultivating a relationship to the Self: by listening to dreams and bringing to consciousness one's shadow, complexes, contrasexual nature (anima/animus), and ultimately, the Self.

CONTINUING INCARNATION

Jung built upon the archetypal theme of incarnation in Western religion by proposing a continuing incarnation through the process of individuation, in which the individual becomes aware of the Self and begins to live out of this awareness. In the course of the individuation process, one encounters and reconciles opposites and holds the tension of this conflictual birthing of the Self. This coincides with Meister Eckhart's notion of the birthing of God in the soul. Ultimately, this leads to individuation, the full flowering of one's potential within their personality. In order to hold the tension of the opposites and enter into a dark night of the soul a strong ego is required. It is left to each of us to incarnate the unique aspects of our relation to the Self and coalesce an individual *Imago Dei*. In one of his late books, *The Undiscovered Self*, Jung exhorts people to recognize the critical role of individuation that each person must engage in the new dispensation.

> "So much is at stake and so much depends on the psychological constitution of modern man...does the individual know that he is the makeweight that tips the scales?"[124]

The furthering of individuation also entails embracing the suffering of the opposites. As Jung writes: "...we don't know of, how much of God...has been transformed...it can be expected that we are going to contact spheres of a not yet transformed God" ...the transformation of the "not yet transformed God"

[124] Jung 1964, CW 10, para. 586.

entails the suffering of the *Complexio Oppositorum* (Jung, Letters II, 1975, p. 314).

6. COMPLEXIO OPPOSITORUM

Man's suffering does not derive from his sins but from the maker of his imperfections, the paradoxical God (Jung 1980, [CW 18, para. 1681]).

Jung's concept of the Self is based on inherent contradictions: light and dark, spirit and matter, good and bad, etc. The Self is by definition paradoxical. It is important to point out that the Self cannot be known fully, so we cannot speak about the contradictions within the Self, but only about the contradictions, or duality of the Self as reflected in ego-consciousness. The image-dimension of the Self, as collected by humankind during the course of history, often reveals complexities of opposites.

Totality of The Self

The Self is manifested in visions, dreams, religion, mythology, and tales in the form of the superordinate personality, such as savior, ruler, king, priest, prophet, and the like. The Self in Jungian psychology is considered a symbol of totality and wholeness often represented by the circle, mandala, square, *quadratura circuli*, cross, star, etc. The Self, as a representation of one's *Imago Dei*, presents as a *complexio oppositorum*, a union of opposites. Jung puts it this way:

> There is an old saying that 'God is a circle whose center is anywhere and the circumference nowhere.' God in his omniscience, omnipotence, and omnipresence is a totality symbol par excellence, something round, complete, and perfect. (1959, [CW 10, par. 622])

The process of differentiation (analysis and dissolution) and "unification" (integrating and synthesizing), the two phases of analysis, was described by Jung as the transformational goal of individuation; a process that culminated in the birth of a new symbol (image, disposition, attitude, perspective, etc.) which represented an amalgam of the opposites. Jung borrowed the term *complexio oppositorum* from alchemy. It is similar to Chinese philosophy in which the Tao, a way of achieving balance, is the product of the interplay of opposites: yin and yang. In fairy tales, we find the totality of the Self in the twinship-conflict (two opposing forces) of the hostile brothers, or of the hero and his adversary. In Goethe's' (1819) work, it is Faust and Mephistopheles. The Self appears as an interaction of opposites: light and shadow. However, in the Self, the opposites are united and interdependent.

Dividing The Experience of The Numinosum

The opposites, however, can be divided or split off by a psychological maneuvering in the psychic system of the individual. Because the experience of the Self (the numinous) can be terrifying and fascinating at the same time, the ego can selectively block (split off) one "pole" (i.e., terrifying) from its perceptive sphere. If the archetypal "Complexio" is approached in an excessively selective manner, then each pole can be experienced in its extreme. Jung's research on Otto's (Jung 1938, [CW 11, para. 6]) ideas pertaining to the experience of the mystery of the "Holy" leads one to the realization that the emotional response of the ego to "The Holy" was either one of excitement or ecstasy on one hand or one of terror and dread on the other. Thus, an experience of ecstasy may lead to possession by the "light" side of the Self, which in turn can lead to *hubris*. On the other side, experiences of dread and terror can lead to possession by the "dark" side, bringing feelings of humiliation, alienation, and most importantly shame. Bradford (Bradshaw 1988) calls this kind of shame a "toxic shame." The ancient Greeks used the term "*aeschyne*" to describe the experience of possession by the "*tremendos*" of the Self. Compaan (2007) then describes hubris as possession by the light (fascinating) pole of archetypal energy, while *aeschyne* as a possession by the dark (awful) side of the archetypal energy, (p.8). Shame, according to Compaan, is the key emotion that determines how the ego deals with strong archetypal energies.

Inadequate Regulation of The Numinous Energies

One of the functions of the ego is to mirror the image of the Self and regulate the feeling of shame, which naturally arises as a result of facing the numinosum. However, there are instances in which the ego's regulation is insufficient and inadequate. This can lead to possession—unconscious identification with one side of the Self. Compaan (2007) says:

> Where the mirroring is inadequate, the result is that the individual becomes possessed by polarized affects, either dread/terror (*aeschyne*) or excitement/interest (*hubris*). The transcendent function does not develop and the opposite affects are not held in tension. (p. 8)

Holding The Tension of Opposites

So, psychological and spiritual health has to do with the ego's ability to *hold* the tension between the extreme poles of energies within the Self. The ego must be able to *relate* emotionally to both *aeschyne* (the personification of shame) and *hubris* without being possessed by either. The resilient ego remains flexible as long as it is aware of these intense energies that press against it. If the ego is in a state of psychological "holding" and enduring the archetypal affect, one can experience a deep depression, be overwhelmed by a frantic idea, or become paranoid yet still not succumb or be possessed by these forces. Rituals and religious practices can be viewed as natural attempts to provide structures and practices that facilitate affect regulation and instruct the ego on how to relate to "The Holy" without falling into possession. Possession by archetypal affect means that the ego has "insufficient perceptive and discriminatory abilities to be able to adequately handle the intensity of the shame affect aroused in psyche by the numinous" (Compaan 1997; Coen 2002). Spiritual practices are used to increase and deepen one's self-knowledge and skills; this includes knowledge of the complex aspects of the impact the numinous exerts upon the ego. The ego's ultimate task is to bring the inherent contradictions of the Self together, to transcend polarities. This is not a maneuver of the mind; it is the fruit of the spiritual life. Alchemists described this process metaphorically as the work to create the lapis, the philosopher's stone, or "The Wisdom Stone". Jung says:

> We find the crucial importance of self-knowledge [for the sake of the transformation process] expressed most clearly [by the alchemist Dorn] ...The transformation is brought about by the *conjunctio*, which forms the essence of the work... The union of opposites in the stone is possible only when the adept has become One him/herself. The unity of the stone is the equivalent of individuation, by which [we are] made one; we would say that the stone is a projection of the unified self. (...) It does not, however, take sufficient account of the fact that the stone is a *transcendent unity*. (1950, [CW 9i, para. 256]; emphasis author's).

Defensive Religious Stance

It follows that an inability to unite opposites can be expected to lead to unhealthy religious phenomena. Fanatical religion can be conceived of as the creation of a defensive ideology when it comes to dealing with the paradoxical nature of the numinosum.[125] The ancient Greeks understood that *hubris* fostered identification with god-like power and provoked excessive pride or grandiosity and *aeschyne* perpetuated feelings of shame in relation to the religious attitude. *Aeschyne* is an attitude toward oneself that is utterly shameful and engenders feelings of having no value before God—self-loathing, disgust, shyness. *Aeschyne* ignores and turns away

[125] Ego-defense systems operate as survival mechanisms, not unlike other biological defense systems that have evolved over millions of years.

from the fullness of the *Imago Dei.* A person under the influence of Aeschyne [goddess] rejects the notion that he or she is an image bearer of the divine and could be thought of by the Greeks as lacking *aidos*, a humble religious attitude. In contrast, *hubris* exaggerates the human role in the encounter with the numinous and inflates the individual. It overreaches the boundaries of reality and natural law. *Hubris* can propel a person into magical spheres where the archetypal world of the collective unconscious encourages a person to act as if God imparted to them some special privileges or tasks. A flexible and open ego that nurtures a connection to the archetypal world is unlikely to blindly embrace a radical religious perspective and or engage in extremist conduct.

V.
ANALYTICAL PSYCHOLOGY AND THE DYNAMICS OF EXTREME RELIGION

1. DELINEATION OF THE CONCEPT OF STRONG RELIGION IN JUNGIAN PSYCHOLOGY

The creativity of consciousness may be jeopardized by religious or political totalitarianism, for any authoritarian fixation of the canon leads to sterility of consciousness (Neumann, 1970, p. xix).

Strong religion, as fundamentalists understood it, is not beholden to the mainstream religious establishment or to conventional religious authorities, weakened as they are by deadening compromises with secular powers (Almond, Appleby, & Sivian, 2003, p.17).

In this chapter we attempt to explain how religion becomes strong, inflexible, excessive, or abnormal. A depth-analytical inquiry naturally focuses on the relationship between the ego and the unconscious. This relationship is examined through a lens of the ego's capacity to withstand the encounter with unconscious numinous energies.

Strong Religion

We use the term "strong religion" to refer to rigid or fierce adaptation to archetypal energy in an *unhealthy way.* We are borrowing the term "strong" from the *Fundamentalism Project* because it describes the use of religion that exceeds healthy limits.[126] "Strength" in this respect does not mean vitality and health, but maladaptive rigidity when relating to the archetypal affect and *Imago Dei*. In depth psychology, when something becomes abnormal or excessive it is often recognized by the shadow lurking behind. In other words, unconscious or split-off parts speak (or often shout) via actions; enactments that we have spoken about earlier. The unconscious, split off parts of the psyche are enacted in some fashion—and are seen to be determinants in a person's actions. Every individual, at times, manifests disharmony, imbalance, or pathology in unique ways that are influenced by various subjective factors. Everyone employs his or her subjective feelings and opinions about what is abnormal and unhealthy. Consensual reality, however, provides a frame of reference for judging what may be abnormal and unhealthy and, in addition, points to the possibility of making changes. A phenomenological analysis of ego-Self relations allows Jungians to see commonalities among impaired adaptations while preserving a pragmatic view. Jungians regard all aspects of the phenomena of a person's life as worthy of examination. Truth is preeminent. It is tested by the practical consequences of belief and the degree of one's personal development, the culture, and the times through which we judge them.[127] Jung might have said that the real is what works and how something works makes it very real.

---

[126] *The Fundamentalism Project*: Project sponsored by the American Academy of Arts and Sciences; an international scholarly investigation of conservative religious movements throughout the world. The project began in 1987 and ended in 1995. Martin E. Marty and R. Scott Appleby directed the project.

[127] For example, human religious sacrifice is not only illegal in the western world, but a person who insisted on practicing it as part of their personal religious belief would be considered insane. Nevertheless, in some parts of the modern world women may be subject to stoning for infidelity or other alleged acts.

Imbalance Is not Pathological: The Psyche as a Holistic and Homeostatic System

The psyche is a system that naturally seeks balance, yet relative states of imbalance are also natural. Like other living systems, occasional perturbations from a homeostatic state are not necessarily indicative of illness or disease. Transitional periods and in-between states of occasional dysregulation create opportunities for change and reorganization. However, within the psyche such periods have dangerous potential if they are met with rigidity or are relegated to the unconscious for too long a time.

> As we have seen, the inherent tendency of the psyche to split means on the one hand dissociation into multiple structural units, but on the other hand the possibility of change and differentiation. It allows certain parts of the psychic structure to be singled out so that, by concentration of the will, they can be trained and brought to their maximum development. In this way certain capacities, especially those that promise to be socially useful, can be fostered to the neglect of others. This produces an unbalanced state similar to that caused by dominant complex—a change of personality (Jung 1937, [CW 8, par. 255]).

Rigid ego positions are typical for people who hold strong beliefs. Behind this strength is often an inferior function, complex, or archetype that seems like it must be kept in abeyance. When these elements erupt and penetrate into consciousness this can be experienced as a psychological breakdown. Periods of chaos, confusion, or depression should not automatically be viewed as pathological. There are numerous instances in which the dark night of the soul is followed by a beautiful sunny day. Negative periods or life events might eventually prove not to be negative at all when we revisit them later. Negativity may possess the seeds of positivity. The encounter with the numinosum may appear to be inevitable and provides the impetus for the emergence of consciousness.[128]

Compensation: Psyche's Self-Regulating System

While developing a concept of psychic compensation, Jung drew upon multiple sources, including Heraclites' concept of enantiodromia, the Eastern concept of yin-yang, and findings from Alfred Adler.

Compensation naturally inclines the psyche to complement maladaptive processes by new, hitherto unutilized potentials—an attempt to establish balance and equilibrium. Jung said:

> In dreams, for instance, the unconscious supplies all those contents that are constellated by the conscious situation but are inhibited by conscious selection, although a knowledge of them would be indispensable for complete adaptation (1921b, [CW 6, para. 694]).

Unsuccessful adaptation leads to negative ego-positions or neuroses. The neurotic posture exerts effect on emotional and cognitive processes and on the constitution of the personality.

The Unattainable Ideal

The ideal of perfect psychological health is unattainable — one can only be on the journey *toward* such an ideal. That journey requires a flexible capacity to embrace new experiences and respond to them adaptively. It requires openness to constant learning and growth with humble acceptance of our

---

[128] "In a truly complex system no single aspect as adequate information to represent the whole, nor can any single part statistically predict the dynamic behavior of the system, especially when it self-organizes. Symmetry is broken in what are called phase transitions, rapid, abrupt reorganizations of a dynamic system that radically restructure the system, allowing new forms to emerge. Bearing the psychological equivalent of a phase transition and reorganization can be highly stressful for an individual even if ultimately positive in transformative effect." (Cambray, J., *Synchronicity*, 2009, Texas A&M)

smallness. Like Socrates who claimed to be wiser than another because he did not pretend to know what he did not know, the person who acknowledges the elusive nature of complete psychological health may appear healthier than the one who claims to have achieved ideal psychological health. Human development is always a work in progress.

The same is true with radical religion. The radical fundamentalists are at great risks in reifying their religious ideals. A person possessed by radical, fundamentalist religion may come to believe they have attained to the highest idea. When this belief becomes concretized the search for the ideal ceases—a person does not continue searching for something that has been secured. A system of beliefs that achieves unquestioned certainty and that seems to have manifested in the material world places a person at risk of becoming entrapped. This is an untenable position. A belief system that loses its ability to change or incorporate feedback grows stagnant. The capacity to experience the numinous and interact with the environment is impeded. This can lead to increasingly maladaptive, one-sided beliefs.

Unhealthy Ego-Positions

In relation to strong fundamentalist attitudes, the ego adopts one of several basic positions. The ego's posture we propose are based on Andrew Samuels' (1985) and our own findings. Some of the postures include:

1) *Participation mystique* Characterized by poor differentiation of the ego from the original state of unity with the Self, this a primitive identity.

2) *One-sidedness* Involves identification with an ego-consciousness that erroneously believes itself to the one and only self. This posture produces a compensatory pressure whereby the unacknowledged, unconscious contents become inflated.

3) *Identification* This position involves over-identification with a particular ego-position that cuts off other possibilities.

4) *Possession* Here the ego becomes engulfed by unconscious contents resulting in the defeat of the ego, which becomes overwhelmed and carried away.
5) *Possession by the inferior function* This occurs when the ego comes under the influence of the unintegrated inferior function. Under such circumstances infantile and archaic adaptations are produced.
6) *Concretistic adaptation* When this ego-posture is assumed, the ego-complex loses its ability to relate objectively to unconscious content (ideas, affects, complexes, archetypes) in healthy adaptable and symbolic ways. This results in a sterile imagination and developmental rigidity.
7) *Lack of aidos* (a Greek word that connotes the feeling of reverence). This ego-posture is characterized by a haughty ego that is unable to adequately contain and integrate archetypal energy.
8) When the Self possesses the ego, a sense of being inspired by God may be ushered in. This can engender such God-confidence one unleashes destructive deeds that are not constrained by a fear of God's disapproval or retribution. Jung demonstrated that from an empirical perspective there is no difference between the Self directly experienced on a psychological level and the experience of a supreme deity, or God. The Self "might equally be called the 'God within us'" (1928b, [CW 7, par. 399]). If the Self, as an autonomous psychic content (i.e., archetype), takes hold of the ego, the result is a specific sort of possession— *theocalypsis*—possession of a religious nature.

All the above outlined ego postures lack balance; one aspect or another becomes dominant at the expense of a complementary aspect. This lack of balance or departure from the unity—*complexio* of the numinosum—is the key concept of Jung's theory and practice.

2. CONCEPT OF ONE-SIDEDNESS IN JUNGIAN PSYCHOLOGY

The tendency to separate the opposites as much as possible and to strive for singleness of meaning is absolutely necessary for clarity of consciousness, since discrimination is of its essence. But when the separation is carried so far that the complementary opposite is lost sight of, and the blackness of the whiteness, the evil of the good, the depth of the heights, and so on, is no longer seen, the result is one-sidedness, which is then compensated from the unconscious without our help (Jung 1955, [CW 14, para. 470]).

It can generally be stated that psychological processes become unhealthy when they reach a certain degree of "*stuckness*." This can be the result of the activation of a complex or an archetype, or by the rigid adherence to an ideological structure via attitude of the mind. In describing these psychological dynamics, Jung coined the term "one-sidedness."

Genesis Of The Concept of One-Sidedness In Jung's Work

Jung was inspired by the teachings of Otto Gross, a disciple of Freud who coined the phrase in writing in 1907. Later, Jung (1921, [CW 6.]) used this concept in his theory of *Psychological Types*. There, he elaborated the idea that a poorly developed psychological function—undifferentiated from the unconscious—is only loosely connected to the ego and consequently not under the volitional control of the ego. The more unconscious the function is, the more autonomous it becomes intermingling with, and contaminated by, other cognitive functions.[129] Under

[129] Jung (1921) postulated four essential cognitive functions: thinking, feeling, sensation, and intuition. He says: "Sensation establishes what is actually present, thinking enables us to recognize its meaning, feeling tells us its value, and intuition points to possibilities as to whence it came and whither it is going in a given situation." (*Psychological Types*, CW 6, par. 958)

certain circumstances, the function that is disconnected from conscious processes behaves like a purely unconscious dynamic factor—a sort of wild, untamed, self-directed stallion. This dynamic factor can produce all sorts of undesired phenomena; Jung summarized this notion by stating:

> In one case the conscious function is transported beyond the limits of its intentions and decisions, in another it is arrested before it attains its aim and is diverted into a sidetrack, and in a third it is brought into conflict with other functions ... (Jung 1921c, [CW 6, para. 118]).

Superior psychological functions are well integrated into the ego complex and freely at the disposal of the will. They stand in opposition to inferior functions. These attitudes or cognitive functions can become one-sided if the ego excessively identifies with them in its attempts to defend against unconscious fantasy activity. To the extent that a function develops one-sidedly, the inferior function becomes correspondingly primitive or undeveloped. The overly determined dominant primary function takes conscious energy away from the inferior function. The result is that the inferior function "falls" into the unconscious where it tends to be activated in a primitive way, giving rise to symptoms of a psychic imbalance. Inferior functions are always represented as autonomous, compulsive energy. For example, inferior feelings will burst out as anger, or strongly defended judgments, inferior thinking can take the form of sacred opinions, prejudices, and inferior intuition can take the shape of "pseudo-prophecy."

Compensation and One-Sidedness

Psychological one-sidedness results in the accumulation of increased energy in the unconscious that can intrude into consciousness in a compensatory fashion. As Jung said:

> The contents that are excluded and inhibited by the chosen direction sink into the unconscious, where they form a counterweight to the conscious orientation. The

> strengthening of this counterposition keeps pace with the increase of conscious one- sidedness until finally ... the repressed unconscious contents breakthrough in the form of dreams and spontaneous images ... As a rule, the unconscious compensation does not run counter to consciousness, but is rather a balancing or supplementing of the conscious orientation (Jung 1921, [CW 6, para. 694).

The problem of one-sidedness lies in the fact that the navigating space of the ego becomes too narrow, too limited to embrace broader aspects of reality (1954a). The solution offered by one undergoing Jungian analysis is "to compensate [for] the one-sidedness and narrowness of the conscious mind by deepening its knowledge of the unconscious" (p.756). For example, an overly determined thinking person, with the help of his or her own unconscious (i.e., dreams, slips of the tongue, interior reflection, enactments, etc.), can develop the feeling function in order to free the ego from an unhealthy and inadequately one-sided rationalistic approach to life. One-sidedness produces rigidity, not only with theoretical stances and perceptions of the world; it can determine how a person deals with a whole spectrum of life phenomena like social interactions and daily tasks. We believe that this phenomenon is responsible for what is known conspiracism (belief in bizarre conspiracy theories).[130] One-sidedness is *neurotic* in nature and it eventually produces unwanted (unconscious) enactments:

> In a case like this the unconscious usually responds with violent emotions, irritability, lack of control, arrogance, feelings of inferiority, moods, depressions, outbursts of rage, etc., coupled with lack of self-criticism and the misjudgments, mistakes, and delusions which this entails (Jung 1954b, [CW 13, para. 454]).

A person possessed by such one-sidedness may appear to be missing something essential, as if his or her soul has

[130] See: Šolc, V., Kde se rodí konspirační teorie, Vesmír, 2016

wandered away. It appears like a loss of freedom and creativity; as if one was denied access to some of the most basic expressions. Metaphorically, we might say that such an individual has been expelled from paradise.

War Trauma

One of my patients (V.Š.), who recently came home from his second tour in Iraq, was unable to reestablish an emotional connection to his wife, children, and to nature in general. Skills and perspectives that were so valuable in the battlefield were suddenly useless upon his return home. His emotionality was covered by a warrior-like thinking accompanied by strict organization. His feelings of love had become buried beneath layers of bloody memories. He wanted to go "back home," back to himself, but he was unable to cross to the other side. He had experienced too much of the *tremendos* in the form of a numinous terror and it kept him sequestered from the *fascinans* that might have afforded him access to experience the fullness of his soul.

Missing Parts of Numinosum Are Projected Out

> *The present day shows with appalling clarity how little able people are to let the other man's argument count, although this capacity is a fundamental and indispensable condition for any human community. Everyone who proposes to come to terms with himself must reckon with this basic problem. For, to the degree that he does not admit the validity of the other person, he denies the "other" within himself the right to exist – and vice versa. The capacity for inner dialogue is a touchstone for outer objectivity* (Jung 1981, [CW 8, para. 187,]).

One-sidedness is typically accompanied by an unconscious longing for wholeness, a longing for the missing aspects of the psyche. A person who is unable to adequately claim those inaccessible feelings that are naturally associated with both aspects of the Self tends to project the unclaimed elements onto other people. The recipient of the projection is then supposed to act as *re-collector*, and they are assigned the task of restoring the lost soul-part. Projection is founded upon the psyche's natural tendency to dichotomize phenomena in ways that the unacknowledged, unclaimed soul-parts lead to extreme idealizing or vilifying the person upon whom the projection is cast. When the unclaimed aspects take the form of idealized projections, the recipient may be revered as a *savior or deliverer*. The opposite valence of a projection tends to render the recipient of the projection as a villain possessed by the *awful (dark)* aspects of the numinous that may be full of anger and hate. This dichotomizing of projected material fuels the tendency to identify with one side of a polarity of opposites, and this obscures a person's ability to recognize that the source of enmity and conflict as originating from within. As a result, the other person inadvertently becomes a container of the split-off archetypal energies.

Susan

I recall a story of a client whose mother was depressed and suffered from various health issues. Susan's mother was a devout Christian, and her religion strongly dictated the right worldview, proper behavior and morals, all in accordance with biblical teaching. Susan's mother devoted herself to controlling the smallest details of her daughter's life. Susan found herself in a web of carefully designed ideologies, indoctrinations, and rituals. This became unbearable as Susan grew older, and finally when she was strong enough, she responded with her own oppositional views against her mother's manipulation and control. In desperation, she ran away from home and married a man who was an outspoken atheist. In the aftermath of her daughter's rebellion, Susan's mother broke down and began treatment. (V.Š.)

Psychological work at times is an attempt to re-collect scattered pieces of the soul and rebuild psychic unity. This can only be accomplished by a conscious realization of the one-sided entrapment(s) to which we have become subject. This can foster and allow a balancing of opposing forces.

Even though Jung (1921) originally understood one-sidedness as an imbalance pertaining to the differentiation of four psychological functions, he later extrapolated from this typological perspective and applied one-sidedness to any phenomena when consciousness acquires an excessive sum of energy originating in a function, persuasion, complex, or archetype. A one-sided mind can hypostatize abstract concepts or feelings. Unconscious content that breaks loose from a complex can produce an excessive amount of energy that is at the disposal of other unconscious content and, without one knowing, can contribute to and fuel the formation of a strongly held ideology that defies reason.

Substituting Symbol

According to Jung, the mind can adhere to a "substitute sign" that replaces the living, natural symbol. Religious institutions, for example, can create stereotyped concepts and signs that over time replace natural symbols of the unconscious with empty conventional signs. These barren symbols and substitute signs often mislead the individual and simply support institutional hierarchies of power— fostering one-sided dominant hegemonies. One example can be found in the exclusive dominance of an all-male clergy over the feminine dimensions of faith. This yields a system of hierarchies in which matter dominates spirit, male clergy rule over laity; the redeemed/saved individual is esteemed over the infidel/damned, and other similar splits. To this end, Jung said, "*The symbolic concepts of all religions are recreations of unconscious processes in a typical, universally binding form*" (1921d, [CW 6, para. 80], emphasis ours). These symbolic images and concepts become ideas and customs, which function as expressions and containers of the numinosum for the collective. From a developmental perspective, such containers are *indispensable*. Living symbols are archetypal containers and, as such, are humanizing principles giving cultures and societies direction and structure. Symbols that have been established by cultures over thousands of years play a key role in human religiosity. What makes them living is that they work, profoundly speaking to and affecting people soulfully. It is the relationship that makes them alive, not a property of symbols as such. Through ritual, worship and contemplation, living symbols mediate numinous feelings and foster the creation of higher consciousness. In this very function they are alive. However, substitute forms and stereotyped concepts are bereft of life: restrictive, blinding, and suffocating. They end up narrowly defining and limiting one's experience of life and the numinosum, turning living symbols into a form of magic. For example, one often sees professional baseball players making the sign of the cross as they approach home plate to bat. What determines if this is truly a symbolic (ritualistic) gesture or a good-luck gesture to provide a little juju to ward off anxiety and ensure a base hit, one's internal disposition and relationship to the symbolic.

Creating and substituting a sign for a symbol denies access to the inner sources of the numinosum and the renewing energy it supplies. The journey of discovering one's own symbolic reality can be disorienting and painful, but its benefits always outweigh the consequences of being a pawn, unconscious and vulnerable to the effect of the collective mass-minded. Many of our religious patients today are seeking psychotherapy and analysis due to loss of meaning and the inability of their symbolic systems to mediate connection to the renewing power of the numinosum. For many, the collective religious symbols no longer reveal or carry the power of the numinous for them.

Peter

A patient of mine (G.J.D.) who was a minister in his church, sought analysis due to a feeling of malaise in regard to his personal and spiritual life. He was also undergoing spiritual direction. However his work with his spiritual director was not reaching the depths of his concerns and malaise; it tended to focus on theology and church doctrine. He spoke hauntingly about the hierarchical leadership's emphasis on the letter of the law, which he followed, and how it deadened the spiritual life of his fellow parishioners. After the first year of his analytical work, Peter had the following dream:

> I found myself involved in a baptism of a newborn child in a church I wasn't familiar with. The baptism took place right in the pews (which was quite unusual) toward the middle of the church. The church was very large. The child had a very unusual name.

After several years of work in analysis, Peter underwent an initiation (baptism) and transformation of his religious attitude. He was seeking to establish a more personal relationship (a re-engagement with his own images and symbols) to his own soul; this was signified by the baptism of the child, in the pews of the church with the unique name. After years of service and loyalty to the institutional church, its symbols had lost their revelatory power to reveal, engage and inspire his ongoing spiritual journey. Peter needed to re-establish a deeper connection to his own personal myth and symbols, the source and wellspring of the life of the spirit. After several more years of analysis in exploring and working with unconscious images and accompanying emotions, he began relating to undeveloped parts of his soul (e.g. issues of Eros in relating to the feminine), which had the effect of re-energizing both his psychological, sexual and spiritual life. This process was one of reestablishing a deeper reconnection (baptism) to soul through the living symbols that spoke personally to him, challenging him to claim his inner spiritual authority as opposed to projecting his authority onto the hierarchical church.

Strong Creed As a Defense

The phenomenon of compensation ensures that the vigorous exclusion of certain components of one's totality ultimately contributes to its emergence on a different level. Take for example a compensatory prophetic vision that is forcefully imposed on its beholder. In the case of religion, the creed has to be very *strong* to keep out the compensatory, numinous energy that seeks to surface and push against the defensive structures of the ego. Although these energies have a deep archetypal origin, their compensatory projection is directed toward anybody who disagrees with one's creed or one who appears to have secret doubts.

Radical religious wings build their defense on a strong demarcation from other religions, sects, and ideas. In their book on strong religion, Almond, Appleby, and Sivian (2003) explain why a fundamentalist's religion has to be *strong* in demarcating their adversaries:

> Religion must be strong because its enemies are perceived as powerful and potentially overwhelming. Foremost among these enemies is the modern state, which projects itself as omnipresent, omniscient, and omnipotent. How could an entity possessing these three properties avoid becoming the object of a religion and being fervently worshipped, fundamentalists worry, especially when its existence is beyond any doubt? (p. 19).

Religion As Container of Archetypal Affect: Bruce

I remember (V.Š.) a patient who experienced a spiritual breakdown. Bruce experienced trauma as a little boy. When he reached his teenage years, that trauma reemerged with great intensity. His ego defenses broke down under the power of his previous unresolved trauma. Bruce's thought process became incoherent, full of bizarre and archaic fantasies, and his behavior was erratic and aggressive. Bruce was increasingly paranoid and believed that the CIA was tapping his phone. It was the onset of schizophrenia, as became apparent years later. Bruce was hospitalized and put on the medication. After that, over the course of several years, he was in and out of hospitals. During that time, he developed a relatively concise and complex philosophy, or we should say, theology in which he addressed, in a very naïve way, the basic questions of religion, such as life after death, the problem of will and morality, theodicy (the problem of evil), or the relation between mind and matter. Before this episode, Bruce was an atheist, very irreligious, and an a-philosophical man who was not interested in the great questions of life. We can hypothesize that the sophisticated defensive ego-system he developed allowed him to *contain* the wound of his early trauma and its archetypal energies. In the face of the numinosum, his ego substituted and replaced living symbols with the immovable and locked-down ideas that functioned as protectors against disintegration. As often occurs in cases of chronic posttraumatic stress, Bruce's religion did not gradually evolve; it erupted and thus clashed repeatedly with reality. When the impenetrability of his creed carried him away, the goddess of righteous indignation, Nemesis, stepped in and brought him back to the hospital. As Bruce became ever more trapped in his own creed, he could not find his place in life. In order to avoid getting burned each time his grandiosity overwhelmed him, he adapted to his surrounding reality by adjusting his persuasions and beliefs accordingly. Over time he learned that he was not indestructible and all-powerful. He learned that anger against another kept him from getting his basic needs met. Bruce's case is a dramatic condensation of the life-story of a man seeking relative freedom from the influence of archetypal forces while preserving the vital benefits they provide.

An open-minded, dialectical communication with the archetypes appears to be the best option left to us. Unceasing adaptation and striving toward the optimum of *complexio oppositorum* (a union of opposites), or what Jung calls life with *paradox*, is far less psychologically dangerous than the belief that the ideal has been already reached.

The Complex and Neurotic One-Sidedness

The "complex" is a fundamental tenet of Jungian psychology. In fact, the idea was so important to Jung that he originally considered calling his theory "Complex Psychology." (Shamdasani, 2003, p. 12) A complex is a splinter psyche or a fragmentary personality that was originally split off from the ego because of the intensity of overwhelming affect. Clinically, we would refer to one's complex as a personal wounding, a situation in which a child was not able to process or master powerful emotions.

Basically, a complex is a collection of images and ideas centered around a core derived from one or more archetypes and is characterized by a unifying emotional tone that acts like glue holding it together. A complex is capable of seizing control of a person. According to Jung (1937), one-sidedness and the influence of the complex on consciousness may be viewed as different aspects of the same phenomena. They both result from splitting or fragmentation of the totality of the personality, and both are representations of inhibited adaptation and consequent isolation of affect. When constellated, both are manifested through a sudden shift in personality. This change is, as a general rule, negative, because every split or dissociation produces regression and increases the energy of shadow. Complexes "behave autonomously and interfere with the intentions of the will, disturbing the memory and conscious performance,"[131] and while not negative per se, their effect is typically experienced negatively by others.

Complexes are the core constituents of psychic life. An experience dangerous to life or health "imprints" a complex in order to better recognize it in the future. While some complexes may foster learning, some may be helpful in specific situations, and some are plainly dysfunctional and outlive their usefulness. So-called *negative* complexes are unwanted and they cause psychological and interpersonal distress. The less a complex is under the control of one's will, the more "contentious" it becomes.[132] They tend to emerge or be activated when triggered by a situation similar to the original wounding. Complexes can feed into one-sidedness. For example, a child often criticized for

131 CW 8, par. 194 - 219.
132 CW 8, par. 255

being "lazy" and compensates in life by overachieving, might later develop an anti-welfare philosophy. Failure to recognize the complex often leads to others being subjected to it.

Paul

Paul was a patient (V.Š.) who sought therapy to deal with his angry outbursts toward others, particularly at work. He also reported anxiety, procrastination, obsessive thinking, indecisiveness, and excessive preoccupation with the little details of his daily tasks. This derailed him to the point that he "never got anything done in time" and "could not be perfect." Paul grew up in a family of Christian fundamentalists where his father played a dominant, patriarchal role. His father was extremely religious, controlling, and punitive and like his father he was a religious fundamentalist. Paul was a very critical and angry man who was in the grip of a critical father complex, but his criticism was always directed toward the *unrighteous* people around him. He believed himself to be a "very religious man," following an evangelical branch of Christianity that did not believe in symbolic expressions and considered the Bible to be the literal truth. Paul was *stuck* in his own inferiority: secretly doubting himself all day long. He did not doubt his religion he doubted his actions. My patient showed a strong resistance to anything new, and the only area of study that he was willing to consider was the Bible. He dwelt on traditional patriarchal values: where the father is the head of the family, and the mother stays home with the children. He ascribed to traditional beliefs including the view that homosexuality was a sin, and he identified himself as a "pro-lifer." When Barack Obama was elected president, my patient sighed that the "American dream of the white Christian man has died." His philosophy lacked nuance and this black-and-white attitude produced frequent conflict with his loved ones. He was unwilling to look within, but obsessed with ways to change or convert the others. This patient's father complex manifested in his general attitude and reinforced his one-sidedness. The Zeus-like qualities of his overly strict father brought about his own one-sided father complex. Perhaps, he was defending himself against it by identification, but it did not help him in the long run. When he came to see me, he was not ready for change and unable to recognize his own inner critical voice—he remained unable to move past his projections. He terminated therapy prematurely, being angry at the world.

The complex stands between the archetype and the ego disturbing the healthy flow of energy.

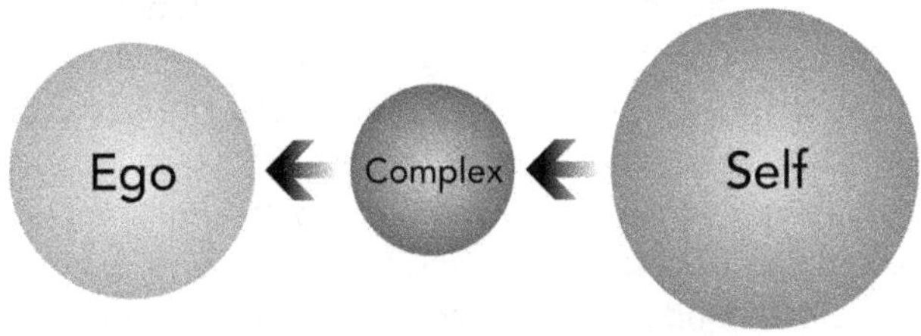

Complex Stands Between Ego and the Self

Jung (1937) distinguished between deformations of persona that are the result of a complex and those caused by one-sidedness, but he made it clear that they are interrelated:

> People often fail to see that consciously willed one-sidedness is one of the most important causes of an undesirable complex, and that, conversely, certain complexes cause a one-sided differentiation of doubtful value. (Jung [CW 8, para. 255])[133]

[133] Jung understood the "persona" as both an archetype and a complex. It is an archetype because it is universally human and it is a complex because it is filed with individual experience that is connected to ego consciousness. Thus the persona is a social mask or the face a person puts on to engage one's social world—it stands between the ego and the outer world. The persona is not to be thought of as pathological or false. It is a compromise between the demands of the social environment on ego consciousness balanced with the structures of one's inner landscape.

Refuge To Safety

An escape to one-sidedness can produce comfort since this psychological state is experienced as free of ambiguity. The Self that seeks to unite opposites in tension inevitably encounters ambiguity and persistent tension. One-sidedness distances a person from his or her inferior side, the shadow. The one-sided mind wants to avoid change and flees from higher truths found in the unity of opposites. Typically, one's ego wishes to maintain a narcissistic state of idealization and omnipotence. The ego may attempt to do this by clinging to soothing one-sided views of archetypal imagery and corresponding thought structures. To this end, the ego selects only those aspects of archetypal imagery that confirm its views and goals and ignores the unwanted parts. Such archetypal ideas and images, with which the one-sided mind identifies, according to Jung (1943, [CW 7]), "can acquire powerful amounts of energy that draw the ego into its service." Possession by the archetypal idea can be as equally strong and equally destructive as possession by the complex. We say that the complex has an "archetypal core." A religious idea has to be equally justified, but its energy is much greater; therefore it holds with a much greater force.

The recently emerging movement in many Arab countries called ISIS builds on such archetypal religious ideas. ISIS promises paradise on earth, a "Perfect Mohammedan Islam" after the just war resulting in unified Islamic governance. An apocalyptic vision feeds into an ideology that is not afraid to put everything at stake. An early ISIS statement calls upon the "believers" to join the final fight:

> O soldiers of the Islamic State, be ready for the final campaign of the crusaders. Yes, by Allah's will, it will be the final one. We will conquer your Rome, break your crosses, and enslave your women, by the permission of Allah, the Exalted. (*Inquisitr*, September 11, 2014, p. 1)

Behind any powerfully held religious idea lies an archetype. Ideas were originally instincts, then spirits endowing natural objects, and later gods. There cannot be an idea without the archetypal background, and it is also true that where there is an archetype, there is an energy that can be manifested in various ways through the spectrum from an urge through emotion and feeling, to image to abstract and complex ideas.

Shamanism, A Cradle of Mythology

The evolution of consciousness can be viewed as a process during which the unconscious becomes discriminated and formed into conscious structures. Prototypical images that were revealed originally to shamans were *purified* by their minds to constellate early cosmology, which much later became a theology for the tribe. Eliade (1951) discovered that mythology was not consciously created, but rather revealed to shamans who used various techniques to lower the threshold of consciousness allowing unconscious images to emerge.[134] Shamans basically worked with lowered defenses (lowered level of consciousness: *abaissement du niveau mental*[135]) of the ego, in order to evoke an openness to the unconscious and, in particular, to the images of numinosum. Shamans were traditionally initiated into tribal mythology and thus into the secrets of how to deal with forces of the numinosum. The transformation of archetypal material into spiritual form corresponds to the evolution of the mind. That is to say, over the course of history ideas emerged from the emotional laden archetypal images and were assimilated to the philosophical and theological concepts of their times. Pre-Socratic philosophy is still practically based on imagery and mythological motifs, while

[134] See Eliade, M., *Shamanism: Archaic Techniques of Ecstasy*, Princeton University Press, Princeton, 2004 (First published in 1951)

[135] *"Abaissement du niveau mental,"* was first used by French Professor Pierre Janet and refers to a relaxation and uninhibited lowering of consciousness or letting go of psychic restraints characterized by an absence of concentration and attention. This psychic state can be brought about either involuntarily (e.g., possession by complex, physical and mental fatigue, shock, etc.) or voluntarily through fostered preparation for active imagination and/or forms of mediation.

Platonic philosophy begins to deal with more abstract and isolated ideas and explains the world through a more sophisticated process that adds a reflective thinking element to the feeling-based image.

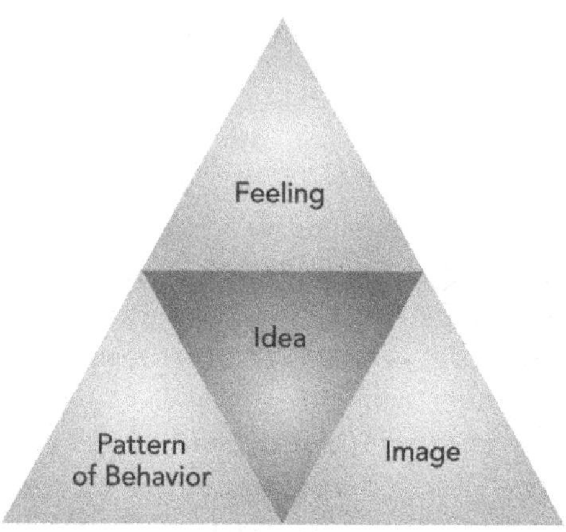

Archetype as Composed from Feeling, Idea, Image and Pattern of Behavior

Archetypes Are Sources of Ideas

The very notion of Jung's theory of archetypes is only a continuation of the development of the concept that started at least 2,500 years ago. No systematic thinker is able to come up with an understandable theory without connecting the dots of how the theory was distilled through the historical accumulation of ideas. Thinkers like Goethe, Kant, Schopenhauer, Nietzsche, Hegel, Hartmann, Carus, Burckhardt, Levy-Bruhl, James, Helmholtz, Driesch, Stahl, Haeckel, Fouillée, Lorenz, and Adolf Bastian whose theories provided a basis for Jung. And this list of philosophers owes a debt to the philosophers of antiquity like Zeno of Citium, Dionysius the Areopagite, Socrates, Plato, Saint Irenaeus, Philo of Alexandria, Saint Augustine and others. Jung's theory is not an exception to this. His genius wasn't in creating something totally new, but in his ability to connect ideas in a meaningful way and apply them to modern depth psychology. Those who accuse him of creating a new theology need to understand that Jung merely explained human phenomena through an already-established frame of reference, separating metaphysics and theology from empirical science. We can say that Jung provided a psychological methodology for framing the numinosum rather than postulating it.

Abstraction and Concretism

Understanding how archetypes become ideas, phylogenetically speaking, is crucial to developing a clear concept of the differentiation of psychic functions as ontogenetic process. Whenever a psychic function as a cognitive tool is "closer" to consciousness, the easier it is manipulated by will, or in Jung's (1921b) words, it is at the "disposal of consciousness." Passive and active thinking are distinguished by the presence of volition. All functions were originally, so to speak, fused in the unconscious. We can best observe these phenomena in children and ancient people who do not separate feelings from perception and thinking. For them, their own feeling or emotion *is* a fact; their own projection is reality. Jung referred to the state of undifferentiated cognition as archaic to describe its developmental origin. Imagery and perception can be fatally "contaminated" by the unconscious, i.e. fused with functions that are activated but not integrated by the ego. Jung said:

> An image has an archaic quality when it possesses unmistakable mythological parallels. Archaic, too, are the associations-by-analogy of unconscious fantasy, and so is their symbolism. The relation of identity with an object, or *participation mystique*, is likewise archaic. Concretism of thought and feeling is archaic; also compulsion and inability to control oneself (ecstatic or trance state, possession, etc.). Fusion of the psychological functions, of thinking with feeling, feeling with sen-

> sation, feeling with intuition, and so on, is archaic, as is also the fusion of part of a function with its counterpart (1949, [CW 6, para. 684]).

Abstraction is a form of differentiation with a simultaneous presence of conscious awareness, and therefore it is the process of "counterfusion." It is a selective process of (active thinking) forcing certain ideas to associate with others and also consciously excluding some ideas due to their irrelevance or with the intention to narrow the content held in the mind (see Jung, *Definitions*, CW 6, par. 678). *Concretism is the opposite of the process of abstraction*. Concrete concepts are not differentiated but are still embedded in the material world and they are transmitted by sensory perception. (ibid.) Jung said:

> Primitive thinking and feeling are entirely concretistic; they are always related to sensation. The thought of the primitive has no detached independence but clings to material phenomena ... The primitive does not experience the idea of the divinity as a subjective content; for him the sacred tree is the abode of the god, or even the god himself (1921b, [CW 6, para. 697]).

Concretism, as a way of cognitive operation, is related to Levy-Bruhl's concept of *participation mystique*. Concrete cogitation is bound by physiological stimuli and the perception of outer, so-called, material reality. Ancient humankind and children likely saw material objects as full of power and they used apotropaic (magic to ward off evil) rituals to diminish their influence (Jung, 1921b).

For contemporary people, concretistic thinking consists of the excessive conception of facts that have been transmitted by the senses and the consequent inability to discriminate between subjective feelings and objective property, which often results in superstition or dogmatism. Fetishism as a type of sexual deviation, but also as a mana-worship could be based on the unconscious fusion of thinking, feeling, and perception.

Unconscious Is Always Projected

Simply put, concretism results in projection because physiological stimuli that are not the only fabric of human cognition and parts that are unconscious are not accepted as other than sensual facts (Jung 1921b, [CW 6, para. 69]). Cognitive aspects that are part of symbol, but not recognized as such, then lead to strong projective compulsory and uncritical attachments of either negative (terrifying) or positive (fascinating) charge. Archetypal reality, when projected, inevitably appears as a concrete fact. Withdrawal of projection, reversely leads to de-concretization: the symbol.

Joey

An adult analysand (G.J.D.) named Joey was fondly recalling his early religious experiences he had as an elementary student. Joey was raised in a very large, Roman Catholic family. As a young boy he often felt lonely and unacknowledged in the midst of all his eight siblings. His dad was often working or else preoccupied with other avocations, while his mother favored his older sisters. As a student at the Catholic elementary school attending daily mass and other religious rituals during the school year was mandatory. Joey enjoyed participating at mass and other religious liturgies, stating that they provided a sense of comfort and connection to God the Father and the Blessed Mother. One day while serving as an altar boy during Benediction (adoration of the Blessed Sacrament), Joey saw an image of the face of Jesus on the large consecrated Host. At first this frightened him, but as the image continued to present itself both at Mass and Benediction, he became accepting of it identifying the personal experience as being connected to and known by the Lord. It also gave him a sense of being loved and feeling special; he slowly acclimated to this ongoing numinous experience. He continued to "see" this sacred image while viewing the consecrated Host, until his mid-teens. These apparitions had a deep affective and devotional impact on his early developmental life. They served his self-object needs to be mirrored and seen, and the need to merge with a loving idealizing Other. As Jung writes, "The Church represents a higher spiritual substitute for the purely natural, or "carnal," tie to the parents. Consequently it frees the individual from an unconscious natural relationship" (CW 7, [par. 172, p. 105]). Joey's experience also illustrates how the numinous is often experienced and revealed through one's personal wounding or vulnerability leading to healing and wholeness.

As Corbett suggests,

> Subjectively, the self-object experience is a kind of *participation mystique* (a shared consciousness or merger) with an unconscious diffusion of normal boundaries in which soul-to-soul communication occurs which is analogous to shamanic healing... (1996, p. 124).

This is a beautiful case of the religious function of the psyche: the image of the *inner-Christ* figure (i.e. archetypal Self) being projected for identification, merger, and growth. Over time, this young lad developed a symbolic function that allowed him to understand and integrate this experience into his own symbolic religious imagination and the projection ceased.

The unconscious initially appears fused with the outside world; but the task of individuation is to proceed through continuous differentiation and separation between the conscious and the unconscious, together with the choices one faces guided by their moral responsibility and spiritual growth. Regression, however moves one toward states of outer divisiveness, where things are simple and concrete; this is only a step away from overt conflict in the outer world. Any idea that is bound to a concrete worldview is inherently dangerous. As a rule, an inner split at first appears outside and can be reconciled only through work inside.

Because concretism is based on symbolic illiteracy, the remedy lies in freeing concrete ideas by symbolic insight. At their core, messianic and apocalyptic religious attitudes are intolerant and tend to impede the process of personal symbolic insight. Even some of the most revered persons in the Christian tradition, such as Paul or Saint Augustine, are guilty of rigorous persecution of those with varying views. When an idea's archetypal background is not registered and analyzed by ego-consciousness the archaic qualities become more pronounced. In such cases, the ego is at the mercy of the archaic (i.e., numinous) forces, automatically concluding that all that it produces belongs to it as a noble and moral invention—as if the archaic force is the voice of God! However, these types of ideas stand in a compensatory relation to symbols. Since the ego does not get the hint, the ideas easily become tools by which a person discharges his or her projections. Many fundamentalist movements seek to destroy religious symbols that are polyvalent and multifaceted, due to the belief that only their symbols are efficacious; can bring them closer to God.

A conscious relationship to living symbols is essential for the healthy development of a balanced worldview and one's individuation. The radical mind typically lacks balance, and because it is unconsciously supported by rigid images of the numinosum, it continuously produces imbalances that lead to further isolation and conflict. Behind the scenes here, will be found the phenomenon that Jung (1950a) calls the *inferior function*; this plays an important role in constellating a one-sided position.

3. THE INFERIOR FUNCTION: A TYPOLOGICAL ASPECT OF EXTREME RELIGION

A man who is possessed by his own shadow is always standing in his own light and falling into his own traps (Jung, 1950a, [CW 9i, par. 222]).

One of the mind's crucial functions is the principle of discrimination (Jung, 1950a, [CW 9i, par. 178]).

Anything that is conscious (i.e., discriminated in consciousness as separate entity) is inevitably, to some extent limited: separated off from the whole. Every subjective content is inherently incomplete, and imperfect. Overly discriminated content thus becomes fixed. This is similar to the idea of balance (Jung 1921, [CW 6, para. 694] and 1937, [CW 8, para. 425]). Ego operates on the principle of attempting to attain balance between psyche's opposites, but it is constantly counter-balanced by psyche's natural propensity to identify with one side or another—after all energy must flow in some particular direction. Because perfect balance is an unattainable ideal, there is always a certain degree of *entropy* that operates in our psychic system. Some degree of one-sidedness is therefore normal and desirable. One-sidedness becomes problematic only if certain content distances itself so far from the middle, (a sort of Golden mean) that it gets stuck. Several questions arise. How does an idea or complex of ideas develop into an unshakable position in a person's mind? What happens in the psyche that allows one position to dominate another, at the expense of the well-founded reasoning of an otherwise intelligent person? How do we understand one's religious belief in the concrete existence of, let's say, Noah's Ark, or miracles that proclaim to stand outside of natural laws? Or further, how do we explain the reasoning of religious fanatics who committed an honor-killing of their own daughter and sister, because she trespassed Allah's law by working and going to school—this happened in England in 2010?

Jung's theory of types, particularly his concept of the superior and inferior functions of consciousness, can help us understand the processes.

According to Jung (1950a), some functions can be used more consciously when they are *adapted* to external reality and *differentiated* from the i.e., unconscious. However, the inferior function is by definition not under conscious control. Therefore, the ego-will has very little or no control over it. The inferior function is rooted in the archaic "primordial stratum" of the psyche, and that makes it accordingly primordial when one becomes influenced by such a function. Jung states:

> The essence of the inferior function is *autonomy*. It is independent, it attacks, it fascinates, and so spins us about that we are no longer masters of ourselves and can no longer rightly distinguish between ourselves and others. (1928b, [CW 7, par. 85]; author's emphasis)

On another hand, this inferior function conceals aspects of the wisdom and symbolic meaning of the archetypal world; thus making it conscious is a necessity of individuation. Being unconscious, it is always in a contrary relationship with the superior function. The inferior function is, according to Jung's later writings, basically identical with the shadow side of human personality.[136] One's inferior function is like a voice of nature within. If it is listened to and not hindered, a transformation of personality can take place; however, if defensive processes are actively creating a resistance against its integration, the trapped inferior function gains an even more archaic and primitive quality. If its manifestations are not made conscious, these very qualities will be projected onto an object—a person, group, or even another set of beliefs. Kramer's *Malleus Maleficarum* (1486, *Hammer of the Witches*) or Hitler's *Mein Kampf* (1925) are infamous examples of what happens when the forces of the dark Self take hold of the psyche and are projected onto somebody else.

In The Name of God

It is not an accident that religious imagery is frequently used in cases when the mind is possessed by the inferior function and its archetypal energy. The inferior function is rooted in the "depth" of the unconscious so it brings about archetypal themes and archetypal affect. Thus, a person under the influence of the

[136] CW 9i, par. 222: "There are still other factors which may take possession of the individual, one of the most important being the so-called "inferior function." (...) I should only like to point out that the inferior function is practically identical with the dark side of the human personality."

inferior function can easily identify with the imagery, because it enforces itself compulsively without the individual having to employ any moral effort. What we call religious is natural. The collective psyche simply cannot speak any other language than a symbolic one. The language of the collective unconscious is built up with its own fabric of symbols. The collective psyche cannot be held responsible when it is misused by the ego for the purposes of building its pseudo-power. By "hiding behind" the supposedly greater cause (i.e., one's God), one is stripped of all moral responsibilities and the perils of doubt. It is as if the ego declares, "If there's an almighty God mastering my will, how can I object!" The Self is like a nuclear power station; In the name of God, humankind can reach its deepest potentials and is capable of committing the worst atrocities. One does not have to revisit history to see evidence of this drama; religious clashes proclaiming God's mandate are being acted out at this very moment. Modern examples of such confrontations include: the conflict between Roman Catholics and Protestants in Northern Ireland; the Bosnia-Herzegovina conflict where three religious groups (Muslim, Roman Catholic, and Serbian Orthodox) clashed; the civil war in Sudan where Muslims and Christians killed each other in the name of their respective God; or the upsurge of the quasi-religious fundamentalists movement of ISIS that has been spreading throughout the Middle East along with the sectarian conflicts between Shia and Sunni Muslims.

Bin Laden's Inferior Thinking

Osama bin Laden was widely acknowledged to be a religious fanatic. The following transcript of a speech bin Laden gave illustrates his interior function at work:

> In the name of God, the merciful, the compassionate. A message to our Muslim brothers in Iraq, may God's peace, mercy, and blessings be upon you. O you who believe fear Allah, by doing all that He has ordered and by abstaining from all that He has forbidden as He should be feared. Obey Him, be thankful to Him, and

> remember Him always, and die not except in a state of Islam [as Muslims] with complete submission to Allah. We are following up with great interest and extreme concern the crusaders' preparations for war to occupy a former capital of Islam, loot Muslims' wealth, and install an agent government, which would be a satellite for its masters in Washington and Tel Avijust like all the other treasonous and agent Arab governments. This would be in preparation for establishing the Greater Israel. Allah is sufficient for us and He is the best disposer of affairs. Amid this unjust war, the war of infidels and debauchees led by America along with its allies and agents, we would like to stress a number of important values: First, showing good intentions. This means fighting should be for the sake of the one God. God Almighty says: "Those who believe fight in the cause of Allah, and those who reject faith fight in the cause of evil." So fight ye against the friends of Satan: feeble indeed is the cunning of Satan (Al-Jazeera, 2003, p. 1).

Notice here an apparent mythical pathos and ornate poetry that is typical for prophets, but also psychotic individuals. This "poetic" language is common to many terrorists. An archetypal background forms thinking into the shape of the primordial symbols, and it also influences emotions and feelings so that they take the form of passionately naive attachments, reminiscent of early idealistic love toward parents. Ideas remain simple because they are based on the same feelings, often following pre-verbal rules of idealized projections. "Neocortical sophistication," the realms, from which reason presumably emerges, is either retreated from or devalued in this process because the inferior function dominates thinking. The highest amount of psychic energy is summoned by the unconscious, and thinking is undifferentiated from the various parts of the activated archetypes. This state of mind can be understood as a regression to the original state of unity when the ego is fused with the Self. Bin Laden identifies his own will directly with that of Allah and encourages his followers to do the same. Hence, the object (God) and subject (the individual) are merged—the speaker does not distinguish between them. Because of this identity, the ego harbors feelings of grandiosity: being as important as the Self. In this grandiose delusion, roles of master and servant are reversed. The ego thinks and feels *as if* it is "the center of the universe" (Edinger, 1973). Beneath the veneer of seemingly great (fanatical) ideas are often hidden the primitive emotions of fear, grief, shame, rage, envy, and the like. Bin Laden does not appear to be aware of being possessed by the archetypal Self. Consequently, he uses the energy springing from the archetypal Self for his own egocentric purposes. In effect, he is hiding his basic humanity behind the veneer of the grandiose, inflated ego.

As a rule, undifferentiated functions stand in as compensations for the complexes. They pretend to create a very rational basis for something that is inherently motivated by irrational forces. In light of this, even the murder of a child can be justified in the mind of a fanatic. For example, self-destructive acts by a suicide bomber are outweighed by the idea of a holy sacrifice rewarded by eternal bliss. Symbols and symbolic reality no longer subtly inform the individual's life and actions, they are consciously embraced or rejected for the sole purpose of supporting the fanatic's creed and preconceived action. Reflections and aspects of images and ideas that do not align with the ego's inflated perspective are selectively and defensively split off. When actions are based on images of wholeness with all the attendant richness and paradoxical complexity of the numinosum, a person is less likely to be led to the destruction of self or others. The return to home, to more complete consciousness leads to love and inclusion.

When ego chooses to hide behind the falsely constructed images of self/Self, the facts of reality and the ideas abstracted from lived experience take on magical qualities. The ego's field of perception is reduced to experiencing simple emotions, where dealing with ambiguities becomes straightforward and black-and-white. The calls for martyrdom and sacrifice in Bin

Laden's speech are not to be understood symbolically but literally. This kind of heroism lacks a true spiritual dimension and is only experienced through submitting one's will to the awful (i.e., terrifying) aspects of the numinosum. Such submission is typically accompanied by projective demonization of the [outer] other. Demonizing the other goes hand-in-hand with the failure to recognize and integrate the daemonic qualities of the archetypal affect associated with an *inner* other. Note the inner other is the depository of the unacknowledged aspects of psyche and is the source of what is projected onto the *outer* other For Bin Laden - all who oppose him also oppose Allah and therefore *must be* evil. Instead of the focus being on the moral quest of insight and change of character, this demand is projected outside—in this case the infidel. In the act of projection, nuances and ambiguities are sacrificed and are replaced by a single judgment accompanied by a strong calling to act. One feels compelled to enforce one's will on the other in the same way as the *will* of the Self was imposed on oneself. It should be noted that as feeling, thinking and sensation are merged there is strong adherence to specific locations (Israel, Islamic State, etc.). Thus places acquire numinous qualities. The *territory* of Tel Aviv is demonized or worshipped as holy land (Greater Israel). A piece of land, a nation-state, an ethnic group, just like a specific individual can all be the recipients of demonic or idealizing projections.

Archetypes and complexes transmute its contents into feelings of consciousness, but if there is insufficient "distance" between consciousnesses and the archetypal affect, then feelings drag with them an archaic tail that deploys a possessive effect. Without the protection of a spiritual outlook and container—teaching and practice—the ego is more vulnerable to being overtaken. The lack of a spiritual structure opens the fanatic's ego to the influence of basic instinctual urges for power and sex. Mehdi Hasan points out in his article "How Islamic Is Islamic State?" that many terrorists are actually illiterate regarding their own religion. He quotes findings of MI5 stating that religion in its healthy countenance assures protection against fundamentalism. Hasan (2015) writes:

> (...) in 2008, a classified briefing note on radicalization, prepared by MI5's behavioral science unit, was obtained by the *Guardian*. It revealed: 'Far from being religious zealots, a large number of those involved in terrorism do not practice their faith regularly. Many lack religious literacy and could . . . be regarded as religious novices.' The MI5 analysts noted the disproportionate number of converts and the high propensity for 'drug-taking, drinking alcohol and visiting prostitutes.' The newspaper claimed they concluded, 'A well-established religious identity actually protects against violent radicalization.' (p. 1)

Archetypal energy possesses ego consciousness when the ego loses a reasonable narrative through which it can have a relationship with them. A healthy religion that is endowed with genuine spirituality provides a container and "interpreter" for those energies, as it teaches a person how to navigate and relate to a complicated and seductive endowment from the archetypal realm. Jung said:

> The primordial images [archetypes] are awakened from their slumber and emerge as operative factors in the thinking process . . . rather like invisible stage managers behind the scenes (1921, [CW 6, para. 513]; note authors).

The conscious mind can decide to either follow the allure of the archetypes or it may question them. The worshipping of a God Image that only fits specific ego desires is one example of inadequate ego adaptation to archetypal energies. Sexual desire, the will for power, and greed are all masked by noble ideas. Real prophets speak about something bigger, connected to the collective, while fanatics are at mercy of dark ideas serving their egoistic interest. Terrorists, typically, appear fearless and free of anger, but that is because they displace their emotions onto the object they attack. Analysis of the available historical material reveals that their painful emotions were redirected to the other by indoctrination, brainwashing and other techniques. The indoctrination into the inflexible and excessively passionate held beliefs or creeds allows the terrorist to "store" split-of painful emotions outside of their awareness.

Prazis Images/Shutterstock.com.

Dogma

Conflicting emotional pressures create a subliminal state of high anxiety that seeks an "intellectual home." Quasi-intellectual processes attempt to stabilize anxiety through a soothing and reassuring technique: an adherence to doctrines. As a rule, the inflated positions are subject to unintended self-ridicule; they are undermined by their own deceptions and inconsistencies. Quasi-intellectual positions can be sustained only by maintaining ideas that might otherwise seem irrational or be outright lies. These non-rational aspects of the unconscious can, in a certain sense, be intuited or "grasped," but only symbolically. If interpreted literally, they are easily transformed into strong beliefs or "truths." The connection with archetypal imagery enhances the attractiveness of strong beliefs. Some conservative people like radio commentator Glenn Beck skillfully conflate political and religious semantics for their own purposes. This type of conflated manipulation is often complex-ridden, and can only relate negatively to the other (the opposite of the consciously held beliefs). What is required to foster a dialogue is the willingness to embrace one's shadow: to look into the mirror. Unfortunately, the more one's shadow is backed by strong archetypal energy, the more dense and oppressive it becomes, sometimes to the point of "evil." This is why there is a lack of higher emotional relatedness, including empathy, compassion and forgiveness when it comes to views emerging from a narrow ego-space that has been squeezed by the archetypal shadow. Archetypal power can be a source of renewal, healing and transformation. However, if the capacity to hold the tension of the opposites of the numinosum together is missing or not developed, archetypal power can produce venomous ideas.

This type of thinking (e.g., Beck's conflation) is primarily based on selective identification with certain numinous contents. It is selectively identified with the positive and projects the negative. The subjective factor, as Jung called the archetypal *inner other*, determines the nature of the perception of the objective world. This unconscious subjective factor is always bound to one's judgments; thus an implicit premise of every judgment. The question is, to what extent is it influencing one's perception. These findings are supported by modern brain research. Knox (In Cambray, 2004) states:

> Jung constantly emphasized the emotional basis of the complex. He also recognized that emotion is not merely a visceral or physiological experience, but is inextricably bound up with cognition, a view which has been independently elaborated within an information-processing framework by George Mandler (1975:47) and reinforced by neuroscientists such as Daniel Siegel who argues that 'there are no discernible boundaries between our 'thoughts' and 'feelings' (Siegel 1998:6), (p. 67).

We can assume that in the case of the religious beliefs of the fundamentalist, the feeling component is unconscious but represented in the ego as an idea totally devoid of its emotional basis. This kind of thinking identifies the numinous power as solely good and completely submits to its cause. The bad, the Satanic, or the so-called evil, is radically denied and has to be eliminated or conquered. In this splitting process the ego becomes inflated due to the *merger* between the archetypal and the personal. The ego traces everything good back to the highest ideal and projects everything bad to the outer enemy. This is a regressive maneuver, which is morally decadent because it does not require nor ask for personal responsibility. It is a regression to a magical state without moral conflict. As Jung said:

The real existence of an enemy upon whom one can foist off everything evil is an enormous relief to one's conscience. You can then at least say, without hesitation, who the devil is; you are quite certain that the cause of your misfortune is outside, and not in your own attitude (1948, [CW 8, para. 518]).

Hypocrisy

The word *hypokrisis*, from which the English word hypocrisy is derived, means acting or playing.[137] A person assumes a role or pretends that something that he or she does not actually believe is true. Although projection originates from the

---

[137] Hypocrisy: c.1200, *ipocrisie*, from Old French *ypocrisie*, from Late Latin *hypocrisis*, from Greek *hypokrisis*,ὑπόκρισις "acting on the stage, pretense," from *hypokrinesthai* "play a part, pretend," also "answer," from *hypo-* "under" (see *sub-*) + middle voice of *krinein* "to sift, decide" (see *crisis*). The sense evolution in Attic Greek is from "separate gradually" to "answer" to "answer a fellow actor on stage" to "play a part." The *h-* was restored in English 16c. "Hypocrisy is the art of affecting qualities for the purpose of pretending to an undeserved virtue. Because individuals and institutions and societies most often live down to the suspicions about them, hypocrisy and its accompanying equivocations underpin the conduct of life. Imagine how frightful truth unvarnished would be." (Benjamin F. Martin, *"France in 1938,"* 2005) (Online Etymology Dictionary, n.d., p. 1)

unconscious, it is often close enough to consciousness that the recipient of the projection can be recognized as somewhat significant—this allows the projection to be recovered and possibly withdrawn. With hypocrisy, there is often a permeable boundary between projection and conscious recognition that one's unacknowledged psychic content is being projected The capacity for recovering projections depends upon the intensity of the one-sidedness and how open the ego is to accepting that it is the source of its own projection.

A few examples come to mind. Former Attorney General of New York, Eliot Spitzer, was known for his contempt of prostitution, and during his term as AG, he worked vigorously to break and prosecute several prostitution rings.[138] Meanwhile, he was seeing and buying the services of multiple prostitutes until the FBI uncovered his secret. We might surmise that his own disdain for sexual desire was merely projected onto the entire domain of prostitution, but that very disdain intensified the allure prostitution held for him and it intensified his compulsion to act out his desires. When the ego can no longer continue in denial, the split-off parts come back to consciousness to be re-experienced and integrated; often experienced as an emotional and spiritual break-through. Thus, Spitzer, in the midst of his shame and tears, experienced himself in a new light.

Similarly, Pastor Ted Haggard, an American evangelical preacher who was known for his public rebuke of homosexuality and drug use, was ironically caught using illegal drugs with a male prostitute. Where there is a strong and overwhelming passion against (or for) something, it is important to remain vigilant and watch for its opposite. The more our minds become attached to *bonum*, the stronger the *malum* grows in the shadow. If there is a *Summum Bonum* behind an idea that somebody adopts as the truth, then the shadow becomes so relativized that it energizes an individual to such a degree that

[138] See movie: *Client 9: The Rise and Fall of Eliot Spitzer*, 2010.

it permits one to do almost anything. For the person possessed by the image of God, as *sum of goodness*, the shadow is waiting to be activated. No deed is ever dark for the religious fanatic if it is done in the name of God. Of course, the shadow does not disappear; it is simply cast onto the other with corresponding intensity.

This can be demonstrated by a recent example from the University of Michigan. Andrew Shirvell, an assistant state's attorney, followed Chris Armstrong, the University of Michigan student body president, who is openly gay. Shirvell followed Armstrong around campus and the town of Ann Arbor as a form of protesting against him; he also created a blog where he attacked Armstrong's "radical homosexual agenda," calling him a radical Nazi activist while labeling him "evil."[139] Armstrong was forced to seek a restraining order against Shirvell, who believed he acted in the name of God.

An even stronger example of hypocritical extremism occurred when a radical anti-abortion activist, who also claimed to be acting in the name of God, killed Dr. George Tiller for providing abortions. This same phenomenon is seen in the case of religious terrorists who kill women and children in the name of God. When the mind is psychologically eclipsed by a one-sided image of God, even the most extreme acts become justified. Throughout history most if not all religious wars and crusades occurred in the name of God. The lighter side of religious expression has been noble and glorious, whereas the dark side has been bloody and hellish. How is the loving and compassionate human soul capable of atrocities? According to Jung (1955/1956) an atavistic vestige of *participation mystique* that can be described as *psychological externalism*, combined with the unwillingness of humankind to look deeply into the murky depths of its own soul is responsible for such divisiveness:

[139] SHIRVELL v. DEPARTMENT OF ATTORNEY GENERAL, FindLaw for legal professionals, January 8, 2015, p.1

> The view that good and evil are spiritual principles *outside* us, and that man is caught in the conflict between them is more bearable by far than the insight that the opposites are the ineradicable and indispensable preconditions of all psychic life, so much so that life itself is guilt. Even a life dedicated to God is still lived by an ego, which speaks of an ego and asserts an ego in God's despite, which does not instantly merge itself with God but reserves for itself a freedom and a will which it sets up outside God and against him (1955, [CW 14, para. p. 205] emphasis ours).

Allowing religiosity to exist outside of ourselves, we may be unwittingly consumed by it.

4. POSSESSION AND INFLATION

> *It is an axiom of psychology that when a part of the psyche is split off from consciousness it is only apparently inactivated; in actual fact it brings about a possession of the personality, with the result that the individual's aims are falsified in the interest of the split-off part* (Jung 1951, [CW 9i, para. 277])

Possession can be defined as the mastery of certain unconscious contents, complexes, or archetypes over the ego. The ego's reaction that ensues, as a result of possession, becomes principally identical with the forces. The personality of the individual is changed, and he or she acts and thinks under strong and mostly unshakable convictions. Typically, individuals who are possessed by unconscious contents are not open to correction by normal means. Only very strong emotionally corrective experiences can produce change. A change of attitude can come about as a result of experiencing powerful emotions. Typically experiencing the opposite pole of the numinosum has the potential to compensate one-sided affect.[140] If the change is

[140] Ancient techniques of exorcism were performed with intention to drive

progressive and results in the enlargement of consciousness, it generates new, and more-integrated psychological positions. A thesis and antithesis is embraced so that a new synthesis emerges. This is the gold of analysis. As Jung states:

> ...the main interest of my work is not concerned with the treatment of neuroses but rather with the approach to the numinous. But the fact is that the approach to the numinous is the real therapy and inasmuch as you attain to the numinous experiences you are released from the curse of pathology...

Archetypes and complexes typically compel one to actions that are fueled by strong ideas, images, and feelings. These ideas, images and feelings remain functional only within established frames of reference (e.g. historical, cultural, and religious contexts) unless the work of conscious integration (individuation) is undertaken. For example, a patriarchal system, based on the dominion of masculine energy, may be supported by the collective consciousness of certain communities, but it proves to be seriously flawed in societies where feminine consciousness is more integrated. Personal and cultural complexes provide the means for archetypes to be embodied—this is why individual psychopathology is never independent from its collective dimension.

Complex-Archetype Continuum

Manifestations of particular feminine archetypes, for example, Persephone or Aphrodite, are not only representations of collective experiences of phenomena that are universally valid regardless of place and time, but can also emerge as individual complexes of a very personal nature. For example, we have reason to believe that a complex manifested in a woman as an overbearing, controlling, and stifling mother would not be

---

out evil by allowing the positive influence of God's presence. (from Greek ἐξορκισμός, *exorkismos* - binding by oath)

so firmly established had it not had an archetypal basis. What we view as pathology are also archetypal exaggerations of otherwise beneficial patterns. Because they became possessive and lost their counterbalancing feedback, we view them as being rooted in a negative mother complex. Possession by a complex, therefore, entails possession by some aspect of archetypal energy. Because archetypes are revealed through stories, they contain prescriptions for resolving conflict with and possession by complexes. This calls for the uncovering of the whole and not just the part attached to ego. Conversely, it is precisely the singling out or splitting off certain elements that accounts for the possession.

Tales and myths reveal archetypes in their interplay with the "Other" (archetype or ego) and often offer solutions capable of freeing humans from various trials, tribulations and possessions. In order for the woman possessed by the negative mother archetype above to individuate, it will be necessary to integrate aspects of the positive mother archetype.

Righteousness Aspect of Possession

As a rule, possession forms a naïve persuasion that often asserts a claim for finite truth. The resulting behaviors and actions feel as if they are not only intelligible but also justifiable. A patient, from a cultural background where the use of physical punishment of children is still the norm, recently relocated to the United States came to see me. (V.Š.) Her husband urged her to seek treatment for her rage and physically aggressive behavior against their daughter. Only after recovering and re-experiencing the memory of her parent's aggression did the possibility of change really open up to her. Therapy allowed her to re-evaluate the personal, familial, and cultural aspects of her parental complexes. Until then, there was no doubt in her mind that she (and her parents) was right. Possession creates isolated and unquestioned conviction and if it is attached to religious matters it becomes a dogma.

Aidos Function of the Ego

Where does religious righteousness come from? It is important to recognize that archetypes and complexes function psychologically function in similar ways to the gods— powerful forces that are not easily comprehended. They are like totalitarian rulers insisting on unquestioned obedience. They are relatively singular structures and entities that represent absolutes. We could compare them to instincts, which have fixed and specific functions. When complexes acquire an excessive amount of libido, they can easily overwhelm the ego making it difficult to impossible for it to use its resources to adequately adapt and thus it becomes ruled by archaic material that normally is found within the lower levels of the psychic hierarchy. There were evolutionary reasons for why psyche developed certain functions that we call archaic today. In tribal organizations stereotypes were protective and guiding mechanisms. Survival depended on tribal cohesion; therefore consensual ideas had priority over individuality.[141] Thence factual accuracy (rational logic) was only secondary to tribal identification. Brain structure is still such that emotions are the primary source of information contrary to what we rational think. Neuroscientist Antonio Damasio (2005) in an interview for *Scientific American* said:

> I continue to be fascinated by the fact that feelings are not just the shady side of reason but that they help us to reach decisions as well. (...) In everyday language we often use the terms interchangeably. This shows how closely connected emotions are with feelings. But for neuroscience, emotions are more or less the complex reactions the body has to certain stimuli. When we are

---

[141] Aidos (Aedos), Greek: Αἰδώς) was the Ancient Greek goddess of shame, modesty, and humility. Goddess Aidos was often thought of as a companion of the goddess Nemesis. Aidos, as a psychological quality or as a personified spirit (*daimónia*), was experienced as the feeling of reverence, respect, shame and dread, which was needed to restrain people from acting foolishly and doing wrong..

> afraid of something, our hearts begin to race, our mouths become dry, our skin turns pale and our muscles contract. This emotional reaction occurs automatically and unconsciously. Feelings occur after we become aware in our brain of such physical changes; only then do we experience the feeling of fear. (p.1)

With the development and differentiation of our cognitive functions one of the primary roles of the ego became one of balancing the various forces imposed on it. When the balance between the ego and archetype is lost, the ego becomes truly a slave to the power of the archetype. The role of the ego is to create a dialoging bridge between the different complexes even in the midst of demanding forces. In the face of the Other and its magical powers, the ego must keep heroic integrity and that we call religion. The ego accomplishes this through the creation of consciousness and meaning. If the ego becomes even partially identified with archetypal content it begins to move toward one-sidedness, or into possession. A possessed ego, by definition, cannot hold the balance between opposites when it purposely or inadvertently surrenders its authority to the unconscious. We can say that possession happens when the ego loses a specific spiritual *attitude* toward the unconscious. Compaan (2007), in his research on archetypal shame, identified a psychological notion known as *aidos* in ancient Greece. *Aidos* represents the respect, humility and honor needed in one's attitude toward that which is superior—the archetypal, the holy.[142] *Aidos* regulates and coordinates the feelings of inferiority and inadequacy that arise when the ego is exposed to the perils of the numinosum. The absence of *aidos* leads to hubris—the antithesis of *aidos*. Compaan (2007) said:

[142] Aidos (Aedos), Greek: Αιδώς) was the Ancient Greek goddess of shame, modesty, and humility. Goddess Aidos was often thought of as a companion of the goddess Nemesis. Aidos, as a psychological quality or as a personified spirit (*daimónia*), was experienced as the feeling of reverence, respect, shame and dread, which was needed to restrain people from acting foolishly and doing wrong..

> The possibility when aidos is absent is to be possessed by the affective energy of divine/archetypal excitement and curiosity with the result that one is inflated, hubristic. Hubris is the affective state where one feels superior to all other humans and is totally captivated by the excitement and pleasure of the new and unknown. When so possessed, the ego senses little danger in the new and the unknown. ...This is a position of shamelessness, of *inadequate shame*. Shame affect is not available to assist in the modulation of the excited feelings. Rather the person is possessed, driven by this energy. Clinically it appears as mania or, as Jung preferred, as a mana personality (Compaan, p. 6; Jung, 1966; author's emphasis).

Eugène Delacroix - La liberté guidant le peuple; 1830, Ve jménu Boha.

A State of grandiose excitement, where the fear of death is absent, is a natural precursor of psychological change; thus the equipment of heroes. Without it, no social revolution would be possible. People flee to the streets and protest against their oppressive governments because of the lack of fear and shame. However, the dark side of this development is when the ego is possessed by this archetypal energy, then it loses its moral boundaries and becomes rude: without regard for human life.

It is also true that a lack of *aidos*, shamelessness, can bring about change. It provides momentum for breaking up narcissistic defenses and may lead to a new level of consciousness. If it becomes chronically one-sided, then the danger of a painful, hubristic (Icarus) fall is just a matter of time. The question of maintaining a dialogue with numinous energies is, of course, not a simple one. There is no straightforward recipe for how one should go about it. It is a spiritual process *par excellence* that is needed to maintain an attitude of remaining true to oneself. From time-to-time it is only natural that one may fall into the grip of unconscious powers; it is actually desirable for our growth. As Joseph Campbell reminds us:

> "It is by going down into the abyss that we recover the treasures of life. Where you stumble, there lies your treasure." (p. 26)[143]

It is not the state itself, though, but how we deal with it in our intimate and conscientious self- awareness that determines if it's a spiritual endeavor or not. Denial of what *is* never leads to wholeness. It is not the cross we carry that makes us stronger, but the process of awakening to what makes our cross heavy.

Hubris and The False Self

Edinger (1973) said, "(...) hubris is the human arrogance that appropriates to man what belongs to the gods" (p. 31). Possession (as a collapse of a relational attitude) and hubris have a common denominator. In fact, hubris expresses a state of mind, while possession is a phenomenological, internal happening. A possessed ego does not operate in the realm between opposites but identifies itself with one position or the other where it seeks soothing refuge. But in the shadowy domain, intense feelings of inadequacy creep in.

When feelings of inadequacy are denied and suppressed, perceptions of real inadequacies and inferiorities also disappear

[143] An Open Life: Joseph Campbell in conversation with Michael Toms, 1990.

from consciousness, which eventually leads to the formation of a false self—one that is not authentic. Donald Winnicott introduced the term *false self* to describe an infant's defensive self-organization formed in the very early stage of development—as a result of inadequate (not good enough) mothering or other failures of empathy by the caregiver. Because of these early wounds of rejection and moments of abandonment, the infant naturally develops a compensatory system of accommodation to provide for his or her own needs. The infant compulsorily and later by desire accommodates to those upon whom he or she is dependent. The creation of a false self is primarily a defensive, self-preserving act. (1960a, p. 145)[144] According to Stern, the false self serves as a protective system that safeguards the true self from the mother's neglect while maintaining a connection with the mother (Stern, 1985). Winnicott states that the "not-good-enough mothering" results in:

> (...) the process that leads to the capacity for symbol-usage does not get started (or else it becomes broken up), with a corresponding withdrawal on the part of the infant from advantages gained). (...) in practice the infant lives, but lives falsely. The protest against being forced into a false existence can be detected from the earliest stages. (1960, p. 146).

Winnicott's concept of the false self provides several useful, though loosely related insights of our examination of the self that becomes possessed by religious contents. Winnicott's false self is distinguished, among other characteristics, by its limited capacity of comprehending, forming, and employing the use of symbol. The phenomena that we have described above, namely the possession by unconscious contents as they pertain to the creation of strong religious convictions could be understood as symptoms related to aspects of the false self. From a Jungian perspective, these correspond to a persona that is identified

[144] Winnicott, D. W. (1960a), *Ego distortion in terms of true and false self*. In: *The maturational processes and the facilitating environment*. Madison, CT: International Universities Press, 1987.

with the Self. Because the false self compensates for all unrecognized and unintegrated numinous feelings that the ego is wounded and confused about, is probably why it is often accompanied by all sorts of enactments and inferior exploits. A person living out of the false self can be very charismatic and intelligent, but there is always a sense of false spirituality accompanied by narcissistic irritability that is readily available for enactment as soon as something touches the inferior part hidden behind a carefully groomed persona. *Vana sollicitis incutit umbra metum* (Latin: A slight shadow alarms the nervous). An inflated position is often attended by an excessive vulnerability to shame. Thus, the inflated person is driven to stay in a place of false adequacy with minimal shame. Such a person needs constant narcissistic reassurance from his or her environment to maintain the false persona and to ward off feelings of inadequacy. Typically, members of fundamentalist traditions are intolerant of feelings of inadequacy and therefore, collectively set about creating an environment of high confidence and superiority based on their *righteous* beliefs. They are often idealized by others because most people would like to be free of feelings of shame and actual inadequacies (Compaan, 2007, p. 10).

The Self, the goal of individuation, an aspiration for the whole individual is always present in the deepest realms of the psyche and is felt as a sort of paradisiacal voice that whispers its insistent call to greater consciousness and integration. Jung says:

> Here one may ask, perhaps, why it is so desirable that a man should be individuated. Not only is it desirable, it is absolutely indispensable because through his contamination with others he falls into situations and commits actions which bring him into disharmony with himself. From all states of unconscious contamination and non-differentiation there is begotten a compulsion to be and to act in a way contrary to one's own nature. (...) But the disharmony with himself is precisely the neurotic and intolerable conditions from which he seeks

> to be delivered, and deliverance from these conditions will come only when he can be and act as he feels is conformable with his true self (Jung 1943, [CW 7, para. 373]).

The stronger the emotional investment in the false self, the harder it becomes to maintain objectivity regarding one's own psychological process. Change is difficult, especially when a person's investment in a particular religious persona is nurtured over long periods of time or under circumstances that feel desperate (e.g., poverty, lack of social options, etc.) with few other options for a wider perspective. For example, poor and illiterate minorities, blacks, Muslims, and Hispanics, among others, often have less opportunity for development and growth and thus are more vulnerable and susceptible to being "radicalized." Dispositions accumulate behind the tenuous religious persona that create a one-sided personality or false self to complement the undeveloped parts and that hinders movement toward wholeness. This brings us back to Jung's theory of compensation:

> All those psychological tendencies that suffer under [its] repression become grouped together in the unconscious, and form a counter-position, giving rise to paroxysms of doubt. As a defense against doubt, the conscious attitude grows fanatical. For fanaticism, after all, is merely overcompensated doubt. Ultimately this development leads to an exaggerated defense of the conscious position, and to the gradual formation of an absolutely antithetic unconscious position; for example, an extreme irrationality develops, in opposition to the conscious rationalism, or it becomes highly archaic and superstitious, in opposition to a conscious standpoint imbued with modern science (1921b, [CW 6, p.41).

Leaders who are imbued with a confident persona prove to be attractive to people with the attitude of guarding against doubt, described above. Others feel that they have found somebody with answers who has figured it all out, a person free from doubt. Hiding behind archetypally backed ideologies can end up being very attractive and inspiring. So-called religious truths offer a seemingly impenetrable identity and offer refuge seen as lasting religious inflation. A person inflated by the archetypal energy of the Self, acts as if he or she has a mandate from God, so any effort to question this absolute authority is typically in vain (Edinger, 1973).[145]

Hiding Behind God

Possession by the Self can form hubristic religious inflation. That is to say, the ego is under the influence of various aspects of the Imago Dei: thinking, feeling, imagery. Hiding behind the authority of God gives a person the delusional belief that whatever action is taken is done in the name and with the permission of God.[146] The ego has such little regulating power when it comes under such possession that suicide, or violent attacks on others appear entirely justified. Efforts to persuade or to engage in critical dialogue with someone in such inflated states prove to be ineffectual. Even a commandment that forbids killing and that ordinarily preserves healthier states of mind fail because they are replaced by a new *God order* adopted by the fanatic mind. This helps explain why religiously fanatic stances are very rarely subject to correction. Because the Self enthralls, and this enthralling quality releases tremendous amounts of energy, it can only be corrected by an equal or greater degree of energy of the opposite valence. Any attempt to change this sort of religious one-sidedness is constrained by the hallmark of the highest ideal (*Imago Dei*). The consciousness that accompanies individuation tends to refrain from identification with the contents of the Self simply because it sees the other side and recognizes its own ownership. This insight provides a natural boundary and defense for the ego against possession by the Self. Individuating

---

[145] Possession can be distinguished from inflation by the intensity of unconscious influence, or degree of ego-consciousness.

[146] Extreme form of this possession is theomania. In this psychotic state of mind one believes that he or she is the God himself. (Origin, 1855-60).

consciousness does not produce a counter-pressure but participates in a "discursive cooperation between the ego and the unconscious" (Jung, 1948, p. 21). Jung specifically refers to this as a "moral strength." (Jung 1946, [CW 16, para. 469])

Ideology backed by archetypal energy can become an extremely dangerous weapon. The conspicuous thirst for power and other narcissistic desires displayed by religious and political leaders who are playing with archetypal contents easily turn their ideas into coercive tools wielded over people who trust them (Jung, 1954). Many who have sought totalitarian power quickly learn that it is easy to hide behind mythical themes simply by repetition and accentuating their implicit nobility. As an idea becomes inflated, the archetype garners greater power regardless if it contains obvious lies. Conspiracy theories and their steadfastness are typical examples of this. The greater one's experience of emptiness felt by the individual who projects onto the leader a promise of fulfilling a *noble* spiritual quest, the greater will be the individual's susceptibility to possession by the numinosum. As Jung pointed out, only those who are as well organized in their individuality as mass ideology is organized in its structure can effectively resist the archetypal energies presented by the masses. Beginning at birth, the ego develops its psychological anatomy through the interactions with caregivers. The role family complexes play in creating religious extremism is likely to prove fertile ground for our examination.

5. FAMILY COMPLEXES AND THE DEVELOPMENT OF RELIGIOUS EXTREMISM

Our first relationships of attachment provide the original blueprint of the mind. The patterns of interpersonal communication in these relationships are internalized as the collection of structured patterns known as the self (Wallin, 2007, p. 84).

The unrelated human being lacks wholeness, for he cannot exist without its other side, which is always found in a 'You' (Jung 1946, [CW 16, para. 454]).

An early childhood experience that includes *good enough* (Winnicott, 1971) parental objects is of crucial importance for healthy development.[147] Parents modify and channel archetypal energies for their child. A newborn baby has practically no ego; therefore, the caregiver is the one who *holds* the virtual ego for the child and teaches the child how to relate to the world, relate to its self and relate to and regulate numinous energies that envelop it. Good enough parenting also provides a safe container for the child's nascent archetypal projections of the Self onto the parents. This is a major symbolic development, for if the parents are psychologically mature (i.e., comfortable with their own narcissistic elements and power), they will receive these projections, foster their development, and at the right moment in time, relinquish the projection, pointing the child's projections in the direction of symbolic [religious] development. A good enough family that loves and responds consciously to the needs of their children promote a safe balance between the establishment of healthy defenses, the ability to integrate new experiences into the budding ego structure, and the appropriate mirroring of the child's incipient self.

Religion, mediated through religious communities, has supported and shaped parenting functions for thousands of years. It is important to stress that religion, understood as a quest for consciousness, is a naturally emergent phenomenon that came into existence out of human developmental needs and that it was not arbitrarily created as a tool for manipulation. Religion was and is the system of promoting individuation. In most occurrences, creed—as delineated earlier in this book—has also been used to nourish developmental needs, but for one reason or another its original purpose becomes deformed. Natural religious symbols, used by both, religious institutions and families, promote, among other functions, the development of the mythic and symbolic functions.

---

[147] "The good-enough mother, (...) starts off with an almost complete adaptation to her infant's needs, and as time proceeds she adapts less and less completely, gradually, according to the infant's growing ability to deal with her failure." (D. W. Winnicott, Playing and Reality, 1971, p. 5)

Mary Mother of Jesus, Giovanni Battista Salvi da Sassoferrato, between 1640 and 1650. Public domain, via Wikimedia Commons.

Shadow phenomenon lurks behind the places where parental or religious control is too tight and too distant from one's instinctive roots. Strong systematic indoctrination and selective access to information and emotions nurtured by family, society, and the like create a predisposition for a one-sided ego—this is wounding to the child's developing ego-Self axis. Children often internalize parental complexes, and if there is constant monitoring, or a lack of appropriate mirroring, or a rigid guarding and condoning of an ideology, a child's ego-structure will be left with no choice but to resemble and mirror the structure of the parent's ego-Self axis. This adaptation by introjection is sometimes accomplished in ways that resemble absorbing a whole complex structure. The child's complexes sometimes mimic parental complexes and sometimes develop in response to parental complexes. The stronger the external control, the firmer the complexes are embedded in the child's psyche, leading to greater dissonance and disconnection between experiencing one's true self and one's experience of identifying with individual or cultural complexes. Hence one is more vulnerable to be preyed upon by certain group factions and cultural complexes and their representations through phantoms narratives. (Kimbles, Sam 2014) For example, a tribal or group identity may arise in which collective (complexes) forces easily supersede one's individual identity and experience of their true self. This type of manipulation constellates very strong attachments, which can be worked with and dissolved only after years of conscious work. People attempting to liberate themselves from the shackles of oppressive, early indoctrination into firmly held beliefs and paradigms, backed by what we might call mythic structures, battle a sense of inadequacy and shame comparable to the shame created by early trauma. The change is followed by the development of a new identity (loss of earlier myth) that is anchored in a new arrangement that is more effectively organized. For example the documentary movie, *Jesus Camp* (2006), provides insight into the process of group thinking and control by means of religious indoctrination (Ewing & Grady, 2006). Becky Fisher, the leader of the Christian Camp who desired to teach children how to be better Christians, stated in the documentary:

> It's no wonder, with that kind of intense training and discipline, that those young people are ready to kill themselves for the cause of Islam. I wanna see young people who are as committed to the cause of Jesus Christ as the young people are to the cause of Islam. I

> wanna see them as radically laying down their lives for the Gospel as they are over in Pakistan and Israel and Palestine and all those different places, you know, because we have... excuse me, but we have the truth! (2006, p.1)

The sectarian and fundamentalist organizations use their coercive teachings to create a self-identity based on fellowship forged within a unilateral mythic system of beliefs—typically a system that radically departs from traditionally proclaimed beliefs (See Sharlet, 2008, p. 4-5). Psychologically speaking, one cannot prescribe *the right myth*.

Imago Dei Used As a Tool

Organized religions often develop a plethora of effective tools for dealing with the numinosum that are used for maintaining hegemony. Power, understandably, is a necessary means of structural development and necessary for maintaining order for any intrapsychic, familial, or social structure. This is why a family cannot exist without some measured employment of power. In normal, healthy development, the expediency of power comes from archetypal energy that is modulated by ego. This process promotes growth and asserts boundaries that prevent enmeshment while preserving interconnectedness. It also prevents other unhealthy obstructions to the process of individuation. If archetypal energy is channeled by the natural order, family members proceed through the stages of development relative to their individual and environmental proclivities. Instinctive mechanisms ensure connection and affiliation, as well as freedom and separation. Healthy families do not imprison their members in *uroboric states*,[148] to use Neumann's term for the incubation state of development prior to

[148] The uroborus symbolizes the developmental stage that exists prior to delineating and separating the opposites. Without delineating and separating boundaries from one's family, one does not become an individual.

separation. At their best, the family and its internal and external relations should serve as a mirror of the internal and external relations that point to and illuminate the numinous Self. That is perhaps why Neumann (1970) stated, "The existence of the family is of paramount importance for the preconscious and transpersonal psychology of the child" (p. 437). Often, a family utilizes power in a way that is a hindrance to individuation; from Neumann's perspective, power is used "unethically." In these case the archetypal energies of the Self are channeled improperly causing "projective grips" that serve the perpetuation of control within the parental hierarchy. Thus, the family ends up creating an identity which attempts to compensate for missing (healthy) parts of the whole. It may be stated, that the greater the dysfunction in the family, the greater is the temptation to play god. But, as we know, that is humanly impossible, so the flaws and shortcomings of the parental couple are transmitted to the children. Oppressive parental control is often insistent on children either surrendering or disavowing the power of archetypal projections. In such cases parents often believe there is only one God Image—the one provided by them. Oppressive power often produces the "rebellion" of suppressed elements. Which in turn leads to differentiation through the mechanism of compensation. One of my patients, Betty, illustrates this. (V.Š.)

Betty

Betty's family of origin was a very strict and traditionally religious family who wielded a lot of influence on her. Nonetheless, she fell in love with a divorced man with liberal values who had excellent family relations that were quite differentiated and functional. Betty eventually married this man but it took many years for Betty's family to come around and formally accept her husband. It took Betty six years of analysis to ease her enormous shame and to come to terms with her guilt about departing from her family's strict religious views. It became apparent that the beliefs built on parental complexes, when confronted with healthy principles furnished by her husband, began to disintegrate despite the fact that they had previously offered a stable and safe refuge. The creation of a new attitudes is never a painless process; new life can only come after the death of the old attachments that originally provided refuge. In the course of her analysis, Betty found a new religion that was no longer based on sinfulness, restrictions, adherence to dogmas; but a religion based on love and compassion.

Iva

Iva was another patient of mine; her father was an abusive alcoholic. (V.Š.) Her mother did little to protect her because she was suppressed by her husband's pathological control. As a young woman, Iva found refuge in a new family of Jehovah's Witnesses. For many years after her conversion, Iva had not fully realized that she replaced one system of control with another. The benefits of belonging that included protection, mutuality, and a promise of salvation, gave Iva what she lacked in her family of origin. She gradually developed a strong attachment to her new family and described it as her new identity. However, this new identity began to shatter many years later when Iva realized that she had married an abusive man and seven years later found the courage to divorce him. Her Jehovah's Witness family considered it unacceptable and dis-fellowshipped her. Iva divorced her husband at the cost of being expelled from her adoptive church. Her expulsion was followed, by a period of deep depression and loss of meaning in her life. Iva said she felt "like a zombie," as if something in her "died, and for a long time, [she] thought it could not be born again." Her own identity, merged with the group, became a reason for her blindness, which allowed her to ignore some essential aspects of her reality that lead to her entering into another abusive relationship. For a long time, she did not want to admit that her escape to freedom was really not freedom at all. This is often the case when one is possessed by an idea that is irreconcilable with their experience. No matter how idealized paradise may be conceived by the human mind, reality proves to be a stumbling block. Psyche is present even if she is not seen. Neumann (1969) writes:

> The tyranny of the content by which consciousness is possessed leads to the repression of such elements in reality as are incompatible with the idea that has obtained "possession"; and the ignoring of these factors then results in disaster. As is demonstrated by a wealth of historical examples, every form of fanaticism, every dogma, and every type of compulsive one-sidedness is finally overthrown by precisely those elements which it has itself repressed, suppressed, or ignored... The individual's essential *non-identity* with the transpersonal is in fact the basis of his life (p. 43, emphasis author's).

Atë, the Heroes' Fall

Ancient Greeks recognized this natural law, the overthrowing of one-sidedness in the principles Nemesis and daimona Atë[149]—as goddesses of righteous indignation who punish acts of hubris. Out of these mythological ideas and images the idea of *Dike* or justice, was further developed in Greek mythology. (Gilkey, 1993, p. 116)[150] We will examine more thoroughly the dynamic concerning the *consequences* of possession by the Self in a later discussion of theonemesis. Neumann (1969) continues:

> The uniqueness and individuality of man is realized precisely by the self-differentiation of the creaturely and limited from unlimited power of the creator. In *inflation* this basic situation is by-passed, and man becomes a chimera, a 'pure spirit' or disembodied ghost (pp. 42-43, author's' emphasis).

---

[149] *Atê* refers to deception. (*Greek*)

[150] Gilkey, Landgon, *Nature, Reality, and the Sacred:The Nexus of Science and Religion*, Fortress Press, 1993

Trauma: A Source of One-Sidedness and Openness to The Spirit World

Traumatic experiences are also roots of poor adaptation. Early trauma or overly controlling parenting promotes a split in the child's ego that often creates an inadequate self-structure. Ego, which task is to modulate archetypal energies, becomes captured in the feeling-tone memories that led to a one-sided autonomy. Due to the high autonomy of one-sided contents, psychological organization loosens. Loosely organized self-structures are open to inflation by archetypal contents and cannot hold well a relation between the opposites. Some inferiorities are too crude for the ego and pushed-off from consciousness, thus creating—a complex.

Jung stated:

> But [this] one-sided development must inevitably lead to a reaction, since the suppressed inferior function cannot be definitively excluded from participation in our life and development. The time will come when the division in the inner man must be abolished, in order that the undeveloped may be granted an opportunity to live (1923, [CW6, para. 112]).

How can this be understood from a developmental perspective? Edinger (1972) defined the Self as the *ordering* and *unifying* center of the total psyche. According to him, the Self is the seat of an objective identity, while the ego can be understood as the seat of subjective identity. (p. 3) From Edinger's perspective, the Self is a central source of life energy, the fountain of our being, which is most "simply" described as God (but conceived psychologically as a God Image). In this respect, his concept of the Self encompasses all the archetypes and the whole unconscious, including that which eventually becomes conscious. Archetypes are, in his view, only different aspects (or components) of the ultimate unconscious archetypal reality, i.e. the Self. According to Edinger, during the development of human consciousness, the ego slowly emerges, and then is separated from the Self, through differentiation, and then remerges to achieve conscious unity in the process of individuation. In the process, unconscious unity becomes conscious unity. Viewed from this perspective, trauma-induced complexes influence the separation of the ego from the Self in a way that parts of the ego are left at the mercy of the split-off, dark, unconscious Self. What makes the Self *dark* is the extreme degree of the polarization into opposites. The misguided ego, which has lost its reference point, hides itself behind the Self, and uses its authority to fill out developmental gaps. The ego can adapt an omnipotent position and disguise itself behind what presents itself as a great universal truth, but this comes at the cost of critical thinking and other higher functions of reason. Inflated logic is rigid and hard-to-penetrate by rational means, but at its core it serves a protective function. It protects feelings that are hiding in the unconscious. Archetypal imagery becomes disconnected from its source and becomes an encapsulated fantasy serving as a soothing balsam, keeping those feelings quiet. In the family, fantasy can find refuge in the transitional space.[151] In the case of relatively good enough parenting and normal development of the ego, the child can utilize the space provided by good enough parenting to play and to eventually use symbols that are neither connected nor disconnected to the real world (Winnicott, 1986: *Playing and Reality* pp. 10-19). It is a space of make-believe and magic, where the child can safely create and then attempt to bring these creative fantasies into reality.

With perpetuated trauma, the fragile ego is split-off from the totality of the psyche, and the person ends up trapped in a space between illusion and reality. This transitional space serves as the container for fantasy, but also can also foster states of

[151] Transitional space: "'in-between space' - the transitional area, to Winnicott, or das Zwischenmenschliche to Buber. This is a meeting-ground of potentiality and authenticity, located neither within the self nor in the world of political and economic affairs. In this space, one finds the most authentic and creative aspects of our personal and communal existence, including artistic, scientific, and religious expression." (Laura Praglin, Universitas, Volume 2, Issue 2, 2006)

dissociation; it is "a kind of melancholic self-soothing compromise—a defensive use of the imagination in the service of anxiety avoidance," says Kalsched, (1997, p. 106). Numerous pioneers in depth psychology have given an account of "spiritual" phenomena becoming visible "through a gap created by trauma," (Kalsched, 2013). One caveat, however, is that these discoveries have remained on the periphery of mainline thinking and theorizing.

Fantasy and Imagination

Kalsched (1996) stated that one of the functions of the archetypal psyche is to keep the ego-germ alive and in life, to support the "personal spirit[152]" when otherwise life has forsaken it, (p. 49). Kalsched says:

> Building on what Fordham called 'defenses of the Self,' I suggest that in cases of early trauma, we see a remarkable wisdom in the psyche to assure survival of what I call the *imperishable personal spirit*, the essence of the person. (2003, p. 1; author's emphasis)

Archetypal Imagery, including the *Imago Dei* is often used by fundamentalists supporting and preserving the protective fantasies that keeps one's ego encapsulated. There is a crucial difference between fantasy and imagination in this respect. While fantasies are produced by the psyche to keep the ego from fragmenting, basically keeping the ego shielded from reality, imagination is the capacity to connect with those parts of the Self that can return the ego to a realistically anchored life (p. 187). The *System of fantasy*, as Kalsched, (2003), termed it,

[152] Jung writes, "Spirit, like God, denotes an object of psychic experience which cannot be proved to exist in the external world and cannot be understood rationally...From the psychological point of view, the phenomenon of spirit, like every autonomous complex, appears as an intention of the unconscious superior to, at least on a par with, intentions of the ego. If we are to do justice to the essence of the thing we call spirit, we should really speak of a 'higher' consciousness rather than of the unconscious" (CW 8, par. 626 and 643).

is a protective system that basically substitutes the imagination. (p. 5)[153] Fantasy protects the ego from splitting-off the affect completely, but in order to accomplish this the affect becomes detached from the reality of life.

A powerful example of Kalsched's archetypal self-care system is a patient of mine (G.J.D.) who taught me the tragic but intricate subtleties of long-term trauma bonding and the years of attachment in analysis needed to address and heal the wounded soul. At the time she entered into psychotherapy, she was in her mid-30s. As an 11-year-old grade school girl, her sixth-grade teacher psychologically groomed her for over a year, then while babysitting for his children one night, he sexually abused her. Uniquely, this illicit sexual relationship and trauma bonding continued for over 25 years; not only with the initial perpetrator but with numerous other men. She could not break, resolve, heal or integrate this "trauma bond." In the early years of our work, she would pejoratively state: "I am his sex slave; he listens to me. I give him sex." In the early years of analysis, she would often dream of a young girl who was locked away and trapped in a basement. While on the upper level of the house, there was an elderly woman who was the keeper of keys and kept the little girl locked downstairs; the little girl in the basement became known, affectionately, as "BG:" basement girl. BG was an image of a part of her soul that was split-off in order to protect her from further emotional trauma and the ultimate fear of bondage (again) in relationships, particularly in relationship with her husband. One day I asked why she never wore her wedding ring? She responded saying, "I do not want to be a kept women"! She could not integrate her powerful sexuality and her need for emotional intimacy and attachment. That is, the profound and traumatic split between her vulnerable emotional self and her sexual self would need to be healed and integrated before she could give herself to another. The older adult woman appeared to play the role of the protector/

---

[153] An *Interview with Donald Kalsched Contributed* by *Anne Malone*, Friday, 28 November 2003, C. G. Jung Page, p.5.

Girl with the Matches, Public domain.

persecutor part of the defensive archetypal self-care system. In this context, phantasy serves the same function as ideology and strong belief for the fundamentalist's. Some semblance of connection to archetypal affects is preserved but the connection to reality is lost. Ideology can become the carrier of one's personal spirit; and it functions, among other things, to protect one's vulnerable spirit, often keeping a person from fragmenting. It serves as a psychological and spiritual prosthesis, but it cannot function like the real, original organ.

Splitting the poles of the Self

The archetypal world, when reflected by the ego, yields structures that are manifested as bipolarity. Bipolarity, the tendency for phenomena to be experienced as a dichotomous, polarized pair, can be considered a basic characteristic of the unconscious. A healthy psyche balances these bipolar psychic structures within the limits of normal identification. There may be an oscillation between the polarities and some degree of fluidity and interchangeability between them; this is a hallmark of healthy psychic development. Contrast this with the inflated ego that splits the original bipolar archetype and overtly identifies with only one side of the polarity.

Categories of good and evil and other such oppositional concepts, which Immanuel Kant identified as antinomies of pure reason, may become concretized in the psychological life of fundamentalists. With identification directed toward only one pole, dogmatic positions develop. This underlies the propensity to hide behind the authority of the Talmud, the Bible, or the Koran. Identity that is predicated upon convenient, effortless adoption of dogmatic beliefs does not require the individual to engage in genuine moral work. In this respect, inflation is a state of regression to a time before rational capacities had developed and could be called upon to work through and resolve personal moral dilemmas. As Harris aptly pointed out,

> "... Once we abandon our belief in a rule-making God, the question of why a given action is good or bad becomes a matter of debate" (p. 170).

For the ego caught in inflation, initially, the resolution of ambivalent or paradoxical positions relies on denial, projection, rationalization, or other defensive adaptations. I recall discussing the authority of the Bible with a therapist I met at a conference. (V.Š.) This Episcopalian woman based her counseling on fundamentalist beliefs that homosexuality is a sin and counseled her gay patients in accordance with her beliefs (so-called conversion therapy).[154] She stated that she absolutely trusted the authority of the Bible and followed what the Lord advised in her life via Scripture study. I opened a Bible to a passage in Deuteronomy and asked her if she would strictly follow the advice it contained.

> "If any man takes a wife and goes in to her and then hates her and accuses her of misconduct and brings a bad name upon her," saying, I took this woman, and when I came near her, I did not find in her evidence of virginity, then the father of the young woman and her mother shall take and bring out the evidence of her virginity to the elders of the city in the gate ... But if the evidence of virginity was not found in the young woman, then they shall bring out the young woman to the door of her father's house, and the men of her city shall stone her to death with stones, because she has done an outrageous thing in Israel by whoring in her father's house. So you shall purge the evil from your midst (Deut. 22:21, *English Standard Version*).

First, she could not believe that it was a regular Bible, and later she said she would have to consult her priest to come to terms with this question. I never heard back from her.

Inflation Is Natural

It is important to stress that archetypal one-sidedness should not be considered pathological. Normal processes are oscillations between opposites. Naturally, adaptation is rather a fluid process. The symphony of the human mind is a result of the play of endless archetypal instruments emerging and influencing the ego. Like different sections in an orchestral suite

[154] Unfortunately such therapy is not illegal everywhere in the U.S. In April 2015, President Obama called for an end of "repairing" therapies after a transgender youth committed suicide after being forced into the conversion therapy.

that may move back and forth between foreground and background, temporary identifications with one or the other side of a polarity proves to be a very normal part of psychic life. Without archetypes that are inherently bipolar in nature perhaps there would be silence. The rules of understanding reality are based on the *a priori* archetypal background. Our eye cannot see white writing on the white paper. There must be contrast. Similarly, there must be contrasts within the psyche for our consciousness to discern the signs and symbols from which choices emerge. Consciousness, as Edinger points out, is a phenomenon based on relating of two factors: "knowing" and "witness." (Edinger, 1984, p. 36) Consciousness is the experience of a *knower* experiencing something *knowable.* Identification with one side or the other is an inevitable aspect of the process of creating consciousness. It should be remembered that consciousness is basically the unconscious that became conscious. Inflation is sometimes a needed transitional state for healthy development of the reflective function; without inflation the numinosum would have no transformative effect on the personality. The danger ensues if archetypal energy is excessive or if the ego becomes inflexible in absorbing the meaning of the numinosum.

Aeschyne

The person who becomes conscious of their inflated ego will experience a sense of shame, which the ancient Greeks called *aeschyne*. *Aeschyne* comprises a state of shame aroused in the presence of forces that evoke a sense of reverence. It is a quality that is antithetical to ego inflation that results from identification with archetypal contents. If the light side of the Self possesses the ego, it is manifested as mania, unchecked excitement. If the dark or dreadful pole of the Self possesses the ego, the ego becomes shamed and paralyzed. Weakness of the ego stems from its inability to contain numinous experiences meaningfully. Jung said:

> It must constantly be borne in mind that the constellation of archetypal images and fantasies is not in itself pathological. The pathological element only reveals itself in the way the individual reacts to them and how he interprets them (Jung 1950b, [CW 9i, para. 621]).

Humble Attitude Toward the Self

In regard to the vital place of humility in our spiritual journey, Jung himself stated, "The experience of the Self is always a defeat for the ego," (1955, [CW 14, para. 778]). What could he possibly mean by this? The experience of the Self is essentially initiatory and transformative. It heralds the initiate into the deeper mysteries of the archetypal underworld where one discovers new aspects of their human identity and myth that seek incarnation. Of course, this brings about the relativization of the ego—ego death—to its previously cherished structures. Corbett (1966) spoke on this theme and described how an encounter with the numinosum does not produce inflation when the ego is humbled and awed by the experience; rather, it is radically relativized in front of the great and overwhelming power of the Self. In order to fully experience the numinosum, one must humbly submit to the power (tremendum) of the inner other, or the holy; or one may be forced to submit by fate. It is in submitting to the Self that one is stripped of grandiose pretenses and opened to the possibility of a new identity. This is illustrated powerfully in the Sumerian myth of Inanna. However, there is a price for this new reality, and that is the embracing of one's own (finitude) unique suffering. This humbling experience engenders a realization that we are all alike in terms of status before the numinosum and it fosters a letting go of illusive structures of ego-control. This submission not only humbles, but also liberates. It encourages the embrace of one's limited self with its accompanying suffering. Grandiosity can function to shield a person from their own genuine suffering but this blocks access to wholeness.

Corbett (1966) continues:

Suddenly we realize that we are not who we thought we were; our childhood conditioning is loosened a little. We are also thrust into a relationship with the totality of [the] Mind instead of being trapped within an internal solipsism.[155] *This does not feed grandiose pathology, it eradicates it by making one feel very small. In the presence of normal reality testing and reasonably firm self-structures, the numinosum provides the empirical personality with what is missing; it does not produce an experience that will further alienate one from the Self. The exception to the rule that the numinosum does produce inflation found when the self structures are too fragile to contain the experience, and psychosis results because of an identification with the experience as a way of managing terror. Grandiosity as a defensive maneuver then serves to protect an enfeebled self* (pp. 23-24, author's' emphasis).[156]

Expulsion from the Garden of Eden, between 1426 and 1427. Public domain, via Wikimedia Commons.

[155] Solipsism is "a theory holding that the self can know nothing but its own modifications and that the self is the only existent thing"; it can also imply extreme egocentrism" (Internet Merriam-Webster Dictionary, 2009, p.1). (footnote authors)

[156] Image: Masaccio: *Expulsion from Paradise*, Florence, 1425

Corbett's insights provide very important information because it offers the therapist direct advice regarding how to support and consolidate ego-functions, including the regulation of one's suffering and shame. It is this process, including one's symbolic capacity, that allows the ego to integrate archetypal energy. It is essentially a nurturing of the reflective function when the knower of the "Other" gradually develops awareness that life has a symbolic dimension and that paying attention to the subtle nuances of feelings and reveries allows the mind to access symbolic understanding. Through this process, inflation is used progressively because the archetype is metabolized, given meaning, and contained to the extent that it becomes consciously integrated. The function of rituals, faith, and mythology can be viewed as a *symbolic process* intended to establish conditions for the ego to be able to relate to its suffering, integrate unconscious contents and metabolize the archetype. For the human ego, it is a different experience to be awed by the profound meaning that archetypes can channel than it is to be overwhelmed by the power of absolute incomprehensibility. Working on fostering a spiritual attitude of humility, and thus, the ego-capacity to experience and meaningfully integrate the numinous experience, involves working to prevent inflation.

False Prophets

People who have poorly mastered this task of fostering a spiritual attitude are especially susceptible to outside influence. They attempt to restore the modulating faculty of their ego by projecting the missing part onto spiritual leaders. Gurus, priests, and politicians can hold this function for them. In Jungian analysis, we speak of transference in daily life we use the term projection. Trained analysts usually recognize projections and appropriately utilize them in their analytical work until the patient is ready to claim and reintegrate this symbolic psychological function into their own psyche. A guru, therapist or spiritual leader, and for that matter anyone receiving another's idealized projections, who does not recognize that they can be caught in their own countertransference is susceptible to taking blind advantage of the power educed from the relationship with their followers.

Questioning Opens One's Spiritual Door

One needs to be anchored in one's true God to be able to resist the false God. Stated differently, if one is unconscious about the numinous effects of the Self and subsequently projects this onto a leader or an idea, one becomes a victim of the inflation of his or her own inferiority. Thus, he or she gives up his or her identity, or at least part of it, in favor of some other false inflated religious identity or connection with an idealized figure. When the question of God remains fluid and remains a *question*, the ego is conscious of uncertainty and doubt. But when the ego gives up its relational function to the Self, the idea of God becomes ultimately locked down. This process increases the energy of all the unwanted, interfering thoughts. It is exactly the "dark" part of one's own personality that kills off the remaining voice of psychological opposition.

One patient of mine (V.Š.) grew up in a fundamentalist environment where both of his parents were "very devoted Christians." He was continuously hearing as a child: "You cannot question God!" or "You cannot be angry, it is a sin." Later in his adult years he sought therapy for his uncontained anger outbursts.

Feeling unsure, said Jung (1943), is much nearer to the truth than the illusion and bluff of certainty (p. 18). It is no accident that the religious mythology of Christianity placed a snake in paradise. Psychologically speaking, the snake represents the fracturing of unconscious unity by creating duality and self-realization. Original sin, therefore, can be understood as sin against the *unitary unconscious*. Paradoxically, the realization of one's self/Self brings about fear, shame, and feelings of abandonment, but at the same time it enlarges the world by its consciousness: human element, the very gift that came from the sin. (Kohut, 1971, author's emphasis).

Status Quo

Let us now go back to what role the radical religious attitude plays in the creation of defenses. Religious dogmatism can be viewed as an attempt to fend off the fear of "bad" numinous energy and the consequent fear of realizing and suffering ambivalent (or bivalent) ego-states. That is one of the purposes of dogmatism, to preserve the shameless *status quo* and to fend off anxiety. According to Kohut, the fear of fragmentation and loss of self is one of the *core* anxieties. (Kohut, 1971, p. 152) The loss of experiencing a unitary paradisiacal state is perceived by the ego as an annihilating threat. However because everything changes, a paradisiacal state is only a transitory experience (mystical, romantic or otherwise). However, the ego wishes to make it permanent and thus creates a concept (a dogmatic defense) thinking it can capture and control it. The ego fears that this loss will lead to complete annihilation involving a corresponding loss of self, self-esteem and identity. To remain unconsciously merged with the Self is one of the instinctive tendencies that protects the fragile ego or the incubating and virtual ego against those core anxieties. As stated earlier, some degree of reasonable shame and fragmentation are needed for healthy psychological development and wholeness. One's life attitude does not remain nor should remain fixated in the grandiose merged state indefinitely. Sooner or later, life's circumstances will press and archetypal energy will intervene in an attempt to restore the undifferentiated or unacknowledged parts that are hampering adaptation. Corbett (1966) said:

> ... these fragile areas of the personality are precisely those to which the numinosum will address itself, because they are where healing is most needed and where the barrier to the unconscious is most tenuous, so that pressure from the unconscious is felt most keenly ... Because the archetype attempts to provide what is necessary to restore what is missing for the individuation of the self, true religious experience is potentially frightening, and may be related to areas of

> great difficulty. Thus, within analytical psychology, and especially for the religiously oriented therapist, the fear of the numinosum can be considered a core anxiety ... The numinosum does not necessarily respect our view of the world, but rather tends to present us with the need for radical re-evaluation of our beliefs ... When the spirit presses for change in a direction contrary to the ego's established norms, grandiose defenses are threatened. If they cannot withstand the pressure of the numinosum, they collapse, producing depression or anxiety; the spirit is resisted in order to prevent such dysphoria (p. 33).

When the ego intensely fears the numinosum and raises strong defenses against it, then the unconscious is more likely to be activated and may make its voice heard even at the expense of fragmenting the ego. Because the unconscious is projected at first, it feels like it is coming from outside, from the other person: in the form of conflict, or strong attraction. Quite frequently, people begin therapy or seek spiritual renewal due to the onset of anxiety and suffering that the world "imposed" on them. If one is spiritually open, then one is eventually confronted with questions like: *What is the Self (or God) trying to help me to see or understand?* Or, what does this anxiety signal? It is a question pertaining to the purpose (finality, *causa finalis*), not only the origin (*causa efficiens*) of the symptom. Anxiety often lessens when one begins to be receptive and open symbolically to a fuller understanding of one's anxiety. Indeed, the anxiety may act as a prelude to a new phase of psychological and spiritual development that starts with a process of *creative disillusionment*. However, if the ego is overwhelmed by the anxiety, it may split it off into anxiety-provoking elements, creating another illusion: comparable to an autoimmune reaction of the body. The ego then attaches itself to a magical paradigm that is disconnected from reality. In order to prevent excessive shock and fragmentation one must be genuinely relating to the numinosum. Progressive integration of numinous energy that is related to consensual reality increases consciousness and produces a positive, adapted change that fosters growth of the personality. It is a task of therapy and many spiritual practices to promote the growth of consciousness and the incarnation of the Self.

Andrea

Andrea was not a very religious person until her son died tragically before he reached the age of 13. Her pain was immense. She grieved and suffered for many years, and her pain would not depart. She kept his room exactly the way it had been on his last day. Slowly she developed a form of religion, or rather *spiritism* when she communicated with her deceased son through the screen of a turned-off television set, burning candles, or whistling in the wind. She would buy her son gifts and spends hours "communicating with his spirit." One may argue that she was happy and that this practice served her well because she had a meaningful connection to her son's image. However, Andrea was caught in her literal fantasy and spent too much time investing in it; like an addict obsessed with a drug. Andrea withdrew from life and literally abandoned her three other children who needed her more than her son's spirit. Her living sons resented her, but she felt misunderstood and lonely, despite the blessing that she received from God. (V.Š.)

Church: Container For The Archetype of Initiation and Spiritual Development

Support from religious communities and the symbolism they employ can promote healing from trauma and provide a person with tools to discover deeper religious meaning. Unfortunately, many religious institutions use anxiety as a tool of oppression to build a system of hegemony and power that relies on stagnant rituals and dogma.

Ancient rituals and rites of passages were designed for the purpose of containing and embodying numinous energy for the transformation of personality and, along with it, culture. Ritualization and individuation developed together. Churches and their elders were providers of sacred images (archetypes) in culturally specific forms. Their purpose was to lift the dimension of attachment from the purely instinctive, and therefore unconscious form, to a highly conscious relational and eventually divine form. Jung (1917/1926/1943) speaks with respect to this point:

> The Church represents a higher spiritual substitute for the purely natural, or "carnal," tie to the parents. Consequently it frees the individual from an unconscious natural relationship which, strictly speaking, is not a relationship at all but simply a condition of inchoate, unconscious identity (CW 7, [par. 172, p. 105]).

Fear of Numinosum Can Lead to Spiritual Sterility

One of the church's ideal functions is to contain, mediate, and facilitate the embodiment and transformation of numinous energy. A prime example would be the preparation for and celebration of the sacraments as mediating and dispensing of grace, numinous energy. However, many contemporary churches have largely lost their pathway to the great mysteries though they continue operating with a fear of a change. Their dogmas no longer speak to the signs of the times or the needs of modern individuals. Their symbols have dried up and lost their life-soul; a connection to the deep well of the numinous. Today, many perceive this as a major religious crisis in the Western world (Taylor, 2002; Tacey, 2005 & 2015[157]; Heelas and Woodhead, 2005; Bender, 2010). As Jung (1927/1931) realized, when a symbol has outlived its effectiveness, but it is still perpetuated as if it was a living symbol, it becomes an *idol* without relevant personal value. The *sacred dimension* (i.e.

[157] Tacey, D., *Religion as Metaphor: Beyond Literal Belief*, Transaction Publishers, NJ, 2015.

revelatory of the unconscious and transcendent function) over time evaporated, diminishing the potency of the symbol. Unconscious sacred energy has thus lost its container and seeks expression in other areas of human existence (Fox, 2000). Hence, the numinosum, which for many today is rarely experienced in the symbols of the church, naturally bursts forth in uncontained ways outside of the churches, though in forms that are often maladaptive and regressive. Religious name-calling, hatred, demonization of the other, adherence to sectarian teaching, self-bashing, profound feelings of sinfulness on one hand and all kinds of addictions on the other are all attempts to deal with uncontained numinous energy. Like the goddess Psyche herself, the numinosum cannot be avoided or ignored, without dangerous consequences. It is one's relationship to the numinosum and the symbolic expression of the numinosum in healthy religions that promotes individuation. The value of one's religion depends on whether it utilizes numinous energy effectively through ritual and symbol or defends against its various expressions. Choices confront the modern person when his or her mind is freed from the tyranny of delusions, though it also creates moral issues with their corresponding apprehension.

Faith Versus Reason, Religion Versus Science

The gifts and advancements of science have fostered a plurality of worldviews, but with it, seeds have been laid for enormous anxiety, which has confronted individuals with the questions of whether faith worshipped chimeras after all. Jung (1936, [CW 11, [par. 868]) has argued that humans have walked on the path of pursuing science and rationality a little too uncritically—to the degree that the modern person is isolated and detached from their instinctive roots. A split between knowledge and faith follows the same scenario that "every psychological exaggeration" does, "breaks into its inherent opposite," as Jung put it. Both sides offer unsatisfactory answers and provide partial truths respectively. Without scientific knowledge, the world remains veiled by a fog of magical identification and arbitrary beliefs, but a lack of faith turns the world into a corresponding illusion devoid of mystery and enchantment where everything can be understood and explained. Rationality and reason cannot provide a good enough answer to the perennial questions afflicting human beings: *why* are we here and *what* is our purpose? Similarly, faith alone cannot adequately answer *how* the world works. If it adheres to ancient, outdated truths that are irrelevant to modern times, faith risks sinking into increasingly distorted manifestations. Many organized religions tend to postulate absolutes and immutable forms that protect against complexity. Science, on the other hand, encounters complexity eagerly because it is based on the idea of perpetual discovery. Science and religion approach complexity by different means. But these are not mutually exclusive. For example, science proves to be of little help in explaining certain burning questions about the nature of human consciousness, free will, immortality, existence of external reality, or even the rationality of reason alone, as Hume has argued.[158] There are times when one must accept the premises of faith to achieve any rational conclusion. Likewise, faith cannot maintain its integrity if it does not build on rational axioms inferred from practical experience in the natural world. For faith to function optimally, it not only has to be reasonable, it must emerge from a rational cause; otherwise it will not be perpetuated. Scientific inquiry and religion are equally important aspects of the human spirit on the quest for truth. Albert Einstein (1930) said:

> Though religion may be that which determines the goal, it has, nevertheless, learned from science, in the broadest sense, what means will contribute to the attainment of the goals it has set up. But science can only be created by those who are thoroughly imbued with the aspiration toward truth and understanding.

---

[158] Hume, D., *A Treatise of Human Nature: A Critical Edition*, David Fate Norton and Mary J. Norton (eds.), Oxford, Clarendon Press, 2007.

> This source of feeling, however, springs from the sphere of religion. To this there also belongs the faith in the possibility that the regulations valid for the world of existence are rational, that is, comprehensible to reason. I cannot conceive of a genuine scientist without that profound faith. The situation may be expressed by an image: science without religion is lame, religion without science is blind. (See more in *The Einstein Reader*, p. 22)

Einstein was a spiritual person who believed in God. It was his scientific exploration that opened his mind to the numinosum. His great insights show us that science and religion are not contradictory stances, but complementary, and when they are combined this can produce higher synergies. Jung and Einstein are examples of this possibility. Though science and religion each have their limitations, they can mutually enrich each other. Einstein (ibid.) continues:

> It would not be difficult to come to an agreement as to what we understand by science. Science is the century-old endeavor to bring together by means of systematic thought the perceptible phenomena of this world into as thoroughgoing an association as possible. To put it boldly, it is the attempt at the posterior reconstruction of existence by the process of conceptualization. (...) Accordingly, a religious person is devout in the sense that he has no doubt of the significance and loftiness of those superpersonal objects and goals which neither require nor are capable of rational foundation. They exist with the same necessity and matter-of-factness as he himself. In this sense religion is the age-old endeavor of mankind to become clearly and completely conscious of these values and goals and constantly to strengthen and extend their effect. If one conceives of religion and science according to these definitions then a conflict between them appears impossible. For science can only ascertain what is, but not what should be, and outside of its domain value judgments of all kinds remain

> necessary. Religion, on the other hand, deals only with evaluations of human thought and action: it cannot justifiably speak of facts and relationships between facts.[159]

A world devoid of the unfathomable mysteries found in nature would resemble a machine similar to the depiction in the movie *The Matrix* (1999).[160] We cannot comprehend the mystery by adhering to a one-sided position. To avoid getting trapped by the one-sidedness of primitive and superstitious beliefs, we must have the courage to live symbolically—holding opposites within the psyche in tension.

Science, of course, is not free from dogmatic entrapments, it is not free from the influence of the unconscious. There are presumptions such as materialism that have permeated the sciences from its beginning. Science has yet to explain the phenomena of consciousness and unconsciousness, though it has often pretended so.[161] Thus science has to reflect on itself without prejudice and open itself to all of its rationalizations and dogmas that it unwittingly creates. If science is not successful in this task, it will simply revert to its religious source and science will assume a dogmatic approach.

Symbol Connects Unconscious and Conscious

Symbols nourish the human mind when the conscious mind is simultaneously present with unconscious intuition. Without the presence of critical reasoning, a symbol can become an

---

[159] The article by Albert Einstein appeared in the *New York Times Magazine* on November 9, 1930 pp 1-4; reprinted in *Ideas and Opinions*, Crown Publishers, Inc. 1954, pp 36 - 40.

[160] See: Vladislav Šolc, 2007, *PSÝCHÉ MATRIX REALITA, hledání dimenzí reality očima psychologa*, Amos, Praha.

[161] See: Chalmers, D., *Philosophy of Mind: Classical and Contemporary Readings*, Oxford University press, 2002

obsessive dogma, and without the feeling-based and intuitive comprehension, a symbol would be just an empty shell, a sign, referring to nothing beyond the apparent meaning. Symbols, then, if grasped as advocated by Jung, function as a bridge between opposites. This prevents the mind from becoming stuck in one pole of the opposites. Jung (in von Franz, 1964) says:

> Thus a word or an image is symbolic when it implies something more than its obvious and immediate meaning. It has a wider unconscious aspect that is never precisely defined or fully explained. Nor can one hope to define or explain it. As the mind explores the symbol, it is led to ideas that lie beyond the grasp of reason (p. 4).

In our analytical practices, we are amazed over and over again by the unfathomable ways the unconscious speaks. Dreams of our clients, and our own, often bring about symbols that open the depths of soul: feelings and insights that are often awesome in the true sense of the word. Feelings cannot be reduced to anything else, only clarified by amplification. Words are only approximations to something that is already perfect. Here is one example from many. A client of mine (V.Š.) who felt she "could not do it anymore," depressed and overwhelmed by difficult events in her life, had the following dream:

> I am in the old house. Looked like an abandoned building. At the table there is a book. I believe it is a Red Book from Carl Jung. Suddenly the author appears. I am not sure if it is Jung, but it is an old man with grey hair and very charismatic presence. I open the book and see that it is not *The Red Book* I thought it was. The book is half unfinished. I ask him to sign it. He says: sure, but I just honor it by my signature, the book is yours and you have to write it!

After this dream, the client realized that she had to carry her own cross. It gave her strength and understanding that surpassed a description of mere words. A symbol in the role of the transcendent function makes possible one of the most baffling powers of the mind—it allows for the comprehension of something larger by way of something smaller. A part of the limitless universe is mirrored in the limited ego, like the reflection of a starry sky on the surface of a small pond. Is this because the ego and the Self are ultimately one? Is it the ego that reflects the Self or the Self who reflects the ego? Or, the Self who reflects via the ego? The symbolic life provides opportunities for meaning to be elucidated and for the constant correction of the illusory notion that the mystery of life can be fully explained. To paraphrase Immanuel Kant's (1781) dictum on "necessary cognitive complementarity and semantic interdependence of intuitions and concepts," it can be said that there has to be a necessary complementarity and interdependence of consciousness and unconsciousness if a symbol is to fulfill its exhaustive function, (p. 93, A51/B76). A symbol without the unconscious is empty, and the unconscious without reason is blind. From a phenomenological perspective, no conscious realization or perception is possible without some utilization of the symbolic function. Naturally, it is desirable to employ symbols the way they best serve our spiritual needs, (i.e. the way that provides the most freedom for one, while preserving a reasonable level of responsibility and love for the world). A person living an honest symbolic life does not cling to mass dogma nor does such a person reduce reality to a primal, material cause. Instead, he or she lives for and looks for the truth with the highest responsibility while remaining aware of his or her limitations, mistakes and shortcomings. The symbolic life fosters hope that liberating answers can be revealed, even if those answers are eventually replaced.

An Impossible Task

Modern people are asked to undertake this almost impossible leap where truth is found in the depths of their own soul. This is the path Jung traversed in his descent into the underworld, where he discovered his own lost soul. Today, individuals can no longer rely on dogma or science alone. As scholars pore over

Jung's "night sea journey" captured in *The Red Book,* there is growing agreement that *paradox* is the nearly universal theme appearing throughout *The Red Book*. Every individual is called to take a night sea journey of his or her own, replete with paradox, instead of relying on a paradisiacal vision built upon childish magical thinking. This task may be difficult but not impossible. Therapists know what St. Paul meant, "Who will not suffer you to be tempted above that ye are able; but will with the temptation also make a way to escape, that ye may be able to bear it," (Cor. 10:13, *King James*). The temptation to escape the work of holding opposites in tension is almost irresistible. For the modern individual, a regressive move that restores antiquated rules, beliefs and dogma is not a viable option, but neither is the spiritual dread that would accompany the choice to muster no response to the demands of the soul. Each person stands in front of this task alone, and has the responsibility of creating a better world through the ongoing movement that embraces reality rather than nurturing a fantasied world.

Sapere Aude: Dare to Know

A wake-up call came 200 years ago. In 1784, Kant asked: "What is enlightenment?" In German, *Was ist Aufklärung*? His answer was the following:

> Enlightenment is man's emergence from his self-incurred immaturity. Immaturity is the inability to use one's own understanding without the guidance of another. This immaturity is self-incurred if its cause is not lack of understanding, but lack of resolution and courage to use it without the guidance of another. The motto of the Age of Enlightenment is therefore: *Sapere aude*![162] Have courage to use your own understanding! (p.11)

[162] Horatius (20 B.C.) said, *"Dimidium facti qui coepit habet: sapere aude, incipe,"* which translates from Latin to "He who has begun is half done: dare to wise"

Kant's urging is just as relevant today. The succeeding Romantic era added a greater sense of urgency to the question of uncovering the moral implications of self-incurred immaturity—a form of self-deception as a choice. Jung's teaching presents the psychological processes of individuation as a hopeful and optimistic choice. Jung began to understand and envision the human being as an active player in bringing about a spiritual awakening; one that far exceeded the simple necessities of adaptation. In a similar vein, Friedrich Nietzsche, a post-Kantian philosopher, furthered the idea of moral responsibility. He appealed to one's own conscience and urged the individual to seek the meaning of life by *living* it. He believed that reason alone is not enough. The meaning of life is revealed by living authentically, not by submitting to abstract systems of thought or dogma, even if that system is of our own making. Nietzsche (1888) said:

> Judgments, judgments of value, concerning life, for it or against it, can, in the end, never be true: they have value only as symptoms, they are worthy of consideration only as symptoms; in themselves such judgments are stupidities. One must by all means stretch out one's fingers and make the attempt to grasp this amazing finesse, that the value of life cannot be estimated. (TI, *The Problem of Socrates*, 11: 2)

Nietzsche promised that when we throw away systems that bind us to somebody else's beliefs and instead rely on our own inner authenticity, we would find freedom. But the promise of authenticity and moral freedom also comes with a warning, especially when combined with advancing technology, because our destructive capacities have grown exponentially. The increasing speed of socio-economic changes, the rise of science, conspiracism and atheism, the rapid commixture of cultures and religions, the loss of historical knowledge, and the estrangement from nature all contribute to heightened confusion and fear. This often pushes one to choose old, familiar paradigms. However, this sort of regressive movement that fosters a self-imposed blindness empowers the darker elements that can easily coalesce as secular and religious "isms." This is precisely what Jung warned against.

It is a paradox that religion can be an instrument that equips humans to deal with the perils of the soul, as well as arousing very destructive psychological elements. According to Erich Neumann (1974):

> We know that the core of the neurosis of our time is the religious problem or, stated in more universal terms, the search for the self (the Self, authors). In this sense neuroses, like the mass phenomena resulting from this situation, are a kind of *sacred disease*. Our whole epoch is full of it, but behind it stands the power of a numinous center, which seems to direct not only the normal development of the individual, but his psychic crises and transformations as well – not only the disease but also the cure, both in the individual and in the collective (pp. 132-133; emphasis added).

God and evil, along with many other polarities, must be kept in balance because they are inherent properties of the Self. Religion is misused and misapplied when it emphasizes one polarity at the expense of the other within the psyche; this too hinders one's spiritual development.

6. JUNG'S TAKE ON PRIVATIO BONI DOCTRINE

If we are convinced that we know the ultimate truth concerning metaphysical things, this means nothing more than that archetypal images have taken possession of our powers of thought and feeling, so that these lose their quality as functions at our disposal. The loss shows itself in the fact that the object of perception then becomes absolute and indisputable and surrounds itself with such emotional taboo that anyone who presumes to reflect on it is automatically branded a heretic and blasphemer (Jung 1955, [CW 14, para. 787]).

Jung discovered a cornerstone for his own understanding of archetypal numinosity in Rudolf Otto's teachings. The interpretation of the idea of God as *Summum Bonum* (Sum of the Good) did not fit Otto's findings nor Jung's clinical experience.[163] So how can a sensible and spiritually open-minded person come to terms with the fact that the experience of the Holy is not only awesome but full of terror, all at the same time? Ancient heroes of Greek mythology stood up to their gods and challenged their hypocrisy, corruption, weaknesses, inconsistencies, and lies. Sometimes they even fought them. Many Christians would be outraged if anyone recommended a similar approach to the Christian God. And yet Jung wrote that sooner or later Jesus Christ would have to find God, as such.

> ..."difficult to love, as a kind father, a God whom on account of his unpredictable fits of wrath, his unreliability, injustice and cruelty, it has every reason to fear." (Jung 1952a, [CW 11, par. 665])

In the New Dispensation, Jung proposed that individuals would look at Christ in a *new*, depth-psychological way. To be true to one's individuation as Christ was true to his is to live one's own experiment! Jung believed that his time was one of epochal changes, and Christians would have to discover new ways of interpreting biblical teachings in order to find their meaning and one's own myth. Jung (1952a) spoke about the end of the Christian aeon and even referred to himself as a modern Joachim di Fiore for introducing the idea of the coming of a new global spiritual revolution. Murray Stein (1985) argued that Jung tried to heal the one-sidedness of Christianity by reinterpreting and transforming it in a fashion that would speak to the contemporary world and the spirit of the times.[164]

---

[163] "There is none good but one, that is, God." (Mt 19:17)

[164] Joachim of Fiore, (c. 1135 – 1202), was the founder of the monastic order of San Giovanni in Fiore. Fiore was a mystic and a theologian. Fiore was an official in the court of the Norman kings of Sicily when he went off on pilgrimage to the Holy Land and had a spiritual vision of some great calamity (perhaps an outbreak of pestilence) that led to his conversion "from the world."

A Good God?

Christ, Jung says, looked at God, the father, with fear, and at the same time, he mediated the knowledge of his own earthly existence to God the father. Christ had an ambivalent relationship with God. He loved him and acted as his advocate, but in the end, he did not understand why his father abandoned him:

> About three in the afternoon Jesus cried out in a loud voice, "*Eli, Eli, lema sabachthani?*" Which means "My God, my God, why have you forsaken me?" (Matthew 27:46)

Jung (1952a) said:

> It is exactly as if God the father were a different God from the son, which is not the meaning at all. Nor is there any psychological need for such an assumption, since the undoubted lack of reflection in God's consciousness is sufficient to explain his peculiar behavior. It is quite right, therefore, that fear of God should be considered the beginning of all wisdom. On the other hand, the much-vaunted goodness, love, and justice of God should not be regarded as mere propitiation, but should be recognized as a genuine experience, for God is a *coincidentia oppositorum*. Both are justified, the fear of God as well as the love of God" (Jung 1952a, [CW 11, para. 664]).

Let us repeat possession happens when the ego no longer has a meaningful relationship with archetypal content, i.e., the Self (Jung, 1954a). For example, a conscious position or predominant adherence to (or identification with) a superior psychological function or content can literally produce the archaizing, inferior attitude. The Christian concept of *privatio boni* is one of Jung's examples of how the banalization of evil through calling it nonexistent paradoxically gave evil even more power.[165] Omnipotence and the absolute goodness of God are two important Christian premises. In the Christian arena, these were popularized by St. Augustine, but it has its roots in the pre-

[165] From Latin, privation of good.

Platonic philosophy that Plato further developed in his philosophy of ideals. St. Augustine of Hippo writes (1887):

> And in the universe, even that which is called evil, when it is regulated and put in its own place, only enhances our admiration of the good; for we enjoy and value the good more when we compare it with the evil. For the Almighty God, who, as even the heathen acknowledge, has supreme power over all things, being Himself supremely good, would never permit the existence of anything evil among His works, if He were not so omnipotent and good that He can bring good even out of evil. For what is that which we call evil but the absence of good? In the bodies of animals, disease and wounds mean nothing but the absence of health; for when a cure is effected, that does not mean that the evils which were present—namely, the diseases and wounds—go away from the body and dwell elsewhere: they altogether cease to exist; for the wound or disease is not a substance, but a defect in the fleshly substance—the flesh itself being a substance, and therefore something good, of which those evils—that is, privations of the good which we call health—are accidents. Just in the same way, what are called vices in the soul are nothing but privations of natural good. And when they are cured, they are not transferred elsewhere: when they cease to exist in the healthy soul, they cannot exist anywhere else. (Chap. 11, *What is called Evil in Universe is but absence of Good*)[166]

The teaching of *privatio boni* implies that evil is not real and that evil does not rest in substance, it is only *accidental*. Plato taught that evil does not possess its own ontological status, but that the good is real (*bonum et ens conventutur*). Evil, on another hand, is only the privation (deficiency) of good (*privatio elicitus particularis boni*). Evil, thus, is not a *thing*, it is only a

[166] St. Augustine, *Anti-Pelagian Writings: Nicene and Post-Nicene Fathers of the Christian Church*, 1887, Kessinger Publishing, Jan 1, 2004, p. 240.

temporary state of affairs, a deviation from the right path, which will be corrected through eschatological happenings. According to this teaching, evil is a mere illusion, a shadow of good. This Platonic concept later finds its place in the teachings of Neoplatonism, Origen, Pseudo-Dionysius, Areopagite, and St. Augustine, all of whom hypostatized those concepts into theological truths. Thereafter, Christian theodicy was always built on this premise. God only allows good, but the source of evil is man: *Omne bonum ab deo, omne malum ab homine*!

Reality of Evil

Even though the *privatio* doctrine is rather a metaphysical speculation, it can have real psychological implications. It is an idea that attracts a high value of energy in the mind. We know that developing a name or concept for certain phenomena fosters its conscious recognition that allows a concept to take on very real properties. For example, William Gladstone (1858) noticed that Homer's entire *Odyssey* lacked the word "blue." He then researched ancient Icelandic sagas, the Koran, an ancient Bible, Vedic hymns, and found out that the word blue was likewise missing in them. It was as if mankind was colorblind long after the naming of other colors: red, green and yellow. He discovered that ancient humans were only able to see darker shades of green, or "wine," for which they had a vocabulary.[167]

The ability to perceive the color blue (to see it) appeared only a few thousand years ago along with its appearance in the broader vocabulary of humans. Even though the human eye was equipped with an ability to see blue, the brain was not able to conceptualize it due to its inability to conceive of a concept that would *hypostatize* it, making it visible for consciousness. He discovered that the blue sky (and ocean) was not perceived as blue because it was literally too broad and lacked specific

[167] The only exception to this was an ancient civilization of Egypt that used the word blue and used the blue paint in their crafts. (Business Insider, February, 27, 2015, p.1)

dimensions. The color blue was unconscious because of the lack of formal recognition. Similarly the concept of evil can become unconscious without its proper conceptualization by ego.[168]

So what happens if not only colors but also emotions are seen but not recognized? In *Mysterium Coniunctionis*, Jung (1948b) speaks clearly to the process of the "dogmatization" of psychic content. The process of dogmatization consists of building a wall on one side of a content against the split-off energies of the other side of the content in the collective unconscious which leads to the creation of theoretical statements (ideological structures of the *Imago Dei*) that are organized in the mind in the form of *dogma* to ensure that the opposite *side* does not reach consciousness and does not threaten the fragmentation of the established quasi-unity. The assumption of any metaphysical *truth* can be equated to an unconscious identification with the contents that are not known to ego-consciousness. Thus, whenever the human mind postulates any metaphysical truth, it is always a result of the influence of the Dark Self. Such statements are always confessions of a more or less subjective value, and therefore, they reflect the nature of transcendental reality with respect to very narrow human aims. Even though the reasons behind those rationalizations are apparent, projecting onto God what we would like God to be does not make God in that image. Jung said:

> It is difficult to avoid the impression that apotropaic tendencies have had a hand in creating this notion, with the understandable intention of settling the painful problem of evil as optimistically as possible. Often it is just as well that we do not know the danger we escape when we rush in where angels fear to tread (Jung 1948b, [CW 11, par. 247]).

Throughout his whole life Jung advocated strongly for "the revision of religious formulae by the aid of psychological insight" (Philp, 1959, p. 21). He believed that the process of individuation

---

[168] Gladstone, William, Ewart (1858), *Studies on Homer and the Homeric Age. I.*, Oxford, United Kingdom: Oxford University Press.

required a new hermeneutic in understanding religious doctrines through the acquisition of depth psychology and conscious insight. This process was left for the New Psychological Dispensation.

Recognizing the Reality of Evil

From the psychological perspective, dualistic religions make more sense and provide more favors by assigning evil *real* destructive potency. It is healthier to recognize the nature of so-called evil for what it is. Jung saw a major insufficiency in the *privatio boni* teaching because, in the hands of idealistic theologians, evil was perhaps simplified and reduced to something unreal and illusory. Thus it was split-off and held in the unconscious, where, based on one of the most significant principles of analytical psychology, it has not perished, but only gained more power proportional to the strength of the defense. In answering a man who was caught in the "unreality" of evil, Jung suggest:

> If your evil is in fact only an unreal shadow of your good, then your so-called good is nothing but an unreal shadow of your real evil. If he does not reflect in this way he is deceiving himself, and self-deception of this kind [has a] dissociating effect which breeds neurosis ... (Jung 1952b, [CW 11, para. 457]).

For Jung, it is crucially important to recognize the *reality* of evil because believing in evil has direct and real implications in how one lives life. He (1950) says:

> I am indeed convinced that evil is as positive a factor as good. Quite apart from everyday experience it would be extremely illogical to assume that one can state a quality without its opposite. If something is good, then there must need to be something that is evil or bad. The statement that something is good would not be if one could not discriminate it from something else. Even if one says that something exists, such a statement is only possible alongside the other statement that something does not exists. Thus when the Church doctrine declares

> that evil is not or is a mere shadow, then the good is equally illusory, as its statement makes no sense [CW 18, [par. 1592, p. 708]].

Jung believed that it was imperative for the patient's mental health to obtain a proper understanding of the paradoxical nature of the numinosum and the collective unconscious in general. If one does not assign a legitimate place to archetypes in one's life and in one's subjective philosophy, it may result in the unconscious elevation of evil leading to the phenomenon of one-sidedness.

When Jung spoke about the importance of the recognition of evil, he was not only talking about metaphysical evil as a substantive entity of the objective world but more importantly the evil of the deeds we conduct here and now. We can only change our environment and ourselves when we become conscious of how our own shadow impacts the world around us. Jung again:

> ...there is no light without shadow and no psychic wholeness without imperfection. To round itself off, life calls not for perfection but for completeness; and for this the 'thorn in the flesh' is needed, the suffering of defects without which there is no progress and no ascent (Jung 1944, [CW 12, par. 208]).

This is a *conditio sine qua non* of individuation: the confrontation of one's own shadow and thus one's inextricable participation in evil. Such deeds shape and change the image and reality of our world. To create ideological theories that make one's participation in evil and the concurrent responsibility appear banal is psychologically and morally dangerous. There are countless examples of what can happen when evil is suppressed or denied and then projected outwardly as if the content being projected is the property of the *Other*. Wars, persecutions, racism, sexism, domestic violence, social injustices, bigotry, and many other ills that mankind rationalizes by misusing the name(s) of God, are examples of how poorly equipped we are when it comes to handling the evil that we all carry and hide from ourselves.

VI.
THE PHENOMENOLOGY OF EXTREME RELIGION

1. FUNDAMENTALISM PROJECT: AN ANALYTICAL PERSPECTIVE

[A] fundamentalist is the one who is ready to regain territory that had been lost to Antichrist and to do battle royal for the fundamentals of the faith... A war from which there is no discharge (Laws, as cited in Marsden, 1980, p. 158)

The fundamentalism rebuff comes after "big science." Its pervasiveness and militance raises questions about the boast that science and secular rationalism will fully replace religion and the sense of the sacred as approaches to meaning (Almond, Appleby, & Sivan, 2003, p. 5)

What constitutes *strong, fundamentalist,* or *extreme religious* attitudes from a depth-analytical perspective? The history of fundamentalism, when analyzed using the findings gleaned from psychology provides a useful perspective. Almond, Appleby, and Sivan (2003) conducted several comprehensive studies of fundamentalism.[169] Their extensive research looked at religious fundamentalism mainly from a sociological and historical perspective and compared different religions, but it

[169] See the *Fundamentalism Project*, 1987-1995.

also provided rich material for psychological interpretations. Although their findings focused on the modern phenomenon called fundamentalism, we believe those findings can be extrapolated to help explain the radicalization process that occurs with religious belief in more universal and less historically confined ways.

Fundamentalism, the Original Meaning

The term fundamentalism was originally used to describe a return to the *fundamentals* of religious teachings. For Christian those credos were written and inspired as the true teaching of the Bible. Some examples are the virgin birth of Jesus, the doctrine of substitutionary Atonement, the Resurrection of Jesus from the dead, and so on. For other religions, fundamentalist teachings would involve other specific fundamental, or core, beliefs. Although the term fundamentalism originated in America sometime in the 1830s and 1840s, it was, more or less, a Christian millenarian political movement anticipating the second coming of Christ. However, we can trace fundamentalist modes of thinking to many historic periods when one form of worship feuded with another, or where one understanding of the *Imago Dei* clashed with another. God-inspired wars *(Holy Wars),* the persecution of heretics, so called witch-hunts and religious violence are as old as religion itself. King Henry IV of France was killed in 1610 by a man whose passionate Catholicism combined with *visions* led him to regicide, and the killing of Dr. George Tiller in Kansas in 2009 by someone intent on stopping him from performing late term abortions. Religious fanatics were responsible for both assassinations. It can be argued that both ultimately died because of somebody's strong religious persuasions. Research on fundamentalism has shown, among other factors, that *strong religion* is a widespread reaction to change or the threat of change. Fundamentalism conjures up original pristine images of religious purity from the past by selectively recovering earlier traditions that form a basis for a present religious vision; it also struggles against all of that which is considered a threat to the particular religious identity (Tyler, 2009). So, fundamentalists aim to return the world to a state conforming to their view of God's will. Fundamentalism attempts to achieve this in a very proactive way, investing a lot of energy, money, and effort. Fundamentalism is a religious and political movement, however, we will focus on its psychological dynamics and motivations. Politics becomes the secondary vehicle for extending the objective of restoring God's will to society. Psychologically speaking, it is an activated archetype that supplies energy and imagery to a religious ideology while animating follower's behavior. Those who become subject to such forces often act and believe they are *influenced by the spirit* but, psychologically speaking, they really are under the power of the Dark Self. Remembering, as outlined earlier, archetypes (Jung, 1954b) are the very source of the numinosum, so anytime there is a passion or fascination, the archetype is lurking in the background:

> Archetypes have, when they appear, a distinctly numinous character which can only be described as 'spiritual.' It not infrequently happens that the archetype appears in the form of a spirit in dreams or fantasy products, or even comports itself like a ghost. There is a mystical aura about its numinosity, and it has a corresponding effect upon the emotions. It mobilizes philosophical and religious convictions in the very people who deemed themselves miles above any such fits of weakness. Often it drives with unexampled passion and remorseless logic towards its goal and draws its subject under its spell, from which despite the most desperate resistance he is unable, and finally no longer willing, to break free, because the experience brings with it a depth and fullness of meaning that was unthinkable before [CW 8, [par. 405,pp. 205-6]).

Preserving Fundamentals

This very archetypal dynamic explains the radicalization of the religious attitude. Fundamentalism represents the tendency to uphold orthodoxy (right belief) and orthopraxis (right conduct) and aims to defend and conserve religious traditions from what comes to be perceived as erosive societal forces. Fundamentalism claims that it is preserving fundamentals that are foundational principles, but in fact they often formulate new ideologies, methods, and structures (Almond, Appleby, & Sivan, 2003). It is not unusual to see that some of the new methods, structures, and ideologies end up directly violating actual historical beliefs, traditions, interpretative practices, and moral codes that were followed by earlier generations—"or... at the least, a significant departure from these precedents, as well as from praxis of contemporary conservative or orthodox beliefs" (p. 92).

Characteristics of fundamentalism

The fathers of the Fundamentalism Project identified four *organizational* and five *ideological* characteristics of fundamentalism. A closer examination of these characteristics follows with an aim of identifying their psychological dimensions from the perspective of analytical psychology.

The Fundamentalism Project defined four Organizational Characteristics pertaining to the inner structure of a fundamentalist organization:

1. An elected or chosen membership: The belief that the faithful are divinely called.
2. Sharp group boundaries: A tendency to separate the sinful from saved. This can be manifested physically but also metaphorically, via dress code, rituals, hierarchy, etc.
3. Charismatic authoritarian leadership: The typical form of fundamentalist organization is charismatic, a leader-follower relationship in which the follower ascribes extraordinary qualities, heavenly grace, special access to

the deity, complete understanding of sacred texts to the great rathe rabbi, the imam, the virtuous jurist, the minister. One man is set apart from others (p. 98).

4. Mandated behavioral requirements: Members' time, space, and activities are considered to be *group*, rather than individual, resources. "Elaborate behavioral requirements create a powerful affective dimension, an imitative, conforming dimension. This function is closely related to the boundary-setting function of the enclave" (p. 98).

Additionally, five ideological characteristics of fundamentalism were identified.

Ideological Characteristics of Fundamentalism

- Reactivity to the marginalization of religion
- Selectivity (from religion, from modernity, focused opposition)
- Moral Manichaeism (i.e. good vs. evil)
- Absolutism and inerrancy of religious sources
- Millennialism and messianism (i.e. a "miraculous culmination" to history)

1. Reactivity to the Marginalization of Religion

The shadow is a moral problem that challenges the whole ego-personality, for no one can become conscious of the shadow without considerable moral effort. To become conscious of it involves recognizing the dark aspects of the personality as present and real (Jung, 1951b, [CW 9ii, p. 8]).

The first finding of the Fundamentalism Project is that fundamentalism is almost always *reactive*. It is a reaction *to* and a defense *against* the processes and consequences of perceived secularization. Fundamentalists are led to believe that their *true religion* will become debased and impure when faced with new, modern changes and forces. Thus, one of the core values of the fundamentalist movement involves the defense of one's religion, according to Marty (as cited in Almond, Appleby, & Sivan, 2003). The movement reacts to the feared annihilation of their basic principles by opposing the new and exploiting it for their own aims.

2. Selectivity of ideas and ideologies

At the same time, fundamentalism specializes in what we call cherry picking. Fundamentalism is *selective* in three ways:

1) Some perspectives of religious tradition are defended, while others are reshaped, especially those traditions that distinguish their view from mainstream ideology.

2) Some features of modernity are accepted, such as technology, medical views, and the Constitution.

3) Certain texts and ideas are selected to match issues that are in agreement with the fundamentalist's philosophy, and contradictory texts and ideas are opposed.

For example, some biblical stories are selected to support opposition against homosexuality, but stories or theological teachings that may refer to evolution are excluded. Certain aspects of modernity are excluded as well, such as opposition to legal abortions. Other examples can be cited like the willingness of some fundamentalists to accept the authority of the United States Constitution with its proclamations of equality for all, while opposing same-sex couples from marrying. Such adherents are able to ignore the Constitutional mandates regarding the separation of church and state insisting that the document was written with the intent to enshrine and give primacy to a particular religious view, most often a Christian worldview.

The mind naturally strives to preserve the *status quo,* and reactivity and selectivity provide the means to accomplish this. Defenses are most strongly applied where the *dark,* unconscious part of the Self assumes autocratic governance. Similar to the tale of Sleeping Beauty, it is the *omitted* twelfth fairy that puts the princess and the whole kingdom to sleep for a hundred years. It is the omitted unconscious aspects of the Self that keeps a person asleep psychologically.

Religio Means Reconnecting

In normal development, the fragmenting force of the Self counters this (sleeping) tendency. The Self, through its numinous affect, challenges the ego, permeates its walls, and if the ego is able to consciously tolerate the energies, endeavors to re-integrate the missing part(s) of the Self.

A patient of mine (G.J.D.), Michael, was on the threshold of encountering a psychospiritual awakening (return of the repressed) that coincided with the development of a new relationship. During the initial phase of the relationship he had the following dream:

> I am at a large construction company yard. There are many construction vehicles around: trucks, tractors and earthmovers parked in the yard. I am in a small wooden makeshift structure studying blueprints and showing them to a small boy about 8 years old. All of a sudden water begins to flood the yard and then totally submerges the small structure. I am scared. I go over to one of the windows with the boy and press up against it – the structure is strong enough to safely hold the boy and I.

The dream reassured the analysand and me that he could successfully undergo the numinous surge of energies from the Self for transformation and individuation. The new powerful relationship in this analysand's life represented a strong thrust toward individuation, which involved breaking up the old psychological status quo and structure in order to foster the potential for transformation heralding a new level of development.

It is essentially a process of self-knowledge, because the inner *Other* is found within; in the dream above—parts of the boy/Self. The term "knowledge" as used here does not designate mere intellectual knowledge, but the *real* knowledge of the heart—that is love. Meister Eckhart said: "The eye through which I see God is the same eye through which God sees me; my eye and God's eye are one eye, one seeing, one knowing, one love" (Sermons of Meister Eckhart, No: 22).

Difficult decisions of devotion and sacrifice are not made for the reasons that they make practical sense, but because of the depth of feeling associated with a call. Once I (V.Š.) visited a Roma village in eastern Slovakia. It was a very poor village where a 30-year-old mother lived with her 13 children in a dilapidated homemade of clay and hay. There was no electricity or sewer system. But in the village, I happened to meet a Swiss woman who built a house and lived there half of the year ceaselessly helping villagers. She devoted her life to this village and believed that she could make a difference.

Without access to archetypal sources humans would be little more than machines, but the mystery of archetypal wisdom makes us spiritual beings. Thus religion works to transform a personality from within by its persuasiveness and, at the same time, healing touch. Religion is re-remembering (re-connecting, *re-ligio*) of something that works, and works for the right reason! This ability to produce and to be efficacious makes change real. The Self can soften and transform complexes if the ego adopts a humble and loving attitude. Devotion, prayer, and forms of meditation are refined spiritual techniques for opening a person to the possibility of change. Vedic traditions discovered the power of meditation 4,000 years ago. It has been argued that the inexhaustible thirst for connection with the greatest mystery of life is instinctive. Human beings may choose whether or not to heed this call, and this gives the enterprise a powerfully spiritual dimension. Without the inherent duality of virtually everything the human mind encounters, spirituality might become less of a quest and more of a simple working out of formulae, merely a set of actions that are prescribed and proscribed like rules in a computer program. Transformation of the individual is rooted in the tension produced by the inherent duality, the tension between opposites—*complexio oppositorum*.

Through it all, we do well to take heed of Shakespeare's words, "All's well that ends well."

We cannot eliminate evil in part because we cannot fully know evil. It seems evil is not only inherent, to the psyche that dichotomizes everything it encounters—good requires there to be evil—it also seems that evil is necessary for the real awareness and recognition of good to be possible. The harmony and symmetry that are inherent properties of the entire universe, on both the microcosmic and macrocosmic level, are deeply valued within the unconscious. We unwittingly seek visual harmony in the partner we chose, in the objects we surround ourselves with, and in most every phenomenon we encounter. It appears there are engrams in our psychological apparatus that cause us to evaluate a symmetrical arrangement of flowers and the deeply moving images of a Buddhist mandala as beautiful. Our very existence seems to depend on the flow of energy between opposite states like harmony and disharmony.

Edinger (1972) spoke about this [transformative process] in terms of basic mythopoetic imagery, which is represented in Christian iconography by the figures of Yahweh and Satan. Consider the biblical story of Job:

> Since Yahweh and Satan are working together they can be considered as two aspects of the same thing, i.e., the Self. Satan provides the initiative and dynamism to set up Job's ordeal and hence represents the urge to individuation, which must break up the psychological status quo in order to bring about a new level of development. The serpent played the same role for Adam and Eve in the Garden of Eden (p. 80).

The projection of absolutes on God creates suppression of the shadow, and, especially in monotheistic religions, it plays an important psychological role as it pertains to the problem of *privatio boni*. Jung considered Satan to be a natural and important psychic reality whose quality should be viewed without prejudice and rationalization. He said:

> The will to be different and contrary is characteristic of the devil, just as disobedience was the hallmark of original sin. These, as we have said, are the necessary conditions for the Creation and ought, therefore, to be included in the divine plan and—ultimately—in the divine realm. But the Christian definition of God as the summum bonum excludes the Evil One right from the start, despite the fact that in the Old Testament he was still one of the "sons of God" (Jung 1948b, [CW 11, [par. 252])

Later, Jung continued:

> For the same reasons I also criticize the dictum derived from the privatio boni, namely: "*Omne bonum a Deo, omne malum ab homine*" (Lat.: All good is from God, all evil is from man.); for then on the one hand man is deprived of the possibility of doing anything good, and on the other he is given the seductive power of doing evil (1948b, [CW 11, par. 458]).

It is clear that Jung considered this topic important and intended to open a dialogue despite great controversy. Many religions perpetuate beliefs that exclude any possibility of understanding a positive dimension to evil. One-sidedness based on the idealization of any religious message contributes to a religiously split phenomenon, and this is a hindrance to the process of individuation.

If psycho-spiritual development goes well, and one recognizes the nature of his or her own ambiguities and cultivates a relationship to them, one becomes more elastic, tolerant, accepting, and will be more inclined to integrate elements of the shadow. This is not possible when one-sidedness reigns like a dictator. Fundamentalist values provide tools for defensive maneuvers against change. Numinous experiences can generate fear or tremendum that can be very threatening. To live in the midst of perpetual and often enormous ambivalence is a bedrock of the everyday heroic journey that confronts every person. Life involves balancing one's walk on the edge of the abyss knowing that occasionally the courageous person may be swallowed mercilessly.

Idealization

Strong idealization of the object produces strong demonization in the shadow. The more somebody adheres to light, the more he or she fears the darkness. It is typical for fundamentalist communities to avoid teaching their members about the complexity of religious symbolism, the relativity of good and evil, the paradoxical nature of numinous experiences, and the personal responsibility to accept and work through their own shadow. Extreme idealization corresponds to identification with the *fascinans* of the numinosum. The real fear of the *tremendum* is split-off and rationalized through well-crafted mythologies of convenience.

Reality of Death

For example, in the mind of the strongly religious person, death ceases to be a real finality of existence. Death is understood as a temporary transition on the way to eternal life. This creates many sources of psychological complications. Such expedient compromises that the ego makes in order to fend off more nuanced, uncertain, and ambivalent alternatives tends to exert a deadening effect on the ego through identification with the Self (as in the myth of Narcissus). Apart from the possibility of immortality through technological advances, death remains an indisputable and unavoidable outcome for every human being. The fear of death is anchored in physical reality, while immortality is anchored in the archetypal realm and it should be understood as such. The fundamentalists tend to overvalue the immortal, archetypal realms even at the expense of reality. It is as childish as it is dangerous to rely too heavily on this attitude. The unconscious fear of death and the fear of progression toward death can produce a *psychic death* marked by an *absence of feelings and affective relatedness* as to produce a cynical, vulgar disregard for life. Fundamentalists who become intoxicated and fascinated with the promise of immortality rooted in identification with the Self, may end up vulnerable to sacrificing their own life, which is absurdly the very result that immortality promises to cure.

> During an interview with a Hamas activist Muhammad Abu Wardeh, who recruited terrorists for suicide bombings in Israel, was quoted as saying: "I described to him how God would compensate the martyr for sacrificing his life for his land. If you become a martyr, God will give you 70 virgins, 70 wives and everlasting happiness.[170]

Acceptance of death paradoxically sustains life. Jung, in his essay *On the Tibetan Book of the Dead* (1954b, [CW 11, par. 759]; *Bardo Thödol*, 800 A.D.), when talking about the psychological world "beyond" death, in the Eleusinian initiation of the living, states:

> In the initiation of the living, however, this "Beyond" is not a world beyond death, but a reversal of the mind's intentions and outlook, a psychological "Beyond" or, in Christian terms, a "redemption" from the trammels of the world and of sin. Redemption is a separation and deliverance from an earlier condition of darkness and unconsciousness, and leads to a condition of illumination and releasedness, to victory and transcendence over everything "given" (1954b [CW 11, para. 841]).

Obsessive Need For Control Stems From Distorted Self-Awareness

Fundamentalists are very careful and selective to choose values that allow them to maintain the status quo and they reject the things that would challenge or be detrimental to their ideology; yet, the very things they reject are precisely what would allow for a possible integration of the shadow. As a result, the opposites break apart in the unconscious, which leads to

[170] https://www.theguardian.com/books/2002/jan/12/books.guardianreview5

dogmatization of the fundamentalist's position. In this respect, members of radical religious communities are traumatized because they are denied conscious access to the negative side of their own personality, and with that, access to a whole experience of the numinosum. This does not eliminate the negative dimensions relegated to the shadow, they simply becomes inaccessible. This is very conspicuous in children of fundamentalist religious leaders. These children are forced to carry the split-off parts to which their parents have lost access. Beneath the shiny, magnetic, charismatic persona, there often looms the shadow of a punitive, oppressive, and controlling figure. That shadow is anxiously kept hidden—something that becomes necessary to prevent interference with the perceived values. A child reared in such an atmosphere cannot admit that he or she is unhappy—they must preserve the illusion of happiness and contentment. Parents in this configuration remain controlling because anything else would require the parents to relinquish control. Controlling parents, driven by deep unconscious feelings of inadequacy, succumb to the belief that they can perfect their children by more effective control over them. On the conscious level, this may lead to strict adherence to *"good values,"* but what is less apparent is that the values serve the parents' need to strive for perfection. When parents fail to achieve such perfection themselves, these idealized elements are projected onto the child; in essence the child simply becomes a self-object for the parent and their individuation is lost. The child is only permitted to manifest the elements of the idealized pole. The hubris of this idea that perfection can be fashioned in the child is obvious. The fact remains that the way toward deeper self-knowledge is through one's own dark, unknown interior landscape, not around it. As Corbett reminds us, the path is through our very woundedness. Any strong encounter with the other side of the split, might feel like, or, actually produce, a crisis of faith. Corbett (1996) explained why the numinosum evokes such fear:

> This is so because numinous experience is precisely relevant to our pathology, our selfobject needs and our

> areas of woundedness. These are just the places that the archetype tries to enter the personality for the purposes of restructuring and healing (p. 30).

Black Swan

In the 2010 movie, *Black Swan,* the protagonist's mother is central to development of the ballerina's shadowy character development. Nina's mother viewed herself as a very caring, gracious, and concerned parent. However, behind the caring façade lurked the shadow of a devouring, suffocating mother who needed to keep her daughter trapped in a dynamic that mimicked Nina's early childhood. Nina's mother, Erica, a former ballerina who failed to attain what Nina has achieved, lives vicariously through her daughter. Interestingly, Erica paints demonic images of herself, perhaps in an effort to come to terms with her own dark, unacknowledged energies. However, these creative attempts do not suffice to break through Erica's obsessive defenses. The daughter unconsciously identifies with her mother's failed career and attempts neurotically to be the imagined "idealized" dancer that mother abandoned when she became pregnant with Nina. All of these dynamics are powerful shadow enactments in both characters. Nina's ego position as the *good daughter* must be destroyed for her to claim her own passion for dancing. If her mother had been able to look at her own dark side and acknowledge her own shadow rather than projecting the split-off idealized side upon her daughter, she might have been able to let go of the control she wielded over her daughter. Instead, she invests in preserving her conscious self-image of the all-good *mother.* She remains unconsciously attached to her ego-ideal and outwardly enmeshed with her daughter. This leads, ultimately, to the demise of her daughter. However, it was precisely Erica's wounding of Nina that might have provided Erica needed access to her own dark side and, thus, the healing power of the numinosum.

I Must Be Good If My Ideals Are Good

In religious fundamentalism, this process of idealization and unconscious identification is amplified by the worship of the image of the exclusively good God. This becomes a form of idolatry of the positive *Imago Dei*, at the expense of the dark side and thus stands the all-too-human ego bathed only in the light of the *Summum Bonum*. In this scenario, a person can all too easily hide behind the supremely good God in order to perpetuate a delusion of goodness even if that does not concur with their objective actions but coincides with a subjective feeling of identity. With the highest amount of libido accumulated "behind" the Self (*Imago Dei*), this position of identification is psychologically justified and vigorously defended in the mind. Such a person is prone to think: "God is talking directly to me, so how can I change? I cannot betray God! Therefore, all of you are wrong, and I am right." We refer to this type of specific religious inflation by the Self as a *Theocalypsis,* or a hiding behind God.

Reactivity Is a Response to One's Own Shadow

Reactivity is a defensive reaction against the projected shadow. Anything that is split-off becomes compensated by its opposite, and the fundamentalist will project that onto infidels, non-believers and the like. This process not only allows the fundamentalist to preserve his or her untainted self-image; it also allows a release of accumulated psychic energy created by the sharp gradient between the split-polarized numinosum. Enemies end up carrying shadow projections and are labeled with various negative monikers like evildoers, Nazis, and bigots, a particularly ironic moniker in light of the definition of bigot.[171]

---

[171] Bigot: from French *bigot*, "a religious hypocrite." "A person obstinately or intolerantly devoted to his or her own opinions and prejudices; especially: one who regards or treats the members of a group (as a racial or ethnic group) with hatred and intolerance" (Merriam-Webster Dic. 2010, p. 1).

Modern secular society is the unacceptable Other for the fundamentalist, since secular society appears to engage and uncover themes that the fundamentalist keeps locked away under a heavy shroud of untouchable dogmas. Science, atheism, ethical relativism, philosophical plurality, liberalization of sexuality, feminine empowerment, and the recognition of doubt and uncertainty, are frightening to the person devoted to a fundamentalist posture. While the fundamentalist's fear may appear to drive out the elements of the other side of the polarity, that polarity remains as an unconscious fixture in the fundamentalist's psychology. Main (2006) offered an explanation as to why fundamentalist movements react so vigorously against secular society and why they form enclave cultures to create their untainted center. According to Main:

> Fundamentalist movements typically retreat into what has been called an "enclave culture" within whose secure confines religion can be practiced with maximum purity [Almond, Appleby, & Sivan, 2003: 23-89]. It is often only later that such movements launch their counter-offensiveness against the secular or compromised cultures surrounding them [Armstrong, 2001: xi]. The motivation for such counter-offensiveness may be not only the increasing threat to survival of the enclave and its values from external sources but also the *intolerability of the divine darkness and ambiguity that have been accessed by the religious intensity of the group itself, which exerts an overwhelming pressure to be discharged* (p. 161, author's emphasis).

Main concluded that:

> The more deadly manifestation of religious extremism may be a kind of *return* of the repressed of this dark side of God, designated by Otto's tremendum. (p. 162, emphasis added).

Reactivity and selectivity of religious radicalism is, therefore, directly proportional to the intensity of the "ominous cloudiness" on the ego by the one-sided *Imago Dei*.

3. Moral Manichæism[172]

The shadow is a moral problem that challenges the whole ego-personality, for no one can become conscious of the shadow without considerable moral effort. To become conscious of it involves recognizing the dark aspects of the personality as present and real. This act is the essential condition for any kind of self-knowledge (Jung, 1951b, [CW 9ii, para. 14] added emphasis).

If one identifies with the fascinans and believes oneself part of the saved remnant of humanity, while tremendum is projected onto one's opponents, believe them to be different from oneself at the most fundamental eschatological level, and treat them as worthless and therefore legitimate targets for hostile action (Main, 2006, p. 164)

Fundamentalism's worldview is based on the premise that there is absolute good and absolute evil, absolute right and absolute wrong. And there is a belief that ultimately light will triumph over darkness. Furthermore, fundamentalists believe that they are chosen to live within the pure and redeemed world, while others are sinners/infidels who are doomed to face God's punishment. The sinful world "outside" is graded in varying degrees of contamination with evil (Almond, Appleby, & Sivan, 2003). Closer to the fundamentalist center is the greater guarantee that good is present.

We have discussed earlier how the ego's identification with archetypes distorts one's perception. In that case, the perceived world is filtered through the reality of the mythological level of the psyche. That which is inside is also outside. If the illusion of

[172] Manichæism is a religion founded by the Persian prophet Mani during the third century. It purported to be the synthesis of all the religious systems then known (Zoroastrian Dualism, Babylonian folklore, Buddhism and some of the Christian elements). Manichæism is the [Gnostic] theory of the battle between two primeval principles, good and evil, illustrated in The Fundamentalism Project (1991-95). (authors)

one's own perception predominates, the whole world is arranged accordingly. The ability to recognize the source of this illusion—ego attachment to archetypes and complexes that are both personal and cultural—is therefore a crucial spiritual task. Jung noted this in his famous statement: The one "who looks outside, dreams; who looks inside, awakes," (Letter I., p. 33). The ego has its roots in the unconscious that shape and inform its perceptions, but those roots are not conscious. An essential task of ego-consciousness is to permit the inner world to guide and assist the adaptation to the outer world without falling back into the unconscious and embracing a one-sided perspective. The ego maintains balance by dwelling in the in-between psychic regions. Greek mythology recognized that archetypal ideas can be extremely attractive and seductive. The capacity to resist the lure of the archetypal realm is dependent on developing a mature spiritual consciousness. Jung (1954b) said:

> The ego keeps its integrity only if it does not identify with one of the opposites, and if it understands how to hold the *balance* between them. This is possible only if it remains conscious of both at once ... Even if it were a question of some great truth, identification with it would still be a catastrophe, as it *arrests* all further spiritual development, (p.219, emphasis added).

Loss of Soul

What are the implications of giving into one pole of the archetype? One example would be when Odysseus is stranded on the Island of Ogygia where Calypso seduces him. In Homer's opus *Iliad and Odyssey*, (about 840 B.C.) Odysseus forgot about his journey and his wife, Penelope, and being bewitched by archetypal energy, he believed for some time that he had become immortal. In the thinking of the ancient Greeks, immortality was actually conceived as a death. Thus we might say that psychologically, the soul of Odysseus was dead for seven years, or at least laid dormant.

If the ego does not hold its position between the designated opposites, but identifies with the unconscious image, it begins thinking and feeling archaically. Jung stated:

> When one is identified with an archetypal image the perceived world gains archetypal dimensions. Archaism attaches primarily to the fantasies of the unconscious, i.e., to the products of unconscious fantasy activity which reaches consciousness. An image has an archaic quality when it possesses unmistakable *mythological parallels* (1921b, [CW 6, para. 684] emphasis added).

This is typical for religious possession resulting from identification with the Self. It is very important to note here that the world of the fundamentalists is conceived in terms of archetypal imagery and terminology. Their adversaries are often literally considered possessed by [objective] evil—often given the names of the devil—and correspondingly, they perceive themselves as heroic agents of [objective] justice—God's agents and messengers. This phenomenon can be described as: confusing frames of reference. The ego identified with parts of the collective unconscious, assumes the archetypal goal as its own mission without *distilling* the symbolic message. Descending into the unconscious, the ego forgets that it needs to act within the frame of reference belonging to it that is governed by the reality principle. Without a frame based on reality, the ego starts to live the life of the archetypes, acting and thinking in magical ways. The ego becomes blinded by the power of the archetype forgetting its own circumscribed identity, so to speak. And, as we have noted, identification with the Self produces distortions of reality. It is only through realizing and acting in both worlds at the same time—the archetypal and the one ruled by the reality principle—that the ego can be free. In Hindu philosophy, Maya veils the true Self (Brahman). The ego falls for this illusion if it does not distinguish between itself (its own perception; e.g., it's own *Imago Dei*) and its source (the Self). In *Bhagavad Gita* we read:

> Wherever a being is born, whether unmoving or moving, know that Arjuna, as born from the union between the field and the knower of the field. (...) This body, O Arjuna,

> is called the Field; he who knows it is called the Knower of the Field by those who know of them, that is, by the sages. Do thou also know Me as the Knower of the Field in all fields, O Arjuna! Knowledge of both the Field and the Knower of the Field is considered by Me to be *the* knowledge (by Swami Sivananda, Chapter 13, p. 100).

William James documented that profound mystical experience that occur spontaneously or emerge during meditation or prayer, can be distinguished by their purely positive tone. Visions of brilliant light or intuitive experiences of deep truths, or profound meaning are not uncommon during religious practices. These experiences often lead to belief in a supremely good, transcendent entity (God). The obvious question for the analyst is, what happened to the negative aspect of the numinosum? Like falling in love, these profound experiences are similar to an altered state of consciousness. The initial magical and enchanting period is extremely idealistic and alluring but it never endures at the same level of intensity as the more mundane, everyday aspects of reality begin to return to consciousness. Likewise, sooner or later unconscious elements gain ascendancy and weaken or dissolve the blissful experience of perfect union. One cannot grow without confronting the element of real suffering. Jung famously said, "One does not become enlightened by imagining figures of light, but by making the darkness conscious." (Jung, CW 13, 1967:265, par. 335) The greater the unconscious attachment, the more intensely the ego is blindsided by the shadow. Love matures and deepens by embracing and integrating shadow rather than staying in the light. Whether we consider Buddha's teaching of the Noble Truths or Jesus's taking up his cross, there always is suffering. The Self can only serve us as a compass, while the ego has to navigate the stormy waters of everyday reality. The Knowledge or Unity, *Unio Mystica*, that is described by the mystical traditions does not refer to a complete and permanent immersion into the archetypal world, but immersion in the paradoxical experience of duality when ego experiences itself as a Self and, at the same time, as observer.

Complete or permanent possession by the Self results in the loss of the objective observer. In those extreme cases, especially where a person has a fragile or vulnerable ego structure, the person may truly think he or she has divine attributes (e.g., omniscience, omnipotence, etc.) and even that s/he *is* God. This inflation is also typical in some forms of schizophrenia as well as intoxicated states using psychedelics or hallucinogenic agents. This type of thinking is clearly a radical confusion between the ego and the archetypal frames of reference. This is why the Bhagavad Gita teaches the importance of knowing both: the Field and the Knower of the field.

In the Bible, *Joshua 10*, we find the story of Joshua praying to the Lord to stop the moon and sun in order to give him time to finish fighting the Amorites:

> At that time Joshua spoke to the Lord in the day when the Lord gave the Amorites over to the sons of Israel, and he said in the sight of Israel, "Sun, stand still at Gibeon, and moon, in the Valley of Aijalon." And the sun stood still, and the moon stopped, until the nation took vengeance on their enemies. Is this not written in the Book of Jashar? The sun stopped in the midst of heaven and did not hurry to set for about a whole day. There has been no day like it before or since, when the Lord heeded the voice of a man, for the Lord fought for Israel. So Joshua returned, and all Israel with him, to the camp at Gilgal (Joshua 10:12, English Standard Version).

If the Earth really stopped rotating, the Earth would have to slow from 1,100 miles per hour to a complete stop in less than 24 hours. In this situation, everything that is not tied down, including people, would continue moving in the direction of the Earth's rotation at the speed of 1,100 miles per hour at the equator. To take this story literally and concretely, onw would have to accept a miracle of enormous complexity. One would have to accept a God who operates outside of natural law. Further, this God would be acting arbitrarily in his choice with respect to the people for whom he would grant such a favor. This would also have enormous implications for the power and effectiveness of prayer. Religious scriptures are full of miraculous stories. One can accept them at face value—as if they are literal—or one can accept them as symbolic expressions of something equally important in the realm of psycho-spiritual reality. The symbolic understanding has a more grounded bearing for it calls upon one's responsibility based on insight and understanding of the implications of one's psychological and spiritual life. Great philosophical questions concerning life after death, freedom of will, and the existence of God are irresolvable mysteries within one frame of reference, but they can be absolute certainties in other frames of reference. The task of consciousness is to preserve the best possible relationship between the rational and irrational, the concrete and abstract, the literal and the symbolic and so on.

Inflation by the Self

When the ego is inflated by the Archetype of the Self, some functions of the ego are connected to the reality principle and other sectors harbor grandiose persuasions based on archetypal imagery (*Imago Dei*) and emotion. Typical with this type of inflation, one feels with great excess, indestructible (protected by God), absolutely justified (having God's mandate) in his or her action, and free from psychological shadow (being supremely good). We termed this type of inflation theocalypsis and will talk more about this concept later in this book.

Bipolar Complex

Manicheistic divisiveness is the psychological expression of the process first described by Perry (1970). He introduced the idea of the *bipolarity* of the complex in his seminal paper on complex theory. Perry wrote about the everyday ego as being different from the ego that is possessed by a complex in the Jungian sense of the word. Anytime there is an activation of a complex, one half of its bipolar property, affect and perception, takes hold of the ego and contributes to what Perry calls "the affect-ego." The opposite part of the bipolar complex is projected onto the object—usually toward someone with whom one is caught in a complex dynamic, who then become what Perry calls an "affect-object." The affect object represents the unconscious part of the subject's own personality (p. 3). As Jung (1948b) noted, all projections provoke *counterprojections* when the object is equally unconscious of the quality projected upon it by the subject, so the highly charged and affective interaction between the parties involved (affect ego vs. affect object) ensues. Singer and Kimbles (2004):

> "This bipolarity of the complex leads to an endless round of repetitive skirmishes with the illusory other – who may or may not fit the bill perfectly" (p. 20).

We can see this example with many individual conflicts, but also in cultural conflicts involving broader social disagreements. The division between the so-called East and West or the Muslim and non-Muslim world is derived from their culturally based shadowy projections onto each other. Consequently, the opposing side often demonizes that which is culturally suppressed and hence unconscious. Singer (2009) gave the following example:

> George Bush made a slip of the cultural unconscious when he first referred to a "crusade" as the American response to the World Trade Center and Pentagon bombings. Bush's slip was reflexive and automatic, backed up by a centuries-old memory. A crusade is the West's cultural complex answer to a holy jihad or vice versa (p. 6).

Likewise, Jung (1948b) stated:

> "The more clearly the archetype is constellated, the more powerful will be its fascination, and the resultant religious statements will *formulate* it accordingly, as something 'daemonic' or 'divine'" (Jung 1948b, [CW 11, para. 223] emphasis added).

Archetypal Excitement

The phenomenon of bipolarity applies not only to every personal complex and cultural complex, but also to archetypes.

From the ego's perspective the archetypes have positive and negative poles. Archetypes manifest their opposites via feeling-tones whose value is assigned by the ego and the actions they produce. A mother's love can be very positive, but when it is excessive, it can hinder her child's development. We recognize this motif in the Mother Goddess Demeter in her nurturing and devouring qualities. Again, the positivity and negativity are only relative categories determined largely by personal and cultural norms. The human ego, through its discriminating function, assigns a good or bad valence to experiences. The degree of conscious awareness of the process of assigning a negative or positive valence can shape the ego's later capacity to integrate things into consciousness. Depression, for example, can be personally experienced as very negative, but from the teleological standpoint can be viewed as a positive process or moment in one's individuation. Jung has clearly shown that neurosis can often serve as a means to higher level of development and individuation that could not happen any other way. By unifying negative and positive elements (experiences) an individual is able to "extract" greater meaning from life.

Because our perspective represents the perspective of the subjective observer, *exempli gratia*, we can state that every archetype produces various degrees of the numinosum: distinguished mostly by the polarity of its manifestation. It has been stated that *tremendum* and *fascinans* are naturally opposing properties of the archetype. The unconscious part of the pair is the part that becomes capable of possessing the ego. Compaan (2007) described the possession by the archetype in terms of the affective influence on the ego as "divine/archetypal excitement." Archetypal excitement only happens when the ego is not fully present (by its reflection), and therefore, unconscious (reflexive) power takes over. He said:

> When so possessed, the ego senses little danger in the new and the unknown. Consequently the individual moves without hesitation into the exploration of the wonderful world out there, much as the unknowing child easily ventures away from mother until encountering

> the experiences of fragmentation in the face of the wholly other. This is a position of shamelessness, of inadequate shame. Shame affect is not available to assist in the modulation of the excited feelings. Rather the person is possessed, driven by this energy. Clinically it appears as mania or, as Jung preferred, as a mana personality ... we may say that one aspect of analysis is working with those encounters with numinous archetypal energy where there has been a failure of adequate human mirroring of the unavoidable shame affect. Where the mirroring is inadequate, the result is that the individual becomes possessed by polarized affects, either dread/terror (*aischyne*) or excitement/interest (*hubris*). The transcendent function does not develop and the opposite affects are not held in tension. Aidos is not possible (pp. 6-8).

Fear of One's Own Profaneness

Main pointed out that the ability to hold the *wholly other* or the divine pair together decreases where there are high levels of *ambiguity* and *intensity* together (Main, 2006). This is typical for strongly religious communities because of the high idealization of [only one pole of] the numinosum and the subsequent suppression of its other (typically dark) side. Main goes on stating:

> Understanding such splitting and projection is especially helpful for... fundamentalism, where one projects onto others [the] terrible and damned (the *tremendum*) and identifies with the blissful and saved (the *fascinans*), either directly or by subordinating oneself to a charismatic leader onto whom miraculous redemptive knowledge and powers have been projected (p. 163).

According to Main the level of hostility is proportional to the amount of shadow (i.e., the suppressed of the part of numinosum):

> Hostility towards the godless of secular societies could be a horrified defence against and projection of the inability of the fundamentalists themselves to maintain a *credible* God Image (p. 165; emphasis added).

Religious fundamentalism is an expression of "ascendant secularity," to use Main's term. The profane and the sacred are a naturally existing pair and it seems more apparent in the modern era. Reconciliation cannot lie in submerging one of these aspects, but in establishing a new paradigm where both aspects of a paradox coexist and are recognized as valid and mutually complementary. He concluded:

> The very place where the inalienable but lost religiousness might be recovered is in the dual sacred *and* secular selves that are cancelling themselves out along with others (p. 165, emphasis added).

Commonly, the government may be the recipient of the fundamentalist's projections. Religious fanatics often aim their anger at the state and government officials, perceiving them as liberal or progressive, and decadent. For example, in U.S. politics the Religious Right vilify liberals in general and Democrats in particular for the secular values they embrace. Jared Loughner's shooting of US Representative Gabby Gifford in 2011 is an example of the escalation of the phenomenon of reactivity (and hostility)—it was a *righteous* act intended to punish or remove the unfaithful, the non-adherents, and the infidels.

Hostility is an outward expression of the alienation a person is suffering from his or her own shadow. Instead of recognizing the hostile emotions as originating in disowned, unacknowledged, elements within oneself, a person is simply aware of their hostile sentiments. In their inner dialogue, subjectively, the person explains even the worst act in a positive light. Active shooter might be feeling like a god while taking lives of other people. In his grandiose moment of killing he might be feeling triumphant, powerful and in complete control. Compassion and love is utterly split off in this God-possession delusion. The recent clash in Charlottesville, Virginia between white supremacists and counter-protesters seeking to stand up to the white supremacists in the summer of 2017 was an ugly display of how hostility can erupt when people become alienated from their own shadow-feelings. This phenomenon is easily amplified when a group and its members are subject to unconscious induction. Groups create an atmosphere of mutual understanding that evokes feelings of righteousness. French author Le Bon (1894) noted this phenomenon and element of mobocracy, which states that a mass soul regresses to the level of its most primitive member. For example, when a car plowed through a crowd of individuals assembled to oppose the white supremacist's assembly in Charlottesville, the same sort of fanaticism was on display in Nice, France one year earlier. The white supremacist and the ISIS supporter behind the wheel share quite a bit in common including a passionate belief that their mission was so righteous that it justified killing people who did not share their fanatical views but were otherwise innocent.

The Role of Cultural Complex In Fundamentalism

The group soul as a whole is gripped by the collective archetypal image, and the whole group tends to behave in *conformity* with the image. When Singer (2002) spoke about cultural complexes, he referred to the same process:

> Sometimes groups as a whole behave as if they are in the grip of a specific type of cultural complex. This type of cultural complex mobilizes in the group's behavior, emotion and life a defensive self-care system akin to that described in individuals by Kalsched. In the group version of the complex, however, the goal of the self-care, defensive system is the protection of the collective spirit, not the personal spirit. The Daimones are mobilized to protect the traumatized divine child or other symbolic carrier of the collective spirit of the group and can do so with a mixture of sheltering kindness and persecutory attack, which directed inwardly results in self-loathing and directed outwardly results in impenetrability and hostilities to other groups (p. 22).

Religious ideas and teachings of certain fundamentalist groups assume the archetypal/ mythological position of the collective spirit which often mirrors specific properties of the *Imago Dei* that accords with the group's ideology. A defense of this kind should, therefore, be conceived as archetypal. On a mythological level or within the archetypal frame of reference, such individuals and groups are not only protecting their own identities or collective identities, they are executing a divine plan.

The ability to deal with the archetypal influence of the Self requires moral effort. Overly religious identification with the Self creates powerful and seductive traps in which true morality is translated into submission to the archetypal powers.

4. Absolutism and Inerrancy

> *Religious statements are, however, never rational in the ordinary sense of the word, for they always take into consideration that other world, the world of the archetype, of which reasoning in the ordinary sense is unconscious, being occupied only with externals* (Jung 1948b, [CW 11, para. 222])

Fundamentalists believe that God does not only inspire their sacred scriptures but the texts are considered inerrant and indisputable. The fundamentals of a tradition are passed on through many vehicles, which the sacred texts are often central. Deviations from a strict interpretation of the sacred texts are tantamount to challenging the faith. Anything new, including new interpretations of the texts and scientific investigations, is judged as an unacceptable deviation from the truth. For example, on June 26, 2013, the U.S. Supreme Court struck down the 1996 law blocking federal recognition of gay marriages and allowed gay marriage to resume in California by declining to decide a separate case. The Supreme Court canceled the Defense of Marriage Act, which denied federal benefits to gay couples who are legally married in their states, including Social

Security survivor benefits, immigration rights and family leave, (MSNBC, 2013, p.1). This issue continues to be litigated and in a 2015 decision, Obergefell v. Hodges, the court held up a 5–4 decision that the fundamental right to marry is guaranteed to same-sex couples.

Michele Bachmann, a former member of the United States House of Representatives and a fundamentalist and outspoken Tea Party member, issued a statement shortly after the 2013 decision:

> Marriage was created by the hand of God. No man, not even a Supreme Court, can undo what a holy God has instituted. For thousands of years of recorded human history, no society has defended the legal standard of marriage as anything other than between man and woman. (New York Times, 2013, p. 1)

After the 2015 decision, Governor Mike Huckabee, an ordained minister and past presidential candidate, went so far as to question the authority of the court:

> The Supreme Court can no more repeal the laws of nature and nature's God on marriage than it can the law of gravity. Under our Constitution, the court cannot write a law, even though some cowardly politicians will wave the white flag and accept it without realizing that they are failing their sworn duty to reject abuses from the court (statement on June 26, 2015).

It might seem that conservative adherence to the inspired text and various religious doctrines comprises only a fraction of the population, but this may not be accurate. While in the United States there are estimates that upwards of 72% of the population believe the Bible is the Word of God, 40% of that group believe that the Bible should be interpreted literally. Nearly two-thirds assert that they are certain that Jesus Christ was resurrected, and three-fourths report that they maintain a belief in life after death. And almost 50% of the population believe that God created the world within the last thousand years (Marty & Appleby, 1991). It is important to distinguish between fundamentalism and religious conservatism. Conservatives are *softer* in their beliefs and do not share many of the strongly held core beliefs to which fundamentalists ascribe. Religious conservatives and fundamentalists share a great deal in common regarding how the ego deals with archetypal energies and images. If recent estimates that twenty percent of the population of the United States are fundamentalists, that is more than 60 million people. When the number of religiously conservative and deeply religious people are added to these numbers, the final tally is likely to be much higher. A survey of commonly held religious beliefs in America reveals that 60 percent of Americans are "absolutely sure" that heaven exist, 52 percent believe that there is life after death, and about 50 percent believe that hell exists (Putnam & Campbell, 2010).[173]

Call for Obama Certificate Billboard, Public domain, via Wikimedia Commons.

[173] Conspiracism could be viewed as fundamentalism *sui generis*. About 50% of American population believes in some kind of conspiracy theories. Some of them are truly bizarre and could be explained by possessions by unconscious contents. To mention a few: 25 percent believe in the "birther" conspiracy about president Obama, JFK conspiracy is endorsed by 50%, 19 percent believe in a conspiracy about 9/11 (that attack was orchestrated by US government), the theory that the FDA is deliberately withholding natural cures for cancer is endorsed by 40 percent, 20 percent believe that global warming is a hoax, and 4 percent believe that mutant lizards control politics. (*The Washington Post*, February, 2015 & *Public Policy Polling*, 2013)

Five Fundamentals from the 19th & 20th Centuries

The following five fundamental beliefs of Christian doctrine were identified in *The Fundamentals* (Niagara Bible Conference of 1878 and the 5-point statement of the Presbyterian General Assembly of 1910):

1. Biblical inerrancy – a doctrinal position claiming that Bible is absolutely accurate and free of errors.
2. The divinity of Jesus.
3. The virgin birth of Jesus (parthenogenesis).
4. The belief that Jesus died to redeem humankind.
5. An expectation of the Second Coming or physical return of Jesus Christ to initiate his thousand-year rule of the Earth, which is known as the Millennium.

Anytime there is a belief that a symbolic or psychological reality is concretistically factual, we are dealing with literalism. Literalism and concretism are symptoms of an unreflected unconscious.

In the fundamentalist worldview, the Virginity of Mary is taken literally as a physiological virginity; it does not allow the possibility of considering virginity symbolically. While the symbol of virginity denotes purity of soul, being without sin, innocence, it also points to the great psychic mysteries. However, an undue preoccupation with the literal notion of virginity often leads to the oppression of women within radical religious societies.

Because of its excessive one-sidedness, radical creed does not allow for the development of what Jung termed, the *transcendent function*, a natural psychological process that mediates between opposites. Essentially, the transcendent function enables each member of a pair of opposites to encounter one another on equal grounds and to express their distinct point of view without denying the opposite. By nature it is a force, "a manifestation of the energy that springs from the tension of opposites," (Jung 1943, [CW 7, para. 121]) that will only function and express itself where there is a true dialogue between ego-consciousness and the unconscious. Thus, when one consciously engages opposites, the transcendent function acts as a bridge or a link between the rational and the non-rational, thus creating a living symbolic relationship between the conscious and the unconscious. In the process of engaging and confronting one another, a third thing (i.e., symbol, attitude, metaphor), a new synthesis, which transcends time and conflict and which is capable of uniting the opposites, is created. Therefore, the worlds of consciousness and unconsciousness are intimately joined to form a greater whole. Jung considers the transcendent function to be one of the most significant factors in psychological transformation. It is important to note that Jung uses the word "transcendent" as expressive of the presence of a capacity or function to transcend the destructive tendency to identify with and be pulled to one side or the other of a polarity. The destructive tendency arising from an over-identification with a one-sided perspective is precisely what the mind of the fundamentalist does.

It is to be expected that a fundamentalist are prepared to spend more energy in disputing and challenging a perspective opposite to its conscious identification than would be required to embrace the opposite—that might lead to a more inclusive, charitable and divergent view. Literalism, as a psychological expression, also reflects a natural stage of cognitive development, which reflects a degree of separation between the ego and the collective unconscious. Naturally, for a child or archaic person (a so-called primitive person, an expression used in 19th and 20th Century in the West), the reflective function of consciousness is not yet fully developed, and therefore, everything is experienced as external, literal, and concrete. Jung says:

> Primitive thinking and feeling are entirely concretistic; they are always related to sensation. The thought of the primitive has no detached independence but clings to material phenomena. It rises at most to the level of analogy (1921b, [CW 6, para. 420]).

At this stage of development, outside objects are considered powerful and magical; but because of the strong unconscious identity, the differentiation between the ego and the other is not made. My friend, who visited indigenes tribes in Borneo, communicated that for them the biggest sources of fear were not wild animals or other tribes, but spirits and ghosts emerging after sunset. This would be an example of the phenomenon of "participation mystique;" which consists in the fact that the person cannot distinguish him or herself from a psychic object and hence is bound to it by a direct relationship —which amounts to partial identity. It is a natural phenomenon because it reflects the evolution and developmental (stages) of consciousness. Jung, elsewhere says:

> Everything that is unconscious in man is projected by him into an object situated outside his ego, so that the phenomenon of projection is a part of the natural life of the psyche, a part of human nature itself (1936/1954, [CW 9i, par. 142]).

However, the source of the projection, without critical self-awareness, often goes unrecognized. Here there will be an acknowledgement of a subjective dimension to powerful spiritual experiences—everything is experienced as though it has divine origins and therefore demands to be treated as sacred. Intense spiritual experiences are external to the ego. This is true with the radically religious person, but there is a crucial difference concerning the origination of the experience. The extremely religious person acts *as if* the powerful spiritual experience was literally and concretely present because they believe things ought to be that way. This little epistemological trick allows fundamentalists to navigate this reality quite well. It allows them to have a "dual mind" and be selective of which aspects of reality are allowed to be magic and which are not. Children are learning to make these distinctions during their early cognitive development. In Wisconsin, in 2012, two twelve-year-old girls lured their friend into the woods and stabbed her nineteen times as part of a sacrifice to Slenderman, a fictional horror character whose existence arose on the Internet. They reported to police that they simply "believed he was real," and wanted to please him. Is it possible that the young girls got caught in the literal stage of development and not able to access or think symbolically? This type of thinking and reasoning is typical for the fundamentalists where the symbolic is collapsed into the concrete and literal interpretation.

Fowler (1976) observed such thinking in children and called it the *Mythic-Literal Faith stage*. He wrote:

> The gift of this stage is narrative. The child now can really form and re-tell powerful stories that grasp his or her experiences of meaning. There is a quality of literalness about this. The child is not yet ready to step outside the stories and reflect upon their meanings. The child takes symbols and myths at pretty much face value, though they may touch or move him or her at a deeper level (p. 36).

Fowler noted that the child is "trapped" in his or her own narrative. It is a well-chosen expression because projections basically isolate the subject from the environment. They create an illusory world of the *Other,* and in so doing, they omit their own intersubjectivity as an equally real aspect that co-creates reality. Jung puts it:

> "Projections change the world into the replica of one's own unknown face" (1951b, [CW 9ii, para. 17).

Projection is *de facto,* a process of dissimilation, by which the unconscious becomes alienated from the subject (ego) and is, so to speak, embodied in the object, (See Jung 1921, [CW 6, para. 783]). And with that comes a moral albinism because if everything, light or dark, is considered to be outside, the locus of responsibility is also outside. The object becomes contaminated by the unconscious, and because of the lack of a reflective distance, (i.e., consciousness), it results in possession and consequently literalism and externalism, which are logical antinomies of morality! The projection of moral authority outside the soul keeps "all God outside," to use Eckhart's (1320) expression. Further, it robs the soul of its vitality and thus denies ego the uncontaminated experience of the numinous dimension of the psyche and the sacredness of the world itself. So, if God is viewed as totally outside the human person, then so are evil and the devil. If that is the case, then how can self-knowledge result in moral improvement? Dourley (2006) puts it this way:

> With theologians or not, the consequence of externalism is to empty consciousness of the soul's sense of its natural relationship to God without which no humanizing connection with the divine could eventuate (p. 12).

One can only escape from the trap of one's own narrative, when the realization that God speaks from within the soul, becomes an obvious truth. It moves the soul from the state of embodiment to moral responsibility. The fundamentalists' approach lacks precision and is reduced to an attempt to please or avoid angering the seemingly arbitrary forces that are responsible for imposing good nd evil on the world. The fundamentalist mind does not concern itself with the symbolic dimension of biblical texts; therefore, it misses one of the most important dimensions of spirituality: the relative *sovereignty of* moral decisions. The fundamentalist's modus operandi imitates —in lieu of refining the true gold that is uncovered through the symbolic life. A symbol is true gold if it connects the inner and outer in a meaningful way. Such gold brings real spiritual prosperity in the form of wisdom and love. *"Aurum nostrum non est aurum vulgi"*—our gold is not an ordinary gold, reads the secret rule of alchemy. Dourley later stated:

> The spiritually debilitating consequences of externalism are tragically apparent in the related pathology of historicism. In its Christian variant, historicism reduces the figure of Christ to a past historical figure and not a present psychic force. The imitation of Christ becomes the slavish reproduction in the individual's life of the details of a past life instead of the ongoing rhythm of archetypal death and resurrection in the now of psychic life (p. 12).

Atheism Can Serve as a Defense Against The Numinosum

Some [atheist] critics of religion, such as Sam Harris (2005), Lawrence Krauss (2013) or Richard Dawkins (2006), criticize religious worship on the same basis that fundamentalists adhere to it.

Haught (2008) argued:

> Both scientific and religious literalists share the belief that there is nothing beneath the surface of the texts they are reading—nature in the case of science, sacred scriptures in the case of religion (p. 30).[174]

The atheist and the fundamentalist rely on a literal understanding and therefore miss the symbolic message of religion. They are caught in the same predicament and problem of concretism; they just happen to focus on the opposite aspect of it. While being possessed by the numinosum marks the fundamentalist attitude, along with an uncritical adherence to an *Imago Dei* defined for their specific purpose, those who criticize religion based on the absurdity of symbols are excluding the *Imago Dei* perhaps due to their failure to access their own inner world. The atheist can be caught in his or her own material narrative of the world (See Casement, 2008). An atheistic position, by excluding the numinosum as a legitimate, autonomous source of transcendence for the ego, displays a high degree of one-sidedness like the fundamentalist they seek to dispute. The scientific attitude may impart flexibility and openness to the unknown that is better aligned with spirituality than what the fundamentalist approach permits, though an excessive adherence to a scientific perspective risks throwing out the baby with the bathwater. It will prove shortsighted to discard the powerfully symbolic spiritual experiences entirely. Though many atheists assail fundamentalist religion as infantile, they too may come up short in attaining to the maturity of a religion that can hold the numinous and the material interpretations in dialogic tension. The scientific mind may not acknowledge that religion emerges from the inherent reality of the psyche in ways that are similar to the way natural laws emerge within the physical, material world. Instead, they see it as sort of atavism pertaining to an undeveloped individual lacking in *sober* rationality. They criticize the need for a Creator-

---

[174] Haught, J. F. (2008), *God and the new atheism: A critical response to Dawkins, Harris, and Hitchens* (1st edition), Louisville, KY: Westminster John Knox Press.

God, something that affronts their own beliefs. In some respects, certain scientific constructs associated with quantum mechanics, theories of multiverses, and string theory are essentially mythology presenting themselves as products of pure reason. Many atheists hubristically rationalize the spirit of the numinosum by applying so called scientific knowledge to the phenomenon. But they omit the fact that science is a tool for approaching, not explaining the mystery. Science has made little progress in explaining what consciousness is and how it works from a purely materialistic perspective and even less progress regarding the vast unknown of the unconscious (See: *The Ghost in the Machine*, Koestler, 1967; *The Problem of Consciousness,* McGinn, 1991). Some mysteries may remain essentially unsolvable and are best approached through myth and symbol. Jung's new myth and Edinger's new dispensation address these questions.

Organic Unity of Conscious and Unconscious

When human decision-making is vested in any outside authority, people stand to lose their natural autonomy and freedom. People embedded in concretistic worldviews unwittingly forfeit their autonomy and decision making power to the authority of the unconscious. By seeking balance between the opposing polarities, including the connection between the conscious and unconscious realms, rather than excluding or projecting outwardly one or the other poles, one secures freedom and avoids subjugation to outside authorities (See Dourley, 2004).[175] Jung repeatedly cautioned against the *blind* following of the unconscious as if it was the only source of supreme wisdom per se. The unconscious is just as amoral as the Greek gods. The unconscious provides a reference for

[175] Dourley (2004) said: "Jung denies that divinity should be conceived as an 'absolute' somehow beyond the human. Rather the divine and the human should be imagined as a 'function' of each other dialectically related and contained within the organic dynamic of the psyche."

the development of a true morality based on freedom of the will. It can sometimes be experienced as very persuasive and imperative, sometimes as supremely wise, but despite its limited perspective, the ego is left to choose how it will be informed by the unconscious as it develops what is moral. Morality is not an *a priori* faculty—it is a function and task that is organically bound with consciousness. Jung says:

> If man were merely a creature that came into being as a result of something already existing unconsciously, he would have no freedom, and there would be no point in consciousness. Psychology must reckon with the fact that despite the causal nexus, man does enjoy a feeling of freedom, which is identical with autonomy of consciousness. However much the ego can be proved to be dependent and preconditioned, it cannot be convinced that it has no freedom. An absolutely pre-formed consciousness and a totally dependent ego would be a pointless farce, since everything would proceed just as well or even better unconsciously. The existence of ego consciousness has meaning only if it is free and autonomous. By stating these facts we have, it is true, established an antinomy, but we have at the same time given a picture of things as they are. There are temporal, local, and individual differences in the degree of dependence and freedom. In reality both are always present: the supremacy of the self and the hubris of consciousness (1942, [CW para. 259]).

Freedom and servitude are inextricably connected and both the ego and the Self share an interest in how these two polarities are lived out. As Edinger (2002) said:

> "... [T]he supreme psychological goal has not only a divine archetypal begetting but also has an earthy ego begetting. Or, to put in Jung's lapidary phrase, 'God needs man'" (p. 20).

Morality as the Expression of Freedom

In order to be able to seek freedom, the ego has always danced between the world of potentials and the world of absolutes. Attributing great religious ideas to an absolute, external authority brings about a question of the ultimacy of one's moral position. Kant (Hick, 1970) asked the following question: How good is it to do the right thing for the wrong reason, if the only motivation is fear of punishment? (Paraphrased). Kant pointed out that good deeds could not be considered as true morality if they are done for wrong reasons. The fear of punishment is the maxim for preconventional morality in Kohlberg's (1958) theory of moral development. If fear motivates moral conduct, as is often the case with religious fundamentalism, this only causes individuals to shirk the duty to develop a real morality choosing instead to simply avoid damnation and strive for salvation. When fear, threat and punishment come as the imperative that I do not understand, then free will cannot be exercised. The decision to obey an external ruler is itself a moral choice in which the ultimate value is diminished to the point that it is no longer moral. When external authority is the provider of the imperatives irrespective of the circumstances, we are in the area of ethical dogmatism.

Ideals can serve as prescriptions of actions, by providing symbolic outlines of human ethics and morality, but any identification with them impedes their function.[176] That's because identification with the unconscious reduces a symbol

[176] Symbol: early 15c., "creed, summary, religious belief," from L.L. symbolum "creed, token, mark," from Gk. symbolon "token, watchword" (applied c.250 by Cyprian of Carthage to the Apostles' Creed, on the notion of the "mark" that distinguishes Christians from pagans), lit. *"that which is thrown or cast together,"* from syn- "together" + bole "a throwing, a casting, the stroke of a missile, bolt, beam," from bol-, nom. stem of ballein "to throw". The sense evolution in Greek is from "throwing things together" to "contrasting" to "comparing" to "token used in comparisons to determine if something is genuine." Hence, "outward sign" of something. The meaning "something which stands for something else" first recorded 1590 (in "Faerie Queene") (Harper, 2010).

to a sign and changes a complex idea to a concrete fact, and consequently an imperative. [177] This could happen with any symbolic image, if any part of the symbol is concretely comprehended. The symbol's meaning is dictated instead of abstracted, and the unintegrated, complementary part of the symbol supplies the *shadowy* energy characteristic of moral Manichaeism; this fuels the demonizing of the Other. The world of ideals and the world of the gods are similar. Once we bring them into the human realm, we risk misunderstanding and disappointment. If ideals are understood to be literal properties of the world and not entities a person runs headlong into their own inferiority again and again. Schleiermacher (As cited in the *Encyclopaedia Britannica*, 1907) said:

> Conscience, as the subjective expression of the presupposed identity of reason and nature in their bases, guarantees the practicability of our moral vocation. Nature is preordained or constituted to become the symbol and organ of mind, just as mind is endowed with the impulse to realize this end. But the moral law must not be conceived under the form of an "imperative" or a "*Sollen*"; it differs from a law of nature only as being descriptive of the fact that it ranks the mind as conscious will, or *Zweckdenken* (English expediency; authors), above nature. Strictly speaking, the antitheses of good and bad and of free and necessary have no place in an ethical system, but simply in history, which is obliged to compare the actual with the ideal, but as far as the terms "good" and "bad" are used in morals they express the rule or the contrary of reason, or the harmony or the contrary of the particular and the

---

[177] Jung defines the symbol as the essence and the image of archetypal psychic energy, which cannot be perceived directly. It is the expression of something unknown. Thus, symbols are alive, they possess many meanings, and they arise from the unconscious to reconcile opposites. A true symbol possesses the psychic power to transform the conscious attitude and therefore can only arise from the unconscious (CW 6, par. 814-829).

> general. The idea of free as opposed to necessary expresses simply the fact that the mind can propose to itself ends, though a man cannot alter his own nature (p. 430).

Principles like absolutism and inerrancy remove the burden of moral responsibility from the shoulders of the individual. Reliance on an objective, infallible agent reduces the pain and weighty burden of the morality that emerges from consciousness. Tragically, this does not resolve the problem; it only creates a façade, a false impression of the solution.

5. Millennialism and Messianism

What does the "Apocalypse" mean psychologically? My essential answer is: the "Apocalypse" means the momentous event of the coming of the Self into conscious realization ... This is what the content of the Apocalypse archetype presents: the shattering of the world as it has been, followed by its reconstitution (Edinger, 1999, p. 5).

Fundamentalists believe that history has a purpose and culminates in a miraculous conclusion. Good will triumph over evil, and likewise, immortality will conquer mortality. Essentially, history will be accomplished in an act of eternal justice.

Fear of the Unknown

The unknown, with its unpredictability, lack of order (chaos), apparent arbitrariness, and absence of meaning naturally produces anxiety. Meaninglessness alone is one of the major causes of unrest, fear, and anxiety. We observe that the human endeavor seeks to eliminate anxiety and fear while creating meaning and hope for the future. Because the finality of death breaks all attachments with the "known" produces the greatest anxiety. This is the reason that death is one of the central themes for every religion. But the fear of death should be considered only a symptom, not the real driver of religion.

Immortality could be "believed in" in terms of a continuation of consciousness, or it could be understood as a continuation of a reality that has an infinite possibility. Schleiermacher (1799) said:

> Religion is the outcome neither of the fear of death, nor of the fear of God. It answers a deep need in man. (...) Similarly belief in God, and in personal immortality, are not necessarily a part of religion; one can conceive of a religion without God, and it would be pure contemplation of the universe; the desire for personal immortality seems rather to show a lack of religion, since religion assumes a desire to lose oneself in the infinite, rather than to preserve one's own finite self (p. 26).

God—psychologically speaking—is a reality that cannot be avoided. "If God did not exist, it would be necessary to invent Him," said Voltaire (In Roger Pearson, *Voltaire Almighty*, p. 338). Archetypes are the background in the human's striving for meaning; where there is a lack of meaning, there is a lack of meaningful relationship to any archetype. Archetypes do not provide answers nor do they encapsulate meaning in some Lamarckian twist whereby acquired characteristics are inherited. Instead, archetypes organize otherwise chaotic experience into meaningful patterns. They facilitate the ego's work to abstract meaning from experiences, but the archetypes do not answer the question of what meaning *is*. It falls to the relationship between the conscious ego and the unconscious, not some prescribed imperative, to bring the archetypal energy and image from the background into the foreground. In between the conscious ego and the unconscious, one discovers meaning and consciousness: one's unique world, one's own religious myth, and one's *raison d'etre.* Fundamentalists often *lock* their meaning into very specific commands or events, thus eliminating the potential (*in potentia* - archetype) for ongoing personal revelation, one's raison d'etre. Because they do not view archetypes as precursors of meaning but rather as prescriptors of meaning and they interpret images in specific and concrete ways, their meaning is not unique, therefore not free. The faith of a fundamentalist is bereft of any symbolic interpretation of the apocalypse; it is a fact that WILL happen, literally and exactly as described in the scriptures, and it will happen in our physical and material world.

Apocalypse

Edinger (2002), in his book, *The Archetype of the Apocalypse*, explored and amplified the meaning of the apocalypse from a depth-psychological perspective. Accordingly, the apocalypse represents an extension of consciousness with the realization of the Self. The Book of Revelation, or any biblical or religious statement, can be understood from four basic angles.

1. Preterit's interpretation: *The Book of Revelation* is a picture of recent (1st Century A.D.) events in the Roman Empire.[178] This is not a prophetic viewpoint; preterism believes that the *end time*s were already fulfilled with the destruction of Jerusalem. This belief is based on historicism and concretism.
2. Historical interpretation: This view looks at Revelation as a symbolic representation of the entire course of Church history leading up to the final consummation. This perspective somehow spans the whole idea of Revelation and places the individual inside the historical sweep rather than placing Revelation somewhere in the future.
3. Futurist interpretation: This view looks at Revelation as an event that is yet to come, in the Christian tradition, in the form of Christ's return.
4. Idealistic interpretation: Revelation is more or less an allegorical description of the eternal conflict of "good and evil" in the world, and it has been happening already throughout time. This interpretation understands "good and evil" as rather autonomous and objective forces,

[178] From Latin *"praeter"* – something past.

> rather than aspects of human experience on one hand and products of human actions on the other. According to Edinger, this is essentially a Platonic viewpoint, which is very close to being symbolic, but it still has many concretistic and reductionistic elements; it also excludes the human psyche as the central player of this drama.

All of these approaches lack the essential symbolic dimension; they are grounded in naïve and inadequate psychological conceptions of reality. In their roots, they are sterile and very limited with respect to the amount of insight they offer. Dourley (2006) put it this way:

All of these approaches lack the essential symbolic dimension; they are grounded in naïve and inadequate psychological conceptions of reality. In their roots, they are sterile and very limited with respect to the amount of insight they offer. Dourley (2006) put it this way:

> Literalism combines historical externalism to look upon the life of religious figures as literal accounts of past events and not symbolic expressions of the unconscious which creates these figures and their deeds as triggers to their reenactment in the internal forum of the living psyche. Revelation as the deepest poetry of the soul is turned into history and its transformative power all but lost (p. 12).

When symbols are stripped of their revelatory dimension, they lose the vitality and potency (numinosity) needed for transformation and thy can become trapped in the collective unconscious. It is like a motif in a fairytale where the imprisoned princess can only be rescued from the dragon by the heroic triumph of consciousness, not by its sacrifice. Literalism, historicism, and concretism, as explored by Dourley, are the manifestations of the decanting symbol; that is, the shrinking of the embodied life spirit that become expressions of an inanimate and bloodless spiritual reality.

Pleroma - An Archetypal World

Edinger's (2002) "pleromatic" designation is to a certain extent an extrapolation of the last scholarly viewpoint.[179] He believed that Revelation can be an expression of "events" that are in motion "somewhere" outside of time and space, in the collective unconscious: pleroma. So, he called this belief "pleromatic," but [he] did not use the word in the Gnostic sense (Webster's Online Dictionary, n.d.). Edinger suggested that events of revelation take place in the "realm" of the collective unconscious, but they might not be registered at the level of ego-consciousness. Archetypal reality, for that matter, is constantly being expressed in the world, even though it might not be registered in a person's individual consciousness. For example, an alcoholic possessed by Dionysian archetypal energy might act out its power *reflexively* by self-destructing but never fully bring it to consciousness *reflectively*.

Key To The Soul Is Symbol

Edinger thus identified a category of interpretation, which is the key to understanding Jungian psychology. This perspective

---

[179] Pleroma (Greek πλήρωμα) generally refers to the totality of divine powers. The word means *fullness* from πληρόω ('fills') comparable to πλήρης which means 'full,' and is used in Christian theological contexts: both in Gnosticism generally and by Paul of Tarsus in Colossians 2.9. Gnosticism holds that the world is controlled by archons, among whom some versions of Gnosticism claim is the deity of the Old Testament, who held aspects of the human captive, either knowingly or accidentally. The heavenly pleroma is the totality of all that is regarded in our understanding of "divine." The pleroma is often referred to as the light existing "above" (the term is not to be understood spatially) our world, occupied by spiritual beings who self-emanated from the pleroma. These beings are described as aeons (eternal beings) and sometimes as archons. Jesus is interpreted as an intermediary aeon who was sent, along with his counterpart Sophia, from the pleroma, with whose aid humanity can recover the lost knowledge of the divine origins of humanity and in so doing be brought back into unity with the Pleroma. The term is thus a central element of Gnostic religious cosmology. (*Webster's Online Dictionary*, p. 1, n.d.)

not only conceives of revelation, but all mythological and biblical events as the psychological ground of the soul: symbolically. Revelation is then understood, in terms of depth psychology, as a symbolic expression of the coming of the Self (*Das Selbst*) or the coming of the Self "into conscious realization in an individual psyche" (p. 10). Of course all events recorded in the Bible stimulate the mind to contemplate their actual historical possibility, if we talk about the life of Jesus or Revelation. Symbolic reality is a dynamic force, thus, a relationship to the symbol is not simply a mechanical process where we are automatically informed and told what to do and think. Rather, we can compare it to a relationship between human beings where hearts and minds are ceaselessly involved in seeking relationship to the numinous. In depth psychology, the symbolic mediates the deeper psychological realities regardless of the process concerned. Jung explained:

> "Every psychological expression is a symbol if we assume that it states or signifies something more and other than itself which eludes our present knowledge" (Jung, 1921b, p. 475).

Symbol Versus Sign

Understanding the concept of the living symbol is one of the most crucial aspects of this book. Radical creed does not use symbols as transcendent functions between the rational and irrational worlds but more or less as a divine sign, prescribing a way of thinking and feeling in an *a priori* designated way. Symbolic attitudes, as understood by Jungians, are at their essence constructive and prospective because they give priority to understanding the meaning or purpose of psychological phenomena.

Jung (1921b) understood symbols as products of a highly multifaceted nature, products that basically mirror the complexity and profoundness of the human psyche. A symbol, he taught, subsists as the expression of the passionate yearning of the human mind and the product of the unconscious at the *same* time. He said:

> ...Because the new symbol is born of man's highest spiritual aspirations and must at the same time spring from the deepest roots of his being, it cannot be a one-sided product of the most highly differentiated mental functions, but must derive equally from the lowest and most primitive levels of the psyche (Jung 1921b, [CW6, para. 824)].

Thus, clearly, if there is a subordination of one part, the symbol will turn into a symptom. One will live out [unconsciously] the symbolic image without the meaning being reflected in consciousness. To the extent that a symbol is merely a symptom, it lacks a redeeming effect. It fails to express the fullness of the symbol within consciousness. Instead it serves as a constant reminder of the antithesis of the symbol, though consciousness may not register it, (Jung, 1921b, [CW 6, para. 817]). Often, in a therapeutic relationship symptoms are manifested as aspects of the transference-countertransference before they transfer into a symbolic image. If the real symbol is created, it has the quality of a compensatory relation to the thesis and antithesis of psychological processes, particularly as they pertain to the creation and use of the transcendent function. The transcendent function allows an "organic transition" (Jung, 1916, [CW 8, para. 152]) from one attitude to another. Even though the transcendent function arises autonomously from the psychic system (as the tension of the opposites is held) the ego must do the necessary work to allow the meaning to be integrated into one's specific life.

Jon

I remember a client of mine, Jon, who sought analysis about five years after his father died. (V.Š.) His grieving process got stuck, and he became bitter, angry, detached from others; he lost his vital energy. We started to pay attention to his dreams. In many of his dreams he was driving a beautiful Volkswagen. It was the car that his father used to drive, took care of, and loved. The car was "incredibly beautiful," and Jon felt safe and happy driving it. This car came up over and over in his dreams. He spoke about his father's car with tears in his eyes. It brought about memories and feelings that he had forgotten. This car was something that lived beyond his father's physical existence. Jon came to understand that the soul, the car, of his father continued—symbolically—in the form represented by the car. Jon's relation to and experience of his dreams and images provided an organic transition to the depths of his own experience: soul.

Mountains of Slovakia

Shortly before my own father died, I had a dream in which he came to me and said that he had a secret to share with me. (V.Š.) Then he took me to the mountains. We found ourselves high in the mountains, perhaps, of Slovakia. The weather was rough, with a strong wind and scattered snow flurries mixed with cold rain. This made it difficult to hike up the slippery slopes. Then we got to the point from which we could see a long staircase carved into the rock. It was huge, stretching deep down the mountains until it was out of sight in the valley. I thought to myself: "This is immense, majestic! Who in the world carved those in this mountain?" My dad and I were standing right where it ended. Then my father said: "I carved those. I am tired now. I have come to this point. You have to continue where I left off." This dream filled me with feelings of awe and joy, sadness and humility. It helped me to accept the mystery of life and death better. I cannot adequately put into words the effect this dream had upon me, but it allowed me to unite opposites that previously had seemed irreconcilable.

The Great Reflected In the Small

So, the symbol is a bridge that forges a dynamic unity between consciousness and the unconscious. Symbols allow for the mysterious processes of human consciousness fostering, containing, and reflecting the greater within the lesser, the larger within the smaller, the macrocosm in the microcosm. Anytime a symbol is used to designate only a partial phenomenon, it becomes detached from either its instinctual roots or its imaginal and spiritual origins and deteriorates to a sign. Jung (1921b) said:

> The interpretation of the cross as a symbol of divine love is semiotic (a sign), because 'divine love' describes the fact to be expressed better and more aptly than a cross, which can have many other meanings. On the other hand, an interpretation of the cross is *symbolic* when it puts the cross beyond all conceivable explanations, regarding it as expressing an as yet unknown and incomprehensible fact of a mystical or transcendent, i.e., psychological, nature, which simply finds itself most appropriately represented in the cross (1921b, [CW 6, para. 479]).

Consider, for instance, a symbol of the Self, respectively *Imago Dei* as the image representation of the Self and the philosophical structure that is bound with it. Jung said,

> Hence in its scientific usage the term 'self' (the Self, authors) refers neither to Christ nor to the Buddha but to the totality of the figures that are its equivalent, and each of these figures is a symbol of the self (Jung 1944, [CW 12, para. 20]).

It is not the quality of the content that determines if something is symbolic; rather, it depends upon the observing mind's ability to understand a phenomenon symbolically rather than merely as a sign. The experience of the numinous energy grips a person being confronted with symbolic reality. Symbolic reality is engaged when the ego is able to contemplate and reflect on the content of the symbol. The ego is simultaneously drawn to feelings and other images that open it to the unknown and incomprehensible reality of a mystical or transcendent nature. A symbol is connected in its essence to that which Kant (1912) called a *noumenon*: the thing in itself, which is postulated to exist but is unknowable independently from the mind's operation (*an sich*) even though it is presupposed for its effect. *Phenomenon*, on the other hand, is the appearance of things that are perceived in our senses (from *phaien* – to show, reveal). Senses determine how the phenomenal world is perceived, and it is through this faculty that the psyche borrows sense impressions that are the building blocks for fantasy and through which unconscious images are constructed. Fantasy activity is the highest form of psychic activity and is the key psychological process that unites conscious and unconscious contents. Edinger (1996) said that fantasy:

> ...corresponds internally to the phenomenological object in the outer world. Any presumption to such absolute knowledge as metaphysics or knowledge of the thing in itself is just that, a presumption (p. 7).

A symbol cannot be known in and of itself, but as an ideal it can provide functional relevance to the noumenal world. Meditating on symbolic reality, confronting and wrestling with its many-faceted and eternal vicissitudes, is the essence of (spiritual) life. Thus, symbolic reality is an inexhaustible well of knowledge and energy; and an indispensable fabric for individuation.

Further, symbols can unite all psychic functions and thus be their quintessence. Jung said:

> Its profundity of meaning is inherent in the raw material itself, the very stuff of the psyche, transcending time and dissolution; and its very configuration by the opposites ensures its sovereign power over all the psychic functions (Jung, 1921b [CW 6, para. 828.]).

Symbols and archetypes represent holographic images of the unconscious. Every true symbol embodies archetypal qualities. The mystery of a symbol enjoys close kinship with the mystery of religion. In mystical states, the mind tends to experience symbols in their fuller scope. Consciousness grows out of the unconscious, like a plant emerging from the soil. It can be seen that whatever is outside is also found inside. Symbolic processes furnish a meaningful context for the relationship between consciousness and the unconscious. The degree of spiritual consciousness—individuation—is proportional to the degree of synchronicity between the subjective and objective world. When there is a great deal of disharmony between conscious and unconscious it results in fear and superstitious worldviews detached from actual reality. Inadequate symbolization, for example, typifies fundamentalist beliefs resulting in denying the evidence of global warming, even as a natural condition, or the continuing decline of elephant populations deriving from the belief in the magical power of ivory.

Schleiermacher (1988), whose teaching had a very significant impact on Jung's thoughts, provides phenomenological insight into the symbolic unity as apperceived before it differentiates into the separate cognitive functions:

> That first mysterious moment that occurs in every sensory perception, before intuition and feeling are separated, where sense and its objects have, as it were, flowed into one another and become one, before both turn back to their original position—I know how indescribable it is and how quickly it passes away. But I wish that you were able to hold on to it and also to recognize it again in the higher and divine religious activity of the mind. Would that I could and might express it, at least indicate it, without having to desecrate it! It is as fleeting and transparent as the first scent with which the dew gently caresses the waking flowers, as modest and delicate as a maiden's kiss, as holy and fruitful as a nuptial embrace; indeed, not like these, but it is itself all of these. A manifestation, an event develops quickly and magically into an image of the universe (pp. 31-32).

Inadequate Relationship Between Ego and the Self

The Fundamentalists' religious position, which we termed theocalypsis, can be understood as an inadequate and dysfunctional relation to the symbol. Certain psychological maneuvers of the psyche can thwart the actualization of one's deeper symbolic relationship to the Self. The relationship to the symbol can be distorted by ego-defenses in two elemental ways.

1) First, the ego *identifies* with the symbol that results in a symbolic image being lived concretely; creating the illusion of a *magical* world that is endowed with images, emotions, and thoughts springing from the archetypal world. With ego-identification, the source of the symbolic perception (the Self) is not recognized or honored. This is the situation of the Millennialist and Messianic approaches to understanding the world. In this case the archetype of the Apocalypse operates concretely, creating beliefs that the events in Revelation will someday occur as objective events. A person given to such belief can reason that destructive actions might hasten the day when the events of Revelations will transpire. This can be extrapolated from any belief system (e.g. World Religions: Christian, Islamic, Jewish or Buddhist, etc.), pertaining to archetypal reality. Biblical texts are *a priori* inspired by archetypal reality; that is why there is a correlation between sacred scriptures and archetypal images produced by human unconscious. It is not an accident that heroes around the world have had to descend (the myth of the Eternal Return) into the depths of darkness to rescue the fair maiden or princess, or discover the hidden treasure. This motif of descent and return is nearly universal, and is powerfully exemplified in the lives of the Egyptian god Horus and Jesus of Nazareth.[180]

---

[180] To mention just a few similarities: Jesus and Horus were both conceived of a virgin. They both were the "only begotten son" of a god (Osiris, Yahweh). Horus's mother was Meri, Jesus's mother was Mary. Horus's foster father was called Jo-Seph, and Jesus's foster father was Joseph. Both had their coming announced to their mother by an angel. Ancient Egyptians celebrated the birth of Horus on December 21 (the Winter Solstice). Chris-

Naturally, many such parallels between the world's mythologies could be attributed to the historical transfer of knowledge where societies learn from each other, but Jungian psychology has demonstrated that there are very similar mythologies among indigenous tribes separated by oceans, and that makes the literal sharing of ideas a less likely explanation of the phenomenon. The deep rivers of the archetypal realm inhere to the human psyche. The case for the collective unconscious is strengthened by the probability that societies would have been unlikely to perpetuate similar motifs in mythologies from different cultures if there were no psychological and spiritual benefit. Holy scriptures (Christian, Islamic, Buddhist, Hindu, Jewish, etc.) or any mythological beliefs are archetypally inspired. Despite the discussion among Jungians as how to understand the collective unconscious, there are still strong reasons to consider it the primary medium from which mythologies emerged in consciousness. One can often observe how a psychotic person develops a quasi-spirituality full of mythological symbols that were previously relevant.

Images and symbols spring from the deep well of unconscious activity that governs human behavior from its most basic and primary functions to it most lofty and spiritual ideals and goals. But when the ego becomes possessed by them and loses its

---

tians celebrate the birth of Jesus on December 25. Horus was visited at birth by "three solar deities" and Jesus was visited by "three wise men." After the birth of Horus, Herut tried to have Horus murdered. After the birth of Jesus, Herod tried to have Jesus murdered Both were baptized at age 30. Anup baptized Horus the Baptizer. Jesus was baptized by John the Baptist.

Both Anup and John were later beheaded. Both have 12 disciples. Both walked on water, cast out demons, healed the sick, and restored sight to the blind. Both were crucified. Both were buried in a tomb. Horus was sent to Hell and resurrected in three days. Jesus was sent to Hell and came back "three days" later (although Friday night to Sunday morning is hardly three days). Both are supposed to return for a 1,000-year reign. Horus is known as KRST, the anointed one. Jesus was known as the Christ (which means "anointed one") and the like. (Hub Pages, p. 1, n.d., See D.M. Murdock, *Christ in Egypt: The Horus-Jesus Connection*, 2009, Stellar House Publishers)

inspiring connection to the archetypal images and symbols, they are often taken at face value, *prima facie*. People who adhere to biblical text literally understand biblical events as historical facts. While their mind is not literally possessed by the text, it may be fair to say that their mind is possessed by something that is *backing* or supporting the interpretation of the text, a real, unknown metaphysical entity, which is the source of psychic energy and not only a source of rational information (Edinger, 1996, p. 7). This psychic energy is the real reason why religion has so much potency; a fire can be a good servant but a bad master. On this note, Jung said,

The tremendous effectiveness (mana) of these images is such that they not only give one the feeling of pointing to the *Ens realissimum*, but also make one convinced that they actually establish it as a fact and can express it as such (Jung 1952, [CW 11, para. 558]).

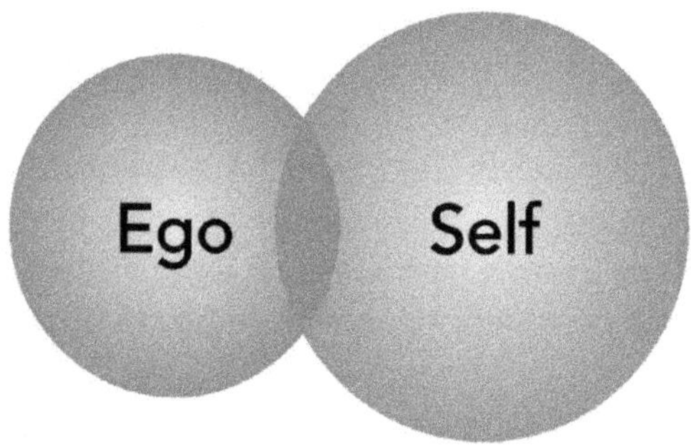

2) The second way symbols are distorted by ego-defenses is that the ego is *alienated* from the symbol. An alienated ego reproduces symbolic actions and thoughts only in a sterile, automatic, manner bound to the persona that creates the illusion of vitality. For the alienated ego the symbol is missing its energy, potential for growth and transformation. Typically, an ideology *replaces* the symbol, and one clings to its position as if in desperate belief that the stronger the attachment, the more true the belief becomes. By reducing the symbol to a specific set of properties (signs), the ego hides from and avoids

the full power of the symbol. Whatever pathos emerges is false since it is not based on the real power of the symbol. This forgery creates a mana personality. Jung said:

The ego has appropriated something that does not belong to it. But how has it appropriated the mana? If it was really the ego that conquered the anima, then the mana does indeed belong to it, and it would be correct to conclude that one has become important. But why does not this importance, the mana, work upon others? ... It does not work because one has not in fact become important, but has merely become adulterated with an archetype, another unconscious figure. Hence we must conclude that the ego never conquered the anima at all and therefore has not acquired the mana. All that has happened is a new adulteration (1928b, [CW 7, para. 380]).

3) A third possibility is the so-called *adequate* position of the ego-symbol. The ego is separated here from the archetypal psyche by its reflective function, not a defense, and therefore, it is able to continue dialectic communication with the Self. Edinger (1972) said:

"The symbol is then able to perform its proper function as releaser and transformer of psychic energy with full participation of conscious understanding" (p. 110).

It is a position of "conscious-cracy" (governance by consciousness) when the ego employs insightful reviews of its own tendencies and applies both, the choice of how the Self-energies are conceived and the *action* as a response to them.

Theologian Rudolf Bultmann (1961), in his book *Kerygma and Myth,* questioned a literalistic dimension of Christian religion. He famously stated that the myth is not a Kerygma. He relied on an "existential element" in the Christian faith. Bultmann said:

> "The real purpose of myth is not to present an objective picture of the world as it is, but to express man's understanding of himself in the world in which he lives" (p. 171).

He passionately expressed that the real theological question was not whether the Christian myth is true but whether the *understanding* is true:

"... Faith ought not to be tied down to the imagery of New Testament mythology" (p. 10).

Critics say that he changed the course of the interpretation of the New Testament. Even though he presented his ideas long after Jung presented his, Bultmann's voice is important because it comes from within the Christian tradition. Real change can arrive only from the inside. Outside pressure always carries with it the stigma of arising from the enemy, something that is hard to overcome. Many theologians understand the importance of the symbolic approach. Therefore, a theologian like Bultmann was able to convey his message to his religious community more effectively than a depth psychologist whose findings seem to come from outside.

When I was presenting a Czech version of this book (V.Š.), an elderly man came up to me during my book signing. He had been reading it for about 20 minutes when he put the book back on table and said: "Very interesting, but I do not want one." I asked him why. He replied, "I am an old man and I'd like to keep things the way they are."

Edinger called the inadequate relationship between symbols and the ego a *fallacy*. While people gripped by a concretistic fallacy consider everything symbolic to be literally real, people suffering from a reductive fallacy reduce symbols to signs or other knowable content. The lighter forms of this phenomenon may not otherwise impact them, but extreme forms of the

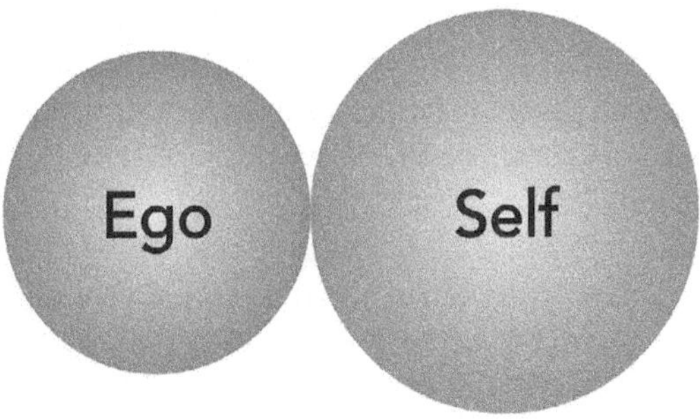

concretistic fallacy are manifested as psychotic delusions or hallucinations. In anthropology, the concretistic fallacy in primitive societies is called *animism,* but it is not technically a fallacy, but rather a stage of ego-development. Extreme forms of the reductive fallacy include materialism and some forms of gnosticism. They create the illusion that one is able to read or interpret all the meaning behind the symbol correctly and to exhaust all of its meaning in a rational way. Classical Freudian psychology appears to be caught in the mode of the reductive fallacy because it considers everything symbolic only in terms of the primitive, archaic, pre-logical functioning of the ego and denies the psyche as an autonomous, teleological, and intelligent agent. Jung's epic split with Freud was grounded in this fundamental difference in understanding the symbol.

Jung came to understand how important symbols are in the life of the individual and made the symbolic process a supreme goal and a key to his psychology of Individuation. The aim of Jungian analysis is to operate exactly at this "third adequate possibility of ego-symbol relations." If one has identified with (or is possessed by) the symbol, it will simply be lived out in a very concrete and undeveloped level. If one is detached from the symbol, one split's off its energy (it stays in the unconscious), resulting in phenomena similar to possession, and, all the while, the mind will be stuck in its own construct. At times, this phenomena may be called religion and at other times an form of an "ism." The numinosum is volatile and dangerous whenever the ego identifies with it or suppresses it. In both cases, it finds a way to manifest in the form of various expressions seeking power. Jungian psychology, as noted, advocates for the spiritual cultivation of symbols–where instinct is transformed into meaning. Edinger (1972) said:

> It is the symbolic image, acting as releaser and transformer of psychic energy, which lifts the instinctive urgency to another level of meaning and humanizes, spiritualizes and acculturates the raw animal energy (p. 115).

VII.
THEOCALYPSIS AND THEONEMESIS

Let us briefly recap the material that has been presented. We have reviewed the phenomenology of extreme religion and reviewed some the relevant concepts of Analytical Psychology in order to understand the psychological dynamics underlying extreme (strong) religion. Having introduced the term theocalypsis it may be helpful to know how we arrived at the term and how it is applied to the concept of extreme religion.

1. THEOCALYPSIS

On psychological grounds, I would recommend that no God be constructed out of the archetype of the mana personality. In other words, he must not be concretized, for only thus can I avoid projecting my values and non-values into God and Devil, and only thus can I preserve my human dignity, my specific gravity (Jung, 1928b, p. 236).

A. Calypso

Before we introduce the term "theocalypsis," the etymological background to the term "calypso" will be surveyed and in the process will illuminate the use of the term theocalypsis (theocalypse). Calypso was, according to Hesiod (1914), a daughter of Oceanus and Tethys, and according to Apollodorus, a daughter of Nereus. In the *Homeric Opus*, (Homer, 1871) Calypso is the daughter of Atlas. There, Calypso was a nymph who inhabited the island of Ogygia. Odysseus was cast away on this island when his ship was wrecked. In *The Odyssey*, (n.d.)[181] Calypso imprisons Odysseus on the Island of Ogygia and intends to make Odysseus her husband forever. Calypso, a mythical figure, is a beautiful and seductive Nymph who infatuates Odysseus and becomes his lover, which is illustrated in the following passage:

> But when he had reached the island which lay afar, then forth from the violet sea he came to land, and went his way until he came to a great cave, wherein dwelt the fair-dressed nymph; and he found her within. A great fire was burning on the hearth, and from afar over the isle there was a fragrance of cleft cedar and juniper, as they burned; but she within was singing with a sweet voice as she went to and fro before the loom, weaving with a golden shuttle. Round about the cave grew a luxuriant wood, alder and poplar and sweet-smelling cypress, wherein birds long of wing were wont to nest, owls and falcons and sea-crows with chattering tongues, who ply their business on the sea. And right there about the hollow cave ran trailing a garden vine, in pride of its prime, richly laden with clusters. And fountains four in a row were flowing with bright water hard by one another, turned one this way, one that. And round about soft meadows of violets and parsley were blooming (p.1).

Calypso's power of seduction kept Odysseus hostage on the Island of Ogygia for seven years, and according some sources ten years. On top of such a wonderful place, Calypso promised Odysseus immortality. However, deep within his heart, Odysseus desired to return home to his beloved wife, Penelope. In Book IV of *the Odyssey*, (Butcher, 1909) Odysseus said:

> And on the tenth dark night the gods brought me nigh the isle Ogygia, where Calypso of the braided tresses dwells, an awful ("awe full") goddess. She took me in, and with all care she cherished me and gave me

[181] 725 BCE

> sustenance, and said that she would make me to know not death nor age for all my days; but never did she win my heart within me. There I abode for seven years continually, and watered with my tears the imperishable raiment that Calypso gave me (p. 100).

Odysseus had a choice to make: immortality in the wonderful, soothing arms of Calypso, or the continuation of his journey and the promise of return to Penelope. Each of us faces a similar choice: returning to the blissful state of one-sided identification with the Self or do the work required to overcome one-sidedness and identification with the Self so that we may continue on with *our* journey of individuation. Odysseus' stay at Ogygia was identical (in the Greek conception) with *death* because it represented life with the infinite pain of separation from Penelope and the world of desired reality that she represented.

After seven years, his patron goddess, Athena, asked Zeus to order the release of Odysseus from Calypso's capture. Zeus finally agreed and sent his messenger, Hermes, to order Calypso to set Odysseus free. When Odysseus left, Calypso was sad, as evidenced by the following passage:

> Thus was Calypso affected by the Ithaca's [Odysseus's] departure, when in ages past she wept to the lonely waves: for many days she sat disconsolately with unkempt tresses uttering many a complaint to the unjust sea, and although she was never to see him again, yet she still felt pain when she recalled their long happiness together (Homer, 1871, 5, 4ff).

The Greek word *calypso* (Greek: Καλυψώ, *Kalupsō,* Kalypso) Καλύπτειν (*kalyptein*, "to cover," from which apocalypse is also derived) means "the concealer" (lit. "hider", from Greek kalyptein "to cover, conceal," from PIE *kel- "to cover, save," root of English Hell. *Apocalypse* means the exact opposite: to "uncover") (*Online Etymology Dictionary*, 2001-2011, p. 1).[182]

[182] Apocalypse: Late 14 c., "revelation, disclosure," from Church L. *apocalypsis* "revelation," from Gk. *apokalyptein* "uncover," from apo- "from" (see apo-) + kalyptein "to cover, conceal" (see Calypso). The

The name Calypso or *Καλυψώ* can possibly have its source in the Indo-European language. It relates to the Greek word, *καλύπτ,* which means to conceal and may refer to the bridal veil that conceals her face. The Indo-European name may reference something more sinister. It may come from 'k̑el', which means "to hide, conceal and u̯l̥p—(a carnivorous animal, esp. fox, wolf, etc.)" (Ibid., p. 1). Calypso may have originally been an Indo-European goddess of the underworld whose function was similar to Valkyries or the Hel of Norse myth. Calypso may have been derived from a demon that was devouring heroes and was thus similar to Scylla. Calypso is also similar to the Hindi Sarva (Lincoln, 1991). In many mythologies, there is a god of the land of the dead; the Proto-Indo-European deity *Kolyos*, for instance, impersonated death itself. She would drag people down into the realm of the dead with a noose. Rituals were performed to offer sacrifices to *Kolyos* in order to spare man from death. One of the ancient apotropaic prayers to keep *Kolyos* away goes like this:

> [Kolyos] keep far from us your snare,
> You who lie in wait for us.
> Keep far from us the time
> When you will be our Coverer.
> We honor you; we acknowledge your power,
> But we do not desire your presence.
> Take what we give you and do not return
> (Jack-son, Peter, 2001, p. 61).

Calypso also symbolized death because, like a wolf, she devoured people without letting them finish their journey. Because Calypso could mean "the concealer," "disguiser," or "misleader," she represents the forces that cause a person to be diverted from their goal. Calypso, in Greek tradition, represents the goddess (i.e. archetype) who captures or veils the mind of

---

Christian end-of-the-world story is part of the revelation in John of Patmos' book "Apokalypsis" (a title rendered into English as "Apocalypse" c.1230 and "Revelations" by Wyclif c.1380). (*Online Etymology Dictionary*, 2001-2011, p. 1)

any person on their life's journey. An organized set of beliefs, false religious persuasions, ideological ism-like structures, teachings of cults, etc., that traps a person with seductive beliefs represents this archetypal process.

While [uniting with] Penelope was a goal of Odysseus's journey, the encounter with Calypso was the distraction. But, true to all symbols, her positive aspect consisted of the fact that she saved Odysseus and offered him refuge after Poseidon, the god of the seas and waters, destroyed his ship. She provided the healing needed after his trauma. Paradoxically, Odysseus would have perished without Calypso, and he would have perished if Athena, the goddess of reason, wisdom, heroism and arts, had not rescued him. This myth illustrates the Jungian insight that an ego either devoid of, or possessed by archetypal energies is, psychologically speaking, lifeless. So we have chosen to incorporate the concept of "calypsis" into the neologism "theo-calypsis" in order to express the kernel of what happens in strong religion, i.e., a creed in which the Self and the corresponding *Imago Dei* takes possession of the ego.

B. Mana Personality & Hubris

In the face of this, our pitiably limited ego, if it has but a spark of self-knowledge, can only draw back and rapidly drop all pretense of power and importance. It was a delusion: the conscious mind has not become master of the unconscious, and the anima has forfeited her tyrannical power only to the extent that the ego was able to come to terms with the unconscious. This accommodation, however, was not a victory of the conscious over the unconscious, but the establishment of a balance of power between the two worlds (Jung 1928a, [CW7 para.381]).

Carl Jung developed the concept of a mana personality. A mana personality is a form of inflation, or identification with the archetypal anima or animus[183]. As Jung's quote above suggests, the mana personality is an ego-adaptation with respect to the numinosum of unconscious energy where ego "appropriates" power that "does not belong to it." The anima/animus, according to Jung, can be "developed" into the *function* of a relationship between the conscious and unconscious. When the anima/animus become functions of this relationship, they lose their demonic (i.e., possessive) qualities. If this relationship-making function is not employed, the anima/animus can turn into a compulsive and "bewitching" ruler of the ego. A mana personality is then created according to Jung.

Mana as Numinous Energy

The word mana, which has its roots in Austronesian languages, means literally "power" and represents the magical powers associated with the divine or superhuman ability. Originally, mana denoted objective forces of nature such as thunder, storm, or wind and hence was attributed to gods. Mana can be found in the Melanesian, Polynesian, and Micronesian vocabularies and refers to a numinous and magical quality of gods and, consequently, religious objects. The Jungian concept of the mana personality refers to possession by archetypes and the endowment of the ego by those magical qualities, which create "animation." When the ego identifies with the content that does not belong to it, it becomes infatuated, or inflated. When the anima/animus is not "integrated," the ego identifies with its power, and thus, the ego becomes a "mana personality." Jung used this term to describe the inflationary [unconscious] effect of archetypal energy upon

[183] Anima/animus are archetypes of psyche and arise as basic archetypal aspects of the Self. As the fundamental forms, which underline the feminine aspects of man and the masculine aspects of woman, they are seen as opposites. As psychic images they serve as bridges between ego-consciousness and the Self in the process of individuation. One must come to terms with their inner contrasexual opposite, if one is to integrate their opposite and individuate.

the ego. The ego does not have this power in actuality, and it only becomes "adulterated with the archetype" (Jung 1928b, [CW 7, para. 380]). A mana personality involves the feeling of exceptional power that is unchecked by reality. It is thus an *illusion* of power. The one who acquires a mana personality acts without fear and shame; thus, it is a specific form of *mania*.[184] Numinous archetypal power is, in the case of a mana personality, inadequately regulated in the ego, which results in feelings of grandiosity and superiority. For this, ancient Greeks had the term hubris (*hybris,* Greek ὕβρις).

Hubris

Ancient Greeks considered hubris to be human arrogance that was appropriated to man but belonged to the gods. As Edinger (1972) said, hubris means the transcending of proper human limits. From a psychological perspective, hubris is a state of inflation where there is an absence of adequate insight (vulnerability) into one's limits due to the narcissistic shamelessness of the ego.[185] Murray (1907/1924) stated, "Hubris is the insolence of irreverence; the absence of *Aidos* (reverence) in the presence of something higher. But nearly always it is a sin of the strong and proud" (p. 264f). *Aidos* was conceived by Greeks as an agency, which helped protect against committing sacrilegious acts that would offend the gods, and make them

---

[184] Mania: Late 14c., "mental derangement characterized by excitement and delusion," from Late Latin *mania* "insanity, madness," from Greek *mania* "madness, frenzy; enthusiasm, inspired frenzy; mad passion, fury," related to *mainesthai* "to rage, go mad," *mantis*"seer," *menos* "passion, spirit," all from PIE **men-* "to think, to have one's mind aroused, rage, be furious" (see *mind* (n.)). Sense of "fad, craze" is 1680s, from French *manie* in this sense. Sometimes nativized in Middle English as *manye*. Used since 1500s (in imitation of Greek) as the second element in compounds expressing particular types of madness (cf. *nymphomania*, 1775; *kleptomania*, 1830; *megalomania*, 1890). (*Online Etymology Dictionary*, n.d., p. 1)

[185] See: Cruz, L., Buser, S., et al. *A Clear and Present Danger: Narcissism in the Era of Donald Trump,* Chiron Publications, 2016.

angry and vengeful. It can be understood as the respect and humility that one needs to deploy, in order to handle and avoid the full impact of archetypal inflation. Jung (1928b) said:

> If the ego presumes to wield power over the unconscious, the unconscious reacts with a subtle attack, deploying the dominant of the mana-personality, whose enormous prestige casts a spell over the ego. *Against this the only defense is full confession of one's weakness in face of the powers of the unconscious* (Jung 1928b, [CW 7, para. 391] emphasis ours).

In the state of hubris, one loses a healthy connection to reality and pursues his or her goals irrespective of natural danger. Due to the increased dominion of the unconscious, one acts as if life was [only] a dream; one becomes an actor in mythical drama.

Compaan (2007) said:

> Hubris is the affective state where one feels superior to all other humans and is totally captivated by the excitement and pleasure of the new and unknown. When so possessed, the ego senses little danger in the new and the unknown. Consequently the individual moves without hesitation into the exploration of the wonderful world out there, much as the unknowing child easily ventures away from mother until encountering the experiences of fragmentation in the face of the wholly other. This is a position of *shamelessness*, of inadequate shame. Shame affect is not available to assist in the modulation of the excited feelings. Rather the person is possessed, driven by this energy. Clinically it appears as *mania* or, as Jung preferred, as a *mana personality* (p. 6).

The term mana personality describes the nature of personality under the influence of archetypal inflation, while hubris refers to feelings of extreme pride and arrogance with which the mana personality approaches the world. *Aidos* is a hubris-compensating ego-capacity, which instinctively protected ancient people from acting self-destructively; it was *aidos* that gave them tools to deal with the "perils of the soul."

A mana personality is thus a result of identification with the anima/animus archetype, but if we view those archetypes as partial aspects of the Self, we can say that the mana personality is principally a possession by the Self. The intensity of this possession depends on the amount of archetypal energy involved. According to Jungian theory, the Self represents the "highest amount of libido" and can be understood as "God within" (CW 7:399); this possession by the Self results in the most intense and hence the most hubristic expression. Quoting Jung (1951a):

> It must be reckoned a psychic catastrophe when the ego is assimilated by the self. The image of wholeness then remains in the unconscious, so that on the one hand it shares the archaic nature of the unconscious and on the other finds itself in the psychically relative space-time continuum that is characteristic of the unconscious as such (pp. 145-146).

Imago Dei

Religious possession was earlier distinguished from other forms of possessions by the presence of the image, idea, or other reference to the holy or a superior being. That idea-image object is referred to as the *Imago Dei*, the "image of God." In Jungian theory, the definition of the *Imago Dei* differs from theological concepts referring to human as an image of God. It is rather an image of God (the Self) as reflected in the ego. In Jungian theory, the representation of God can be a very subjectively conditioned concept, although it has its own archetypal imagery developed and collected by human beings over thousands of years. The conscious representation of an *Imago Dei* consists of what one thinks, or how one defines and imagines God, while the unconscious aspect of an *Imago Dei* is the deeper imaginative dimension of God that emerges spontaneously from the unconscious. This can be applied to any transcendent object. In this way, Jung makes a distinction between the image (*imago*) of a person and her actual existence. He says:

Because of its extremely subjective origin, the Imago is frequently more an image of a subjective functional complex than of the object itself. In the analytical treatment of unconscious products it is essential that the Imago should not be assumed to be identical with the object; it is better to regard it as an *image of the subjective relation to the object*. (Jung 1921, [CW 6, para. 812], author's emphasis).

Conscious and Unconscious Image of God

The *Imago Dei,* like any idea, can be used defensively. The *Imago Dei*, the image or symbol of God, refers to the representation of the Self in the psyche. It consists of a collection of representations of images and ideas. It refers, on one hand, to images or content (feeling-toned representations, energy) emerging from the unconscious either spontaneously or induced by techniques designed for that purpose, and on another hand, to symbols that are more or less created by the human mind for purposes of capturing and representing archetypal contents. An example of the former is spontaneous imagery, visions, or dream images of the Self; an example of the latter is a theological description of divine qualities (philosophical ideas about God's nature, intentions, spheres of influence, etc.). In essence, the *Imago Dei* refers to everything that the human mind imagines, intuits, feels, and thinks about God. Many religious traditions prohibit any portrayals of images and icons of God (aniconism) due to the obvious limitations of the human mind and the inexhaustibility of the object.[186] The destruction of images and icons for reverence is called iconoclasm. The danger is that it may lead to a hubristic illusion that the finite mind *knows* the infinite God, while in fact the mind is simply adhering to its own projections.

[186] For example, *Bible*: *Exodus* 20:4-5

C. Defensive Dynamics of the *Imago Dei*

The Self Provides Energy to Imago Dei

The God Image does not exist independently of its unconscious source of energy. One can only have mediated experiences of the noumenon (thing-in-itself), never direct experience. The medium is ego-consciousness. Universal experiences of the Self point toward something empirically real. The Self is an archetypal content that is presumably "behind" all the psychological variations of the apperception of this archetype. The Self, as the source of libido, the center and totality of the psyche, and the image of wholeness, has the potential to employ a tremendous influence on the religious character. The Self has a potential to create, not only the strongest form of possession, but also—due to its archetypal image-structure—the most ideologically established God Image. As an empirical concept, the Self deserves to be called "the God within us" (Jung, 1928b). The Self is the wellspring and source of what we call a religion in the most essential sense. The God Image, as a set of psychological actualizations, refers to the religious understanding and conceptualizations of the numinous energies exhibited by the Self. Because of the inevitable over-lapping of the Imago [Dei] and the [presumed] object, at times, no conceptual distinction is made between the two. This is especially the case with the radical concept of God and radical creed. This leads to an obvious fallacy when God is considered to be identical with God's psychological expressions and experiences. A fundamentalist attitude makes this obvious mistake that leads to an intellectual postulation of God "as if" he [God] were fully known. That is not to say that we cannot "know" God; on the contrary. A God that is wholly unknowable and distant would be useless and impractical, scarcely worthy of mention. We have to be careful when using the word "knowledge." Meister Eckhart says:

> Truly, you cannot be brought to know God divinely by any human science, nor by your own wisdom. To know

> God in God's way, your knowledge must change into outright unknowing, to a forgetting of yourself and every creature (in MacKendrick, 2001, p. 90).

Jungians believe that the process of individuation is the evolution of increasing consciousness and, as such, is the very process through which reality is realized. The Self in its totality represents the unification of the conscious and unconscious (Jung, 1939, p. 173), and precisely for this reason its knowledge will always be a mystery and a paradox. Chicanery and trickiness thus spring from the same problem: Anyone can claim to have the correct and definitive yardstick by which God is measured. The fanatic mind typically refuses to measure its yardstick against the yardstick somebody else uses.

Theocalypsis arouses a blinding eagerness to believe one is right. Its strength is drawn from the fact that the highest authority is postulated as its basis. For a person caught in theocalypsis, the logic goes something like this: "If there is a God behind my intentions, how can I be wrong?" Any intention or deed enacted under such logic is understood as "good."

Imagine a horrible, repulsive act: Let's say detonating a bomb in a day-care center to make a political/religious statement. The process of cognitive dissonance prevents a person under the spell of theocalypsis from keeping two contradictory claims in mind simultaneously: the good God and the horrible deed. Defensive maneuvers hide one's egotistic desires behind the God image. We could observe how [the good] God was used to justify the cruel and inhumane practice of slavery in the U.S. This continued after all the Northern states abolished or set in motion the reduction and elimination of the practice by 1804. Identification with an absolutely good entity who endorses one's actions like owning slaves, does not allow a person to also be aware of the evil nature of the practice of slave holding. There are also cases in which a person identifies with the dark side of the numinosum and proceeds to commit evil deeds under the aegis of this aspect of the numinosum. That was the case of Dennis Rader, known as BTK killer, who claimed that Satan possessed him. The problem with the philosophy of *privatio boni*, (the denial of the reality of evil) is most eminent with theocalypsis. A person who has identified with some partial aspect of a deity can still submit to the authority of a higher deity. However, a person whose psyche is consumed by the idea of one and only supreme God is caught in a singular paradigm with very few avenues for correction.

Achieving insight is only possible by a redefinition of the given paradigm and restructuring of the relationship with God. Polytheism allows for a greater degree of regulation of affect because of the many options (diversity of gods and goddesses) available. Gods and Goddesses were mutually interdependent and could influence each other by their actions and thus, relativize the value of the other. Monotheism denies this option and, by postulating only one supreme God, inadvertently denies the ego access to the functions of compensation. The relationship with God became unified (possibly simplified), but at the same time, it created the phenomenon of *tertium non datur* (No third {possibility} is given). The problem of theocalypsis lies in the fact that there is no higher entity that can offer a refuge or fuel change. Thus, theocalypsis sets the highest demands on one's moral consciousness. Jungian psychology, particularly archetypal psychology as developed by James Hillman, holds the view that the archetypes need to be viewed as phenomenologically separate realities and, hence, could be considered akin to a psychological return to polytheism. Here is a quote concerning polytheism from Hillman (1975):

> Crucial in our move has been the insistence on the mythical polytheistic perspective. Psychic complexity requires all the Gods; our totality can only be adequately contained by a Pantheon. ...the nature of psychic reality: not I, but we; not one but many. Not monotheistic consciousness looking down from its mountain, but polytheistic conscious wandering all over the place, in the vales and along the rivers, in the woods, the sky and under the earth (*Re-Visioning Psychology*, p. 33)

God Image Ought to be in Service of Individuation

One of the crucial functions of religion is to provide guidance for the ego to navigate numinous energies and to be protected against their overwhelming impact that could otherwise lead to disintegration or psychosis. Rituals, sacred teachings, and practices are designed to create a symbolic container through which the energies of the archetypal world can be transformed, humanized, and used for growth. If the *Imago Dei*, within the individual, reflects its source in a way that is not overly defensive, it will promote individuation. It all depends on how the ego contemplates and understands symbolic reality. Donald Kalsched teaches that the imagination transcends the limitations of the human ego and creates experiences by which it can encounter the real world, while on the other hand mere fantasy is a protective escape from the pain, and thus an escape from the real world. In his theory, fantasy keeps the dark aspect of the numinosum apart from the light, while imagination can foster a process that allows for the integration of the true, paradoxical Self. If the ego is to preserve its human role, it has to find a golden *middle* path. The desired position allows permeability between ego and the Self. Jung referred to this position as the *balanced state,* where the ego employs its moral power through virtues and a "humble attitude." If the *Imago Dei* is not "incarnated," to use Edinger's expression (Edinger, 1999), through the process of building ego-consciousness, then it consumes the personality and imposes the power of its idea dogmatically. A person in the grip of the *Imago Dei* has very little leverage to transmute this power and confront it with a compensatory ego-reality idea. When the *Imago Dei* possesses the ego, it feels so right and true that the ego has very little energy left to argue against it.

The Self moves the ego through the energy of emotion, idea and image; these phenomena come to us like a "voice" that has its own life. William James (1902), who heavily influenced Jung in his research, expressed his findings in the following way:

> We may now lay it down as certain that in the distinctively religious sphere of experience, many persons (how many we cannot tell) possess the objects of their belief, not in the form of mere conceptions, which their intellect accepts as true, but rather in the form of quasi-sensible realities directly apprehended (p. 63).

His findings claim that religious experience is always an emotional and a perceptual experience in relation to a transcendent entity [The Self], which is apperceived as a "reality." Created doctrine or rational understandings and explanations are a secondary phenomenon to the primary "raw" affective experience of the numinosum.

Unhealthy Fixation

A rational doctrine is created to *contain* and explicate religious experience. If the rational container excludes some parts or aspects of the experience, then the container is inadequate, incomplete. That is, the process is one of attempting to translate or transpose experience into an understandable linguistic frame, for example, a doctrine. Once the doctrine is established the approach becomes one of attempting to fit one's experience into the formal canon or creed. The defensive use of the *Imago Dei* leads to the *fixation* of certain religious ideas, or views of the deity. If the idea of God is used to foster archetypal defenses rather than to integrate the energy of the Self, it becomes hypostatized in the mind as a rather sterile and empty ideological construct. Such religious content has lost its inherent connection to the numinous and is thus typically closed to the creation or use of the transcendent function. However, the symbol is the exact opposite of such sterile content—it channels living archetypal energy. Jung (1951c) said:

> For without the existence of conscious concepts apperception is, as we know, impossible. This explains numerous neurotic disturbances which arise from the fact that certain contents are constellated in the

> unconscious but cannot be assimilated owing to the lack of apperceptive concepts that would 'grasp' them. That is why it is so extremely important to tell children fairy tales and legends, and to inculcate religious ideas (dogmas) into grown-ups, because these things are instrumental symbols with whose help unconscious contents can be canalized into consciousness, interpreted, and integrated. Failing this, their energy flows off into conscious contents which, normally, are not much emphasized, and intensifies them to pathological proportions (Jung 1951c, [CW 9ii, para. 259).

Fixation of religious content appears in various degrees of intensity. The strength with which the fixation is established corresponds to the intensity of inflation.

D. Theocalypsis: "Hiding behind the God"

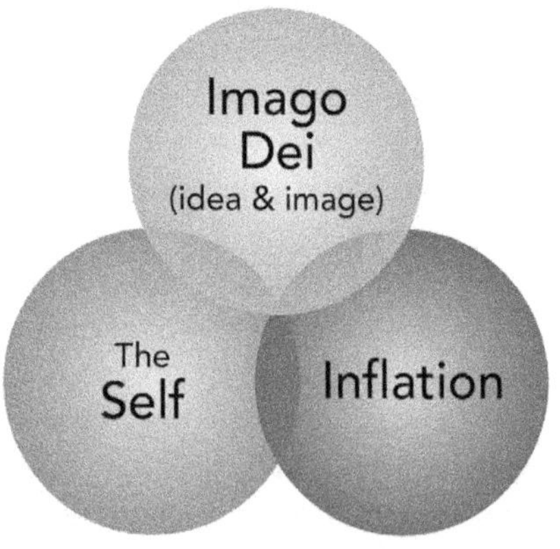

Constituents of Theocalypsis

We chose the term theocalypse or theocalypsis (theocalypsis, Greek: θεόκαλυψις) to describe all phenomena of religious possession. The word *theocalypse* (*theokalypsis*) is presented here to describe the process of:

1) religious inflation by

2) the Self, with

3) the simultaneous creation of specific ideology, beliefs

4) and/or the presence of accompanying archetypal image-symbol (*Imago Dei*) referring to a supreme, transcendent being.

Theocalypsis = Inflation + Archetype of the Self + God Image. The word theocalypse theocalypsis or theokalypsis) comes to mean "hiding behind the god"; to believe one literally and categorically knows God's intentions and thoughts and believes one is acting in God's name.[187] Psychologically, this term can be conceived of as an *ego being eclipsed by the energy of the Self justified by religious imagery, terminology and ideology*. Any of these components could be unconscious and discoverable only by a deeper analysis. For example, some conspiracy theories look very rational on their surface, but within their structure we can find many parallels with religion. For example, the Supreme Being now has a secret society of Freemasons, a secret service or alien civilization. Some parallels between the Imago Dei of conspiracism and fundamentalist religions are as follows:

1. Conspiratorialists believe in a potentially omnipotent director and a perfect plan for a particular conspiracy.
2. All conspiracies have primal cause.
3. Conspiratorialists look for secret signs and clues.
4. Conspiratorialists are chosen to find the secret through their ability to see by the heart.
5. The object of their quest is revealed to them by their ability to read in between the lines.
6. Their knowledge is unshakable and is treated by them as faith.
7. They idolize their own sources and refuse to question their authority. There is only ONE truth (their own).

[187] From Greek: *calypso* – hiding, *theos* – god.

8. They surrender their will and passively accept their responsibility for the states of affair.
9. Conspiratorialists feel an obligation to convert others. Righteousness.
10. Conspiratorialists believe in the struggle between good and evil and they themselves are on the good side.
11. They believe in supreme justice.
12. They believe in the Triumph of the Good.[188]

A mana personality would fall into this category only if it would have it's bearing in religious language and the image of God (*Imago Dei*). Any archetypal process is essentially religious to the extent that it produces numinous experiences and finds a corresponding vocabulary or thought content. For example, the abovementioned conspiracism, dynamics at a football game, technoparty,[189] falling madly in love, or falling blindly for a political ideology are all examples backed by archetypal energies and follow the same psychic rules we observe with religious phenomena.[190] To qualify as *religious,* in line with our definition, it must contain a corresponding ideology or imagery referring to the deity or God. Where possession by the Self is justified, rationalized, or explained by a set of relatively fixed religious ideas, theocalypse is being referenced. These ideas might not necessarily refer to God but to some of God's attributes or attributes of an omnipotent being.

---

[188] See more: Šolc, V., *Kde se rodí konspirační teorie*, Vesmír, April, 2016.

[189] See: Šolc, V., Archetyp otce a jiné hlubinně psychologické studie, (*Mysterium Musicus*, p.13), Triton, 2011, Praha.

[190] Even though it is not so apparent today, in ancient times ballgames were strictly of a religious nature. The oldest literary reference to ballgames dates back to 1000 B.C. But there are reasons to believe that Mesoamerican Mayans were practicing ballgames caled *pitz* more than 4,000 years ago, (Ekholm, 1991). Ancient ballgames should not be considered a sport in our contemporary view, but rather religious rituals whose aim was to initiate adepts (players, i.e., warriors) to the secrets of the sacred world, to win favors from their gods in order to ensure a good harvest and the like. See more in Šolc, V., *Ve jménu Boha*, dodatky, *Psychologie míčové hry*, Triton, 2013, p. 200.

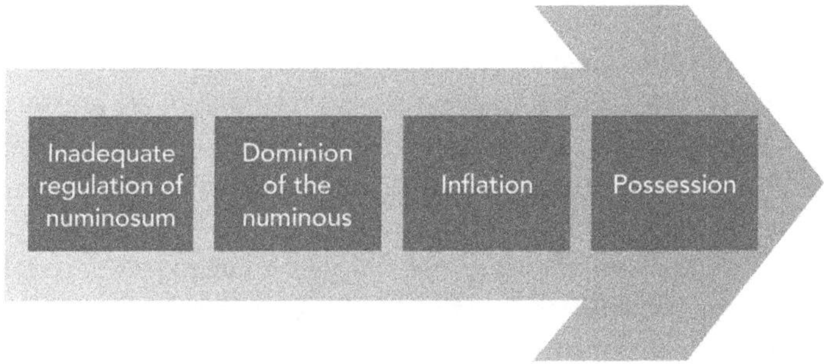

Scope of Theocalypsis

The biblical notion of a *pseudoprophetes* (Greek ψευδοπροφήτης) or false prophets is an idea that pertains to theocalypse. A false prophet is the one who "[acts] the part of a divinely inspired prophet, utters falsehoods under the name of divine prophecies" (New Testament Greek Lexicon, n.d., p.1). This notion appears multiple times throughout the New Testament. For instance,

> "Beware of false prophets, which come to you in sheep's clothing, but inwardly they are ravening wolves" (Matt 7:15 King James);
> "Beloved, believe not every spirit, but try the spirits whether they are of God: because many false prophets are gone out into the world" (1 John 4:1);
> "And the devil that deceived them was cast into the lake of fire and brimstone, where the beast and the false prophet are, and shall be tormented day and night for ever and ever" (Rev 20:10).

"*Probate spiritus si ex Deo sint*": Probe the spirits, to see if they come from God. This advice was given in order to help recognize the energies that came about as a result of one's inflation (antichrist).[191] The ego, which does not critically probe

[191] "Beloved, do not believe every spirit, but test the spirits to see whether they are from God, for many false prophets have gone out into the world." 1 John 4:1 (Bible, English Standard Version, p.1, n.d.)

(i.e., does not have a [conscious] critical distance from the archetypal energies) can free-fall into identification with them. A false prophet is somebody who takes the inflationary pressure of archetypal imagery at face value and considers it to be real. Such a message creates a *false religion* because it is one-sided, quite deceiving, and simply ego serving. It can be of value for the individual and the collective only if the message is decoded and a meaningful connection with respect to the broader, ethical life is made. A false prophet thus advocates for a one-sided *Imago Dei* correspondingly anchored in inflated and false premises.

Mythical Image of Theocalypsis

As stated earlier, we chose the term theocalypsis to describe the process of "being trapped" by the inadequate regulation of archetypal-Self energy and by an insufficient and incommensurate representation of the *Imago Dei*. Like Odysseus trapped by Calypso, the minds of extremists and fanatically religious persons are trapped by unregulated archetypal-Self energy and thus prevented from further individuation.

Penelope represents the correct mean of individuation, the authentic anima, while Calypso represents the distracting, inadequate anima of archetypal illusion. While Odysseus' wife, Penelope, represents a balanced relationship to the Self, Calypso represents a grandiose, power-laden, overly seductive, distorted relationship to the Self. Calypso provided a distraction and was a false refuge, even though she was indeed a refuge, both pleasurable and sweet. Nonetheless, Calypso saved Odysseus and was in some respects very helpful. She played a vital role in his life. Without her help, Odysseus would not have survived. Penelope was Odysseus's true soulmate, his moral duty and [she] embodied his highest spiritual aspiration. Odysseus spent a third of his time in his journey with Calypso, which says something about the significance of his distraction. Nevertheless, in the end, he was freed only by the intervention and message from Hermes.

Theocalypse can be viewed as a process and a distinct state. As a *process*, it refers to a mode of archetypal Self-inflation that easily leads to a corresponding establishment of a religious ideology. Theocalypse, as a *state* of mind, refers to a psychological state of inflation by the Self and the presence of simultaneous religious ideology. Under theocalypsis, one believes God is at all times backing one up. Theocalypsis makes a person feel entitled to speak on God's behalf ("*Vox Dei*": One speaks for God) with an unqualified confidence. Theocalypsis is ultimately a defensive fantasy structure that ensures the protection of the ego from the fragmenting influence of the numinosum.

Self-Care System Preserves Theocalypsis

Donald Kalsched's (1996) research on trauma provides an explanation of the phenomenology of the archetypal processes when fantasy is used defensively. Kalsched called the archetypal mechanism protecting and isolating the ego from further trauma "the self-care system." He compared it to the body's immune system (p. 17). The archetypal self-care system functions as an ego-surrogate that takes over the psychic system when the ego's normal functions are debilitated. When the self-care system gets activated, it not only protects the ego from trauma, but also keeps it from any creative activity (imaginal or otherwise). He says:

> The self-care system performs the self-regulatory and inner/outer mediational functions that, under normal conditions, are performed by the person's functioning ego. (...) Once the trauma defense is organized, all relations with the outer world are "screened" by the self-care system. What was intended to be a defense against further trauma becomes a major resistance to all unguarded spontaneous expressions of the self in the world. The person survives but cannot live creatively, (p. 150).

That explains why so many victims of trauma find refuge in stern religious ideology: It provides a safe haven for them. The negative side of this refuge is that they become prisoners of their own trauma and hence cannot realize that they do not hold the keys to free themselves from their own imprisonment; ironically, the dark Self does. Examined through the lens of Kalsched's theory, theocalypsis is a state of encapsulation of the personal spirit within a world of illusion that serves to prevent it from re-experiencing a traumatic reality and all its consequences (p. 40). Theocalyptic adaptations, or maladaptations, are found widely among trauma victims, particularly where the trauma has been deeply embedded through effecting developmental processes. In the myth explored here Odysseus had suffered multiple traumas. A survivor of Trojan War, on the way home he lost his six best men sailing between Scylla and Charybdis (one per each head of the monster Scylla), then the rest of his crew was killed by the Sun god Helios for disobeying his orders (and eating Helios's cattle). Then while sailing alone he was practically drowned in the sea by Poseidon. It took seven years on the Isle of Ogygia for Odysseus' healing and recovering from multiple traumas.

Based on etiology, severity and length of duration, we now propose a further classification of various states of theocalypsis.

E. Characteristics of Theocalypsis

We need to distinguish between persistent (chronic) and transitional (acute) theocalypsis and between active (reactive) and passive (withdrawn) theocalypsis. Transitional theocalypsis can serve the ego as an adaptation period during which the ego is consolidating its strengths against numinous energies. If this stage becomes unnecessarily protracted and the ego is seized by one-sidedness, we speak of chronic maladaptive theocalypsis. The biblical story of original sin reveals the serious consequences of breaching this taboo. While the land of childhood promises bliss, the adult world promises greater wholeness where pain gives joy its true dimension. God would not have put the tree of knowledge at the center of paradise if he had known that Adam and Eve would never use its resources.

Increased consciousness bears with itself suffering and moral responsibility. This is the heroic task of individuation. Theocalypse manifests in varying degrees. Mild forms of theocalypse should not be considered inflationary but essentially a form of adaptation through the regulation of Self-energy via a more or less rigid ideological (religious) system. A moderate form of theocalypse represents a more passionate religious adherence. At the extreme end of the spectrum theocalypse manifests as religious possession observable in terrorism. There is an even more extreme form and degree of theocalypse; *theomania*, a form of psychosis, (psychotic disorder) that occurs when one believes he or she is literally God himself, or God's obedient messenger. Mark David Chapman, who murdered John Lennon, in his defense in 1980, stated that he was instructed by God to do so.[192] For the milder forms of theocalypsis, it is typical to be God-inspired. For the moderate type, it is typical to be God-advised. However, for the more severe forms, individuals tend to be God-ordered, and in the most extreme cases, God-willed. Active forms of theocalypsis have more to do with possession by the *fascinans* quality of the Self, while the passive forms of theocalypsis are predominantly based on shame and thus associated with the *tremendos* quality of the Self.

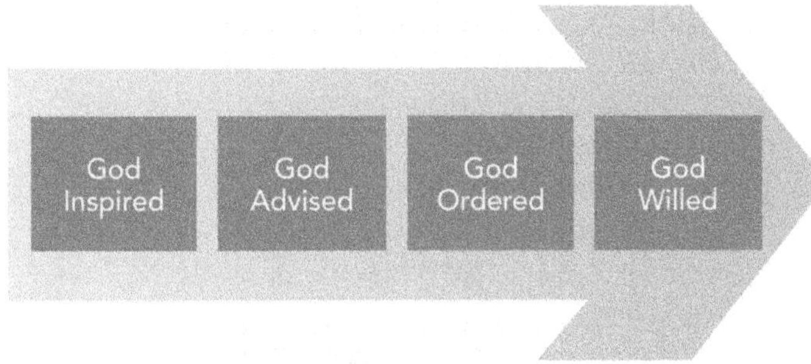

Scale of Inflation by the Self and Its Efect on Ego

[192] CNN Library, 2014, p. 1, n.d.

Below we offer some characteristics typical for theocalypsis. Some of these characteristics of theocalypsis have been discussed above, while others have not.

Basic characteristics of theocalypsis

The first group of characteristics, or should we say symptoms, are called *general*. General characteristics for theocalypsis have been discussed above and can be found in Jungian literature.[193]

General conditions include:

1) Hubris
2) Ethical Infantilism
3) Unconscious Identity (*participation mystique*)
4) Lack of *Aidos*
5) Relinquishment of Will
6) Inadequate Relationship to Paradox
7) Identification with the Self
8) Inferiority of Consciousness

The second group of characteristics is concerned more with the *cognitive* processes and the approaches to religious products (texts and teachings). These attributes can be described as cognitive characteristics, which include:

1) Concretism and naive literalism
2) Historicism and externalism
3) Selective rationality
4) Inconsistency and intellectual rigidity
5) Quasi-intellectualism
6) Absolutism and inerrancy
7) Moral superiority and moral Manichaeism
8) Millennialism and messianism
9) Dogmatism

The third group of characteristics refers to the way one deals with the affective (emotional) quality of the numinosum. These

[193] Their categorization should be viewed rather imprecisely because some of the characteristics could fit more than one category.

characteristics are classified as *affect* characteristics, which include:

1) Asymbolism
2) Inadequate Relationship to Paradox
3) One-Sided Orientation of Consciousness
4) Inadequate Regulation of Numinous Energy
5) Externalization of Numinous Energy
6) Dissociative Selectivity
7) Reactivity
8) Fear of Change and Fear of the New

Let us examine six of the characteristics in more detail.

Selective rationality.

The rationality of the mind that has been influenced by theocalypsis operates on rather loose principles. Some facts are presented as rational, but their rationality only extends to the point that they fit the *a priori* idea (premise) accepted by way of faith. Therefore, it would be more appropriate to call them rationalizations. Archetypal authority subordinates the thinking process under its preconceived feeling-toned agenda. This results in a thought process that is rather selective. Facts that confirm the *a priori* beliefs are accepted easily, without reflection. At the same time facts that are incongruent with accepted premises are rejected. For instance, creationism is accepted as a valid scientific theory, while evolution is dismissed as only one of several possible explanations of the origin of the species. To support the rational basis of their deduction, proponents of Intelligent design use terms such as experiment, analysis, theory, scientific proof (e.g. scientific creationism), and the like.

Because there is an already accepted idea in the background of their thinking, this form of rationality is closed to anything that might contradict it. For example, the human contribution to global warming is easily dismissed because of the belief that God is in charge of climatic changes, and man's influence cannot override God's will. Ultimately, all unexplainable, contradictory, or complex issues and questions are explained by the proposition of the "incomprehensible will of God." For example, even though the tragic death of a child contradicts the idea of an all-good God, it is often explained as something that the human mind cannot comprehend—resorting to the idea that God has a plan or some ultimate positive (!) goal.

Cognitive Dissonance

Leon Festinger (1957) explained the above example as *cognitive dissonance*.[194] The reduction of tension (discomfort, dissonance) caused by the simultaneous presence of contradicting ideas (i.e., bad/evil events and the idea of an all good God) is accomplished through rationalizing a selective explanation (consonance). If the reduction of tension cannot be accomplished by simply resolving the internal dissonance, the mind will use other psychological maneuvers (defenses) to avoid it. Some members of the Tea Party proclaim a strong respect to the Constitution of the United States, but at the same time, they oppose the right for gays and lesbians to marry, and oppose the separation of Church and state when it concerns the Christian Church.[195] The dissonance such people feel is eased by the belief that the Supreme Court's support for the separation of church and state is tainted and corrupt. A devoted traditional Catholic mother, in attempting to resolve a conflict between her lesbian daughter (V.Š.) and herself, stated: "We will not talk about that honey, OK?" It is a basic axiom that in the case of theocalypsis, cognitive processes are always subordinated to the rule of an unconscious authority and only secondarily to the authority of pure logic. Logic is twisted to justify the *a priori* authoritarian claim. It is the privileged and "sacred" belief that is often secretly harbored. It is always an unconscious "higher" authority that rules over individual autonomy.

---

[194] Festinger, L. (1957), *A Theory of cognitive dissonance*, Stanford, CA: Stanford University Press.
[195] See: Šolc, Vladislav (2011), *Tea party a fundamentalismus*, MF Dnes.

Many fundamentalists in the United States, for example, appear to vote against their own interests in what looks like blind obedience to their conservative religious and political leaders. *Sacrificium intellectus* is thus accomplished in the name of God but follows the order of a leader with whom one is unconsciously identified. For example, during his campaign and after, one of President Trump's (who attracted 80 percent of evangelical votes in 2016 elections) favorite phrases was "believe me;" it typically followed a false or misleading claim.

Magical Thinking Is Anchored In Fantasy

When God is postulated as a rigid, one-sided, dominant, idealized, and leading principle, then the *reality principle* is relegated to a secondary position.[196] When the mythical unconscious is overvalued, magical thinking predominates, and miracles are considered the norm and not the exception. In the state of Wisconsin, the parents of Leilani Neumann fervently prayed for their daughter when she developed severe diabetes. They never brought her to a medical doctor, despite the gradual deterioration of her health because they believed that God would heal her. Their daughter eventually went into a coma and died; nonetheless it did not lead to a change in their beliefs. Along similar lines, members of the Westboro Baptist Church praised the killer in the Arizona shooting in 2013. Beginning with the axiom that the God they worship is all-good, the act of shooting someone perceived to be opposed to God is believed to be desirable. The will that underlies such acts is attributed to God and is reinterpreted as evidence of God's revenge against the wicked and sinful.

---

[196] We are not using the term "reality principle" the way Freud used it. By reality principle we mean the ego's ability to recognize psychological and physical laws of reality in a broader sense. Examples of deviation from the reality principle are magical thinking, superstition, uncritical beliefs in miracles, and so on. If the ego's capacity to distinguish between fantasy and reality is poor it is dealt with by projection, rationalization, and other defense mechanisms.

Fanaticism Is Never Logically Consistent

Because of the influence of irrational unconscious contents, these types of thought processes areis often selective, inconsistent, and quasi-intellectual. Inflation causes that irrational element to possess a high degree of energy that results in influencing cognition without the awareness of the person concerned. As one's thinking is influenced by strong faith (archetypal energy) from the unconscious, the person cannot argue against it because the actual source goes unrecognized. A similar selectivity applies to the Holy Bible that is considered the direct word of God, yet certain passages that contradict modern values can be put aside as being outdated or illogical (i.e., slavery, stoning of prostitutes, an eye-for–an-eye, etc.). Once I had a discussion with a Jehovah's Witness about the Book of Job. (V.Š.) We discussed the idea of a just and all-good God. She claimed that God was good, omnipotent, and always knew the future. I asked her for an explanation as to why God listened to Satan when bringing suffering onto Job. She told me it was a mystery and my human intellect could not comprehend God's reasoning. That might be true, but what value does the idea of justice have if it is not anchored in some consensual, intelligible concept? Such an explanation is selective because it excludes some phenomena from logical exploration. Naturally, there are many irrational or mysterious aspects to life and existence, but if so, we ought to be able to call them such. Calling something an *a priori* good, or bad for that matter, does not allow for awe, because it is already decided. An example of quasi-intellectualism might be the pursuit to present an Intelligent Design theory as a valid scientific theory. Faith and the rational process are conflated to the detriment of both.

In The Name of God

In the dynamics of theocalypsis one is hiding behind God. We might say that consciousness is hiding behind, or in, the unconscious. As suggested earlier, it is typical for religious fanatics to confuse their own will with the will of God. Extremists respond that God *told* them to do certain things, or they say they *know* what God wants them to do. Absolute certainty and a sense of righteousness are the very characteristics of theocalypsis. In this regard, a person who commits an act of terror that takes other's lives may have identified with God's right to take a life. In their hubris, the terrorist believes they are beyond good and evil and, like God, they know truth. Doubt must be suppressed because it might interfere with an a priori chosen goal. The mind of the fanatic is eclipsed by the *Imago Dei* and all urges, no matter how destructive, are ennobled by what is perceived as God's will.

Asymbolism:

The inability to think symbolically can turn the otherwise profound meaning into a goal of one's selfish intentions. The symbol, as a transcendent function, provides a bridge between the ego and the unconscious. It is thus a crucial constituent of psycho-spiritual development. Symbols, as they are the best possible expression of something unknown (not yet conscious) and therefore ever emerging, can be a source of continuous deepening and understanding of all things religious.

Symbol appears to be the representation of unconscious knowledge and expression. Consciousness is a process of abstracting that knowledge. Jung asserts that a symbol is an "expression of an intuitive idea that cannot yet be formatted in any other or better way" (CW 15, para. 105). Therefore, symbols are always "only indistinct, subsidiary associations to a thought, which obscure it rather than clarify it" (CW 3, para. 136). If symbols are understood and viewed as truly transcendent phenomena, and not simply as objective and established facts, they serve as tools for enlarging consciousness. A symbol considered on a subjective level provides meaning and opens many doors for the ongoing constructive process, while the symbol understood literally reduces the living psychic event to a command or a dogma. Individuation cannot take place without true engagement and confrontation with the symbol. Without the symbol, introspection may be incomplete, and without introspection, there's no individuation. In contrast a sign provides a definite explanation, so it's meaning is fixed in a definite way. A symbol opens one to unknown perspectives and is the source of a deeper sensibility and appreciation of reality; it is the mother of the ongoing birth of consciousness. The mother of a nine-year-old girl was referred to me (V.Š.) because she complained that her daughter was "bothering her," and would "not let her be" and "argued" every time her mother needed space for herself. Her father had died a year ago. It soon became apparent that the daughter and mother's behavior were deeply affected by this loss. Mother had not grieved; she simply put on a "strong-woman" persona. Her daughter, who was frighten by the loss of her dad, became very insecure and compensated by developing a clinging attachment to her mom – wanting to make sure that she was not going lose her, too. I helped mom to view their communication from a deeper and broader perspective, understanding her daughter's behavior symbolically and allowing her feelings of grief, fear and loss to be shared in their relationship. That helped remarkably.

Without symbolic understanding, the ego easily becomes an "automated thing." Computers, like the ego, can compute all kinds of mathematical and rational truths, but they do not possess the ability to engage or become affected by a symbol with feelings such as awe, guild, grief, compassion or love.

In the case of theocalypsis, the symbol may be strongly valued, but its most important function—to allow not only the creation of collective meaning, but also individual meaning—is missed. Though the symbol mediates potential psychic energy, in states of theocalypse that energy is not utilized to create new meaning, it only perpetuates the *a priori* established idea. Where meaning is lacking, the unconscious steps in with its archetypal energy that can often be to partial and raw, providing the ego simply with instinctive and therefore one-sided guidance. The whole is fragmented, and the symbol *in potentia,* cannot fulfill its function to transform or to elevate. When the symbol is interpreted literally, its meaning is omitted and even defended against. The symbol carries power, but when it cannot be utilized consciously; it declares itself through projection. Rather than increasing insight, the disconnected symbol increases bias and divisiveness. Dourley (2006) asserts:

> And yet even when symbol and myth are stripped of their spiritual vitality, they continue to exercise a truly possessive power over their victims in linking faith with collective unconsciousness. For they provide the instant truth and collective identity so appealing to the human lust for saving certitude to counter the authentic agony of doubt and ambiguity hanging over the human situation. Though it appeals to this baser spiritual instinct, fundamentalism is for that very reason likely to continue its present growth (p. 13).

If a symbol is used as an explanation for objective and extramundane events pertaining to God's work and intentions without a personal and intimate connection to one's soul, it does not bring about insight and consequent individual responsibility. A patient of mine, who was gradually becoming romantically involved with a very self-destructive drug addict, had a dream in which the water in the river was rising and she could only escape if she used her tools to build a boat (V.Š.). Her psychic, whom she went to see prior to coming to therapy, interpreted her dream in terms of a prediction of a possible objective flood in the future and cautioned her from traveling to risky areas. This type of interpretation provided little space for her personal growth. But if she was to contemplate the symbols in her dream, they would give her insight into why there might be a flood, which could also give her practical instructions of how to deal with it. Her troubles only worsened. In the meantime, her boyfriend went through a lot of her money. Eventually, she decided to leave her psychic and begin analysis.

When religious symbols that are not connected to the reality of the psyche their potential meaning remain tools of isolation. This has contributed to the ongoing split between different religions and within factions of many religions. Today, there are over 43,000 denominations worldwide in Christian religions alone![197] Each and every act aimed at hindering the spring of the numinous energy without its conscious integration risks producing another compartmentalization and dogmatization. The Self is as essential to a human being as life-sustaining water is for survival. As the great Dominican mystic Meister Eckhart stated: "Divinity is an underground river that no one can stop and no one can dam up."[198] We can and ought to compassionately share our religious experience with others, though without imposing it. However, if we are not able to recognize the value of others' religious experience, we are simply feeding into another split. As Matthew Fox states, "There is one underground river—but many wells into that river". Indeed, there is a Hindu well, a Christian well, a Buddhist well, a shamanistic well, a goddess well, a Jewish well, a Muslim well, and one might say an endless number of wells that all reach deep into the river of the collective unconscious.

If we decide to embrace a particular well and embrace its traditions, we ought not confuse the particular well with the great source, the archetypal underground river of the collective unconscious. Instead, we ought to celebrate the symbolic particularities and traditions of the well we embrace. Such a perspective brings to humanity the flowering of many hidden treasures that take bloom in the varied and multicultural wells of humankind. And thus, in the end, it unites all the religions under the most fundamental common denominator: the living Self.

Richard

A patient of mine (V.Š.), Richard, was struggling with some teachings of his church. His church was a very important source

---

[197] "These numbers have exploded from 1,600 in the year 1900." Center for the Study of Global Christianity at Gordon-Conwell Theological Seminary, 2012

[198] Fox, M., 2000 p. 5.

of community providing real spiritual guidance, but he struggled with a teaching that he suspected was "outdated" and "tendentious." He looked with skepticism on the church's financial practices, its position with the role of women, and on homosexuality. He grew up without a father, and his pastor was a strong authority figure for him. One day he had a dream:

> "We are in our church, and our pastor is explaining that in order to proceed to the remote Great Cathedral, an even greater place than our church, we must squeeze through the narrow tunnel. Pastor is instructing worshippers one by one to enter the tunnel. As I am getting closer in line, my anxiety is rising. I am asking myself why not exit the church and take the open streets. When I get to the opening of the tunnel, my pastor says: 'You must enter!' Then I feel it is not a good idea and head toward the door to take my *own* route."

One-Sided Orientation of Consciousness:

Theocalypsis is the manifestation of one-sided development; that represses the other side. When Odysseus was held hostage on the island of Ogygia, Calypso's main agenda was to make him lose sight of his goal. She did this by encouraging his psychological one-sidedness. She wanted to elevate and exaggerate one side of his experience and make him forget the other side. Calypso wanted to make her island the supreme experience for Odysseus. She almost succeeded, but then Hermes, Zeus's messenger from the other side, reminded him of his goal and ordered Calypso to release Odysseus. One-sidedness implies that something is suppressed or undeveloped and possibly feared. One side is elevated while the other remains unconscious. A pair of opposites that ideally are held together in tension are unnaturally broken apart. One side sinks into the unconscious, where it becomes potentially dark and destructive, while the other side becomes idealized. It is an unhealthy position precisely because it prevents the ego from having a conscious relationship with both sides. The voice of the unconscious side is being silenced and is denied its proper expression. However, this process does subdue the moral struggle of holding the opposites in tension, instead the entire process is made static and comes to a standstill in the individuation journey—this is the sweet illusion of the Isle of Ogygia.

We Cannot Run Away From Ourselves

The more a particular psychic content is repressed (anger, sexuality, etc.), the more compulsive that content becomes in one's life. In the religious paradigm, it is all too common to label compulsive elements as demonic—elements that need to be disposed of: suppressed.

Neal

I recall a case where a male patient came to see me about his sexual fantasies and to deal with his intense attraction to Internet pornography. (V.Š.) He hated himself for it because it was "against my church's principles." He asked me if I could cure him of his abnormal sexuality and said that his pastor could not help him nor had his prayers proven effective. He reported that his wife did not want to have an intimate relationship with him, and he only wanted to restore things to how they had been when he was a happy member of his church. Perhaps too early in the treatment, I hinted that his sexual obsession might be an expression of some vital need he was overlooking or denying to himself. He never came back.

An Inadequate Relationship To the Paradox:

Jung wrote:

> Oddly enough, the paradox is one of our most valued spiritual possessions, while uniformity of meaning is a sign of weakness. Hence a religion becomes inwardly impoverished when it loses or cuts down its paradoxes; but their multiplication enriches because only the paradox comes anywhere near to comprehending the

> fullness of life. Non-ambiguity and non-contradiction are one-sided, and thus, not suited to express the incomprehensible (1944, [CW 12, par. 18]).

According to Jung, paradox is an inherent natural property of all archetypal phenomena. It is the only expression of an otherwise indescribable nature of the transcendent. We can say that paradox is an expression of reality before consciousness, even though we cannot call anything paradoxical until discrimination by consciousness ensues. Things are just the way they are. A symbol always represents the unity of opposites, because without opposites, there would be no imperative to seek balance or symmetry. The Image of God is, in virtually all religions, paradoxical: God is simultaneously loving and punitive, a creator and a destroyer, immanent and transcendent.

That is to say that everything appears in conjunction with its opposite and that there is no clear line dividing these opposites. Just as there is no clear dividing-line between the four seasons, consciousness seldom finds precise criteria in making distinctions. The role of consciousness is to discriminate between the opposites of a paradoxical unity; however, we should keep in mind that it is always an individual act dependent on one's perspective. Opposites commonly reverse their positions. What seems to be clearly positive can emerge as negative, and what appears negative can emerge as positive; opposites perpetually fluctuate. As a result, absolute judgments are elusive. Take a virus for example. As an organism, it can be viewed as a negative, a nuisance, but occasionally viral invasion of a cell facilitates more rapid evolutionary changes. There are countless phenomena in nature that are rendered as bad or *evil* despite the fact that in a wider sense, there is an underlying paradox.

The collective unconscious is beyond good and evil and the only way for us to come to terms with it is to develop a relationship embracing the inherent paradoxes that arise. What does not work is to try to conform the collective unconscious to our individual likes and preferences.

Conflict of Opposites As Natural Process

Consciousness springs forth as a result and fruit of the conflict between opposites. Conflict itself is natural and purposeful; as Pascal stated, it is also the steadiest and most certain aspect of human nature. The process of individuation proceeds via the tension of opposites. What is first a black-*or*-white perspective becomes black-*and*-white. Jung's analysis builds on the knowledge that if the tension between the opposites can be *held* consciously, then the internal psychic process will restructure our consciousness in ways that resolve the conflict. The solution is based on inclusion and acceptance rather than on exclusion and rejection. This kind of solution is informed by the Self, not the ego, and therefore carries an irrational element within itself. It arises as a new and more comprehensive and adaptive attitude simultaneously with a sense of resolution and relieved tension between opposites (i.e., a higher relationship to the paradox). The paradox transcends the individual opposites; what was previously locked in a state of constant indecision and oscillation between opposites is released in a more complex, nuanced, and ultimately peaceful experience of reality. Acceptance comes about with ego's letting go of its insistence on perfection, or the ideal, or on a one-sided perspective.

The ability to live with paradox corresponds to the process of individuation. Another way of saying this is that the process of individuation suffers the conflicts consciously and leads to the unification of opposites. If the tension is too great and the ego is unable to withstand that tension, then the opposites may be constellated even more powerfully, with the result that the conflict will continue expressing itself in regressive ways, such as splitting, projection and acting-out. The conflict continues to be rendered as an externalized matter.

Unrecognized Conflict Is Projected Outside

De-externalization of the conflict, that is, the withdrawal of projections combined with understanding the reason the conflict exists, returns us to the original source of conflict—the inherent nature of opposites that exist at the collective unconscious level.

Betsy

One clinical example comes to mind. (V.Š.) A woman in her 40s had been trying to conceive children with her husband for 16 years. They both were devoted members of the Catholic Church, law-abiding citizens, and good people. Over the years, they spent a great deal of money on infertility treatments and doctors with no results. They were informed that there was nothing wrong with them physiologically, so they should be able to have children. My patient's husband encouraged his wife to see me when her sister became pregnant with her first child. As a result of this, Betsy became very angry with her sister and brother-in-law, and the conflict escalated to the point that the family broke apart. Betsy stopped communicating with her parents and accused her sister of all sorts of imaginable evils. My patient and her husband could not understand how God could have blessed her *bad* sister with a baby, but left the two of them barren! It took two years for my patient to work through this situation and restore her relationship with her sister. In the end, she was able to express her anger toward God and express compassion for her sister. Betsy eventually became pregnant and has a daughter. Betsy's externalizing of her internal conflict led to her vilifying her sister and projecting onto her the negative, resentful aspects of her own conflicts. Her anger was displaced in part because of the one-sided idealization of the *Imago Dei*: the light side of the Self. With the recovery of her negative (dark side) projections, her relationship with her sister and brother-in-law was healed.

Externalization of the Self or Systematic Blindness:

Jung famously stated:

"What one could almost call a systematic blindness is simply the effect of the prejudice that God is *outside* man" (1938, [CW 11, para. 100] emphasis ours).

Making God an entity that is infinitely remote and absolutely different from humankind does not help with the development of a relationship with oneself and the God-within. When divinity is conceived of as wholly extrinsic to the human psyche, the need to submit one's wills to an external, divine authority increases. For Jung, such theology represents contempt for the human soul. (Dourley, p. 25)

It is typical for a theocalypsis to follow a theology where the God Image corresponds to a remote external authority. In this case God is simply an ordering imperative and not a living experience. Jung uses the term "uprootedness," suggesting a disconnection from the very source of spirit. Such an attitude is inimical to psycho-spiritual growth and hinders individuation. Jung's choice of the word "systematic" refers to the institutionalization of the Churches' teaching of the *Imago Dei* as pertaining, primarily, to an extrinsic deity. Such a view is radically one-sided, limited, and one might say, immature, because it is based on identification with the Self. This identification is a patriarchal usurping and control of the autonomous power of the Self. In the Christian Dispensation one might say, the Kingdom of God is not the Church.

Homoousia

Jung spent a great portion of his life showing that, indeed, God manifests himself *in* his creation and *through* man's psyche. A God *within* makes immanent sense psychologically! Without entering into theological discourse, we'd like to point out that Jung agreed with the theological view that a God who is not of the same substance as man (*homoousia*) cannot intimately relate to or engage humankind (p. 58-9). For God to be able to individually touch humans and effect transformation and change, it would be an indispensable condition, *sine qua non*, that there be an ontological unity between the two. Otherwise, God would be wholly unreachable. These considerations are not necessarily Jungian; but are found in the mystical teachings of many religions. Jacob Boehme (1622) recognized the need to seek God *inside* centuries ago. In his *Dialogue*, Boehme wrote: substance as man (*homoousia*)[199] cannot really touch him (pp. 58-59).[200]

> The Disciple said to his Master: Sir, How may I come to the Place that I may SEE with God, and may HEAR God speak - to a Life that is above my Senses and Feelings—to the Supersensual Life? The Master answered and said: Son, when thou canst throw thyself into THAT, where no Creature dwelleth, though it be but for a Moment, then thou HEAREST what God speaketh. Disciple: Is that Place where no Creature dwelleth near at Hand; or is it afar off? Master: It is IN THEE. And if thou canst, my Son, for a while but cease from all thy OWN Thinking and Willing, then thou shalt hear the unspeakable Words of God (p. 4).

More recently, Tillich (1948) repeatedly stressed the importance of God being ontologically continuous with his creation while *not* being "split within himself, as religious

---

[199] *Homoousia* is a Greek (ὁμός, *homós*, "same" and Greek:οὐσία, *ousía*, "essence, substance") theological term used by the early Church Fathers in discussion of the Christian understanding of God as Trinity. The Nicene Creed describes Jesus as being *homooúsios* with God the Father — that is, they are of the "same substance" and are equally God. The Nicene Creed describes Jesus the Christ as being *homooúsios* with God the Father — that is, they are of the "same substance" and are equally God.

[200] Jung is not referring to the Godhead but a God Image: "It would be regrettable mistake if anybody should take my observations as a kind of proof of the existence of God. They prove only the existence of an archetypal God Image, which to my mind is the most important and influential archetype, its relatively frequent occurrence seems to be a noteworthy fact for any theologia naturalis." (Jung, CW 11, par. 102, pp. 58-59)

dualism has asserted" (p. 116). Tillich called such assertions that divide the divine into two irreconcilable parts — god and evil— "supernaturalistic," based on "a distortion of genuine manifestation of the mystery of being" (p. 117). Autonomous products of the psyche— images and symbols— must be connected and intrinsically related to man if they are to have any meaning. If they were arbitrary, then what would be God's role after all? Jung taught that humans are of a conscious and an unconscious nature, and if a symbol brings them together via reflection and action, it has real implications on the person's life and well-being. Religion that reflects the deity within is connected with one's core and encourages introspection and dialogue; religion that keeps God as *wholly other* and extrinsic remains authoritarian, and as a result, socially divisive. Dourley (2006) said:

> Jung's understanding of the psyche rests on a conception of containment which tolerates no invasion of the psyche by agencies beyond the psyche. This imperative demands that responsible religion recall the Gods to their psychic origin, where dialogue with them would continue on an individual basis (Jung, 1940, p. 85) ... This dialogue would be at once socially safer and personally more harrowing. It would be socially safer because it would undermine the conflict between religious communities who claim a universal truth for one or other of their competing, still-transcendent Gods. The dialogue would be more harrowing because it would face the individual with an inner critique more personal, rigorous, and defiant of evasion than any religion can muster (p. 46).

Organic Unity of Psyche and Spirit

Individuation is not only a process of adaptation, it is also a deeply spiritual flowering of a person: It brings God closer to one and one closer to the divine. Human maturation and human deification are two sides of the same coin. Psychologically, individuation originates and proceeds from the Self. Thus, the

Self is the common source of spirituality and psychological growth. Symbols and rituals that have been the cornerstones of religious systems throughout the ages, are not superficial synthetic, man-made images, but deep organs of the soul on which psychological functioning fundamentally depends. If we look at Tertullian's dictum that (*Apol.* 17.6; *Patrologia Latina* 1:377), *Anima naturaliter Christiana est* (The soul is by nature Christian), via a Jungian understanding of the psyche, we naturally conclude that psyche is sacred by its very organic arrangement: *Anima naturaliter religiosa est* (The soul is by nature religious). This leads Dourley (1984) to state: "religious and psychological experiences are *organically* one" (p. 85). Dourley also stresses the importance of recognizing that 1) [an] "ability to experience God is the most valuable natural *endowment* of the psyche and 2) that the intensification of this experience is *functionally* identical with the process of psychic, and so spiritual and human, maturation" (p. 86). Dourley recognizes Jung's deep insight that human life is a religious process. Revelation proceeds through the same channels as psychological growth does. Consequently, denying or eliminating the sacred from the psyche produces dissociative phenomena.

Dissociative Selectivity:

Unadapted and unintegrated psychological functions result in poor adaptation to the environment. Archaic qualities of the unconscious find expression through compulsive and uncontrollable urges (enactments). The ego, being neither aware of, nor willing to admit to, the dangerous quality of archaic unconscious content, cannot find a way of regulating the unconscious content in ways that would be revitalizing. It becomes a *fait accompli*—the ego becomes assimilated by the Self. When the ego loses its regulating function, the unconscious has a way of possessing the ego. Jung reflected:

> The image of wholeness then remains in the unconscious, so that on the one hand it shares the archaic nature of

> the unconscious and on the other finds itself in the psychically relative space-time continuum that is characteristic of the unconscious as such. Both these qualities are numinous and hence have an unlimited determining effect on ego-consciousness, (1951a, [CW 9ii, para. 45]).

Suppressed or poorly integrated archetypal energies work with increased energy once they become autonomous and lose their connection with the ego As the personality succumbs to the dictatorship of archaic, instinctive qualities, the ego loses mastery in its own house and submits to the unconscious.

Von Franz (1993) said:

> [This] barbaric quality of the inferior function which is mixed up with the other attitudinal type is one of the great practical problems and constitutes the great split of the human personality ... one risks (or even cannot avoid) being temporarily possessed by the opposite attitude and thereby become barbaric and unadapted (pp. 123-124).

Von Franz also noted that the inferior function, like Pac-Man, "eats up" all the rest of the personality (p. 53).

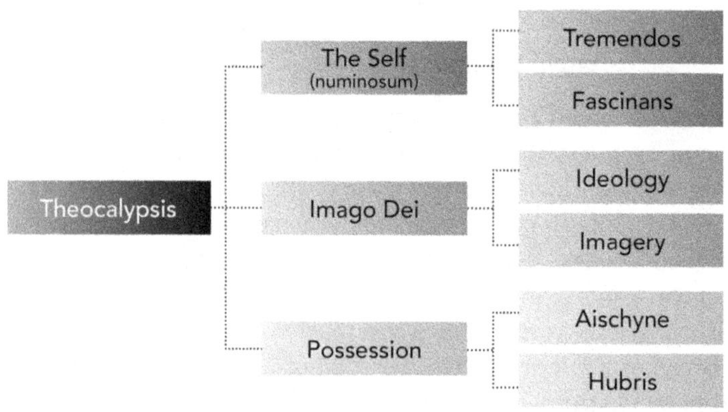

go eclipsed by the energy of the Self justified by religious imagery, terminology and ideology.

Theocalypsis

Excessive adherence to one's *Imago Dei,* as seen in religious extremism, serves as a catalyst for this process. Those whose religious persuasions are based on the selective demonization and suppression of certain psychic qualities are more vulnerable to the effects of the inferior function. In the case of theocalypsis, we often find a high idealization and adherence to an *all-good God Image*. Everything that does not fit the definition of a *good* God inevitably becomes split-off. This process of splitting adds to the development of one's shadow, resulting in the accumulation of excessive, split-off energy. Over time, this excessive energy will eventually be unleashed unconsciously in one destructive form or another. A sexual impulse, for instance, can be cognitively categorized as a *tremendum* and thus be fearfully avoided and not acknowledged, accepted, and consciously worked with. Recent uncovering of the sexual abuse scandals within the Catholic Church confirms Jung's theory on the inferior function. There is reason to believe that the non-credible (i.e., not corresponding to reality; Main, 2006) God Image and the resulting inadequate channeling of the archetypal energies (*numinosum*) are behind *compulsive* acts in strongly religious communities. The case of Pastor Ted Haggard, who publicly denounced homosexuality while secretly, seeking homosexual encounters, provides an example of this phenomenon.

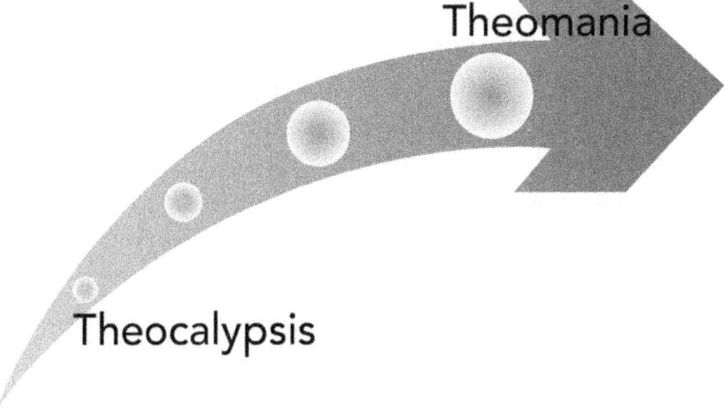

Intensity of Theocalypsis

An extreme case of theocalyptic dissociation is theomania. In this situation, the ego's capacity for regulating the energy of the Self (*aidos*) is very poor or nonexistent. The autonomy of the collective unconscious usurps the ego and its functions and thereby takes control and does what it will.

Jacob

I treated a man with the psychotic form of theocalypsis—theomania. (V.Š.) When under an acute psychotic attack, the patient believed that he was a messenger of God. He became possessed by a spirit and was writing "prophecies" for days. He would write in ancient Russian and stop only when totally exhausted. When possessed by the archetype of the Self, my patient exhibited manic features: he would not sleep, he was overly excited, and he did not communicate with other people. His writings were always concerned with knowledge of the future. His visions were apocalyptic; he wrote about the Antichrist's coming and causing World War III. His visions were messianic and culminated in the second coming of Christ: when the elect are saved and the righteous live forever. His notes were extremely detailed. His writings contained names and dates and filled of hundreds of pages. When he was in one of his cyclic florid states, he was absolutely identified with his noble role. One of his short poems read: "Look, look, can you see? God almighty that is me!" He believed he was God's messenger and believed that what he wrote was literally true; he could not view it symbolically. It WILL happen! Wittgenstein (1953/2001) defined faith as compassionate adherence to the frame of reference. In the case of my patient, the concrete adherence to his beliefs, equals identification with the Self. His blind passion that sprang from the Self was so strong; he was unable to gain any ego-distance without the aid of medication.

When stabilized, he was able to reflect on the "voice within" and was able to partially regain his "earthly" identity. Thus, our therapeutic work involved strengthening his ego in order to help him contain and transform these energies. I considered it successful when this patient was able to have some relationship with these autonomous powers—that were "making him write." The ability to regulate his experience of the *fascinans* of the Self remained poor. Without the capacity to hold these energies, he fell into direct identification with them. We can view his "prophecies" as unconscious Self-compensations for his violent urges—this helped him cope. When he discovered religion, he felt "saved." He suddenly was not alone, and his suffering started to have meaning. Nonetheless, his religion remained fundamentalist, lacking a symbolic dimension, while never learning to have a constructive relationship with the numinosum. His father had

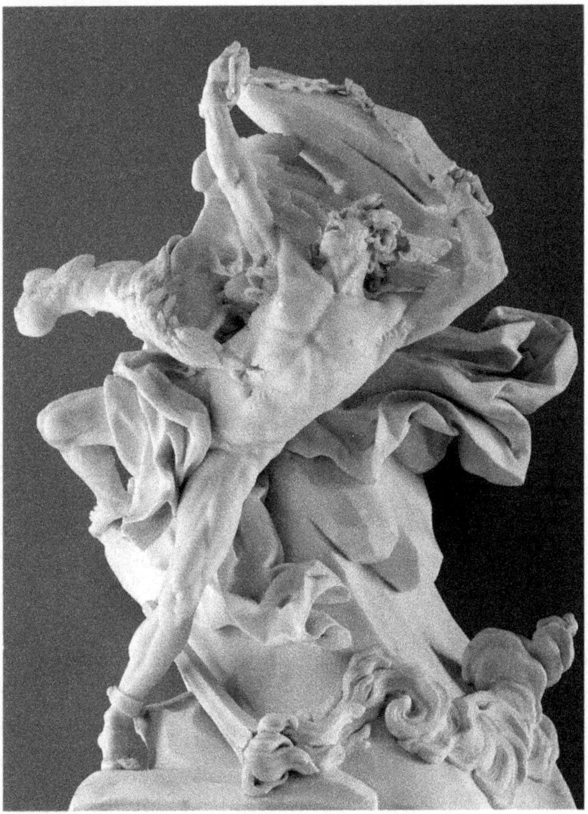

Prometheus on the Mountain, Public domain, via Wikimedia Commons.

been physically ill, mentally abusive, and emotionally uninvolved. Jacob had virtually no positive image of his father or of the world. A very painful and negative chain of experiences in his life had a fragmenting effect on his self-structure. Religious imagery spontaneously emerged as a protective mechanism that was continuously attempting to heal his soul. Without the individuating ego, even nature remains limited in her power.

2. THEONEMESIS: THE CONSEQUENCE OF POSSESSION BY THE SELF

The psychological rule says that when an inner situation is not made conscious, it happens outside as fate. That is to say, when the individual remains undivided and does not become conscious of his inner opposite, the world must perforce act out the conflict and be torn into opposing halves (Jung, 1959, [CW 911, para. 126]).

Ancient Greeks believed that hubris always resulted in punishment by the gods. In the myth of Icarus, his hubristic state is punished by falling out of the sky. Prometheus is punished for stealing fire from the gods. Zeus tied Prometheus to the Mount of Caucasus and an eagle ate from his liver each day.

What is hubris? When one acts without *aidos* (reverence), toward the archetypal forces, he or she experiences hubris. The ancient Greeks, feared hubris, due to the belief that once embodied it provoked a strong reaction from the gods (unconscious). The goddess Nemesis mediated that reaction, since she was charged with overseeing the righteous distribution of consequences. As gods and archetypes are interchangeable phenomena and represent psychic energy capable of impacting the human body and psyche, it proves helpful to understand them in order to live a healthy, fulfilled life. Murray (as cited in Edinger, 1972) considered *Aidos* and Nemesis mutually related emotional concepts experienced by the Greeks. *Aidos* represented an experience of awe when one approached the gods, but it also included feelings of shame when one transgressed the gods' powers. Nemesis represented an experience of the goddess pushing back in response to a person's uncontained inflation, disrespect, and hubris towards the gods (transpersonal forces).

Nemesis

The Greek word *nemesis* (Νέμεσις) can be translated as just indignation, jealousy, or vengeance—more literally, distribution. It is related to *nemein*, meaning to distribute, allot, apportion one's due, from PIE base *nem- "to divide, distribute, allot, to take" (cf. O.E., Goth. *niman* "to take," Ger. *nehmen*; see nimble). When nemisis is written using a lowercase "n", as is sometimes seen in literature or literary criticism, the word connotes a sense of retributive justice. The general sense of the word nemesis means, "anything by which it seems one must be defeated" (Harper, 2010). The term corresponds to 1) *feelings* of doing something arrogant or inappropriate while acting in hubris, but it is also a 2) subjective *experience* of retribution for doing something arrogant. Nemesis can also be found in literature as the feeling of an envying god. Etymologically, the original concept of the word nemesis derived from the feeling one has toward the *other* when they are doing something wrong. It originally meant something between fear, awe, shame, guilt, blame, but later it was applied to the concept of divine retribution (Murray, 1924, p. 85).

Murray said:

> The word Nemesis very soon passes away from the sphere of definite human blame ... Nemesis is the haunting impalpable wrath of the Earth and Sun, the Air, the Gods, the Dead ... It is not the direct anger of the injured person: it is the blame of the third person who saw it (p. 85).

He further explained:

> Aidos is usually translated 'Shame' or 'Sense of Honour', and Nemesis, by an awkward though correct phrase, 'Righteous Indignation.' The great characteristic of both

> these principles, as of Honour generally, is that they only come into operation when a man is free: when there is no compulsion. If you take people such as these of the Fifth Age, who have broken away from all their old sanctions, and select among them some strong and turbulent chief who fears no one, you will first think that such a man is free to do whatever enters his head. And then, as a matter of fact, you find that amid his lawlessness there will crop up some possible action which somehow makes him feel uncomfortable (p. 83).

Public domain, via Wikimedia Commons.[201]

[201] Image: Gheorghe Tattarescu, Goddess Nemesis, 1853.

Goddess Nemessis

There is an archetypal power behind the affect of nemesis, or more aptly nemesis *is* an archetype. Nemesis refers to a concept of equalization of archetypal energy and balance in nature. It is based on an old observation that every phenomenon has its opposite. From an elementary perspective, nemesis refers to a law of action and reaction, from a psychological perspective, nemesis represents the dynamics of compensation. In its essence it represents the concept of justice. Justice came, in the original view, from a higher source, as the gods distributed it. One did not have to take justice into his own hands because Zeus was in charge of this domain. This concept continued in the Christian religion when God performed acts of justice. God simply knew what was right and morally correct, because God is good and one of God's functions is to distribute punishment in order to preserve the very ideal of justice. In Romans 12:19, the Apostle Paul restates unequivocally that vengeance is not man's domain: "Beloved, do not avenge yourselves, but rather give place to wrath; for it is written, "Vengeance is Mine, I will repay," says the Lord. (The phrase "Vengeance is mine" appears earlier in Deuteronomy 32:35.) Adam and Eve's expulsion from the Garden of Eden is the earliest biblical example of justice being meted out in response to hubris. Adam and Eve wanted to be like God and as a result, they become sinful and are made conscious of their humanity. This narrative must not be interpreted only as an historical event; it can be understood as an ever-repeating principle of divine justice—a justice that is always happening *here and now*.

The *Old Testament* is full of examples of divine justice in response to human sin. For example:

> How much worse punishment, do you think, will be deserved by the one who has spurned the Son of God, and has profaned the blood of the covenant by which he was sanctified, and has outraged the Spirit of grace? For we know him who said, "Vengeance is mine; I will repay." And again, "The Lord will judge his people." It is

> a fearful thing to fall into the hands of the living God (Heb. 10:26 American Standard Version, n.d., p.1).

Nemesis was the Greek goddess of indignation against, and retribution for, bad conduct and undeserved good fortune. (Akin to goddesses; *Ate,* who ruled over mischief, ruin, and folly; and *Erinyes*, also known as the Furies, who exacted vengeance on those who transgressed the natural order.) Originally, the word nemesis meant the distribution of fortune, no matter it if was good or bad. Nemesis literally meant "the one who distributes, or deals out." Nemesis was referred to as *Adrasteia*, the one from whom there is no escape. Nemesis was also associated with Aphrodite, who is sometimes depicted bearing the epithet Nemesi. (*Encyclopaedia Britannica*, University press, 1911, p. 369) The goddess Nemesis was worshipped by Roman generals during the time of victory and was the patroness of gladiators. During the Hellenistic period, there were festivals in Athens held in the name of Nemesis (hence Nemeseia, Genesia). (Sophocles, *Electra,* 792; E. Rohde, *Psyche,* 5907, i. 236, note 1). The Greek words *nemêsis* and *nemô* mean "dispenser of dues." In ancient languages, there was a thin line between words designating emotions or objective daimons or gods. Similarly, Nemesis was, on the one hand, a personification of the emotion of resentment aroused in a person by the one who committed crimes with the apparent impunity or the one who had excessively good fortune, and on the other hand, the personification of consequences that were brought about by such deeds. The goddess Nemesis also measured out feelings of well-being, such as happiness or sadness, joy, and shame. Her role was to make sure that emotional experiences of desire, success, and elation were not excessively one-sided —she compensated for Hubris. The goddess Aidos was typically accompanied by Nemesis; together they formed a dyad of righteous accomplishment:

> [At the end of the Fifth Age of man:] And then Aidos (*Aedos*) and Nemesis with their sweet forms wrapped in white robes, will go from the wide-pathed earth and forsake mankind to join the company of the deathless gods: and bitter sorrows will be left for mortal men, and

> there will be no help against evil. *Hesiod, Works and Days 170 ff (trans. Evelyn-White) (Greek epic C8th or C7th B.C.,* Theoi, n.d., p. 1)

While the goddess Aidos, refers to the archetypal affect of reverence or shame that protected a person from the consequences of unwise actions, the goddess Nemesis was the personification of righteous indignation aroused by the realization of corrupt living and undeserved good fortune. (*Theoi*, n.d., p. 1) If somebody acted with hubris (lacking *aidos),* Nemesis would bring about loss, pain, and suffering. Nemesis was regarded as an *avenging* and *punishing* goddess. In some versions of the Trojan War, Nemesis was the mother of Helen, and seduced Paris. Nemesis sometimes appeared as a winged goddess. Some attributes of Nemesis are an apple-branch, reins, a lash, a sword, and a balance. The Romans took over the name Nemesis, but there are other Latin expressions for her: *Invidia* (Jealousy) and *Rivalitas* (Jealous rivalry). Nemesis was to be feared, particularly if one *forgets* about the power of the gods. An Orphic Hymn to Nemesis went like this:

> Thee, Nemesis, I call, almighty queen, by whom the deeds of mortal life are seen: eternal, much revered, of boundless sight, alone rejoicing in the just and right: changing the counsels of the human breast for ever various, rolling without rest. To every mortal is thy influence known, and men beneath thy righteous bondage groan; for every thought within the mind concealed is to thy sight perspicuously revealed. The soul unwilling reason to obey, by lawless passion ruled, thine eyes survey. All to see, hear, and rule, O power divine, whose nature equity contains, is thine. Come, blessed, holy Goddess, hear my prayer, and make thy mystics' life thy constant care: give aid benignant in the needful hour, and strength abundant to the reasoning power; and far avert the dire, unfriendly race of counsels impious, arrogant, and base (Taylor, 1979, p. 129).

Karma

The idea that every act has a consequence is an idea that can be found in nearly every religious tradition. In many eastern traditions the concept of karma is a central idea that traces its origins to the ascetic traditions of ancient India in the *shramana* (*sramana*) tradition. This tradition was influenced Brahmanic religion in the early Vedantic movement in the first millennium B.C. Karma was originally understood as a kind of force generated by human action to perpetuate the transmigration of souls. It brought to bear ethical consequences for human actions that determined the nature of one's next form of existence. The idea of karma is a cornerstone in both the Buddhist and Hindu religions that originated in Upanishads (a genre of the Vedas). The Vedic theologian Yajnavalkya articulated what later became known as the central core of the concept of karma: "A man turns into something good by good action and into something bad by bad action." (*Encyclopaedia Britannica*, University press, 1911, p. 680) Bedi and Matthews (2003) explained Karma in the following way: "Life is a series of choices. Choices lead to actions. Actions carry consequences. Action plus consequences is what we call *karma*" (p. 9).

Karma refers to the totality of man's actions and their concurrent reactions. Present acts determine the future. Allan Watts points out that the concept of Karma is interpreted more causally in the West. According to him Buddha's statement, "this arises that becomes" refers to interdependent origination of all the forms and phases of life: Pratityasamutpada. It is bondage between past and future events, a none-causal way where not only a present act determines the future, but also the other way around.[202] The understanding of the concept of karma varies among different religious and philosophical streams, but they all share the belief that karma is the supreme spiritual principle that pertains to natural law. To the Hindu, salvation is, to put it simply, deliverance from the negative or unwanted power of

[202] Alan Watts: *The Real Meaning of Karma*, published, 2016

karma. Unlike the idea of nemesis or the Christian's idea of justice, karma should *not* be understood as punishment imposed from some independent deity, but as the continued delivery of natural consequences of human acts and the choices a person makes. Karma can also be translated as action or deed. Karma describes the universal axiom that everything is governed by cause and effect. Therefore, an action is followed by a reaction, good or bad respectively. Every effect can be determined by the action taken beforehand.

The nature of consequences is not inevitably predetermined, but it is determined by a set of laws that somehow correlate action and consequence. Karma, therefore, is different from the concept of fate, where everything is predetermined or predestined and therefore not subject to change. With karma, human actions are determined by decisions, and thus an individual's destiny can be changed. According to the *Vedas* (c. 1500 B. C.), if one sows goodness, one will reap goodness; if one sows evil, one will reap evil. The mystery of evil and human suffering can never be fully understood, yet we know that much of it is a result of selfish cravings and desires stemming from the ignorance of the laws of reality. This ignorance is called *avidya*. An *avidya* results in human's moving away from the self (*atman*), which obscures his knowledge of the truth. *Avidya*, from a psychological perspective, is the state of unconsciousness, an unreflected life.

Karma in Fairy Tales, Epics and Biblical Stories

The ancient tale of Sleeping Beauty illustrates the concept of divine consequences. Because the king forgets to invite the wicked fairy, she curses the little baby princess with death. Although the curse is eventually reversed and nobody dies, the kingdom must pay a price in the form of lasting sleep for the king's oversight that offended the fairy.

Oedipus

In the Greek myth of Oedipus, King Laius, the ruler of Thebes, receives a prophecy from an oracle. The oracle told King Laius that his son Oedipus would kill him and then marry his own mother. Laius feared the prophecy and commanded a slave to abandon his son on the mountainside. Oedipus was found by shepherds and raised by King Polybus and Queen Merope. Much later, Oedipus consulted the oracle of Delphi after a friend revealed that Oedipus was adopted. Oedipus asked where his real parents came from, but the oracle didn't answer directly. Instead, he was told to watch out lest he kill his father and marry his mother as the prophecy had foretold. In the end, Oedipus ends up killing his actual father, King Laius and marrying his mother, Jocasta. Upon learning of the fate that he had been unable to avoid, Oedipus put out his own eyes in despair. Here, Oedipus is punished by his own actions and his inability to understand his fate. His fate became inevitable because he misunderstood the prophecy correctly.

Job

The biblical story of Job, the potential consequences of one's ignorance of God is revealed in the form of Job's physical diseases, mental, familial, and social hardship. Job demonstrates naïveté and does not accept the fact that God would listen to Satan and bring suffering upon him. Job only learns the truth when brought to trial and faces the "living God."

> Then answered the LORD unto Job out of the whirlwind, and said, "Gird up thy loins now like a man: I will demand of thee, and declare thou unto me. Wilt thou also disannul my judgment? wilt thou condemn me, that thou mayest be righteous? Hast thou an arm like God? or canst thou thunder with a voice like him? Deck thyself now *with* majesty and excellency; and array thyself with glory and beauty. Cast abroad the rage of thy wrath: and behold every one *that is* proud, and

abase him. Look on every one *that is* proud, *and* bring him low; and tread down the wicked in their place. Hide them in the dust together *and* bind their faces in secret." (*King James Bible*, 40:6-9)

Literature is full of stories where justice is eventually served—wherein evil is punished and goodness is rewarded. However, we believe that this view is not only inspired by a desire for justice, but also by an observation and experience of actual laws operating in nature. People often jump to the conclusion that justice has been meted out by God, or accident, or in their ill-defined imagination. There is sufficient reason to conclude that an individual is the author of the consequences of his or her choices

Making Unconscious Conscious Is a Process of Self-Exploration

Viewing this phenomenon from the perspective of a law of psychic dynamism, we can say that the consequence is contingent upon conscious engagement. Naturally, we cannot ever grasp all the potential players involved in the laws of karma; whether that includes some ultimate deity or not, it is only a matter of faith that distinguishes between the causes of nature as such and the cause of God as a supreme intelligence. From an empirical point of view, the knowledge of psychological processes is important in the same way that knowledge of physical processes is important. Our own life experiences and work have taught us that the unconscious is very real. Through developing our consciousness, it is possible to avert consequences. The authors' clinical work has verified this as a very real effect. We do not wish to pretend to fully understand the laws governing the archetypal dynamics of theocalypsis and theonemesis or any archetypal processes in general, but that should not stop us from making theoretical assumptions based on outcomes. As Stein & Corbett (2006) said:

We do not know the nature of the archetype, or spirit, any more than we know the nature of gravity. Never-

> theless, the depth psychologist can discern the operation of archetypal principles without understanding their origin, just as the physicist can do good physics without knowing the origin of the laws of physics. (p. 2)

In Jungian psychology, fate, as a blind drive, only exists if the ego loses its ability to reflect upon conscious influences. Under such circumstances, life proceeds without conscious realization and is govern sovereignly by the [unconscious] Self. The human will is complex, and human beings have the capacity to act with a certain degree of free will. This fact has real and practical implications. We can say that animals and plants live their fate. A dog does not make a choice to avoid acting on its instincts; only a conscious being can do that. A conscious being can change future happenings by reflecting on the present. When the ego's ability to utilize the reflective function is reduced, the potential for ego inflation increases. Once the ego loses its regulating function, the unconscious moves in with greater freedom, and that is the moment when fate takes over. With the loss of will, the autonomous archetypal forces then operate in accordance with the laws of our pure instinctual nature. The world, Jung reminds us, exists only to the extent that we reflect it consciously. The conscious world derives from the unconscious; thus it will be seen as different and subject to its own laws. As we await the development of a comprehensive theory that unifies matter and psyche similar to the efforts to unify all versions of superstring theory that is known as *M-theory*, we may develop a better understanding of the problem of free will; for now it remains a mystery that evokes a sense of awe.

Nemesis, as an archetypal phenomenon, can be viewed as an aspect and a representation of the laws of psychic dynamism. From a psychological perspective, nemesis represents the consequences for the ego when it is not mindful of the unconscious and its dynamics. As observed by the ancient Greeks, nemesis is initially observed by somebody else, or the body, before it becomes evident to the subject being afflicted by her. Stories abound in which the gods/God become envious of one's success or become angry at one's breaches of the rules; which typically results in consequences. This can be psychologically understood as retribution coming from the split-off or unrecognized parts of the unconscious. Looked at strictly from the human perspective, god's/God's envy is the representation of his inflation. A person, who transgresses in ways that could offend the gods, *feels* the gods' envy because they *know* that they have done something *wrong*. In fact, a person nearly always feels entitled to act in the ways they do that provides gains. This propensity to feel entitled to act with impunity is the root Nemesis's retributive justice when mortals fail to realize that choices will bring consequence. Anyone who ventures too far is stopped and reminded that overstepping human boundaries brings consequences.

Herbert James Draper, The Lament for Icarus, 1898, *Ve jménu Boha.*

Compensation

A consequence, in the broad sense, is a result of the psychic mechanism outlined earlier called compensation. Jung believed that a compensatory relationship exists between the conscious and the unconscious. Alfred Adler (1907) introduced the concept of compensation to psychology in his work titled *Study of Organ Inferiority and Its Physical Compensation*. He considered compensation a natural process of "inner striving to overcome inferiority," meaning it was a functional *balancing* mechanism to compensate feelings of inferiority. This could happen on an organic, psychological, or social level. Adler (1964) stated:

> As soon as the equilibrium, which must be assumed to govern the economy of the individual organ or the whole organism, appears to be disturbed due to inadequacy of form or function, a certain biological process is initiated in the inferior organs. The unsatisfied demands increase until the deficit is made up through growth of the inferior organ, of the paired organ, or of some other organ which can serve as a substitute, completely or in part. This compensating for the defect through increase in growth and function may, under favorable circumstances, achieve overcompensation; it will usually also include the central nervous system in its increased development. (Adler, A., *Individual Psychology*, pp. 25-26)

Jung (1921b) further elaborates on his ideas and conceives compensation as a "functional adjustment" and as an "inherent self-regulation of the psychic apparatus," He says:

> In this sense, I regard the activity of the unconscious as a balancing of the one sidedness of the general attitude produced by the function of consciousness (...) The unconscious compensation does not run counter to consciousness, but is rather a balancing or supplementing of the conscious orientation. In dreams, for instance, the unconscious supplies all those contents that are

> constellated by the conscious situation but are inhibited by conscious selection, although a knowledge of them would be indispensable for complete adaptation (1921b, [CW 6, para. p. 694]).

Psychoanalysis aims to rescue the ego from neurotic one-sidedness and to allow the natural compensation process to happen with minimal damage. Compensation can also take place without the conscious participation of the ego, but then it is in the form of an imperative force. The less conscious the ego is of potential unconscious dynamics, the more powerful and influential the dynamics become. When ego is not listening the compensation has to shout more loudly in order to get the ego's attention. Jung says:

> When the separation is carried so far that the complementary opposite is lost sight of, and the blackness of the whiteness, the evil of the good, the depth of the heights, and so on, is no longer seen, the result is one-sidedness, which is then compensated from the unconscious without our help (1955, [CW 14, para. 470]).

Theonemesis

How does Jung's theory fit into the findings presented thus far? If a *theocalypsis* is a process of archetypal inflation by identification with the Self, what consequences, if any, can be found for this particular state of inflation? We believe that such a consequence is a very real phenomenon, and we have named this phenomenon, *theonemesis*. Though Jung spent considerable time documenting and describing this process, apparently he never gave it a specific name. He believed that the consequences of inflation by the Self are dire. Because individuals possessed by the Self are not in full communication with their bodies and they tend to live (one-sided out of) partially out of concretizing mythical reality, they easily overlook the properties of consensual reality. Jung says:

> Ego-consciousness, [is] differentiated, i.e., separated, from the unconscious and moreover exists in an absolute space and an absolute time. It is a vital necessity that this should be so. If, therefore, the ego falls for any length of time under the control of an unconscious factor (the Self, *authors*), its adaptation is disturbed and the way opened for all sorts of possible accidents (1951a, [CW 9ii, para. 194]).

Theonemesis is a manifestation of an attempted change where a *theocalypsis* no longer provides sufficient adaptation. A *theonemesis* can be understood as a compensatory reaction to an ego that is possessed by the archetypal Self. Both a *theonemesis* and a *theocalypsis* are equally symptomatic of a lack of (or hindered) individuation—they could be considered as two sides of the same coin. At the same time however, both *theonemesis* and *theocalypsis processes* can serve the function of individuation, in fact they are a necessary part of it. Consciousness could arise out of a *theocalypsis* by the experience of a *theonemesis*, but at the same time *theonemesis* can lead to a *theocalypsis* in the form of a defense against individuation. A *theocalypsis* can also be conceived of as a stronghold against the numinosum, while a *theonemesis* is a consequence of the defense against consciousness. A *theonemesis* comes in various forms, from mild to severe, depending on how early one is able to detect warning signs, such as compensatory dreams, wrong conduct/enactment, accidents and injuries, and all sources of psychological and psychosomatic symptoms including anxiety, despair, depression, meaninglessness, etc.

Jung (1943) speaks:

> One of the commonest forms of danger is the instigating of accidents. A very large number of accidents of every description, more than people would ever guess, are of psychic causation, ranging from trivial mishaps like stumbling, banging oneself, burning one's fingers, etc., to car smashes and catastrophes in the mountains. I have examined many cases of this kind, and often I could point to dreams which showed signs of a

> tendency to self-injury weeks beforehand. (...) In the same way, bodily ills can be brought into being or protracted. A wrong functioning of the psyche can do much to injure the body, just as conversely a bodily illness can affect the psyche; for psyche and body are not separate entities but one and the same life. Thus there is seldom bodily ailment that does not show psychic complications, even if it is not psychically caused. (CW 7, par. 194)

Theonemesis can be manifested in various forms outside of the conscious field as a symptom or an unconscious act (an enactment). Its intensity or severity depends on the degree of possession and the lack or inability of conscious reflection. More severe forms of *theonemesis* include bipolar symptoms, physiological (chronic) pain, physical illness, in which case all of these can lead to serious health problems or self-destructive behavior. Notably, symptoms of *theocalypsis* are often initially registered by significant others—spouses and children. Family members of people suffering from a *theonemesis* are more likely to seek therapy than the ones impacted. Those impacted by *theonemesis* often end up in emergency rooms or inpatient settings. Signs of *theonemesis* are always present, but if the ego is not paying attention to them, their intensity gradually increases. One of the tasks of analysis is to predict (and potentially avert) consequences and assess risk.

Fairy Tale Parallel

In the German fairy tale, *Faithful Jan and Maiden Mahulena*, (Grimm's Brothers, 1850) also known as *Der Treue Johannes*, the prince rescues the beautiful maiden from captivity (symbolic of possession) by the Golden Ruler (the dark, unconscious aspect of the Self) in his golden mountain (perhaps the inflation by the Self). The Golden Ruler becomes furious and tries to kill the maiden, Mahulena, and her beloved, the prince. While Mahulena is running away, the Golden Ruler tried to instigate numerous accidents by setting traps. The prince's brother, Jan, intervened and saved Mahulena's life multiple times when she nearly drowned in a river, fell off a mountain, and fell into a fire. In this fairy tale, the reflective function of consciousness is symbolically represented by Jan, who possessed a magic metal crown, a gift from his father. The crown (symbolizing intuition, wisdom, tradition, and possibly a symbol of individuated consciousness) gave him the gift of foresight and the ability to intuit glimpses of the future, which warned him of the fatal threats against Mahulena. His father's gift (crown) saved their lives and delivered them from the punishment of the Golden Ruler. Virtue and knowledge are needed to escape punishment by the Golden Ruler. Without them, the maiden would die. In other words, without the reflective function of consciousness, a *theocalypsis* would have absolute consequences. The moral of this tale dwells in the recognition of the *theonemesis*, which came about from inflation by the Self. The numinosum that is not engaged by (reflective) consciousness becomes enacted, and [part of] the Self becomes dark and dangerous.

Kalsched and The Dark Self

Donald Kalsched's (1996) research on trauma can be helpful in understanding the phenomenology of the self-attack. He observed that the Self could exhibit destructive qualities in the inner world, but also in the "real world":

> ...inasmuch as the traumatized child has intolerable experiences in the object world, the negative side of the Self does not personalize, remaining archaic. The internal world continues to be menaced by a diabolical, inhuman figure. Aggressive, destructive energies – ordinarily available for reality-adaptation and for healthy defense toxic not-self objects – are directed back into the inner world (p. 19).

According to Kalsched, a highly elaborated system (self-care system) of inner fantasies serves the purpose of protecting the ego from re-experiencing anything that resembles the initial trauma in order to preserve the personal spirit and to prevent re-exposure to trauma affect. He continues:

> Like the immune system of the body, the self-care system carries out its functions by actively attacking what it takes to be "foreign" or "dangerous" elements. Vulnerable parts of the self's experience in reality are seen as just such "dangerous" elements and are attacked accordingly. These attacks serve to undermine the hope in real object-relations and to drive the patient more deeply into fantasy. And just as the immune system can be tricked into attacking the very life it is trying to protect (auto-immune disease), so the self-care system can turn into a "self-destruct system" which turns the inner world into a nightmare of persecution and self-attack (p. 24).

According to him, "fantasy is an unconscious undertow into non-differentiation to escape conscious feeling ... and a "defensive use of imagination in service of anxiety avoidance." Kalsched's insightful observations concerning the use of fantasy as a protective faculty while at the same time isolating the ego from experiencing the authentic Self, is quite useful for our research.

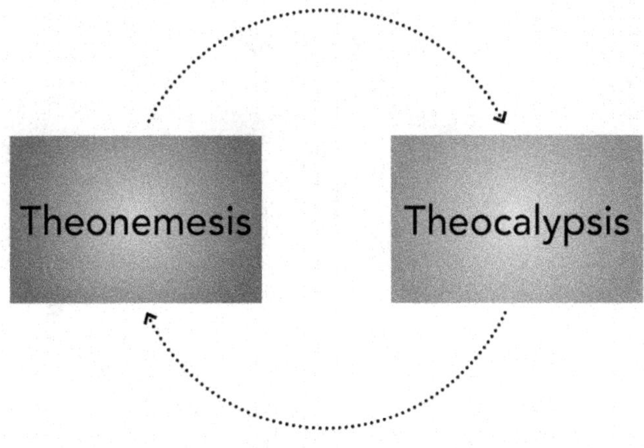

Theonemesis and Theocalypsis

Religious fantasies filled with unadaptive archetypal material used for pacifying purposes are common among people suffering from *theocalypsis*. *Theonemesis* can then be understood as an autoimmune syndrome caused by the dynamics described above. In many cases of religious fundamentalism and fanaticism, *theonemesis* should be understood as various forms of consequences stemming from symptoms of a *theocalypsis*.

Theonemesis As Death of the Soul

Reactivity leads to conflicts and isolation, self-righteousness is arrogance, moral Manichaeism is ethical emptiness, one-sidedness brings about emotional flatness. All these symptoms sooner or later create pain, cut one off from the world, from people, and from the Self. The shadow of a *theocalypsis* is *theonemesis*. Inhibited individuation is one of the commonplace consequences of a theocalypsis. It is psychic death, the death of the soul (Jacoby, 1990).

John William Waterhouse, 1903, Echo And Narcissus, *Ve jménu Boha*.

In the myth of Narcissus and Echo, Narcissus is punished by the nymph Nemesis. According to Greek myth, Nemesis causes Narcissus to die when he falls in love with his own reflected image in the water:

> As he leaned over a pool of water to drink, he was so taken with his own beautiful reflection that he gazed and gazed, transfixed, hypnotized as it were, by his own good looks, in a sense worshipping his own image. Narcissus knew now how others had suffered from his fatal charm. His punishment for his vanity was that he could never leave that image in the pool. Only death could free him from himself. And so it was. Never moving, he lay there until he died. His last words were to his reflected image, 'Farewell—farewell.' (Edgar, 1994, p. 55)

In this myth, as with the myth about Calypso, we understand that mythical death for ancient Greeks did not mean death as we conceive it; instead, it was understood as a process that leads to an eternal, unchanging (unconscious) state, a psychological state without life. Psychic death does not mean death in the physical sense but a lack of change and progression. The Self cannot be killed. The Self always provides communication to the ego, in order to establish harmony. It never ceases in attempting to awaken consciousness to its true light. Although the slumber can be deep, a hope for change persists. Like Odysseus's capture on the island of Ogygia or Sleeping Beauty's deep slumber, the psyche may sleep for a very long time but, hark, it can awaken at any time. *Theonemesis* attempts to reestablish a more adequate *Imago Dei* by attempting to kill the identification with the Self. Theonemesis attempts to radically transform the illusory attachments the ego develops. The sword Nemesis wields is not directed to the very soul. Of course, it is an anthropomorphism to talk about the mortality of the Self. Certainly from a human being's perspective the collective unconscious cannot be annihilated, it is immortal and timeless. If the soul does not listen to Nemesis' attempt to restore equilibrium terrible consequences may follow, including physical death. Once again it is evident that psychic processes are beyond morality, so it would be a mistake to view them as if they had conscious intentions pertaining to revenge, punishment, judgment, and the like. Applying the ego's perspective, *theonemesis* appears as a tool for a higher morality; this is nothing more than a necessary compensatory phenomenon. *Theonemesis* attempts to connect suppressed or unrecognized parts of the *Coniunctio Oppositorum* of the Self. It creates conditions for expanding the conscious field allowing it to take into account a fuller and more complete image of the numinosum which in turn expands the experience of the world.

The biblical account of Job's suffering illustrates this idea. God, acting on Satan's advice, and despite his omnipotence and omniscience, inflicts enormous pain and suffering on Job. Satan's voice can be interpreted from a Jungian view (1954c) as the unconscious, "dark" side of the Self, namely the not-yet conscious aspect of the soul. Similarly, the biblical account of Saul of Tarsus on the road to Damascus was blinded by his encounter with Jesus.

> As I was traveling and near Damascus, about noon an intense light from heaven suddenly flashed around me. I fell to the ground and heard a voice saying to me, "Saul, Saul, why are you persecuting Me"? I answered, "Who are You, Lord?" He said to me, "I am Jesus the Nazarene, whom you are persecuting!" Now those who were with me saw the light, but they did not hear the voice of the One who was speaking to me. Then I said, "What should I do, Lord?" And the Lord told me, "Get up and go into Damascus, and there you will be told about everything that is assigned for you to do." Since I couldn't see because of the brightness of that light, I was led by the hand by those who were with me, and came into Damascus (*Acts*, 22:6-11, Standard American Version).

Theonemesis brings into consciousness the split-off content of archetypal energy, and thus, it supplies consciousness with a deeper, fuller and more adequate religious experience. One is often less conscious of their own state of *theocalypsis*, all the while the more hubristic the attitude is, the more intense *theonemesis* will be.

Prometheus' heroic hubris was such that he was no longer afraid of death, as illustrated in the following passage:

> Chorus: How is it that you are not afraid to utter such taunts [against Zeus]?
>
> Prometheus: Why should I fear since I am fated not to die?
>
> Chorus: But he might inflict on you an ordeal even more bitter than this.
>
> Prometheus: Let him, for all I care! I am prepared for anything.
>
> Chorus: Wise are they who do homage to Adrasteia (Aeschylus, 932)

I recall a patient of mine who suffered from an extreme form of *theocalypsis* when he believed that he was actually God. (V.Š.) He referred to himself as "The One," Jesus, and God. When his psychosis was at its peak, he would not sleep for days and would walk around the city, preaching his own gospel to people. He elaborated his own cosmology and believed that he was the creator of the universe. He became dangerous to others and himself when he drove his car down a hill at a high speed and crashed into a truck driving in the opposite direction. He survived, with only minor injuries. After medical treatment that included a hospitalization, he told me that he wanted to find out if he was "really immortal." Unfortunately, the experience of miraculous survival only fed his grandiose beliefs. He continued on this path until he lost everything, his money, his house, and his friends.

Psychosomatic aspects of theonemesis

"If you do not go along with the unconscious properly, that is, if it finds no expression through consciousness and conscious action, it piles up libido in the body and this leads to physical weakness." Jung, *Letters Vol I.*

Sarah

Another aspect of *theonemesis* is its manifestation as physical illness. Another patient of mine, a woman in her forties, suffered from severe pain in her knees and neck that was accompanied by painful migraines. (V.Š.) Sarah's pain was so debilitating that sometimes she became immobilized. A diagnosis and cause of her pain proved elusive despite numerous medical examinations. Sarah married an abusive partner about seven years before entering therapy. Shortly after their marriage, Sarah's husband began using drugs and abusing her emotionally, especially when he was intoxicated. One day, he physically attacked Sarah and attempted to strangle her. Sarah called police, but refused to press charges. He moved out of the house for a time, but she soon took him back as she relied on his promise to improve his behavior. Shortly after he moved back into their home, it became clear that he had not changed, and the emotional abuse increased. The onset of Sarah's pain in her knees and neck coincided with her husband's return to their home; as their arguments intensified so did her pain. At the time, Sarah remained unaware that her symptoms might be related to her relationship. When Sarah came to see me, it was initially to "find a peace in her relationship"; she hoped that her husband would enter marriage counseling and "change." Sarah was able to make a connection between her physical pain and the conflicts with her husband after she kept a detailed log of the intensity of her symptoms and documented all events surrounding the pain flare-ups. After about six months of therapy, Sarah's pain occurrences significantly decreased. However, the movement was not entirely linear, as Sarah oscillated between ideas of forgiveness and unconditional love on one side and divorce and letting go on the other. Sarah was a member of a fundamentalist church that considered divorce unacceptable. She lived with her mother, who is also a member of the church and did not support Sarah's divorcing her husband. Sarah was under enormous internal and external pressure of guilt and shame if she were to divorce her husband.

When she was eleven years old, her father died suddenly from cancer. For years, Sarah could not accept his death and she refused to believe that he was really, permanently gone. After twenty-six years, Sarah was experiencing a similar problem. She could either let go of her ideal, which was represented by her faith and her church's teachings, or she could accept that her husband was not going to change sufficiently, especially if he refused to seek help for his drug addiction and continued to blame her for their familial dysfunction. The more Sarah clung to her false, religiously ridden persona, the more she overlooked the destructive aspect of her idealized attachment. Jung (1928a) said:

> To the degree that the world invites the individual to identify with the mask, he is delivered over to influences from within. 'High rests on low,' says Lao-tzu. An opposite forces its way up from inside; it is exactly as though the unconscious suppressed the ego with the very same power which drew the ego into the persona (p. 194).

The trauma caused by Sarah's abandonment when she was a child left a deep scar on her ego that was soothed by a superhuman archetypal ideal. She never transformed this to a level where she was able to successfully bear the pain and accept love with all its paradoxical features. When she was young, she did not have enough ego-strength to deal with her father's abandonment, but now she accepted an *Imago Dei*, suffused with promise and protection. Her church offered her a refuge that was also capable of imprisoning her. Like Odysseus on Calypso, Sarah forgot about the malady of her soul and suppressed all *tremendum* to the unconscious. Outwardly, she pursued abusive relationships with fascinating attraction. Before she was married, Sarah was in a similar abusive relationship, yet she had to endure a lot of criticism from her family whenever she left her partner. When she married her current husband, she was determined to show everybody that she was a good mother and wife. She was constantly deluding herself that her relationships were essentially good, but she also blamed herself for all of their evils. When it became very obvious that her husband's conduct was no longer tolerable, she removed herself from the situation but not fully; she remained married and postponed her decision to divorce.[203] Her church provided sufficient protection for her to heal and grieve her father's death, but it was not ample enough to deal with when it became necessary for her to leave her husband and end the marriage. As she was dodging the reality principle, the Self created inflationary pressure to compensate for her one-sided position. She was hiding behind an idea that was unsustainable, so the complementary part still demanded to be heard. Her physical pain was like a loudspeaker announcing that something needed to change. Her psyche maneuvered so as to help her get out of her inner conflict. I called this *theonemesis*. She lacked the courage to face the signals, so her body started to exhibit symptoms. 2r5 (1996) again:

> ...the victim of early trauma. For these patients, disowned material is not psychically represented but *has been banished to the body* or relegated to discrete psychical fragments between which amnesia barriers have been erected. It must *never* be allowed to return to consciousness. A *coniunctio oppositorum* is the most terrifying of all, and the dissociation necessary to insure the patient against this catastrophe, is a deeper, archetypal split in the psyche (p. 34).

Psychosomatic Illness

Theonemesis could be conceived of as an archaic, pre-imaginal process of regulation. It is a form of bypassing the neurotic conflict by hindering conscious access to the parts of the symbol, particularly its feeling and imaginal aspects. Where

---

[203] Sarah discontinued therapy with me shortly after I wrote this due to a change in her insurance coverage. Recently, she paid me a visit and reported happily that she had divorced her husband and enrolled in school. (V.Š.)

there is a lack of consciousness, information is transmitted by other means that can be understood to be at a lower evolutionary level. Psychosomatic illnesses could be understood as expressions of deep archetypal conflicts that draw energy from the *Imago Dei*. Brazilian Jungian analyst and specialist on psychosomatic illness, Denise Ramos, in her book *The Psyche of the Body: A Jungian Approach to Psychosomatics* (2004) introduces a theory about the body registering conflict in its own way. She asks:

> Is the conflict that finds expression in abstract symbols (fantasies, dreams, imagination) closer to consciousness than that which finds more pronounced expression in the organic aspect?

She goes on to provide an answer:

> In the absence of an abstract symbolic representation, the Self would manifest by creating more regressive, primitive, and organismic symbols. (...) The patient who expresses himself somatically has lost his body's connection with his somatic unconsciousness, so that his eidetic fantasy life would be disconnected from his organic life. (...) Perhaps we are dealing here with archaic forms of psychic functioning: pre-verbal symbolic forms, natural at the infantile stage.

Then summarizes:

> In summary, one of the hypotheses we could raise would be that psychosomatic phenomena may be avoided when neurotic forms of organization emerge. (...) The verbal communication of affective states would be disconnected, in general, from the body. Here an archaic form of symbolism is at work, in which the body talks. A symptom that may be corporal ("organic illness") or psychic ("mental illness") would be the symbolic representation of a disconnection or dis-turbance in the ego/Self axis. (p. 33)

From that perspective, a *theonemesis* can manifest also as bodily conflict.

Martha

Another patient of mine, Martha, suffered from physical symptoms of arthritis, lupus, and irritable bowel syndrome. (V.Š.) Martha came from a very religious family and was physically abused by her father, and at sixteen years of age she was raped by a man who kidnapped her and held her captive in the woods. Twenty-seven years ago Martha married a man, but because he was abusive and an alcohol and drug user, she ran away after a few years. Martha found a new partner and lived with him but they never married. She felt guilty and believed that God was punishing her for sinning against God's law. When she went to confession, he confirmed her belief adding to her guilt-ridden religious fantasies. Martha lived in states of constant toxic shame where she believed that God's wrath was justified in light of her sins. Martha was possessed by the dark aspect of the Self, which contributed to her physical suffering. Martha told me when we first met, that she would have killed herself (meted out the ultimate punishment) if it was not for the prohibitions against suicide her church teaches.

Physical Aspect of Mental Illness

The relation between physical and psychological suffering is not only based on intuition, but is supported by various studies. Research shows that there is high correlation between psychological symptoms of clinical depression and physical symptoms.[204] In many cases, depression is considered to be primary to physical illness and not only a secondary consequence of pain and other illness. Depression has also been proven to be a high risk factor in cardiac disease; the American Heart Association in 2008 recommended that all cardiac

---

[204] Madhukar H. Trivedi, *The Link Between Depression and Physical Symptoms,* 2004 and Guy M. Goodwin, *Depression and associated physical diseases and symptoms*, 2006 In: Primary Care Companion to The Journal of Clinical Psychiatry. **Depression and associated physical diseases and symptoms**

patients be screened for depression.[205] Clinical depression is highly correlated with, but not limited to, the following physical symptoms and diseases:

- ✓ Body aches
- ✓ Headaches
- ✓ Abdominal pain (mostly in children)
- ✓ Migraines
- ✓ Fatigue (chronic fatigue syndrome)
- ✓ Diabetes
- ✓ Bone loss (higher bone-breaking occurrences with women)
- ✓ Arterial damage and strokes
- ✓ Irritable bowel syndrome and non-ulcer dyspepsia
- ✓ Fibromyalgia
- ✓ Rheumatoid arthritis
- ✓ Diabetes mellitus
- ✓ High blood pressure
- ✓ Irregular heart rhythms
- ✓ Coronary artery disease
- ✓ Symptoms of weakened immune and neuroendocrine systems.

Research also shows that depression is more prevalent in patients with somatization disorder. Patients suffering from depression and anxiety have been found to have higher mortality rates than nondepressed individuals (See Cuijpers & Smit, 2002).

Again, *theonemesis* should not be understood in terms of morality (i.e., punishment) based on a moral order, but rather

[205] "Over the past 40 years, more than 60 prospective studies have examined the link between established indices of depression and prognosis in individuals with known coronary heart disease (CHD). Since the first major review articles were published in the late 1990s, there have been more than 100 additional narrative reviews of this literature, as well as numerous meta-analyses examining the role of depression on cardio-vascular morbidity and mortality. Despite differences in samples, duration of follow-up, and assessment of depression and depressive symptoms, these studies have demonstrated relatively consistent results." *AHA Science Advisory*, Circulation, 2008, p.1

as a consequence of excessive possession by the Self with a corresponding lack of conscious adaptation. A lack of consciousness and personal responsibility, even a fear of one's body, can lead to the emergence of unwanted phenomena. We generally refer to these experiences as negative because they are sources of suffering or other undesired problems. In extreme forms of *theocalypsis*, the *theonemesi*s comes about in the form of self-destruction or destructiveness directed toward others. An example of this would be a terrorist who detonates a bomb strapped to his body. Though such acts are universally condemned, the terrorist may believe they are acting in the name of God and subjectively their actions may be deemed righteous.

Theonemesis, Criteria

We speak of *theonemesis* in the strict sense only in cases where a *theocalypsis* is present. It should be considered a consequence of unreflected possession by the Self or a consequence of hubris, a result of identification with the Self. In order for phenomena to be called *theonemesis*, an *Imago Dei* in any form needs to be present. We suggest the use of the term *theonemesis* where there is reason to believe that there is a consequence coming from the Self. In Slovakia, three years ago, a woman claimed to be pregnant with baby Jesus. She proclaimed to be St. Mary and found herself at the center of media attention. The birth of her baby-God never happened, though. Shortly before her due date, she stepped out on the street and was killed when a car driving too fast around a curve struck her.[206] Of course, in this case and in many similar cases, it could be argued that it was a mere accident or coincidence, and it had nothing to do with the state of her mind. A careful observer could easily notice how this woman's possession by the Self virtually blinded her and caused her to adapt

[206] TV Markiza, *Archive*, 2008

inadequately to reality with a grandeur that did not serve the protection of her body. She acted with a grandiose persuasion, and she claimed to be the mother of God with laughter, brushing off any attempts for rational exploration of her claim. She was possessed by a messianic idea and could not look at herself or her pregnancy symbolically.

I have seen many accidents resulting from hubris. (V.Š.) I once had a 60-year-old patient who thought, he could jump off a seven-foot-high wall similar to the way he did when he was 18 years old after he believed God cured his alcoholism; he suffered a complicated fracture of his foot in the process. Another patient drove 40 miles over the speed limit while driving to meet a woman whom he "miraculously" fell in love with. (V.Š.) He believed God sent him his "savior femme fatale"; he was in a car accident as a result of his reckless driving. Yet another patient was the victim of an attempted molestation when he was seven years old by a man in a public restroom. (V.Š.) He managed to break free and run into the street. The man ran after him, and when my patient crossed the street, the man followed him. The man was hit by a pickup truck and became a paraplegic. As a very young girl, another patient of mine was raped by her uncle. (V.Š.) A few months later, his decapitated body was found. The police determined that it was retribution from the Mafia because he owed a large sum of money. Jung gave an example of a woman who committed murder, and animals around her became hostile to her (Jung, *MDR*, p. 122). These cases suggest that living in a permanent state of unconscious inflation increases the possibility of accidents. Put differently, life without consciousness and a conscience can become dangerous. As the old saying goes, "Those who play with fire get burned." There's an old Slovak saying, "Who digs a hole for another will fall in it soon."

A patient (G.J.D.) who was befriended and groomed by her 6th grade teacher was then subsequently raped and molested. Their relationship continued for many years. However, one day while working at home, the perpetrator was climbing a high ladder in his garage when he slipped and fell to his death at a rather young age.

Perhaps most of us have experienced or heard about this sort of "*justice*" personally or watch others experience it. We italicize the word justice because we are not assuming to know what is wrong and what is not. It is difficult to be sure whether all such cases or even how many cases are enacted by the shadowy dynamics of the unconscious; nonetheless, we want to bring these phenomena to greater attention for further scientific exploration. If our theory is correct and *theonemesis* serves as a natural mechanism of change and adaptation, then recognizing its different manifestations can help us adapt more quickly, without unnecessary painful consequences. It is up to our consciousness to make this adaptation progressive in order to minimize negative impacts. Some accidents result from broader, more complex causal relations between unconscious enactment and consequences. We know that climatic changes are associated with human behavior. Complex financial dealings on Wall Street that result in low growth may contribute to revolutions in other regions like Egypt and Tunisia (the Arab Spring) as economic hardships reach a boiling point. In these cases, humanity as a whole is called to consciously ponder and reflect on its actions and policy. Sometimes a causal relation between an incident and a person's behavior cannot be found. However, connections might even be acausal, i.e., synchronistic.[207] That would open another theme for exploration and research, which would be beyond the scope of this exploration.

[207] See: Cambray, J., *Synchronicity: Nature and Psyche in an Interconnected Universe, Texas A&M University Press*, 2009.

VIII.
THE PROCESS OF CHANGE

The art of progress is to preserve order amid change and to preserve change amid order (Whitehead, 1991, p. 177).

The birth of the Self results not in displacement of previous psychological center but in complete alteration of one's attitude towards life accompanied by psychological freedom. (Jacobi, 1942)

Because the influence of the numinosum is necessary for transformation and the development of consciousness in general, the ego-attitude toward the numinosum is crucial. Careful examination of various religious teachings reveals a common denominator; they allow the numinosum to be utilized progressively and in accordance with the process of individuation. Although most sacred texts provide templates for individual growth that serve as containers and conduits for spiritual progress, many religious establishments have gradually and selectively adhered to dogmas that perpetuate defensives toward the numinosum. Instead of a gradual and persistent leveling of the fortresses that prevent an ongoing ego-Self axis that would lead to greater spiritual freedom and contentment, the reliance on dogma becomes a hindrance to individuation. We have attempted to answer the question of why and how the ego transits from development to stagnation, and vice versa. Splitting off archetypal affect, leads to the exclusion of, or misuse of logic and critical reasoning which are essential tools for integrating the irrational contents of the archetypal realms into consciousness. This splitting appears to be the *modus vivendi* of many fundamentalist institutions. Jung says that psychological development can come to a halt at any stage; that truth is even more palpable in the case of spiritual development.

Religious Attitude Can Have a Protective Function

When, for various reasons a personality is not equipped, allowed, or willing to deal with numinous affects, all sources of ego-compensation arise in place of integration. Oftentimes there is no other alternative for the ego apart from resisting the seemingly harmful elements of numinous energies by creating a defensive system. Narcissistic defenses may be the only available tool that ensures adaptation to the environment, and possibly the very survival of the ego: ergo person. The adjective "narcissistic" should not be viewed in a pejorative sense, but as a denominator for self-preserving natural processes. Lionel Corbett (1996) stated with respect to the development of one-sided and "dogmatic" positions:

> Narcissistic difficulties contribute to fundamentalist attitude when dogma about eternal verities is used to buttress areas of personal fragility, either it would be intolerable to face the experience of the numinosum, even modified by ritual or symbol, or because dogma is used to defend against problems within the personality (...) For the fragile self, fixed dogmatic assertions help to maintain a degree of narcissistic equilibrium (see Kohut, 1972) by reducing uncertainty (pp. 33-34).

It is important to stress here that the *theocalypse* is maintained and adhered to with stronger effort as more energy is invested into the one-sided understanding of the numinosum. Only an equally courageous energy and attitude that counter-balances this investment—openness to a fuller encounter with the numinous—yields change. A *theocalypse* is built up from personal philosophical and theological foundations to collective levels associated with family, social, and vocational positions. Together these factors form a fine, complex, subjectively-cherished equilibrium that would have to be abandoned or at best restructured in order to pursue individuation. No change will happen without a resilient ego believing that such a loss has meaning, that it is a worthy investment that will bring something of value. When Tom Ham, a founder of the Creationist Museum in Kentucky, was asked by Bill Nye what would have to happen to change his mind with respect to some dogmatic religious beliefs, he answered: "I am a Christian!" Essentially he meant that he cannot change his mind. One can only imagine the degree of emotional pain that would be experienced, should Tom Ham give credence to his biggest enemy: the scientific community. What would change his mind?

Order and Novelty

Whitehead (1991) famously stated that order and novelty are both elements of progress that must be held together. At the core of resistance to change are the fears of deregulation and the loss of order. Change itself is not threatening as long as it produces a higher state while preserving order. Ancient festivals and rites of resurrection and re-juvenescence encompassed this rule. The promise of rebirth and renewal eased the ego's stronghold and allowed participants to let go of the previous order. Numinosum was held in the container of the rite's participation mystique. Jung (1955-56) provided numerous examples of the transformation through the practice of alchemy. The dissolution of the old king was designed to produce a new, more suitable and superior king.

Containment of transformational processes was psychologically very important. Philosopher's (alchemist's) knowledge was an indispensable tool for the containment. Without a sufficient conscious frame (philosophy), any new level of understanding could lose the spirit. Ego-consciousness has to be prepared for encountering the numinosum. Since the numinosum cannot be known beforehand, reliance on teachings and faith can provide assurances. Alchemist and Christian mystic Gerardus Dorneus (as cited in Jung, 1955) stressed that "the first step in the ascent to higher things is the study of faith, for this is the heart of man disposed to solution in water" (Jung 1955-56, [CW 14, para. 363]). Inadequate psychological means leads unwittingly to the phenomena of evasion, stagnation, or regression. In that case, the Self's only access is undesirable; archaic representations that lead to stagnation. The fear of not possessing a psychological apparatus strong enough to withstand the encounter with the numinosum leads to the exclusion of the Self and its natural, transformational work. Corbett (1996) and Jacoby (1990, p. 21) suggested that narcissistic self-centeredness is basically an attempt to hold onto a discrete identity that is not continuous with its transpersonal roots. Ego-consciousness, thus, relies solely on its own means, but those means are inevitably vulnerable, sterile and often rigid without the support of archetypal energy.

Analysis Desires Safe Ego-Self Connection

The process of analysis is a work of art in which the analysand is encouraged to let go of defenses so that the numinosum can proceed to exert its influence and ultimately produce transformation. However, there needs to be a twofold way of approaching the numinosum. Analysis can minimize the intensity of archetypal energies by keeping the permeability of defenses at a level that prevents the effect of the numinosum from becoming noxious and disrupting the ego's integrity.

As a group, religious radicals are more susceptible to the undesirable effects of the numinosum; they invest a great deal of energy into resisting its transformative effect on the ego. This is perpetuated by certain conservative traditions and societal structures, which are designed to create an environment where change is presented as a great spiritual threat and danger.

Looking at the process of change and its perils historically, we can discover how defensive ideologies arose from the attempt to eschew the numinosum often creating false prophets and propagators of quasi-religious messages. Stemming from a rather naïve and intuitive grasp of archetypal reality (as seen in pre-Socratic philosophy), religion naturally encountered obstacles in its movement and developments towards its modern and postmodern positions from which psychological insights are employed to understand and work with archetypal forces. A few examples may be helpful.

Warnings Against Hindrance of Individuation in History

Jesus of Nazareth (cca 5 B.C. – 29 A.D.) pointed out the hypocrisy of the Pharisees to demonstrate faulty logic that led to dogmatic claims (See Matt 23:13, *English Standard Version*). His contemporary, a Jewish intellectual, Philo of Alexandria (20 B.C. – 50 A.D.) was famous for his message of finding harmony between Greek philosophy and Judaism. He taught that reason, which was championed by the Hellenistic tradition, and the message of biblical [Old Testament] teaching were merely two different ways of reaching the same goal. Philo alleged that reason is God-given and, thus, could not be an obstacle in reaching the truth contained in the religious scriptures (Tyler, 2009). He argued against literal interpretation and advocated for critical thinking as an indispensable facility for achieving salvation. It was absolutely necessary, he taught, to read scriptures *allegorically* because the real meaning was to be found "under the surface" of the text. Even though Philo argued for the message of the symbolic interpretation of Holy Scriptures, his views were not widely adopted. Other Christian thinkers, such as Clement of Alexandria (150-215 A.D.) and Origen (185-254 A.D.), adapted his ideas. Origenes questioned the interpretation of claims in the biblical text, such as the six-day creation story and the story of Adam and Eve, as actual descriptions of real events in the physical universe (Roberts, Donaldson, Coxe, Menzies, Richardson, & Pick, 1885). Thanks to the work of the Greeks in the development of the thinking function, the rational and irrational elements of thought began to be discriminated and separated giving rise to theologies dealing with the numinosum, non-mythological and non-ritualistic ways. Anselm of Canterbury (1033 - 1109) spoke about theology as a "faith seeking understanding" (*fides quaerens intellectus*), where he meant that faith is a primary experience of divine reality, but we can understand it only via the property of reason.

Reason Alone is Not Enough

As stated earlier, the symbolic had a primary innate role in giving birth to consciousness from the collective unconscious. Beginning with the Axial Age and continuing through the early Middle Ages, early struggles to integrate the numinosum, at times, turned in the direction of literalism, which tended to exclude the wider symbolic nature of the encounter with the numinosum. Only the liberated function of consciousness pushed this role to a secondary position, which subsequently meant that literalism and the tendency to exclude the wider symbolic nature of any life-concerning phenomena arose as a natural inclination in the early religious minds struggling with the integration of the numinosum; since the beginning of the Axial Age through the early Middle Ages. No progression is immune to unilateral growth, and thus, within the process of the emancipation of the thinking function, one-sidedness did develop and cause an effect inimical to progress. Loss of centeredness accompanies the differentiation of every function. There is no smooth or linear development of anything concerning the natural phenomena of psyche. This fact informs us as to why every achievement claims a sacrifice elsewhere. Spirituality, then, should serve as a function of the constant *equalization* of opposites and the mindful realization of that which was lost. Jung spoke on the enthusiastic valuation of rationality and the use and function of words throughout the historical development:

> One can be—and is—just as dependent on words as on the unconscious. Man's advance towards the Logos was a great achievement, but he must pay for it with loss of instinct and loss of reality to the degree that he remains in primitive dependence on mere words. Because words

> are substitutes for things, which of course they cannot be in reality, they take on intensified forms ...This rupture of the link with the unconscious and our submission to the tyranny of words have one great disadvantage: the conscious mind becomes more and more the victim of its own discriminating activity, the picture we have of the world gets broken down into countless particulars, and the original feeling of unity, which was integrally connected with the unity of the unconscious psyche, is lost (1954c, [CW 11, para. 442]).

Idols

When the numinosum ceases to be a subject of honest exploration, the omitted function may turn nearly anything into an idol. Science, philosophy, or political ideas can then be worshipped with religious devotion. Even the great minds of science, Stephen Hawking and Leonard Mlodinow (2010), pronounced philosophy dead. One can create false belief-structures for basically anything, providing the *Imago Dei* supports it; this type of religious insight makes any object of such devotion unshakable. This is why Jung warned against any "isms," because of their capability to become religiously inspired with all the potential for radicalization and one-sidedness. "Isms" are constituted as ideological castles erected behind strong ideological fortifications. They are defined by the tendency toward *unification* of ideas and hostile intentions toward anything that seems to threaten their unit. What is such a posture defending against? The *other* side; it threatens to disintegrate the existing equilibrium and produce nearly intolerable uncertainty. The unknown is often the thing that arouses the greatest fear. *Theocalypsis* is thus used to bolster grandiose defenses against the new. An idealized posture is substituted for an authentic religion; true aspects of the numinosum lose their potency and are disavowed.

Disavowal

Disavowal allows for the denial or blocking of affect from one's experience (Basch, 1988). This "vertical split" as referred to by Basch, causes a grieving patient to behave, at times, as if he did not lose his loved one. It also allows a strongly religious man to behave as if he was not possessed by numinosum when his ideological stance confirms the opposite. As Corbett (1966) puts it, this "defense allows one to repudiate the meaning of an event which does not fit into a safe category" (p. 35). The potential new meaning is blocked from having an opportunity to be experienced in its full authenticity.

Adherence to the Old Serves as Defense Against New

Looking at the landscape of modern achievements and enjoyment of scientific inventions, we see islands that stand in total contradiction. Even though—and because—we are witnessing the rise of science and reason, we can simultaneously observe the rise of *theocalypsis*: the radicalization of and a strong-holding movement within religious systems protecting their teachings from any modernization. It appears that the increased intensity with which some religious adherents hold tightly to a one-sided position correlates with growing secularization. As Armstrong (2005) pointed out, fundamentalism is essentially a revolt against modern secular society with a tendency to elevate the value of pure faith to the highest level. She said:

> ...Fundamentalists tend to withdraw from mainstream society to create enclaves of pure faith ... Fundamentalists build a counter-culture, in conscious defiance of the Godless world that surrounds them, and from these communities some undertake a counteroffensive designed to drag God or religion from the sidelines to which they have been relegated in modern secular culture, and bring them back to center stage (p. 3).

Armstrong's sociological observation could be read psychologically with respect to the creation of *theocalypsis*. We have speculated that such a phenomenon is motivated by the fear that something substantial (fundamental) is being lost. Their very identity, believed to be the only justified identity, is threatened by emerging *otherness.* Armstrong's findings can also be applied to the intrapsychic level. The "pure center" may correspond to the false self wrapped in defensive thought-structures. The inner "pure center" may be preventing its adherents from experiencing a more authentic, individual religion; that is, spirituality. It is the formation of noncredible religious positions that are adroitly designed to reduce uncertainty and anxiety by keeping unwanted parts of paired opposites separated. Strong religions ought to be characterized, as ego-religions in that they create impenetrable ideological walls making sure there are no holes through which disavowed archetypal energies can enter. Jung stated:

> Civilized life today demands concentrated, directed conscious functioning, and this entails the risk of a considerable dissociation from the unconscious (1916/ 1957, [CW 8, para. 139]).

The ego that creates fixed structures in order to maintain equilibrium feels a sense of safety and integrity. But it comes with the price of being denied an opportunity to integrate vital aspects of the unconscious. The more those structures become rigid and the more the unconscious is excluded, the more a personality becomes trapped in a rather complex-ridden persona operating from a very narrow range on psycho-spiritual spectrum. The greater the fear of uncertainty and fragmentation, the greater the rigidity in the development of the structure of beliefs and their rationalizations.

Theodicy

Theodicy (from Greek *Theos dike* justice), defined as the defense of God's goodness and omnipotence in the face of the existence of evil, can also be used as a defense against the painful realization of the reality of evil.[208] God's reasoning for the judgment is rationalized as incomprehensible but still considered to be just and good regardless of how heavy-handed in its representations it may be. Goodness becomes disconnected from its bearings in reality because it has no frame of reference in the morality of its holder; this implies an obvious truth that no human being can accommodate to the demands of perfection. The ideal is projected onto the postulate of perfect being, God. The connection, though, is only philosophical, not practical. Despite this lack of the connection, some still believe in the property of goodness in a real sense. Again, the tension stemming from the logical fallacy continues to be resolved by projecting the resolution into God's mind, which knows everything. It is nothing other than an act of alibism through postulation of an absolute unattainability of logic. It is like saying, "Yes, by the judgment of all of my senses, this is dark, but God in his almighty power sees [it] as light; therefore, I have to accept it as light." Jung elaborated on the relativity of good and evil, and concluded that it can only be rendered relative if there is no exclusive goodness hypostatized. If such a paradigm is accepted absolutely, it becomes a hindrance in explaining the problems of evil on an individual level. This is true about any postulated idea, religious or nonreligious. The more uncritically an idea is adapted, the stronger the defense is established, and that prevents the passage of other possibilities. Theocalyptic adherence to the idea then naturally leads to its justification by noncredible means. But a persona built up from identifications cannot hold, and sooner or later, it becomes a victim of its own traps. *Sacrificium intellectus* has enormous practical implications. Because it provides deceitful grounds for problem resolution, it can keep people in abusive relationships (as in the case of Martha and Sarah above) or in the case of larger organizations

---

[208] Theodicy: (from Greek *theos* – "god" and *dike* – "justice") is a theological and a philosophical study which attempts to justify God's intrinsic nature of omnibenevolence, omniscience, and omnipotence, despite the existence of evil. (Authors)

it leads to electing leaders whose platforms are in direct contradiction with the interests of its voters. An idea that is adopted through *theocalypsis* becomes a truth with seemingly profound meaning, a truth, however, that is only available to the chosen.

Another patient of mine who had been in an abusive marriage for many years told me that she could not divorce her husband even though she suffered greatly because "their marriage was meant to be so." (V.Š.) When I asked her what she meant by that, she told me that they swore that they would stay together for better or worse in front of God. She stated that what kept her in the marriage was her faith and hope that one day God would change him, even though in the past twenty years there were no indications of his changing. The irrational elements are often blended into the total picture of one's philosophy of life proportionally to the intensity of *theocalypsis*. For example, the magical beliefs in the power of elephant tusks and rhinoceros horns have proven profoundly destructive to these species that have been decimated. Naturally these are not problems of some so-called primitive cultures but are contemporary problems that are endemic throughout modern culture. Whether belief in sexual potency, money, or power, all of it can be destructive if we are unable to set limits and recognize the difference between what we need versus what we want. This is not to devalue irrationality, as it is a very important and truly indispensable ingredient of human permanence, but it has to have a proper place, to be recognized as such. Otherwise, it would acquire an oppressive gradient instead of serving in the process of individuation.

Middle Path is Golden

Jungian insight teaches us over and over that only the middle position between opposites can be fluid enough to integrate ambivalence and enhance personality (Corbett, 1996). As such, it is arduous and freeing—at the same time—it is terrifying and uncertain, but also mysterious and longed for in the deepest recesses of the human heart. That realization, indeed, is like a heavy burden, which cannot be carried without true moral strength. That experience can be born only by those who are willing to bow deeply and look directly into the eyes of their own darkness and light and not fall in love with it, like Narcissus. Keeping a dialogue with the unconscious is a sacred task of the everyday hero and heroine. True morality does not consist of pretending to be perfect but in accepting all that can never be perfect and encountering it as a spiritual challenge. Trying to hide one's shadow is like releasing toxins in a river, naïvely hoping that they would never make it back to their body. Authentic and genuine spirituality squarely faces the reality of a difficult position in the midst of opposites instead of trying to deny the shadow by projecting it onto others. Paul Tillich (1948) spoke on this note:

> There is no place to which we could flee from God which is outside of God. "If I ascend to the heavens, Thou art there." It seems very natural for God to be in heaven, and very unnatural for us to wish to ascend to heaven in order to escape Him. But that is just what the idealists of all ages have tried to do. They have tried to leap towards the heaven of perfection and truth, of justice and peace, where God is not wanted. That heaven is a heaven of man's making, without the driving restlessness of the Divine Spirit and without the judging presence of the Divine Face. But such a place is a "no place"; it is a "utopia," an idealistic illusion. "If I make hell my home, behold, Thou art there" (p. 40).

Tillich examined attempts to escape the numinosum, to use Jungian terms, and with it, to avoid the shadow. In this *theocalyptic* attitude, the shadow is ultimately the source of fear that is projected in the form of re-activism. Utopia is the place where God's eyes do not see.

Corbett (1996) said, "... The price of this kind of salvation may be dogmatism, intolerance, and lack of freedom to experience the divine in a uniquely personal way" (p. 34). Mystic Eckhart (2000) said that the greatest suffering of the condemned lies in the fact that they recognize heaven in themselves, yet they cannot enter it. More rigid *theocalypsis*, the stiffer the adherence to the one-sided position can only produce a split and a compensatory eruption of the unconsciousness. According to Armstrong (2005), fundamentalism is a reaction to everything modern and secular that arose at a rapid pace. Armstrong stated:

> Culture is always contested, and fundamentalists are primarily concerned with saving their own society. Protestant Fundamentalists in the United States want America to be a truly Christian nation, not a secular, pluralist republic. In Palestine, Hamas began by attacking the PLO, because they wanted the Palestinian resistance to be inspired by Islamic rather than a secular polity. Bin Laden began by targeting the Saudi royal family and such secularist rulers as Saddam Hussein. Only at a secondary stage—if at all—do fundamentalists begin to attack a foreign foe. Thus fundamentalism does not represent a clash *between* civilizations, but a clash *within* civilizations (p. 4).

From a psychological perspective, this tendency to save one's society can be understood as a tendency to preserve the status quo of a socially accepted *theocalyptic.* It is a refusal to change in the face of the numinosum threatening to break established defenses as defined by Corbett (1996) and others (Kohut, Jacoby, Stein). Any direct pressure toward a defensive stance only increases the defenses and enhances the intensity with which the shadow is projected outward. Too direct of a challenge of irrational ideas usually leads to those ideas becoming strengthened. Change can only be successful when it comes from *within,* and that is from within the community, or from within one's personality. When change is pursued through purely external means the result is often distrust and reactivity.

When Odysseus finally left Calypso, it was because he acted on Hermes' message. Hermes was sent by Zeus to release Odysseus from his unwitting captivity. In clinical practice, we see how recognizing the inner other permits a person to use the transcendent function, to hold the pairs of opposites in tension. The messages from within are more potent in their transformative capacity. For example, Pope Francis's call for greater tolerance of gays and lesbians has more influence to persuade change from within the religious community than thousands of messages outside it. Likewise, in a dialogue with an-other, we allow a greater chance of having a successful and productive communication when we start from an [inner] position that we might be wrong all the while trying to find a common ground, (the third thing) the arboth agree. Thus, concurrently, we begin to acknowledge our own shadow and reveal to the other that we have a shared burden to carry together.

It is important that the ego differentiate between possessive energies of the Self in order to change fate to destiny. Jung says:

> Once the unconscious content has been given form and the meaning of the formulation is understood, the question arises as to how the ego will relate to this position, and how the ego and the unconscious are to come to terms. This is the second and more important stage of the procedure, the bringing together of opposites for the production of a third: the transcendent function. *At this stage it is no longer the unconscious that takes the lead, but the ego* (1916/1958, [CW 8, par. 181] author's emphasis)

My patient Martha, was terrified, but also nicely surprised when she began to realize that she could interpret the Bible in her own way and thus redefine what constitutes abuse and redefine the limits on her marital vows. (V.Š.) One day she told me: "Maybe I was abused so much that I came to believe that God wants me to suffer." The transcendent function, a messenger of true spirituality, can melt away the frozen fantasy and allow a more encompassing imagination to replace it. Overcoming the fear of God is the greater challenge for people in the grasp of *theocalypsis*. As Tillich reminds us, "there is no place to which we could flee from God which is outside of God." Thus everything is part of our spiritual journey, *theocalypsis* and *theonemesis*. Good cannot exist without evil, freedom without captivity. In their separateness there is No salvation; a higher and more developed consciousness can only emerge from the acceptance of both sides being parts of the greater unity.

Fear of Change

Let us go back to the role of fear in the history of religion. Individual psychological processes often parallel collective processes. The *other* in the collective and the *other* within the individual are treated with the same psychological mechanisms of refutation if they are not valued as enriching sources of change and individuation.

It is commonly known that the fear of change is so strong that many are willing to kill over it. History gives us countless examples. When Copernicus (1473-1543) discovered new and revolutionary ideas in which the planets revolved in circular orbits around a stationary sun, at rest. The Church considered it heresy, as his claims purportedly contradicted the teachings of the Bible (though the teachings were never recorded that way in the Bible). Anybody who dared to consider the heliocentric Copernican theory as valid was mercilessly attacked. The sad truth is that, according to a National Science Foundation survey (2014) 30 percent of Americans adults and almost 40 percent of Europeans still "believe" today that the sun revolves around the earth. Are there ramifications and consequences involved with this lack of basic knowledge? Is there an increasing debt that humanity will pay in the future as a result?

In 1633, Galileo (1564-1642), a follower of Copernicus, was found guilty of heresy and was sentenced to house arrest for the rest of his life. Three hundred years later (in 1992), the Roman Catholic Church admitted that it had been wrong to condemn Galileo. Another example is that of Giordano Bruno (1548-1600). He held innovative ideas about the universe. Bruno was a firm believer in God and presented his beliefs to Pope Clement VIII (1536-1605) in a well-intended hope that he would be praised for having extended the realm of knowledge of God's creation. Instead, he was tortured for seven years and was then publically burned at the stake at Campo de' Fiori, Rome. (White, 2002) Putting politics aside, the following psychological question can be posed: Why is the human mind willing to invest so much energy to resist change?

Positive Aspect of Theocalypsis

The ego naturally seeks comfort in discovering absolutes and finds refuge in secure ideas, particularly in moments of change, crisis and traumatic events. Even in the face of the emancipation of the human will, it seems that a part of the ego still wants to establish a state of certainty corresponding to the instincts that have firmly established functions and patterns. Perhaps for us it is a tendency and wish to return to a preconscious animal state, archetypally analogous to a return to paradise. Again, in the myth of Odysseus and Calypso, the island Ogygia was the best place to be after the long sea journey and traumatic shipwreck. It is there where Odysseus became stronger. Thanks to Calypso, Odysseus not only survived but underwent transformational individuation: healing and recovering from his trauma and pain. *Theocalypsis* can be a rejuvenating and healthy stage of psychological development; it only begins to become a problem when one resists individuation vigorously after *theocalypsis* has fulfilled its purpose.

It is often during a traumatic event or crisis that one turns to a theocalypsis for its healing properties. A patient of mine (G.J.D.) initiated analysis due to the loss of both of her parents. She was a non-practicing Catholic, quite depressed and anxious and had suddenly returned to her church for solace, healing and understanding. At first she felt like a hypocrite then her initial religious response was, understandably, child-like and hence the return of many aspects of her childhood faith. This was both comforting, at first, then quite unsettling—after working through some of her grief—and coming out of her theocalypsis, she would ask: "How am I using this (religion) and why do I really need it?" Our therapeutic relationship provided a safe transitional space for her to explore and understand from an adult perspective her needed theocalypsis and beyond that the embracing her own individuation. After a number of years of analytical work she developed what Thomas Moore has termed: "a religion of one's own." She questioned and challenged her faith and realized that she could not simply and literally return to her former childhood religion but had to listen to her own soul and need for a particular kind of religious life that was radically different from her childhood faith and that brought tougher many conflicting antimonies in her life.

Animals do not have to consciously deal with contradicting instinctive urges; therefore, their actions may be seen as constantly governed by natural law. However, the human ego steadfastly seeks to maintain some kind of certainty in the *status quo* even though it is never fully attainable. In a way, this is an expression of hubris in its most subtle form. An unchanging state is, just like a perfect harmony, only a futile wish of the ego. Discoveries on a macrophysical and microphysical level reveal that perpetual change and disharmony are essential principles through which the universe comes into existence. Only the Godhead as a theoretical postulate is unchangeable; everything else is subject to *creatio continua*, continuous creation.

Creatio Continua

St. Augustine (426/1982) was well aware that change was an inevitable part of existence. He wrote:

> "Let us, therefore, believe and, if possible, also understand that God is working even now, so that if his action should be withdrawn from His creatures, they would perish" (p. 171).

Human evolution and the development of consciousness proceeds essentially against nature, *contra naturam*. Consciousness is a force that transcends instinct and brings about the need for a different type of adaptation than what was needed for instinct. Jung highlights the paradoxical nature of archetypes as modes of commingled *preservation* and *adaptation*. He says:

> Archetypes are systems of readiness for action, and at the same time images and emotions. They are inherited with the brain structure — indeed they are its psychic aspect. They represent, on the one hand, a very strong instinctive conservatism, while on the other hand they are the most effective means conceivable of instinctive adaptation. They are thus, essentially, the chthonic portion of the psyche if we may use such an expression—that portion through which the psyche is attached to nature, or in which its link with the earth and the world appears at its most tangible. The psychic influence of the earth and its laws is seen most clearly in these primordial images (1931, [CW 10, para. 53]).

Psyche Mirrors Physical World

Elementarily speaking, structure can be found in the atom, which is composed of particles with opposing charges. An opposing charge of electrons and protons basically holds the atom (in other words, matter) together. However, it is also true that this stability is not absolutely changeless because when an atom is "broken," a new substance emerges. Nature seems to be an inherent system of dialectical interaction of opposites; that is mirrored by both the material world and psychological world. It is a rule of nature that opposites cannot exist independently of their counterparts because they are principally dependent on properties of the *other side.*

Bohr (1934) stated:

> "Isolated material particles are abstractions, their properties being definable and observable only through their interaction with other systems" (p. 57).

Since all opposites are interdependent, as stated by Capra (1975), "their conflict can never result in the total victory of one side but will always be a manifestation of the interplay between the two sides" (p. 146). Similarly in the psychological world, phenomena as experienced, derive their meaning by mutual interdependence. Whatever we experience, it can only be experienced as *relative* to something else. We use categories such as good, far, straight, hot, small, unique, chaos, or knowledge with respect to an assumed relative position. The Self and the ego form a similar interdependent unity. The ego without the Self is empty; the Self without the ego is blind. Transformation of personality is possible only by preserving the collective and the individual, not excluding one or the other. As Jung said, the goal of transformation is "attainment of the midpoint of personality," an overlap between the ego and the unconscious (1943, [CW 7, para. 364-365].)

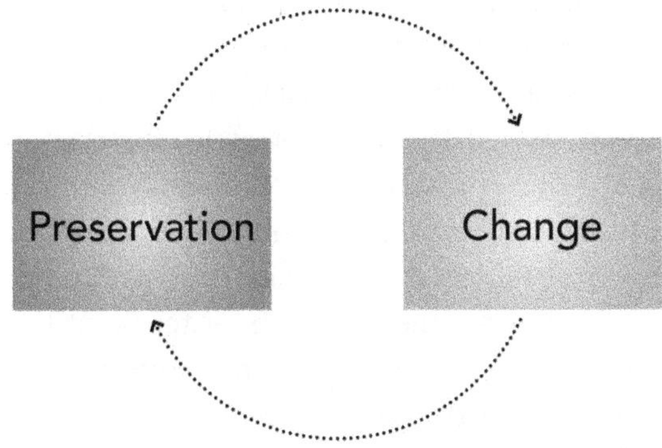

Dynamic of Preservation and Change

Individuation can be considered an expression of the right measure of pushing and pulling between the forces of *preservation* and *change*. Dwelling on unchecked expansion and change can be as destructive as dwelling on unmovable dogma. Such obsessive dwelling on either may be considered hubristic, i.e., attempting to disregard and transcend the law of the universe! It is a fact that the fear of rapid change on the socio-cultural and socio-political scene motivates many to adhere to *strong religion*. It is only human to hide under a secure blanket of familiarity, even if it is predicated on stagnation, rather than face the anxiety of an unknown that could yield growth and maturation; without any guarantee. Jungian analysts know well that there is a human reason behind every decision, no matter how outrageous. Nothing human should be alien to us, (Lat.: *Homo sum, humani nihil a me alienum puto*) as Roman playwright, Publius Terentius (Terence) Afer, stated. One patient of mine, who is a member of a strong evangelical church, explained to me why her creed was so important to her: "In the times when nothing is sacred anymore, when children are using drugs, are sexualized, and doctors are killing babies, I want my family to have firm values and beliefs." (V.Š.) Jung (1954a, [CW 9i, par. 66) once stated that "in all the chaos, there is cosmos, and in all disorder, there is a secret order." But, understandably, the danger of anarchy on the social and individual level, which can be brought about by uncontained destructive forces, is a sufficient reason for adhering to a firm religious structure, *theocalypsis* (p. 32). How do we trust the inherited order of natural happenings, especially when the ego becomes disconnected from nature and nature becomes distant from the ego to the extent that there is no communication between them? We should not romanticize the fear that is caused by the fear of change; it is actually the fear of the loss of identity; loss of the sense of the "I"!

Paradisiacal Past Is An Ideal of The Self, Not the Real World

Strong proponents of rigid and narrow minded rules and order are often project their fantasies on past states and times, namely times of order, security, happiness and presumed stability and peace: Camelot and times of enchantment; the High Middle Ages and "the good old days." Utopian fantasies and consequent belief-expectations are highly influenced and determined by archetypes and are not grounded and based in empirical reality. On the contrary, much of the past was more horrific than many would imagine.

Religious thought structure, cared for by religious institutions, provides a secure container for ego-organization and ego-building

Assisting Plague Victims, St. Borromeo, *Ve jménu Boha*.[209]

processes throughout the stages of spiritual development. It is akin to adapting and securing an identity from ancestors and society. Thanks to instinctive wisdom, ancestors figured out how to read, contain and work with archetypal and symbolic reality without falling into chaos. It is actually *this* very ability of the human mind that allows for the differentiation of the ego from primitive unconscious identification. It becomes problematic

[209] Image: Saint Borromeo assists plague victims. The ancient epidemics killed as many as 4 out of 10 people in the affected areas. Medieval life was for most people painful and short.

when this identity becomes too tightly woven. If there is no reflective distance between the inner and outer spiritual bodies, one can become trapped. Change, therefore, is always a matter of the right use of the specific means of staying connected and letting go.

Secure attachment

Just like a child's secure attachment (which is characterized by the ability to safely leave the caregiver and return for protection and succorance) allows for the development of a balanced relationship between dependence and autonomy, so the secure spiritual development is predicated upon the ability of relating objective religious ideas to inner religious phenomenon and persuasions inferred from individual experiences. This is akin to a balance between reasonable dependence on one's *Imago Dei* and trust and autonomy of one's own spirituality. Stein (In Casement, 2006) says:

> The passion for the spiritual, like all passions, can easily *tip over* into pathos and extreme alienation of other parts of the Self, as we see so well today among religious fundamentalists and fanatics. The goal of individuation, unlike that of the religious quest, is not union with the divine or salvation but rather integration and wholeness, the forging of the opposites inherent in the Self into an image of unity and integrating this into consciousness. (p. 43, Author's emphasis)

It is the spiritual fervor all directed toward the greatest tasks of existence that overshadows daily heroic achievements that are the true building blocks of human spirituality. Similarly philosopher George Santayana (1905) once said, "fanaticism consists of redoubling the effort when we have forgotten our aim." (Original Christian Faith, p. 57) His insight hits the nail on the head; it is, after all, the numinosum and authentic religious experiences that we crave, but in some ways, we can become so needy or thirsty, and out of tune and misdirected we forget that what speaks for the real goal is not an experience detached from the world, but the deed within the world. The gold is not in *having*, but in *being.* Accelerating social change makes increasing demands on the speed of adaptation. This rapid social change practically did not exist for primitive humans. In prehistoric times, subtle alterations on social, cultural or environmental levels were basically spread over hundreds and oftentimes thousands of years, so each generation lived in an unchanged container. Kings or Pharaohs might perish from the physical world, but the ideas were essentially unchangeable. Even during the Middle Ages, a trip from Paris to Rome could easily take several months. Songs or rituals would be changed only after protracted wars and a subsequent domination by the conquering culture that would mix in its creedal paradigm. Even then we observe unyielding effort to preserve religious artifacts, symbols, and ways of life, because with their losses not only religion, but also the whole cultural identity, was threatened. Modernity brought about hasty changes that are very real and noticeable even within the span of one generation.

Humans Are Masters of Incomplete Adaptation

Lorenz (1966) regarded the adaptation of humans unique, because, as he taught, human adaptation was based on *incomplete* or partial adaptation. He believed humans never fully adapt to their environment, and that gives us an advantage over other animals that, as a rule, adapt wholly to their environment, but are unable to readapt expediently when environmental changes proceed rapidly. In that respect, animals —because of their unconscious dependence on their habitat, their lack of conscious comparison between different alternatives, and lack of what Jung defined as reflective instinct, which is manifested as "power of culture to maintain itself in the face of untamed nature"—are exhibiting a one-sided adaptation to the environment par excellence (1937, [CW 8, para. 243]). Strong creeds, viewed through these criteria, are expressions of the failure [of] or a resistance [to] adaptation. A tendency to adhere to radical and strong religious persuasions (*theocalypsis*) might stem from the refusal to adapt fully to new religious, societal and cultural paradigms, and as a result, remain profoundly stuck on the opposite spectrum. It might be the fear that a new paradigm would have to be built anew that causes annihilating anxiety. Annihilating anxiety profoundly inhibits the use of the reflective function in its most basic ability: to balance between opposites.

Around the world, the third rebuff of fundamentalism came after the scientific revolution and the secularization movement —brought about by the Enlightenment—its origin being in the Lutheran revolution. The invention of the printing press played a crucial role in accelerating these dynamics. Such an historical movement was once again accompanied by an almost axiomatic development of dichotomy. Profound scientific discoveries and philosophical insights dissipated many cultural taboos and beliefs, which gave rise to a brighter exploration of the *new*, but inexorably, it also brought a dread that God's wrath would be unleashed on mankind, once again, with iron fist to punish those who dared to diverge from the divine order.

EPILOGUE: PSYCHOLOGICAL PARALLELS OF ODYSSEUS' MYTHICAL JOURNEY

Jung (1916/1957) in his essay "The Transcendent Function" described a process of psychological change in terms of the self-regulatory processes of the psyche. His findings have enormous psychological implications with respect to clinical work. Here, we present his model and add extrapolations pertaining to the archetypal process described in the myth of Odysseus and Calypso.

1. *Difficulty of adaptation*. Little progression of life energy (i.e., libido): Odysseus lost his crew and his ship is wrecked on the Ogygia Isle. Odysseus experiences an acute trauma.

2. *Regression of energy* (depression, lack of disposable energy): Odysseus is exhausted and injured, experiences post-traumatic shock. He realizes he is stuck and mourns the fellow warriors he lost in the sea.
3. *Activation of unconscious contents* (fantasies, archetypal images)/*Compensation*: Odysseus is caught in the fascinating aspect (*fascinans*) of the numinosum and is infatuated with Calypso all the while forgetting the true reason of his journey.
4. *Symptoms of neurosis; theocalypsis*: Odysseus's personality changes and develops a false Self along with fantasies where a paradisiacal stay at the island becomes the highest value. Odysseus creates a belief system to justify his stay and stage at Ogygia and denies love for Penelope.
5. *Unconscious or half-conscious conflict between ego and contents activated in the unconscious*: Odysseus experiences an ambivalence, questions Calypso and attempts to free himself from her influence. Misses Penelope.
6. *Activation of the transcendent function*, involving the Self and archetypal patterns of wholeness, *theonemesis*: Zeus is sending Hermes to free Odysseus. Hermes is talking to Calypso in order to diminish her influence over Odysseus's mind.
7. *Formation of symbols* (numinosity, synchronicity): Odysseus realizes the meaning of his journey in the fuller scope of his life and is now eager to come back to Ithaca to live out his destiny. Odysseus is able to separate from Calypso's seductive influence and is now able to understand the unconscious and negative side of her capture.
8. *Transfer of energy between unconscious contents and consciousness*. Enlargement of the ego, progression of energy: Odysseus is happy and full of energy; he builds up a boat.
9. *Assimilation of unconscious contents*. Individuation: Odysseus sales back to continue his quest.

A POSTSCRIPT
PERSONAL JOURNEY
AND EXPERIENCE OF THE NEW
(PSYCHOLOGICAL) DISPENSATION

George J. Didier

> *Our road may have to take a great swerve that seems a retrogression... We must make a great swerve in our onward-going life-course now, to gather up again the savage mysteries...But this does not mean going back on ourselves. We can't go back.* (Lawrence, 1977)

After years of education and formation in the Catholic tradition (elementary, high school, college, and graduate theology) I was ordained a Roman Catholic priest in 1980. With great anticipation and joy, I was eager to enter the Catholic world of formal ministry. My Weltanschauung and identity was steeped in the sensibilities of the Catholic mythos; the Catholic Church was my spiritual home. At this time, I was, so I thought, deeply fulfilled and would spend my life as a Catholic priest in service to the People of God. Once ordained and involved in parish life, I came to a profound realization of how projection, particularly in the religious realm, functioned. After ordination, people responded to me differently with a deep reverence, deference, and with a great measure of idealization. I was treated as if I literally walked on water. I had a most difficult time with this. My senior pastor was kind but gently persuasive in helping me to embrace this new role or, we might say persona. I slowly came to understand and experience how one's identity can be seduced by the intoxicating power of one's persona. In my situation, the persona was the power of religious authority (i.e., archetype of priesthood) and clerical privilege that accompanies the priestly office. Psychological carrying and holding this symbolic image and numinous energy can be extraordinarily healing (i.e., archetype of healer) and beneficial for the people one serves. Over the years I learned that the caveat was the imperative to remain conscious of the archetypal nature of the religious energy and persona by not over-identifying with it. Becoming aware of and working with these powerful psychological and religious dynamics was deeply instructive. With this awareness, I also began to ponder the source of my own projections onto the Church. It didn't take long before I became restless and very curious questioning my own religious identity and vocation. The balance between one's personal journey and identity and one's relationship to the collective was becoming an ongoing tension in my life. I was beginning to experience this tension concerning my own individual needs and desires and my collective religious tradition in which I was contained. Then something happened. Jung summarizes it is so well:

> So long as all goes well and our psychic energies find an outlet in adequate (symbols) and well-regulated ways, we are disturbed by nothing from within...[210]

This unease and tension slowly increased to where I knew I needed more than my monthly spiritual direction. After several years into the priesthood, my unconscious became highly activated through dreams, moods, synchronicities, and restless questioning of everything. Aspects of my own self that I knew little about were clamoring for consciousness and acknowledgement. Parts of me were crying for awareness and engagement. I was struggling with different facets of my own unmet needs and a deep sadness from within. In this turmoil I was beginning to listen to the glimmerings and stirrings deep within me that

[210] Jung 1931, (CW 10, par. 160).

were previously silenced. I began questioning my priestly vocation as I knew and lived it according to my vows and collective religious identity. Life became enclosed around me as I struggled with questions of celibacy, identity, the institutional Church, its authority, and its exclusivity: *"Extra Ecclesiam nulla salus,"* (i.e., Outside the Church there is no salvation). I slowly began to realize that aspects of my own innate religious function were benignly undeveloped and projected onto the Church, which taught that its way was the only way.

The suffering of the soul forces one to go in search of its own interiority in order to become aware of its larger domain and deeper desires that are seeking ways to be incarnated in one's unlived life. When our collective religion weakens or loses its symbolic power to reveal the sacred, our soul has to find its own symbolic and religious orientation in the depths of one's own being. My own personal and vocational crisis was also a reflection of the present religious and cultural plight of our time. Regardless of what the Church or society may think one is required to make peace with the demands of one's own soul.

Knowing of Jung's great respect for religion and the soul, I entered Jungian analysis and began listening, a bit differently, to the stirrings of my soul, my unlived life, my dreams, and the musings of the unconscious. I became extremely inquisitive and attentive to the energy and images that were awakened from within. In this work, allowance was given for all things human and not so human. This experience was radically different from my spiritual direction, which often would reflect on subjects from an experience-distant[211] perspective, about my struggles with Church policy and religious and theological issues. In my analytical work, I was introduced to the "reality of the psyche" and was confronted by my own living psyche and its shadow. Through this work, I learned to value and honor images and desires of my soul that previously, I would have dismissed or

---

[211] "Experience-distant vs. experience-near" are terms coined by Kohut (Self Psychology) describing one's perspective from being an outside observer vs. the person who is empathically immersed in one's experience.

suppressed. That is, my worldview was completely Christian, however, I quickly learned that my unconscious was not so Christian. In fact, I realized that one couldn't Christianize the unconscious. It must be respected for what it is and how it presents itself.

My relation to my inner world became magnified, up close, and personal. I was focusing directly on my experience of my soul, not on what I think the soul was speaking. In learning to work with the unconscious, I was discerning how to listen to the movement of my soul differently, not simply from prescribed religious exercises (e.g., preordained norms and rules, etc.) or beliefs that I learned or were contained in my religious tradition, but from the images and emotions that sprang from the depths of my own being. Though my traditional religious approach was extraordinarily enlightening, beneficial, and engaging, it did not foster nor encourage the depth of freedom and challenge that I needed in exploring my inner world. In analysis, the depth of my experiential self-knowledge (personal unconscious) and my relation to the collective unconscious increased exponentially. It was threatening, evocative, and exhilarating, all at once.

My initial work confronted me with the dark side of my personal unconscious and the raw and untransformed aspects of my own shadow, which were *hiding behind* the strong persona of my professional religious identity—"Persona Christa." This approach held me more personally accountable for my shadow and its need for transformation. I could not simply confess my sins! I discovered that religious work was about wholeness not perfection! In the second (Christian) dispensation, one strives to be perfect as the heavenly Father is perfect! This was quite a radical change. Wholeness versus perfection encourages one to compassionately face, engage, and work with one's shadow all the while moving toward integration and transformation. In the old dispensation, it was all too easy to end with confession, absolution and penance; resulting in a feeling of relief that all is taken care of. In this Christian dispensation, the God-man, Christ, bore the burden of our sins; however, one can too easily avoid one's responsibility for one's own shadow. In the new psychological dispensation, confession of transgressions (shadow) is only one of the initial moments toward wholeness. The powerful dark side of my own self, my religion, my religious institution, and culture became all the more apparent.

Slowly and painstakingly, I learned that one's authentic spirituality is deeply connected to one's psychological structure and wounds; how could it be otherwise? This factor cannot be overstated. My spirituality at the time was more about putting on the new Christ versus the more arduous task of facing and transforming my inner demons as parts of myself. It is here that I learned that one's religious/numinous experience is always directly relevant to one's personal psychology (the new dispensation!); what one needs for healing and individuation. That is, in short, one's experience of the divine is personally tailored! If one's authentic spirituality is undeveloped, suppressed (e.g., by traditional religious structures) or not related to their own personality, it will usually reveal itself in dreams, symptoms, moods or acting out, ("sin"). Witness the onslaught of sexual scandals rocking the Catholic Church by its own priests. How else are we to understand the radical split between a priest's (otherworldly) spirituality (spirituality from above) and their horrific shadow in sexually acting out (lack of a developed spirituality from below)? It is quite obvious that Christianity's shadow involves the body, sexuality and the feminine.

Often in traditional religions one is not encouraged to discover and relate to one's own inner *Imago Dei*. That archetypal image is often unconsciously projected onto the priest/church who must carry that projection for the Other. Furthermore, if the Holy or Sacred is truly manifested through one's psychic unconscious (the new dispensation), then one can have a direct experience of the sacred and will be less dependent on belief or creed or the intercession of the priest/church. As revealed in my own inner work, the numinous may manifest in ways that are unacceptable or intolerable to one's traditional religion, yet it may be exactly what the individual personally needs for healing and transformation.

The containment of my analytical work allowed me to question my beliefs while opening to idiosyncratic encounters with my soul's God-image, all without worrying about the approval of the Church and its foundational system of orienting beliefs. I experienced my analytic work as religiously and spiritually liberating, exploring and questioning many experiences, images and symbols from my inner work: dreams and active imagination. My own awareness and sense of self greatly expanded as I plummeted my own depths and began to loosen and stretch my egoic identity and beliefs.

During this period, my relation to my own God-within (*Imago Dei*) slowly began to change. What I accepted unquestioningly and, at times, literally, I began to question in the sealed vessel of my analysis. I painfully questioned whose authority was I serving, the Catholic Church, my spiritual beloved mother who had contained and nurtured me since childhood, or the male dominated clerical hierarchy or my own inner experiences and relation to the Self. I found the freedom and authority *within* myself to challenge long-cherished beliefs that no longer fit my experience.

On this journey within, I explored a much deeper relation to my own personal unconscious, whereupon, I stumbled upon aspects of my own being that I never knew existed. For example, I was not aware of my own deep identification with the dominance of the patriarchy, particularly in its suppressing and devaluing of the feminine. As my inner journey continued, I was led into the deeper waters of the collective unconscious, (i.e., archetypal images). The unconscious was the door I had to pass through to discover a deeper connection to my soul (Hillman, 1984). In the new (psychological) dispensation, the unconscious is the royal road through which one will travel to experience, rediscover and honor one's depth. I experienced the living reality of my own psyche that beckoned me to wrestle with it in light of conscious and unconscious conflicts, clericalism, religious narcissism, out dated beliefs, and one-sided attitudes. I befriended my shadow and became aware of my soul, as a living reality and force: not simply a suprapersonal ideal or some otherworldly theological datum. My psyche became like a sacramental altar, its revelations of the sacred images and symbols challenged and nourished me in new ways. In religious circles we talk extensively about one's soul; in analysis one begins to awaken and dialogue experientially with this reality.

Previous to this discovery and liberation, my psyche was part and parcel of a traditional hierarchal religious institution. Nonetheless though, within this religious institution, I had experienced numerous transformations throughout my teens and young adulthood into my late 20's. I was safely contained in that system that provided the substance of meaning for my life. As I began this inward journey I had no idea of the depth and reality of my own psyche, not alone its source of authority (i.e. one's Imago-Dei). While ministering to many parishioners and attending to their pain in trying to "fit their psyche into the Catholic institutional system," I realized that one cannot simply prescribe what the right myth is for each individual without danger to one's very being. I witnessed many parishioners denying aspects of their own soul (i.e., sexuality, authority), in order to "fit in" and be saved within the institutional Church's hegemony. As I struggled with living in a loving and practical world, I became more disenchanted with the Church's practices and beliefs; they became, for me, what Jung has termed "sacrosanct unintelligibility,"[212] (e.g., people forbidden to receive the Eucharist because they were divorced; people forced to live an outdated morality that did not allow expression of who they were; people not allowed to participate fully in the life of the Church due to the continuing denial of women to become ministers/priests; people forced to live in marriages that had died, told that divorce was not an option; homosexuals being marginalized and denied recognition, etc.). The institutional and hierarchical church no longer mediated the divine nor carried the numinosum for me as it once did.

[212] Jung 1948b, [CW 11, par. 170]

In working with the psyche, in the new dispensation, one cannot prescribe what myth is the "right myth" for the other. There is no "one size fits all," no cookie cutter McSpirituality. One's deeper spirituality comes out of one's own deeper (wounded) psychological structure. This does not necessarily mean that one must leave a particular tradition or expression of faith. In traditional religions, people often develop parts of themselves that are not welcomed in the body of the Church. People can and do individuate within traditional institutional religion as long as they are not completely contained with that religion; or as we often say, drink nothing but the cool aid. "Legitimate faith," writes Jung, "must always rest on experience."[213] This is the heart of the new psychological dispensation. One must listen to the depths of one's own experience of the transpersonal psyche/Self.

My analysis turned out to be a deeper experience of coming to know my own living psyche, my soul, which previously was inundated with collective beliefs and attitudes that were not conducive to my own personal individuation. Jung writes clearly of these moments of deeper discovery and confrontation:

> Only then, do we discover the psyche as something that which thwarts our will, which is strange and even hostile to us, and which is incompatible to our conscious standpoint.[214]

The suffering of the soul forces one to go in search of one's own interiority in order to become aware of an unconscious life that is seeking ways to incarnate. When the outer collective religion loses its symbolic power to reveal the sacred, the soul has to find its own religious orientation. Regardless of what the Church or society may think one is required to make peace with the demands of one's soul.

Overtime, my God Image radically changed and challenged me to confront my formal vows of celibacy and obedience all the while accepting and incarnating different parts of myself

---

[213] Jung 1952, [CW 5, par. 345]

[214] Jung 1931, [CW 10, par. 160]

that were excluded in the Catholic mythos. While being contained "in the Catholic Church" and "in the Christian dispensation," I rarely experienced my psyche as a separate entity or reality. I was merely part of a larger collective religious system that contained my psyche. Within that religious structure, I knew who I was; I was securely contained with all the answers to life's questions. This is somewhat similar to religious fundamentalists who are tightly contained within their own belief system. To question one's beliefs and experiences leads to anxiety and fear of losing one's way, one's religious and emotional security and comfort. Leaving the collective to adventure on one's own is indeed a heroic journey.

After years of working on myself and engaging my soul, all the while attempting to adapt and adjust to the religious structures of my tradition and vows (i.e., celibacy, obedience, etc.), I realized, to be faithful to my experience of the divine, I had to formally leave. This spiritual and psychological crisis led to my eventual leaving the Catholic priesthood and setting out on my own personal journey of individuation.[215]

During this reworking of my psycho-spiritual identity and journey, I realized that traditional religious systems of belief were clearly not the only dispensers or guardians of grace and salvation. As I slowly developed a more conscious relationship to my inner Self, I deeply experienced the divine's challenge, love and grace from the numinous images within, what Jung has aptly named, one's inner "church, your cathedral."[216]

It was through this ordeal that I discovered the advent of the new psychological dispensation and became gripped by its power to enliven, change and transform. This change in consciousness and awareness of one's innate religious authority

---

[215] See Didier, (1991), *Vocational Crisis and Transformation: From Ordained Clerical Priesthood to Lay Ministry*, in *Creative Ministries in Contemporary Christianity*, Exploration Press.

[216] In working with his patients, Jung encouraged them to write and paint their own Red Book and discover their inner "church-your cathedral". *The Red Book*, p. 216

and deeper connection (i.e., ego-Self axis) to the divine could be called the Depth-Psychological Dispensation. Working within the new dispensation is an ongoing and evolving process, continuing to make the unconscious conscious, holding the tension of opposites and incarnating the Self. One is no longer driven to have answers to all the existential anxieties and fears; one can embrace the great Unknown.

In my psychological and spiritual work, I began to differentiate from my identity and containment within the Catholic Church. As I did, I became more self-aware, differentiated and, ironically, related more objectively to the Church. That is, psychologically, the Church no longer acted as the container for my spiritual life. One can be highly related to one's church or traditional religion without being entirely contained in it. Containment is an unconscious phenomenon of psychological identification. One can be contained in one's religious life similar to being contained in one's family or other communities.

However, if one is completely contained in their traditional religious life, one risk having no individual living relation to the numinous archetypes, they are totally mediated through the church structure. If one has a personal relationship to the numinosum, one can develop what Edinger (1981) following Neumann, calls an ego-Self axis. In the development of a personal relationship to one's *Imago Dei* (Self), one becomes a carrier of the experience of the Self. This relationship allows one to relate or connect to one's religion out of one's individual numinous experience not by simply assenting to creed or the collective hierarchy. This is practically impossible in the faith of the fundamentalists, where there is little to no room for one's individual experience of the numinosum. In these situations, one's numinous experience is either defensively avoided, or is reinterpreted in light of the religious status quo. One wonders if being completely contained in one's traditional faith is really healthy. The Dalai Lama once remarked that the major problem to interfaith communion and sharing is one's own unhealthy relationship to one's own faith. This is most apparent in fundamentalism, but is also typical of many mainline denominations.

If one is completely contained and identified with a faith community, a new dispensation is practically impossible. Today, we are witnessing a major movement among traditional (and nontraditional) religious people. Many of my religious patients/ clients are in crisis and experiencing what I would call, a crisis in Church-faith. Many traditionally religious people are no longer contained in their faith as in days gone by. Instead, they find themselves in the throes of transition to a new (depth-psychological) dispensation.

What was essential in my own analysis and confrontation with the unconscious, and eventually leaving of the Catholic priesthood, was the discovery of the reality of the psyche. Personally, this was similar to the Gospel story of finding the pearl in the field and then selling everything to buy the field. Previously, the pearl was contained and carried by the Catholic Church and all of its practices, dispensing God's grace through the sacraments, rituals, etc. This discovery of the "reality of the psyche" enabled me to identify and liberate my religious function from the overall domination and one-sided idealization of the Church. Though I still deeply care for and relate to the Church, it is now from a much different point of consciousness.

The reality of the psyche has only been discovered within the last century. Ironically , it is with the decline of traditional religion that the discovery of depth psychology has emerged. This reality of the psyche is the foundational building stone of the new psychological dispensation.

The Emergence of the New Dispensation and the Individual

The emergence of a post-Christian dispensation had been foreshadowed by mystics for centuries. The 15th-century mystic, scientist, and Roman Catholic Cardinal, Nicholas of Cusa, recognized the foreshadowing of a new dispensation. He wrote: "Humanity will find that it is not a diversity of creeds, but the very same creed which is everywhere proposed. ... Even though you are designated in terms of different religions yet you presuppose in all this diversity one religion which you call wisdom." (In Fox, p. 3)[217]

Importantly, the emergence of a new dispensation is not simply a syncretism of fusing different religions or symbol systems together. Contemporary mystic Father Bede Griffiths acknowledged the needed differentiation between faiths when he advised: "We have, of course, to guard against syncretism of any kind, but this only means that we have to learn to discriminate within each tradition between that which belongs to the universal religious tradition of mankind and that which belongs to its own limited and particular point of view." While Father Bede harkens us to honor the differences between religions, he also summons us to emphasize the similarities between them. What he calls "the universal religious traditions of mankind." Jung gives us a phenomenological model of the psyche that orients us to the sensitivities of both collective archetypal religious symbols—world religions—and one's own personal religious symbols and images.

[217] Fox M., *The Hidden Spirituality of Men: Ten Metaphors to Awaken the Sacred Masculine*, New World Library, Novato, California, 2008

THE CONCLUSION AND SUMMARY

In this book, we have explored the questions of religion from the perspective of Jungian psychology. As themes concerning matters of religion are complex and multifaceted, the focus has been on a relatively narrow perspective. Questions of religion were explored from an empirical and naturalistic standpoint, confined to the frame of contemporary depth-analytical theory. Metaphysical and theological speculations have been avoided without dismissing them as unsubstantiated or fantastical. Instead, we rendered them simply irrelevant in terms of this study. Our religious beliefs have not been expressed, nor has the existence of God been debated. However, we stand with humility and awe in front of the great mystery, which reveals itself through the psyche and life as such. Therefore, we harbor the utmost respect for human religiosity and worship with all the diversity it claims to have in human life. Nevertheless, we have attempted to cover the phenomenological and psychological aspects of religion, *not* the object of religion itself. By any means, the current work should not be considered as a critical inquiry into theological questions and alternatively, we offer it as an empirical exploration of religion from a psychological perspective.

Our main goal was to explore the broad question of what religion is from a psychological standpoint and to establish the functions of religion. Here, we closely examined fundamentalist, radical, excessive, and extreme forms of religion and religious worship, as well as the social and individual aspects of religious mindsets. We have drawn important insights pertaining to this matter from various sources, which include Jungian literature, as well as works of social psychology, developmental psychology, philosophy, sociology, anthropology, poetry, spiritual and religious texts, and mythology.

An important distinction between *religion* and *creed* has been made in Jungian theory. Religion is defined as an experience of an *archetypal reality* (the Self) with the concurrent rational assignment of this experience to a transcendent source (i.e., God). Religion, as used in Jungian theory is basically synonymous with spirituality. Rudolf Otto (1917) called this experience *numinous* and postulated two main aspects of the numinosum: *tremendos* and *fascinans*. According to Otto, the experience of the holy is always paradoxical and evokes deep emotions of mystery, fear, and fascination. Otto's concept was adopted by Jung and his followers and has been applied to all phenomena concerning the archetypal, therefore numinous experience. We have attempted to explore the idea of the numinosum and its representation in human psychology. This concept has become the most crucial cornerstone of our paper. We have recognized and delineated religion as the most important modus humans use to apprehend archetypal reality. Religion is *organically* intertwined with the psyche, and therefore, we cannot speak about the psyche without taking the religious function into consideration. *Anima religiosus est:* The psyche is naturally religious, is endowed with religious energy, and is a *container* and a *content* for the numinosum at the same time. Corbett (1996) stated it this way: "Numinous experience is synonymous with religious experience" (p. 15). *Human maturation, therefore, coincides with the maturation of religious conceptions.* Jungian theory refers to this spiritual maturation as the unfolding, in word and deed, of one's individuation. The default position for religion is a primordial state of unconscious identity, which Levy Bruhl (1923) called *participation mystique*. The evolution of religious worship stems from this natural state of the human mind and proceeds through the stages of animism, totemism, and polytheism to monotheism. The phylogeny (and ontogeny) of consciousness advances through the withdrawal of projections of unconscious contents (archetypes) and returning the projections consciously to the projector (the Self). Thus, ego-consciousness is formed. The development of consciousness can be defined as a process of making the unconscious contents conscious. Anytime the unconscious becomes integrated into the ego, we speak about psychic transformation. Consciousness *is* the unconscious that became conscious. Religion (spirituality), from a Jungian perspective, is understood as a tool for transformation. Religion can thus be viewed as a creation of consciousness, a meaning-endowed connection between ego and the Self; what Edinger (1972) called ego-Self axis.

Creed, on the other hand, refers to a scripted, codified and institutionalized relationship to the numinosum. Creed is based on collectively established dogmas; therefore, its main purpose is to provide a universal nexus relevant to the experience of the numinosum. Creed, as doctrine, can provide a container for numinous experiences and thus mediate its content to individuals. However, it can also dogmatize individual experiences in such way that they become *inefficient* with respect to their effect on the process of psychic transformation. Creeds can promote the use of defensive functions in religions resulting in the "dilution" of the numinosum, and the exclusion and rationalization of the numinosum's components.

The function of creed and its relevance to rituals and social structures has been delineated. With respect to ritual, we have demonstrated how ritualistic practices can foster defensive structures, and instead of integrating numinous experiences, they can be used to protect against them. The symbolic process that is crucial to the integration and regulation of numinous energy is missing in many institutionalized religious practices today. Many religious institutions are, thus, unable to provide *adequate* and *credible* religious [psychological, imaginal and ideological] containers for numinous (*Imago Dei*) experiences. That leads to various modes of inadequate psychological ego-adaptation, such as hubris, inflation, possession, mana personalities, and one-sidedness, among others.

These phenomena have been examined from the perspective of Jungian typology, particularly the role of the inferior function, as it pertains to the differentiation of personality and matters of creed. Thorough research has been conducted with regard to the phenomenon of ego-adaptation within the frame of Jungian psychology, and the research followed ego development as reflected in Jung's collected works and the works of von Franz, Neumann, Jacobi, Jacoby, and Meyer, as well as the work of neo-Jungians and other psychoanalysts, such as Corbett, Edinger, Kohut, Kernberg, Winnicott, Kalsched, Hill, Nathanson, Casement, Moore, Main, Compaan, Dourley, Samuels, Hillman and others. Although our primary goal was not to ponder the question of religion from the perspective of progressive, "adequate" or "adaptive" functioning, this book has briefly touched upon it by identifying spirituality as a primary, indispensable aspect of individuation. Spirituality in Jungian psychology has more to do with a practical relationship to the numinosum than with religious faith based on the existence of a transcendent being independent from natural laws and human actions. Jung's theory proposes exploring the psyche and establishing a conscious relationship with various components of the unconscious (complexes and archetypes) and ultimately a relationship with the Self. Further, it opens the door to finding a universal ground for religiosity, stretching beyond the particular religious teachings of any one religious system. The spirituality of Jungian theory and practice seeks to encourage individual accountability as it stands in opposition to the unconscious identification (participation mystique), with mass-psychology and collectively accepted dogmas.

This individuality, however, is not solipsistic nor does it exclude one's individuated relatedness to a particular religious faith. Morality, arising from the Jungian concept of spirituality, is based on a sincere and responsible exploration of the inner and outer world, its corresponding knowledge, and the conscious assessment of consequences stemming from ensuing conduct. This morality is in contradiction to accepting dogmas as only credible premises for spiritual knowledge and also in contradiction to adopting religious beliefs without subjecting them to a critical reality-based rationality. This does not mean the rationality of separate cognitive functions, but *knowledge of the heart* based on the quintessential involvement of all psychic functions (all functions of consciousness including intuition and feeling). This may lead to the deeper and ever-continuous symbolic understanding of reality and the human role in it. Jung called this the individuation process.

Individuation is a process of *becoming* oneself, and therefore, it is the highest goal to which human beings can aspire. Individuation is not a meandering in the river of the collective unconscious, but an *opus contra naturam,* or a conscientious process of slowly accruing self-awareness that requires a strong ego and the willingness to sacrifice. The goal of individuation is not to seek refuge in certain rigid spiritual practices or beliefs that bring the appearance of certainty and familiarity, instead the goal is to create ego-consciousness that is capable of dignified living among the opposites of *Complexio Oppositorum*.

Jung criticized the widespread religious doctrine—*privatio boni*—postulating that God acts as (and is) an all-good being (*Summum Bonum*) without acknowledging the dark, so-called evil part of the divine mysterium (*Mysterium Coniunctionis*). In the formation of one's *Imago Dei*, if one splits-off a part of the Coniunctio, it will have inevitable and severe psychological consequences. Jung presented a theory for the new millennium of growing consciousness that broke a taboo about the Imago Dei and allowed for the emergence of a God Image that more readily corresponds with empirical reality. He dared to know the God Image in its more complex and paradoxical nature. Jung called for knowledge, not for the sake of knowing alone, but for knowledge as a tool for developing and achieving higher consciousness for humanity: a humanity that can live up to the moral demands and obligations presented in the dawn of the 21st century. His message gains urgency with the technological advancements made by humankind and its frightening ability to destroy itself and all life, as we know it.

Acknowledging, holding, and tolerating the tension of the paradox of existence will free the human race from an illusory one-sidedness and the accompanying religious doctrines designed to perpetuate them. This requires a secure ego capable of self-reflection, flexibility, and humility when exposed to the changing demands of life and when it encounters the numinosum and it's archetypal energy. A kind of resilient ego responds to the energy of the numinosum with progressive responses instead of regressive exploit. The consequences of the latter are dire enough that existence as a whole depends on this progressive evolution and incarnation of numinous energy.

The key process for psychological and spiritual change and transformation is the creation of the transcendent function, allowing comprehension of the unconscious via the *symbolic process.* A symbolic understanding allows for a psychologically credible view and explanation of reality. Seeking refuge in religious doctrines that contradict reality does not mean a mere stagnation of intellectual development but leads inherently to destructive phenomena on both the individual and collective level. Rigidly held positions are especially dangerous during revolutionary times. The effects of the numinosum are not eradicated or annihilated by the act of denial. *Au contraire*: The more unconscious those powers are by the unwillingness or inability of the ego (or the collective) to face them, the more archaic, and therefore cruel, they likely become. Religious worship as a natural phenomenon plays an indispensable role in allowing the ego to form a relationship to the numinosum, but like every other tool, it can be used as a defense. Protection against the numinosum is equally important, as is its integration, for individuation. However, when the defenses become the sole habitual function of the creed, neurosis ensues. Henceforth, a spirituality based on reality principles is necessary to resume development. Jungian analysis and a Jungian *Weltanschauung* can play an indispensable role in the resumption of development and growth; they strengthen, inform and make conscious the ego's ability to redefine its relationship to the numinosum, thus forming a new *Imago Dei*.

To a greater extent, we have explored the psychological phenomena of stagnation and distorted adaptation in religious development. To better understand these phenomena, we researched and referenced the work of Almond, Appleby, and Sivan's (2003) on fundamentalism (The Fundamentalism Project, 1987-1995). Additionally, work on fundamentalism and questions pertaining to radical creed by Armstrong, Putnam and Campbell, Hedges, Ehrman, Dourley, among others, were also referenced. Their research furthered our work in elucidating and illuminating the phenomena of fundamentalism and facilitated our work in developing and establishing connecting links between the sociological, psychological and religious aspects. The numinosum was explored with respect to the psychology of the individual and the psychological dynamics of the collective. Besides studying Jung's collected works, as a main source for this book, the work of Main, Casement, Stein, and Corbett were reviewed and included in the present study. In this book, we have identified the major characteristics of "*strong religion*" and we have offered their phenomenology from the perspective of depth psychology.

In addition, the work of Edinger and his concept of the Self became the leading point for the formulation of our own contributions to the question of radical religious dynamics and their expressions.

In Jungian literature, there are different appellations for the phenomenon of possession by the archetypes, creating a *strong creed.* This expression includes fanaticism, radicalism, sectarianism, and fundamentalism. We noted that all of these are expressions for "getting stuck in the land of numen" (Jung, 1935, par. 221). It was discovered that the common denominator for these phenomena was possession and/or inflation by the Self: either by the light, conscious side or dark, unconscious side. We termed this possession *theocalypsis, theocalypse, or theokalypsis*.

The term *theocalypse* was proposed to describe the archetypal process of religious inflation by the Self where a specific religious ideology is present and the ideology is referring to a supreme, transcendent being or beings as God or gods. This ideology can exist in the form of doctrine or individual philosophy and imagery and corresponds to that which is known in Jungian psychology as the *Imago Dei*. We speak of *theocalypsis* only where the phenomena of inflation by unconscious contents of the Self are present: Theocalypsis = Inflation + Archetype of the Self + *Imago Dei*. Typically, *theocalypsis* involves hiding behind god/God while possessed by the archetypal energy of the Self. If inadequate regulation of the archetypal Self-energy is not a part of the process or if a religious ideology is lacking, this state would *not* be considered a theocalypsis; in those situations other terms, such as: possession, inflation, assimilation, one-sidedness, or mana personality would be used. The term *theocalypsis* is used to describe the process of "being trapped" or "deceived" by the inadequate regulation of archetypal Self-energy and by the consequent, insufficient (noncredible), or poor representation of the *Imago Dei*. We believe that the process and phenomenon of *theocalypsis* is universal and archetypal. We have provided an aggregate of historical and mythological examples to support the findings of our examination.

Odysseus's capture on the Island of Ogygia by a nymph named Calypso and his eventual release and return to Ithaca offers a symbolic rendering of both psychological healing and renewal and/or the possibility of psychological stagnation that can impede individuation. Comparisons were made between the unwanted results of losing the relationship with the unconscious, archetypal domain and the dynamics that govern the mind of a religious fanatic; both are trapped by unregulated Self-energy and thus prevented from continued spiritual development. The term *theocalypsis* does not apply to healthy religious expressions (i.e., expressions resulting from the creation of an ego-Self axis, to use Edinger's term). Because we recognize religion as the most essential psychic expression, the term *theocalypsis* is applied only to cases where this function has become *deformed* for various reasons and is a hindrance for the "incarnation" of the Self and hindrance to one's continuing individuation.

We have identified three basic categories (General, Affect and Cognitive) of the psychological characteristics of a *theocalypsis*. Within each category we have identified eight sub-characteristics. The general characteristics pertain to concepts found in the Jungian literature: 1) Hubris, 2) Ethical Infantilism, 3) Unconscious Identity (participation mystique), 4) Lack of Aidos, 5) Abnegation of Will, 6) Inadequate Regulation of the Numinosum, 7) Identification with the Self, and 8) Inferiority of Consciousness. The second group of characteristics which we have called cognitive characteristics, are concerned with cognitive processes and the approach to religious products (i.e., texts and teachings): 1) Concretism and Literalism, 2) Historicism and Externalism, 3) Selective Rationality, 4) Inconsistency and Intellectual Rigidity, 5) Quasi-Intellectualism, 6) Absolutism and Inerrancy, 7) Millennialism and Messianism, and 8) Dogmatism. The third group of characteristics refers to how people suffering from a theocalypsis deal with the affective (emotional) quality of the numinosum. We call them Affect Characteristics: 1) Asymbolism, 2) One-Sided orientation of consciousness, 3) Inadequate relationship to paradox (*Complexio Oppositorum*), 4) Externalization of archetypal Self-energy, 5) Dissociative selectivity, 6) Moral superiority and moral Manichæism, 7) Reactivity, and 8) Fear of the new and fear of change.

Clinical practice and the observation of the phenomena of *theocalypsis* have taught the authors that unconscious possession always yields consequences. Greek mythology recognized this archetypal process in the acts of different goddesses such as Atë, Dike, Nemesis, and others. We borrowed terminology from the Greeks and proposed the term *theo-nemesis* to describe the consequences of *theocalypsis*. The term *theonemesis* was defined as a symbolic manifestation of the Self in an attempt to awaken and change the person where *theocalypsis* no longer provided sufficient ego-adaptation. *Theonemesis,* is thus understood as a compensatory psychic reaction due to the Self. *Theonemesis* and *theocalypsis* are both in service of individuation and are mutually interrelated. Experiencing *theonemesis* could lead to establishing a more adequate God Image and thus a more healthy and realistic religious faith. *Theonemesis* attempts to attack in cases in which the ego is identified with the Self and thus under the influence of unconscious, archaic, and unadapted contents. Examples of this process were likewise found in historical material and our own clinical practice.

Lastly, we have explored the issues concerning psychological transformation and change and have identified the factors inherent in facilitating that change and the basic obstacles to further psychological growth and development. The role of Jungian psychology, its theory, and clinical practice have been noted in the process of facilitating change as necessary conditions for individuation. The numinosum is the alpha and omega of human conscious life; due to its paradoxical nature, it can be a source of psychological freedom or salvation, on the one hand, or the source of the worst destruction imaginable, on the other. Both remain unavoidably present. This is why Jung's work is so vital and important for our time. A hundred years has not diminished Jung's message, in fact, it is more timely and urgent today than ever.

It is our hope that this humble contribution will help perpetuate Jung's message and will inspire others to explore the question of religion, not with iconoclastic intentions, but with the intention to further assist all of us in understanding the power of religion, so it can better serve humankind and the purposes proclaimed by the sages.

BIBLIOGRAPHY

- Almond, G. A., Appleby, R. S., & Sivan, E. (2003). *Strong religion*. Chicago: The University of Chicago Press.
- *APA Handbook of Psychology, Religion and Spirituality,* American Psychological Association, Kenneth Pargament, Editor-in-Chief, Washington, D.C. 2013.
- Armstrong, K. (2005, January). *What is fundamentalism?* Presented at the Intolerance and Fundamentalism Seminar, City, State.
- Armstrong, K. (2009). *The case for God.* Toronto, CA: Random House of Canada.
- Backhouse, Halcyon, (1993), *The Best of Meister Eckhart,* Crossroad Publishing Company, New York, N.Y.
- Basch, M. F. (1988), *The Perception of Reality and the Disavowal of Meaning,* In: *Annual of Psychoanalysis, 11,* 124-154.
- Bechtle, R. (1985), *Convergence in Theology and Spirituality,* in The Way 23, 305-14.
- Becker, E. (1973). *The Denial of Death.* The Free Press: New York, NY.
- Bedi, A., & Matthews, B. (2003). *Retire your family karma.* Berwick, ME: Nicolas-Hays.
- Bedi, Ashok, (2000), *Path to the Soul,* Samuel Weiser Inc, York Beach, Maine.
- Bedi, Ashok, (2007), *Awaken the Slumbering Goddess,* No listed Publisher.
- Bedi, Ashok, and Matthews, Boris, (2003), *Retire Your Family Karma,* Nicolas- Hays, Inc., Berwick, Maine.
- Bender, C, (2010), *The New Metaphysicals: Spirituality and the American Religious Imagination*, The University of Chicago Press: Chicago.

- Berkeley, George, (1982), *A Treatise Concerning the Principles of Human Knowledge,* Hackett Publishing Company, Indianapolis, Indiana.
- Boehme, J. (1622). *Of the Supersensual life (or the life which is above sense): Two dialogues*. London: Holmes Publishing Group.
- Bohr, N. (1934). *Atomic physics and the description of nature.* London: Cambridge University Press.
- Borden, William, (2009), *Contemporary Psychodynamic Theory & Practice,* Lyceum Books, Chicago, Illinois.
- Buber, M., (1952), Eclipse of God: Studies in the Relation between Religion and Philosophy. New York: Harper and Row.
- Bultmann, R. (1961). New Testament and mythology. In H. W. Bartsch (Ed.), *Kerygma and Myth* (10-11). New York: Harper Torch books.
- Burgon, M., (Ed.), (1907). Topic. In *The New Werner Encyclopedia Britannica* (Vol. 21, p. 430). London: Encyclopedia Britannica.
- Burton, Robert A., (2008), *On being Certain,* St. Martin's Press, New York, New York.
- *Business Insider*, February, 27, 2015.
- Butcher, H., S., Lang, *The Odyssey of Homer*, Collier & Son, NY, 1909.
- Cahill, Thomas, (2003), *Sailing in the Wine-Dark Sea,* Anchor Books, New York, New York.
- Cambray J., and Linda Carter (2004), *Analytical Psychology: Contemporary Perspectives in Jungian Analysis*, Edited by Joseph Cambray, Hove, UK: Brunner-Routledge.
- Cambray, J., Carter, L., (2004) *Analytical Psychology, Contemporary Perspectives in Jungian Analysis, Chap. Archetypes: Emergence and psyche's Deep Structure*, Hogenson, Routledge, London and NY.
- Capra, F. (1975). *The Tao of physics.* Berkeley, CA: Shambala Publications.
- Casement, A. (Ed., 2007), *Politics and the American Soul,* Spring Journal, New Orleans, Louisiana.
- Casement, A., & David, T. (2006). *The idea of the numinous.* London: Routledge.

- Chabannes, Jacques, (1962), *St. Augustine,* Doubleday & Company, Garden City, NY.
- Christou, Evangelos. (1976), *The Logos of the Soul*, Spring Publications, Putnam, CT.
- *Client 9: The Rise and Fall of Eliot Spitzer* (2010).
- Cochran, G., Harpending, H., *The 10.00 Year Explosion*, Basic Books, NY, 2009.
- Compaan, A. (August, 2007). *Archetypal shame and its transference/countertransference manifestations in the analytic journey*. Paper presented at the meeting of the XVII International Congress for Analytical Psychology, Cape Town, South Africa.
- Corbett, L. (1996). *The religious function of the psyche*. New York: Brunner-Routledge.
- Corbett, L. (2011). *The Sacred Cauldron*. Chiron Publications, Wilmette, IL.
- Corbett, L., Stein, M., (2005) APA, Spiritually Oriented Psychotherapy, *CONTEMPORARY JUNGIAN APPROACHES TO SPIRITUALLY ORIENTED PSYCHOTHERAPY*, Chap. 3, 200.
- Corbin, H. (1972). *Mundus Imaginalis or the imaginary and the imagina*l. *Spring* (pp. 1-9). Dallas: Spring.
- Cuijpers, P., & Smit, F. (2002). Excess mortality in depression: A meta-analysis of community studies. *Journal of Affect Disorders, 72*, 227-236.
- D. Bruce Dickson (1990), *The Dawn of Belief: Religion in the Upper Paleolithic of Southwestern Europe*, University of Arizona Press.
- Delacroix, Eugène, *La liberté guidant le peuple*, 1830.
- Didier, G. J. (1991), *Vocational Crisis and Transformation: From Ordained Clerical Priesthood to Lay Ministry*, in *Creative Ministries in Contemporary Christianity*, Exploration Press: Chicago.
- Dourley, J. P. (1984). *The illness that we are*. Toronto: Inner City Books.
- Dourley, J. P. (2004). *Jung, mysticism and the double quaternity: Jung and the psychic origin of religious and mystical experience*, Harvest, *50*.
- Dourley, J. P. (2006a). *Jung and the recall of the Gods*. Ottawa: JOURNAL OF JUNGIAN THEORY AND PRACTICE, VOL. 8 NO. 1.

- Dourley, J. P. (2006b, July). *The foundational elements of a Jungian spirituality*. Paper presented at the AGAP Forum on the Symbolic Way in Spirituality, Analytic Practice, and Culture, Zurich, Switzerland.
- Dr. Albert Hofmann (1984), *Stanislav Grof interviews*, Esalen Institute, Big Sur, California.
- Draper, Herbert, *The Lament For Icarus*, 1898.
- Du Boulay, S. (1998). *Beyond the Darkness: A Biography of Bede Griffiths*. Continuum: New York.
- Eckhart. (2000). *Mistr Eckhart a stredoveka mystika.*Praha: Vysehrad.
- Edinger, E. F. (1972). *Ego and archetype*. Baltimore, MD: Penguin Books.
- Edinger, E. F. (1996). *The new God Image*. Wilmette, IL: Chiron Publications.
- Edinger, E. F. (2002). *The archetype of apocalypse*. New York: Open Court Publishing.
- Edinger, Edward F., (1984), *The Creation of Consciousness: Jung's Myth for Modern Man,* Inner City Books, Toronto, Canada.
- Ehrman, Bart D., (2005), *Misquoting Jesus,* HarperOne, HarperCollins Publishers, New York, New York.
- Ehrman, Bart D., (2008), *God's Problem,* HarperOne, New York, NY.
- Ehrman, Bart D., (2009), *Jesus, Interrupted,* HarperOne, HarperCollins Publishers, New York, New York.
- Eibl-Eibesfeldt, Irenäus, (1972), *Love and Hate,* Holt, Rinehart and Winston, New York.
- Eliade, M., (2004), *Shamanism: Archaic Techniques of Ecstasy,* Princeton University Press, Princeton.
- Eliot, Charles W., Jowett, Benjamin, Crossley, Hastings, Long, George, (1937), *The Harvard Classics,* P.F. Collier & Son, New York, NY.
- Ewing, H. (Director), & Grady, R. (Director). (2006). *Jesus camp* [Motion picture]. United States: Magnolia Pictures.
- Festinger, Leon, *A Theory of Cognitive Dissonance*, Stanford University Press, 1957.

- Field, G. W. (1932). *The works of Aristotle: De Anima*. (J. A. Smith, Trans.). Oxford: Clarendon Press. (Original work published 1931).
- Fouquet, Jean, *Job and His False Comforters*, c. 1460.
- Fowler, J. W. (1976). *Stages of faith*. New York: Harper One.
- Fox, M. (2000). *One River, Many Wells*, Jeremy P. Tarcher/ Putnam: New York.
- Franz, Marie Louise von, (1975), *Creation Myths,* Spring Publications, New York, New York.
- Franz, M-L von (1987), *The Process of Individuation*, in *C.G. Jung, Man and his Symbols*, London.
- Franz, M-L, von. (1993). *Psychotherapy*. Boston: Shambala Publications.
- Franz, Marie Louise von, (1980), *On Divination and Synchronicity: The Psychology of Meaningful Chance,* Inner City Books, Toronto, Canada.
- Franz, Marie Louise von, (1982), *Interpretation of Fairytales,* Spring Publications, Dallas, Texas.
- Franz, Marie Louise von, (1992), *Psyche & Matter,* Shambhala Publications, Boston, MA.
- Franz, Marie-Louise von, (1980), *Alchemy*, Inner City Books, Toronto, Canada.
- Franz, Marie-Louise von, (1993), *Psychotherapy,* Shambhala Publications, Boston, MA.
- Fromm, E. (1950), *Psychoanalysis and Religion*, New Haven, Conn., Yale University Press.
- Gallup, G. (2003). *American Spiritual Searches Turn Inward,* Gallup.com
- Gheorghe Tattarescu, *Nemesis*, 1853.
- Gilby, Thomas, (1960), *Saint Thomas Aquinas Philosophical Texts,* Oxford University Press, New York, NY.
- Gilkey, Langdon (1993), Nature, *Reality, and the Sacred: The Nexus of Science and Religion*, Fortress Press, Albany, NY.
- Gladstone, William Ewart (1858), *Studies on Homer and the Homeric Age. I.*, Oxford, United Kingdom: Oxford University Press.
- Goldberg, Michelle, (2006), *Kingdom Coming,* W.W. Norton & Company, New York.
- Grof, S, (2008), *LSD Psychotherapy*, MAPS, Ben Lomond, CA.

- Hannah, Barbara, (1981), *Active Imagination,* Sigo Press, Santa Monica, California.
- Hannah, Barbara, and Franz, Marie Louise von, (2004), *Lectures on Jung's* Aion, Chiron Publications, Wilmette, Illinois
- Harper, D. (2010). *The online etymology dictionary*. Retrieved from www.etymonline.com
- Harris, S. (2004). *The end of faith*. New York: W.W. Norton and Company.
- Harvey, Van A. (1977), *A Handbook of Theological Terms*, Macmillan Publishing Co., New York.
- Hawking, S., & Mlodinow, L. (2010), *The grand design*, New York: Bantam Books.
- Haynal, André, Molnar, Miklos, Puymège, Gérard De, (1983), *Fanaticism,* Schocken Books, New York.
- Heagle, John (1985), *A New Public Piety: Reflections on Spirituality*, in *The Spiritual Revolution: The emergence of contemporary spirituality*, Tacey, D., (2004). Brunner-Routledge: New York.
- Hedges, Chris, (2006), *American Fascists,* Free Press, New York, New York.
- Hedges, Chris, (2009), *Empire of Illusion*, Nation Books, New York, NY.
- Hick, John, (1990), *A John Hick Reader,* Trinity Press International, Philadelphia, Pennsylvania.
- Hillman, J. (1997), *Suicide and the Soul*, Spring Publications, Woodstock, CT.
- Hillman, J. (1975), *Re-Visioning Psychology*. Harper & Row Publishers: New York.
- Hitler, Adolf, (1971). *Mein Kampf,* Houghton Mifflin Company, Boston, MA.
- Immanuel Kant, (1991) *Groundwork for the Metaphysics of Morals*, Edited by Allen W. Wood, Yale University Press.
- International Bible Society, The, (1984), *The Holy Bible,* Zondervan, Grand Rapids, MI.
- Internet Merriam-Webster Dictionary, 2009.
- Jackson, P., (1995), *Sacred Hoops: Spiritual Lessons of a Hardwood Warrior*, Hyperion: New York, NY.
- Jacobi, Jolande, (1951), *The Psychology of C.G. Jung,* Routledge and Kegan Paul Ltd, Broadway House, London, England.

- James, W., *The Varieties of Religious Experience: A Study in Human Nature* (1902), Princeton, Princeton.
- Jaspers, K. (1953). *The origin and goal of history.* (M. Bullock, Trans.). New Haven, CT: Yale University Press.
- Jaynes, Julian. (1990). *The Origin of Consciousness in the Break Down of the Bicameral Mind,* Houghton Mifflin Company, Boston, MA.
- Jung, C.G. (1948), *General Aspects of Dream Psychology,* Princeton NJ: Princeton University. (in CW 8).
- Jung, C.G. (1951), The Psychology of the Child Archetype, Princeton: NJ: Princeton University Press. (in CW 9i).
- Jung, C.G. (1959). *Aion*. Princeton, NJ: Princeton University Press.
- Jung, C.G. (1966). *Two essays on analytical psychology*. Princeton, NJ: Princeton University Press.
- Jung, C.G. (1973). *Letters* (Vol. 1 and 2) G. Adler & A. Jaffe (Eds.). (R. F. C. Hall, Trans.). Princeton, NJ: Princeton University Press.
- Jung, C.G. (1977). C.G. Jung Speaking. Eds. William McGuire and R.F.C. Hull. Princeton University Press, Princeton, New Jersey.
- Jung, C. G., & Von Franz, M. L. (1964). *Man and his symbols*. London: Dell Publishing.
- Jung, C. G., (1959), *Aion*: *Researches into the Phenomenology of the Self*. (in CW 9ii)
- Jung, C. G., (2009). *The Red Book: Liber Novus*, trans. Sonu Shamdasani, Mark Kyburz, and John Peck, W. W. Norton: New York.
- Jung, C. G., (1931). *The spiritual Problem of Modern Man*. Princeton University Press (in CW 10).
- Jung, C.G. (1916/1958). *The Transcendent Function*. Princeton University Press (in CW 8).
- Jung, C. G., (1940). *Psychology and Religion*. Princeton University Press (in CW 11).
- Jung, C. G., Jaffe, A., Winston, R., Winston C., (1963) *Memories, Dreams, Reflections*, Random House, NY.
- Jung, C.G. (1990). *The archetypes of the collective unconscious.* Hull, R. F. C. (Trans.). Bollingen Series XX. The Collected Works

of C.G. Jung, 9i. Princeton, NJ: Princeton University Press. First published in 1959.

- Jung, C.G., (1912/1916/1966), *Appendix: New Paths in Psychology; The Structure of the Unconscious*. Princeton: NJ: Princeton University Press. (in CW 7)
- Jung, C.G., (1921a). *The Type Problem in Poetry*, Princeton: NJ: Princeton University Press. (in CW 6)
- Jung, C.G., (1921b). *Definitions*, Princeton: NJ: Princeton University Press. (in CW 6)
- Jung, C.G., (1921c). *Schiller's Ideas on the Type Problem*, Princeton: NJ: Princeton University Press. (in CW 6)
- Jung, C.G., (1921d). *The Problem of Types in the History of Classical and Medieval Thought*, Princeton: NJ: Princeton University Press. (in CW 6)
- Jung, C.G., (1928a), *On The Psychic Energy*, Princeton: NJ: Princeton University Press. (in CW 8)
- Jung, C.G., (1928b), *The Relationship between the Ego and the Unconscious*, Princeton: NJ: Princeton University Press. (in CW 7)
- Jung, C.G., (1931), *Mind and Earth*, Princeton: NJ: Princeton University Press. (in CW 10)
- Jung, C.G., (1936), *Yoga and the West*, Princeton: NJ: Princeton University Press. (in CW 11)
- Jung, C.G., (1937), *Psychological Factors Determining Human Behavior*, Princeton: NJ: Princeton University Press. (in CW 8)
- Jung, C.G., (1938), *Psychology and Religion*, Princeton: NJ: Princeton University Press. (in CW 11)
- Jung, C.G., (1940), *Psychology and Religion*, Princeton: NJ: Princeton University Press. (in CW 11)
- Jung, C.G., (1943), *On the Psychology of the Unconscious*, Princeton: NJ: Princeton University Press. (in CW 7)
- Jung, C.G., (1944), *Introduction to the Religious and Psychological Problems of Alchemy*, Princeton: NJ: Princeton University Press. (in CW 12)
- Jung, C.G., (1946), *The Psychology of the Transference*, Princeton: NJ: Princeton University Press. (in CW 16)
- Jung, C.G., (1948a), *Instinct and the Unconscious*, Princeton NJ: Princeton University Press. (in CW 8)

- Jung, C.G., (1948b), *A Psychological Approach to the Dogma of the Trinity*, Princeton: NJ: Princeton University Press. (in CW 11)
- Jung, C.G., (1948c), *General Aspects of Dream Psychology*, Princeton: NJ: Princeton University Press. (in CW 8)
- Jung, C.G., (1950a), *Concerning Rebirth*, Princeton: NJ: Princeton University Press. (in CW 9i)
- Jung, C.G., (1950b), *A Study in the Process of Individuation*, Princeton: NJ: Princeton University Press. (in CW 9i)
- Jung, C.G., (1951a), *The Self*, Princeton: NJ: Princeton University Press. (in CW 9ii)
- Jung, C.G., (1951b), *The Shadow*, Princeton: NJ: Princeton University Press. (in CW 9ii)
- Jung, C.G., (1951c), *The Alchemical Interpretation of the Fish*, Princeton: NJ: Princeton University Press. (in CW 9ii)
- Jung, C.G., (1951d), *Christ, a Symbol of thy Self*, Princeton: NJ: Princeton University Press. (in CW 9ii)
- Jung, C.G., (1951e), *The Synthetic or Constructive Method*, Princeton: NJ: Princeton University Press. (in CW 9ii)
- Jung, C.G., (1952a), *Answer to Job*, Princeton: NJ: Princeton University Press. (in CW 11)
- Jung, C.G., (1952b), *Foreword to White's 'God and the Unconscious'*, Princeton: NJ: Princeton University Press. (in CW 11)
- Jung, C.G., (1954a), *Archetypes of the Collective Unconscious*, Princeton: NJ: Princeton University Press. (in CW 9i)
- Jung, C.G., (1954b), *On the Nature of the Psyche*, Princeton: NJ: Princeton University Press. (in CW 8)
- Jung, C.G., (1954c), *Transformation Symbolism in the Mass*, Princeton: NJ: Princeton University Press. (in CW 11)
- Jung, C.G., (1954d), *Concerning the Archetypes and the Anima Concept*, Princeton: NJ: Princeton University Press. (in CW 9i)
- Jung, C.G., (1955-56), *Rex and Regina*, Princeton: NJ: Princeton University Press. (in CW 14)
- Jung, C.G., (1957), *The Undiscovered Self*, Princeton: NJ: Princeton University Press. (in CW 10)
- Kalsched, D. (1996) The Inner World of Trauma: Archetypal Defenses of the Personal Spirit,_London: Routledge.

- Kalsched,D. (2013) Trauma And The Soul, New York, NY: Routledge
- Kant, I. (1781). *Critique of pure reason.* London, Penguin Classic.
- Kant, I. (1784). *What is enlightenment?* Konigsberg, Prussia: 2002 Blackmask Online.
- Kant, Immanuel, (1950), *Prolegomena to Any Future Metaphysics* The Bobbs-Merrill Company, Indianapolis, Indiana.
- Kant, Immanuel, (1983), *Perpetual Peace and Other Essays,* Hackett Publishing Company, Indianapolis, Indiana.
- Kasser, Rodolphe and Meyer, Marvin and Wurst, Gregor, (2006), *The Gospel of Judas,* National Geographic, Washington, D.C.
- Kimball, Charles, (2008), *When Religion Becomes Evil,* HarperOne, HarperCollins Publishers, New York, New York.
- Kittel, G. (Ed.). (1964). *Theological dictionary of the New Testament* (Vol. 1). Grand Rapids, IA: William B. Eerdmans Publishing Company.
- Klemke, E.D., and Hollinger, Robert, and Rudge, David Wÿss, *Introductory Readings in the Philosophy of Science,* Prometheus Books, Amherst, New York.
- Koestler, A. (1967). *The Ghost in the Machine.* New York, New York: Macmillan.
- Kohut, H. (1971). *The analysis of the self.* New York: International University Press.
- Kohut, H. (1977). *The Restoration of the Self.* Connecticut: International Universities Press.
- Krauss, L., A Universe from Nothing, Simon & Schuster, (2012).
- Kuhn, Thomas S., (1996), *The Structure of Scientific Revolutions,* The University of Chicago Press, Chicago, Illinois.
- Lacan, J., Ecrits, (1999). Norton & Company, New York, New York: W. W. Norton & Company.
- Lawrence, D. H. (1977). 'Herman Melville's *Typee and Omoo'* (1923), in *Studies in Classic American Literature*. Harmondsworth: Penguin, pp. 144-45.
- Le Bon, G., *Les Lois psychologiques de l'évolution des peuples* (1894; The Psychology of Peoples).
- Lewis, Charlton and Charles Short (1969), *A Latin Dictionary,* Oxford: Oxford University Press.

- Lorenz, K., *The Foundations of Ethology* (1982).
- Lovelace, Richard. (1973). "The Sanctification Gap," in *Theology Today* 29, 365-366.
- Main, R. (2006). *Numinosity and terror.* In A. Casement & T. David (Eds.), *The idea of the numinous* (153-164). New York: Routledge.
- Malone, A., (2003), *An Interview with Donald Kalsched Contributed by Anne Malone* Friday, 28 November 2003, C.G. Jung Page.
- Marsden, G. M. (1980). *Fundamentalism and American culture.* Oxford: Oxford University Press.
- Martin E. Marty, R. Scott Appleby (1997), *Religion, ethnicity, and self-identity: nations in turmoil*; University Press of New England.
- Martin, Benjamin F. (2005), *France in 1938,* LSU Press.
- Marty, Martin E. and Appleby, R. Scott, (1991), *Fundamentalisms Observed,* The University of Chicago Press, Chicago, IL.
- Massacio, (1425), *Expulsion from Paradise*, Florence Gallery.
- Mathison, K. A. (2001). *The shape of sola scriptura*. Moscow: Canon Press.
- Meier, C.A., (1989), *Consciousness,* Sigo Press, Boston, MA.
- Mercadante, L. (2014). *Belief without Borders: Inside the Minds of the Spiritual but not Religious,* Oxford University Press: New York.
- Merriam-Webster Dictionary. (n.d). *online*.
- Moore, Robert L., and Havlick, Max Jr., (2001), *The Archetype of Initiation,* Xlibris Corporation, United States.
- Moore, T. (2014). *A Religion of One's Own*, Gotham Books: New York.
- Morris, R. C. (1991). *Process philosophy and political ideology*. Albany, NY: Sunny Press.
- Munitz, Milton K., (1990), *The Question of Reality,* Princeton University Press, Princeton, NJ.
- Murdock, D.M. (2009), *Christ in Egypt: The Horus-Jesus Connection*, Hub Pages, Stellar House Publishers.
- Murray, G. (1907/1924). *The rise of the Greek epic.* Oxford: Clarendon Press.

- Nagy, Marilyn, (1991), *Philosophical Issues in the Psychology of C.G. Jung,* State University of New York Press, Albany, New York.
- *National Catholic Reporter* 36, (1999) October pp.11-20. The National Catholic reporter Publishing Co. Kansas City, MO.
- *Nature,* DOI: 10.1038/nature 13962.
- Neumann, E. (1969). *Depth psychology and a new ethic.* NY: P. Putnam's Sons.
- Neumann, E. (1974). *Art and the creative unconscious.* Princeton: Princeton/Bollingen.
- Neumann, Erich, (1969), *Depth Psychology and a New Ethic,* G.P. Putnam's Sons, New York, New York.
- Neumann, Erich, (1970), *The Origins and History of Consciousness.*
- Noll, Richard, (1994), *The Jung Cult: Origins of a Charismatic Movement,* Princeton University Press, Princeton, New Jersey.
- Otto, R. (1958). *The idea of the holy.* Oxford: Oxford University Press.
- Pals, Daniel L., (2006), *Eight Theories of Religion,* Oxford University Press, New York, New York.
- Partridge, C., *The Re-Enchantment of the West.* T & T Clark International, 2004.
- Perry, J. W. (1970), *Emotions and object relations. Journal of Analytical Psychology, 15.*
- Phillp, H. L. P. *Jung and the Problem of Evil,* Robert M. McBride CO., New York, 1959.
- Principe, H. W. (1983), *Toward defining spirituality,* in Studies in Religion/Sciences, 12 (1983), 127-41.
- Putnam, R. D., & Campbell, D. E. (2010). *American grace: How religion divides and unites us.* New York: Simon & Schuster.
- Rackham, Arthur, *Sleeping Beauty,* 1920.
- Repin, I., *Religious Procession in Kursk Province, 1880*–83.
- Roberts, A., Donaldson, J., Coxe, A. C., Menzies, A., Richardson, E. C., & Pick, B. (1885). *The Ante-Nicene fathers: Translations of the writings of the fathers down to A.D. 325* (Vol. 4). NY: Scribner's.
- Robinson, Timothy A., (2002), *God,* Hackett Publishing Company, Indianapolis, Indiana.
- Rogers, Carl R., (1961), *On Becoming a Person,* Houghton Mifflin Company, Boston, MA.

- Rubin, J. (2015), *The McMindfulness Craze: The Shadow Side of the Mindfulness Revolution*, retrieved from www.truthout.org.
- Russell, Bertrand, (1912), *The Problems of Philosophy,* Oxford University Press, New York, NY.
- Russell, Bertrand, (1957), *Why I am not a Christian,* Simon and Schuster, New York, New York.
- Samuels, Andrew, (1985), *Jung and the Post-Jungians,* Routledge & Kegan Paul, New York, New York.
- Santayana, George, (1905), *The Life of Reason or the Phases of Human Progress: Reason in Religion,* Charles Scribner's Sons, New York.
- Schleiermacher, Friedrich, (1996), *On Religion,* Cambridge University Press, New York, New York.
- Schneider, Sandra (2000), *Religion and Spirituality: Strangers, Rivals or Partners?,* Public Santa Clara Lecture, Santa Clara University, Feb. 6, 2000 Vol. 6 No.2.
- Schneider, Sandra, (1989), "Spirituality in the Academy," *Theological Studies*, 50.
- Shamdasani, Sonu (2009). *The Red Book :A Reader's Edition*, W. W. Norton & Company, LTD.
- Shamdasani, Sonu, (2003), *Jung and the Making of Modern Psychology,* Cambridge University Press, Cambridge, MA.
- Shamdasani, Sonu, (2005), *Jung Stripped Bare by His Biographers, Even,* Karnac Books, London, England.
- Sharlet, J. (2008). *The family: The secret fundamentalism at the heart of American power.* Queensland: University of Queensland Press.
- Singer, T. (2002). *The cultural complex and archetypal defenses of the collective spirit. San Francisco Jung Institute Library Journal, 20*, 5-28.
- Singer, T. (2009). *The cultural complex in theory and practice.* Paper presented at the meeting of the Society of Jungian Analysts of Northern California, San Francisco, CA.
- Singer, T., & Kimbles, S. L. (2004). *The cultural complex.* New York: Routledge.
- Šolc, Vladislav (2007), *PSÝCHÉ MATRIX REALITA, hledání dimenzí reality očima psychologa*, Amos, Praha, Czech Republic.

- Šolc, Vladislav (2011), *Archetyp otce a jiné hlubinně psychologické studie*, Triton, Praha.
- Šolc, Vladislav (2011), *Tea party a fundamentalismus*, MF Dnes.
- Šolc, Vladislav (2013) *Psychologie micove hry* in *Ve jmenu Boha, dodatky*.
- Specter, Michael, (2009), *Denialism,* The Penguin Press, New York.
- St. Augustine, (2004), *Anti-Pelagian Writings: Nicene and Post-Nicene Fathers of the Christian Church, 1887*, Kessinger Publishing.
- St. Augustine, and Russell, Robert P., (1942), *Divine Providence and the Problem of Evil: A Translation of St. Augustine's De Ordine,* Cosmopolitan Science & Art Service Co., New York, New York.
- St. Augustine. (1982). *The literal meaning of genesis: A commentary in twelve books*. (J. R. Taylor, Trans.). New York: Newman Press. (Original work published in 401 CE).
- Steffen, Lloyd, (2007), *Holy War, Just War,* Rowman & Littlefield Publishers, Lanham, Maryland.
- Stein, Murray, (1985), *Jung's Treatment of Christianity: The psychotherapy of a Religious Tradition.* Chiron Publications, Wilmette, Illinois.
- Stein, Murray, (2014), *Minding the Self,* Routledge, New York
- Stern, D. (1985). The interpersonal world of the infant. New York: Basic Books.
- Swanson, Max, (2007), *Religion Unplugged: Spirituality or Fanaticism?*, Xlibris Corporation.
- Swinburne, Richard, (2010), *Is There a God,* Oxford University Press, New York, New York.
- Taylor, M. C., (2007). *After God*. University of Chicago Press: Chicago.
- The article by Albert Einstein appeared in the *New York Times Magazine* on November 9, 1930 pp 1-4; reprinted in Ideas and Opinions, Crown Publishers, Inc. 1954.
- Tillich, P. (1951). *Systematic theology*. (Vol. 1). Chicago: University of Chicago.
- Tillich, Paul, (1948), *The Shaking of the Foundations,* Charles Scribner's Sons, New York, NY.

- Tillich, Paul, (1959), *Theology of Culture,* Oxford University Press, London, England.
- Tillich, Paul, (1967, 1968), *A History of Christian Thought,* Simon and Schuster, New York, New York.
- Tippet, K., (2010), *Einstein's God: Conversations About Science and the Human Spirit*, Penguin Books, New York.
- Tocqueville, Alexis De, (2003), *Democracy in America,* Penguin Books, London, England.
- Toms, M., Campbell, J., (1990), *An Open Life: Joseph Campbell in conversation with Michael Toms*, Harper Perennial.
- Tredennick, Hugh, (1969), *Plato: The Last Days of Socrates,* Penguin Books, Middlesex, England.
- Turner, V. W. (1969). *The ritual process, structure, and anti-structure.* Chicago: Aldine Publishing Company.
- Twitchell, James B., (1999), *Lead Us Into Temptation,* Columbia University Press, New York.
- Tyler, R. (2009). *Skeptics and believers: Religious debate in the western intellectual tradition*: NY: The Teaching Company.
- Ulano Ann and Barry, (1994), *Transforming Sexuality,* Shambhala Publications, Boston, MA.
- University of California-Santa Barbara's website.
- Van Ness, P. (1996). Introduction: Spirituality and the Secular Quest, in *Spirituality and the Secular Quest,* Crossroad: New York.
- Wach, J. (1951/1958). *Comparative study of religions*. New York: Columbia University.
- Wallin, David J., (2007), *Attachment in Psychotherapy,* The Guilford Press, New York, NY.
- Watters, Ethan, (2010), *Crazy Like Us,* Free Press, New York, NY.
- Webster Dictionary. (1828). *Word.* NY: Brother's of New York City.
- West, Benjamin, *The confrontation between Telemachus, and Calypso*, circa 1800.
- Wheelwright, P., (1968). *Poetry, Myth and Reality*. In Tate Language of Poetry. New York, New York.
- White, Victor, and Jung, C.G., (1952), *God and the Unconscious,* The World Publishing Company, Cleveland, Ohio.

- Wilhelm, R. (1932). *A Chinese book of life*. London: Kegan, Paul, & Trubner Company.
- Winnicott, D., (1987), *Ego distortion in terms of true and false self*. In: The Maturational processes and the facilitating environment, Madison, CT: International Universities Press.
- Wulff, D. (1998). *Psychology and religion* (2nd ed.). New York: New York.
- Wuthnow, R. (1998). *After Heaven: Spirituality in America since the 1950's*. University of California: Berkeley and Los Angeles
- Zosky, D. L. (2003). *Projective identification, as a contributor to domestic violence*. In: *Clinical Social Work Journal, 31*.

INDEX

ABOUT THE AUTHORS

Vlado Šolc is a professional psychotherapist and Jungian Analyst practicing in Milwaukee, WI. Vlado received training from C.G. Jung Institute of Chicago and Charles University in Prague. Vlado lives in constant awe about the miracle of existence. He is an author of three depth psychology-oriented books published in Czech Republic: *Psyche, Matrix, Reality*; *The Father Archetype* and *In the Name of God – Fanaticism from Perspective of Depth Psychology*.

George J. Didier is a clinical psychologist and Jungian Analyst practicing in Rockford and Crystal Lake, IL. George is a former Catholic priest. He holds graduate degrees in psychology, theology, and spirituality. George studied at Catholic University of America, Washington, D.C., Chicago Theological Seminary, the Illinois School of Professional Psychology and the C.G. Jung Institute of Chicago. He is the author of *Vocational Crisis: Transformations in Ministry*.

CPSIA information can be obtained
at www.ICGtesting.com
Printed in the USA
LVHW111743111218
600081LV00001B/22/P

9 781630 513986